Teaching Counselors and Therapists

Teaching Counselors and Therapists

Constructivist and Developmental Course Design

Written and Edited by

Karen Eriksen and Garrett McAuliffe

BERGIN & GARVEY
Westport, Connecticut • London

MT

Library of Congress Cataloging-in-Publication Data

Teaching counselors and therapists : constructivist and developmental course design / written and edited by Karen Eriksen and Garrett McAuliffe.
    p.   cm.
  Includes bibliographical references and index.
  ISBN 0-89789-795-1 (alk. paper)
  1. Educational counseling—Study and teaching (Higher)   2. Constructivism (Psychology)   3. Student counselors—Teaching of. I. Eriksen, Karen, 1956- II. McAuliffe, Garrett.
  LB1027.5 .T346 2001
  378.1'94—dc21   00-065990

British Library Cataloguing in Publication Data is available.

Library of Congress Catalog Card Number: 00-065990
ISBN: 0-89789-795-1

First published in 2001

Bergin & Garvey, 88 Post Road West, Westport, CT 06881
An imprint of Greenwood Publishing Group, Inc.
www.greenwood.com

Printed in the United States of America

∞™

The paper used in this book complies with the Permanent Paper Standard issued by the National Information Standards Organization (Z39.48-1984).

10 9 8 7 6 5 4 3 2 1

3/14/03

Special thanks to the original think tank group on teaching at the Portland ACES Convention and for ACES' and Dave Zimpfer's encouragement and willingness to publish the first book in the series.

Contents

Preface

TRANSFORMING THE COURSES

The following eighteen chapters offer suggestions for transforming the specific courses in the counselor education curriculum. Each chapter includes (a) an introduction—using ancdotes or student quotes; (b) an overview of the impact of constructivism on the course content; (c) an outline of the course structure, assignments, and activities, with the accompanying constructivist and developmental rationales; (d) examples and anecdotes that illustrate these practices; (e) evaluation and grading procedures that are based on constructivist perspectives; and (f) a description of problems instructors might encounter in teaching a course in this way, and how these problems might be managed.

1

Introduction: Guidelines for Constructivist Teaching

Garrett McAuliffe

THE PARADOX OF THE CONSTRUCTIVIST IMPULSE

"Do not begin another semester without reading this book." So went the insistent phrase in my mind as I contemplated the completion of this volume. Perhaps those words came from the true believer in me, the one who wants to spread the gospel of constructivism to all counselor educators. But how non-constructivist of me! Perhaps I know well enough that I can't talk anyone into anything; nor should I. But I *can* still believe in the impulse behind this work, no matter how temporarily or how tentatively I do so. I *can* make the constructivist commitment to inclusion, to reflexivity, to experience. I *can* hold dear those "thin, flexible words," in philosopher Richard Rorty's (1993) terms, knowing that they might be mistaken—by me and you.

It is, therefore, in the spirit of eternal dialogue that we introduce a book committed to constructivist and developmental teaching in counselor education. This particular dialogue began in 1996 at the national meeting of the Association for Counselor Education and Supervision in Portland, Oregon. There, counselor educators shared their most transformative moments in teaching during five sessions of a Teaching Methodology discussion group. A community of dedicated teacher-thinkers emerged slowly from that first event.

The first product of that conversation was the volume, *Preparing Counselors and Therapists: Creating Constructivist and Developmental Programs,* (McAuliffe, Eriksen & Associates, 2000. That book described principles and program ideas for a constructivist counselor education. The present book expands on that work to emphasize classroom instruction itself. We focus here on teaching from a constructivist orientation. This book is full of practical suggestions for sharing the classroom with learners, for involving students, for transforming counselor education courses. We hope that, through your reading of this work, you will try some of these practices and, more broadly, remain open to the continuing unfolding of what it means to be a constructivist and developmental counselor educator.

We also hope that this book will contribute in some small measure to personal "transformations" (yours and your students') in Kegan's (1994) use of the term as movement across epistemological forms. We hope that, through this encounter, you gain the courage to move away from foundationalist certainty about teaching content and process, and about a "right method" in counseling itself, toward a flexible dedication to inquiry, to listening, to considering alternative perspectives. That is the constructivism that charms me.

Contrary to my initial declaration, I do not believe that anyone *has* to read this book before the next semester, or ever. But if you feel ready to invite an enlivening dissonance into your personal and professional life, please do so. The invitation both to doubt and to believe has been extended by the twenty-some authors of the following chapters.

The Moral Enterprise of Counselor Education

And what a cause we have committed to! It is sometimes easy to forget our ultimate purposes amid the fury of planning, enacting, and evaluating (and being evaluated) that characterizes college teaching. But lest we lose sight of those purposes, let us remember: We are one step away from directly affecting the well-being, even the very lives and deaths, of the children and adults who will be counseled by our charges.

The only certainty that we can ethically rely on is that of being reflective about teaching. An "ironic" stance attunes us to the contingency and fragility of our most sacred practices. But it does not keep us from making the moral commitment to care well for others and to reduce human suffering.

So we push on. The authors in this volume take the act of teaching very seriously, even if they are also wary of "true believerhood." They understand the isomorphism between teaching and counseling: Both practices can include the idiosyncratic and the generalized, the emotional and the intellectual, even the listening and the telling. The authors of these pages see ideal counselor education as an endeavor that brings together the head and heart. What a joy for those of us who consider both dimensions to be central to human knowing and community.

We have written this volume for practitioners of the art and craft of teaching. We want it to be immediately useful for those who labor daily with students of counseling. The book describes seventeen different courses that are part of the canon of counselor education. The teaching methods are grounded in constructivist and developmental principles. We invite the reader to step into the fluid course of constructivist teaching and to pluck the nuggets from these pages.

Implications of Constructivism for Teaching

But, be forewarned: constructivism knows no method, if by method we mean a fixed protocol for teaching practice. It follows from two major traditions: developmental constructivism (Piaget, 1971) and social constructionism (Mead, 1938; Baldwin, 1969). Each tradition places the human being as meaning-maker in the center of the epistemological ring. Piaget and the constructive developmentalists have plotted the evolution of complexity in meaning-making; the social constructionists have emphasized the community creation of knowledge. Both have put an ultimate emphasis on "storying"—the living narration that is meaning-making and knowledge creation. Both recognize that there is no human experience that precedes the act of meaning-making. There is no way to directly apprehend the "there." Our lenses are always on. With this emphasis on story construction, all claims to ultimate expertise and automatic hierarchy are suspect; instead, humility and reflexivity are ultimate.

It is a paradox that constructivist thinking offers no specific method. We are invited thus to stay on our pedagogical toes, never relaxing back onto the heels of essentialist complacency and certainty. In this book, in the previous book, and at conference sessions where we have met with like-minded souls, we have hoped to instigate (and be instigated into) disequilibration, to be unbalanced from any sinecure of position in our work. Instead we have invited ourselves into the permanent whitewater of constructing, deconstructing, and reconstructing our teaching work. Such an epistemological shift means giving up foundations in favor of contingency. Sartre called this a "metastable" position, one in which the only stability is in the conversation. So, welcome to the conversation, and farewell to certitude and control. Remember, a "course" in the original sense of the word means a place of movement.

Despite this seeming amorphousness, we can name some "tendencies" that might be characteristic of constructivist teaching. Some of them echo other impulses in teaching, such as that of the humanistic tradition (Lewin, 1948; Rogers, 1983, 1969, 1951) and of the so-called progressivists (Dewey, 1963/58; Freire, 1994; hooks, 1994). The ten elements that we offer below were initially proposed by Chris Lovell (Old Dominion University counselor educator, personal communication, 1997). They offer direction in this boundary-less journey into meaning-making.

GUIDELINES FOR CONSTRUCTIVIST TEACHING

Question Categorical Thinking

Perhaps this guideline might be subtitled "the danger of nouns," or "the labels we live by." This guideline asks us to model and to encourage in-process, reflexive thinking, in which concepts, once declared, turn on themselves to suggest their limits. Thus, the constructivist teacher is wary of "thick, rigid vocabulary" (Rorty, 1993), in which words—including those such as "nondirective counseling," "social justice," "postmodernism," and "mental disorder"—come to signify supposed entities, ones to which the teacher owes ultimate allegiance. Instead, when we question categorical thinking, all such notions become less final metaphors that we live by, labels that get us through the pedagogical day.

I am reminded of how our language usage has changed over time, and will continue to change, to reflect changes in our culture. That language fluidity is especially apparent in the regularly emerging labels for race or gender. For instance, "hero" has become a gender-inclusive term (as opposed to "heroine"), and "actor" is used for both women and men. Or should we consider words such as "shero," an important neologism, in order to mark out new cultural territory? None are "right," but each carries connotations that can only be interpreted in a historical, political, and social context. That contextual evaluation seems to me to define a constructivist stance.

In the discussion of social and cultural issues, we find the inclination to categorize to be tempting: "European Americans are individualistic;" "Latino/as are family-oriented." To avoid the dangers of such categorizing, we must deconstruct our own reifications and generalizations on the spot, know the limits of language in capturing any notion, and qualify our pronouncements with, "As it seems to me now . . . " or "The story I tell of this client . . . " or "It seems that oppression lies in this practice. On the other hand, it could be seen as . . . . " I often attempt to make my own categories less stable by asking (e.g., in the context of a case conceptualization or of a political position), "How is this view limited? How might others' experiences be different from the story that I have told?"

Recognize that Conflict and Dialectic are the Norm. Encourage Their Expression

This guideline might save someone's life. The emerging counselor might only be able to ask a client the question, "Are you thinking of killing yourself?" If she or he has a "comfort" with the conflict that is inherent in all relationship, with the tension that is the engine of living. Help students to assess their personal and family styles of dealing with conflict in the skills, family, or other courses. Offer them alternate ways to envision conflict. Help them to move through "gumption traps," to use Persig's (1975) motorcycle maintenance term, when they wish to avoid conflict at all costs.

Model comfort with conflict in the present tense by noting "here and now" processes in the room. For instance, an instructor might say, "I think I notice a 'feeling' in the room about this assignment. Would anyone like to express it?" (Or, "Please write down your concern anonymously.") Similarly, I might stir us from our complacency in a course dedicated to social and cultural issues by suggesting, "Let's look at the social 'arrangement' in this very class, by age, gender, or race? Who sits near whom? Who interacts with whom? Who speaks? What functions do these relationships serve? How are they limiting?" It would be easier to avoid the very-present tension inherent in such explorations, but we would miss much by avoiding the potential irritation of checking assumptions.

I recall my own avoidance of conflict while teaching a career counseling class some years ago. During one class discussion of women's current roles in the occupational world, one student shouted at another, "That's b—s—!" I registered my discomfort viscerally but ignored it publicly, moving onto safer discussion ground. I failed to address that tension; yet, all of us in the room noted it. As I learned later, I might have instead seized a "teachable moment" for all of us if I had asked the recipient to report her response to the "attack." We might have probed the emotional dimensions as well as the intellectual disagreement.

Show Commitment in the Face of Doubt

This guideline gives the lie to the charge that constructivism is a relativistic morass and that counseling is value-free. Perry (1970) proposed that there are epistemologically different types of commitments, ranging from the blind, absolutist adherence of the dualist to the contextual commitments of the relativist. Intellectual relativism does not necessarily imply an absence of a moral stance. Quite the opposite: a thoughtful relativism is associated with active moral concern, as the works of Kohlberg (1981) and Rest (1986) attest.

At some point the counselor (and the instructor) must act—that point should ideally be a product of an articulated rationale and a reflexive epistemology. This means that an instructor *can* show concern about injustices and political arrangements that maintain an oppressive status quo. Instructors in the counseling skills and internship courses *do* make clinical decisions and declare case conceptualizations, even "diagnoses," however contingently. We *can*, and should, ask students to acknowledge their "hunches" when they are working with clients, while simultaneously challenging them to find evidence for those inclinations. In the midst of using tentative language, inviting alternative views, questioning ourselves and our certainties, and listening carefully to diverse ideas, we *can*, as instructors, express our current choices and commitments. We *can* ask our students to do the same, always tempering such commitments with the understanding that they will change, that our identity is fluid, in process, progressing as new information unfolds.

Accent Interpersonal Process Commentary, or "Metalogue"

This guideline again draws our attention to "process." The centrality of interpersonal process in the work of counseling, except perhaps for the most ardent behaviorist, is obvious to most. In this guideline, we are charged with directing students' attention, usually through questioning, to interpersonal dynamics. Such attention is most explicit in the group counseling classes. However, during or following any small and large-group work (out-of-class projects), the instructor can ask students to make explicit and discuss, in Lovell's words: "The scripts, the games, the manipulations, the repeated micro-events" that they are experiencing (Old Dominion University faculty, personal communication, 1997). Through a focus on the interpersonal process, Lovell continues, "all these and other indications of the social system at work become evident." This conversation is itself the "metalogue:" the talk about the talk.

Examples of opportunities to attend to process abound. We all know the struggle and frustration that students experience in a malfunctioning small group that is working on a project. Some of us may further know the class rebellions that can rise up from private murmurings. Students who are unhappy with some aspect of a course might consult privately with each other, without broaching their concerns with the professor. Each of these are potential occasions for "public" processing of interpersonal dynamics. We can invite the comments. On a more positive note, students often don't recognize how they are promoting a helpful learning environment. Instructors enhance both students' cognitive development and the classroom environment by inviting students to talk about the talk.

Value Approximation over Precision

This guideline seemingly contradicts the prior dictum of "showing commitment," but it need not. In valuing approximation, we are honoring the elusiveness, indeed the impossibility of ever knowing truth or "reality" in human affairs. We instead speak "in measured tones," to use Belenky, Clinchy, Goldberger, and Tarule's phrase (1986). We thus encourage students to weigh evidence, to problematize what once seemed simple, to recognize bias in case conceptualization. Our constructs are always contingent upon the lenses of our moods, cultures, procedures for knowing, personality styles, genders, ages, and more. We might then modify our seeming certainties—always tending toward, never getting "there" (to a supposedly "final" diagnosis, or social analysis, or treatment plan).

Our responses to students' contributions in class and to assignments can also demonstrate the value of approximation. In class, we can show respect for the "half-formed" ideas that students generate during discussions. We can ask, during brainstorming, that no idea be critiqued. And we can challenge ourselves and students to build on the "partially-forms" until it becomes a "better" formed, more useful thoughts. When responding to assignments, we can recognize students' developmental inclinations as necessary places for them to hold and to move through, respecting their current capacities before moving on be challenged. In these ways we emphasize movement, fluidity, and an ever-emerging progress, rather than emphasizing "truth" as a static place that we will eventually find and attain.

Personalize Your Teaching

As it is described here, "personalizing instruction" means promoting interactions among all participants in the learning environment, as well as making connections between the subject matter and students' personal lives and experiences. In the connected, personalized classroom, participants are encouraged to listen to each other and to build on each other's ideas. The instructor helps to create an atmosphere in which participants can, in Noddings' words: "Nurture each other's thoughts to maturity," versus arguing each other out of positions in a point-counterpoint fashion (Belenky et al., 1986, p. 221).

The presence of the instructor's "personhood" in the classroom further promotes students' empowerment as knowledge creators. As hooks (1994) proposes, teachers can bring their biases, uncertainties, and personal life stories into the learning space. They might show their enthusiasms in the classroom as well. When instructors and students alike show excitement and emotion about ideas, learning is more potent (Bandura, 1986). Such enthusiasm might extend beyond ideas, to, in hooks' words: "Our interest in one another, in hearing one another's voices, in recognizing one another's presence" (1994, p. 8).

A final element in personalizing teaching is simply to be available. In Chickering and Reisser's words: "Frequent student-faculty contact in and out of classes is the most important factor in student motivation and involvement" (1993, p. 374).

Vary the Structure

"Structure" is defined here as the amount of direction and defining framework given to students on assignments and in discussions. The instructor stays on the lookout for the subtle but inevitable fatigue of overchallenge in some students, or the decline of engagement due to lack of challenge in others. This is a deceptively simple guideline; that is, we provide more structure, concreteness, and direction for concrete, authority-reliant thinkers, and less structure for relativistic thinkers.

However, such structure is contextually contingent as well. That is, if learners are unfamiliar with the topic, they will all need simplicity in number and presentation of ideas and will need concrete illustrations. "Layering in" complexity (for example: first learning theories singly before comparing them) and loosening structure (for example, providing suggestions and some references for project topics, but then leaving the content to the students) are ways of meeting situational changes in learners' needs.

Regardless of context, some epistemological tendencies will remain relatively constant across individuals. Thus this guideline might be specified as: "Cycle through a variety of methods of instruction to meet some learners where they are and challenge others to 'stretch' toward less congenial or familiar ideas." Most simply put: Vary your instruction. Give your class the rich pedagogical clutter which Chickering (in Chickering and Reisser, 1993) calls the "junk yard curriculum." Brookfield (1990), an adult education theorist, elaborates on that notion in his book *The Skillful Teacher:* "Given the bewildering complexity of teaching and learning, a good rule of thumb is to use a diversity of materials and methods in your practice" (p. 202).

Value and Promote Experience

Experience can be defined as sensory activity that engages the learner's attention. The power of introducing concrete and emotionally valent experience in order to maximize learning has been demonstrated by recent research (McNamara, Scott, & Bess, 2000). Pictures, sounds, smells, and actions seem to be worth a large number of words. Sensory experience also generates high affect, which has been shown to enhance retention.

The research on teaching and learning, points counselor educators toward instigating experiences for students—through activity, case study, illustration, role play, interviewing, teamwork, and data collection—rather than delivering knowledge largely through lecture and discussion. Counselor educators are especially well-positioned to use these experiential methods to teach. Most counseling practice itself instigates client movement through metaphor, exploration of feelings, in-session experiences, gestalt exercises, role plays, and guided imagery.

Experiential teaching is not, however, a panacea for all instructional challenges. Drawbacks of experiential teaching include its being more time-consuming and "messy" than didactic, abstract instruction. Teachers need to carefully monitor the mix of experience, reflection, and abstraction so that learners aren't focused on unexamined experience, to the exclusion of rational analysis and experimentation.

Emphasize Multiple Perspectives

Constructivist teaching aims at helping the student to become more complex and empathic as a person. Toward those ends, students can be asked to examine each issue, each dilemma, each human story or case, as it arises within the classroom from several angles. At least two ways of promoting such perspective-shifting are available: First, evoke and validate the multiple perspectives represented by the different students in the course; and second, turn to and explore the diverse approaches to the material presented by a particular curricular area.

Some counselor education courses lend themselves quite readily to exploring various approaches to the curricular material. For example, the fairly recent emphasis on multicultural counseling encourages students to seriously consider the impacts of gender, ability, race, religion, ethnicity, class, and sexual orientation on the counseling process. A counselor educator can act as a "critical pedagogue" in these considerations; that is, a teacher who helps students to change their "stagnant or stereotypical views" about groups other than their own (Kanpol, 1994, p. 43). Students can be asked to consider the cultural lenses that they use to judge behavior and values.

A caution is in order. The multiple perspectives approach will match the subjectivist tendencies of many students (the so-called "multiplists" or "subjectivists"). Those students might drown in a sea of multiplicity if perspectives are merely offered side-by-side, without evidence or context for use. We must help students to become sensitive to the relative value of ideas, in context.

Encourage Intrapersonal Process Awareness, or "Metacognition"

Metacognition, or the "conscious monitoring of one's thought processes" (Henderson, 1996, p. 21), is key for the practitioner who would become a constructivist. Metacognition is the process of standing back from one's experiences and thoughts in order to "think about the thinking," evaluating one's internal experiences, and beginning to ask why one might have such experiences. It is with the onset of the constructivist turn of mind that the ability to—and the commitment to—reflect on one's own processes becomes salient.

With coaching, the emerging constructivist therapist or counselor can become alert to the within-session stream of events, the emotions on both sides of the dyad, and the goodness of fit between clinical moves and particular elements of theory or supervisor advice. For instance, one student reflected: "I felt so bored with this client that I could hardly stay awake. What was she doing that I reacted to? What can I do at moments like this while still being alert to my 'automatic' reactions?" *Interpersonal process recall* training techniques, in which a video of a session is stopped and a trainee is asked what her cognitions or feelings were at that point in the session (Kagan, 1980), help to sharpen the trainee's sense of "self-talk" and awareness of affect during a session.

A word of caution is in order, however. Standing back from one's experience or thoughts, making them object, requires a level of development that Kegan (1994) might call "institutional" (or fourth order of consciousness), Perry (1970) might call "relativistic" (Position five), and Belenky et al, (1986) might call "procedural knowing." Many students will not have reached these developmental levels by the time they enter graduate school, and so may have a great deal of difficulty with metacognition. Instructors will need to support such students by matching their developmental level; that is, by giving clear directions about how to reflect, perhaps providing exemplars, and by giving specific feedback and coaching about how to "progress" toward metacognition.

CONCLUSION

These guidelines offer direction for our embarkation into the sea of counseling courses. The guidelines are always present behind the activities of the seventeen courses that follow. The task now lies before us to try to sail these constructivist and developmental possibilities into unknown waters before the next semester appears on the horizon.

We give thanks to the eager author-counselor educators who have patiently abided with us for the four years of this project. Their faith has been rewarded. Many of us have been professionally renewed as a result of our encounters with their thoughts. Now we need you to carry on the work, to rededicate yourself to this labor of love. Perhaps you will contribute to the next edition of this ongoing story.

REFERENCES

Baldwin, A. L. (1969). *The measurement of social expectations and their development in children*. Chicago: University of Chicago Press.

Bandura, A. (1986). *Social cognitive theory*. Englewood-Cliffs, NJ: Prentice-Hall.

Belenky, M. F., Clinchy, B. M., Goldberger, N. R., & Tarule, J. M. (1986). *Women's ways of knowing*. New York: Basic Books.

Brookfield, H. (1990). *The skillful teacher*. San Francisco: Jossey-Bass.

Chickering, A. W., & Reisser, L. (1993). *Education and identity* (2nd ed.) San Francisco: Jossey-Bass.

Dewey, J. (1963/1938). *Experience and education*. New York: Collier.

Freire, P. (1994). *Pedagogy of the oppressed*. New York: Continuum.

Henderson, J. G. (1996). *Reflective teaching: The study of your constructivist practices* (2nd. ed.). Englewood Cliffs, NJ: Merrill.

hooks, B. (1994). *Teaching to transgress*. New York: Routledge.

Kagan, N. (1980). *Interpersonal process recall*. East Lansing, MI: self-published.

Kanpol, B. (1994). *Critical pedagogy: An introduction*. Westport, CT: Bergin & Garvey.

Kegan, R. (1994). *In over our heads: The mental demands of modern life*. Cambridge, MA: Harvard University Press.

Knefelkamp, L. (1984). Developmental instruction. In L. L. Knefelkamp & R. R. Golec (Eds.), *A workbook for using the P-T-P Model* (pp. 29-35). Unpublished document developed for use in the University of Maryland Counseling and Personnel Services Department.

Kohlberg, L. (1981). *Essays on moral development*. San Francisco: Harper and Row.

Lewin, G. W. (Ed.) (1948). *Resolving social conflicts, selected papers on group dynamics*. New York: Harper.

McAuliffe, G., Eriksen, K., and Associates (2000). *Preparing counselors and therapists: Creating constructivist and developmental programs*. Alexandria, VA: Association for Counselor Education and Supervision.

McNamara, D. S., Scott, J., & Bess, T. (2000). Building blocks of knowledge: Constructivism from a cognitive perspective. In G. McAuliffe, K. Eriksen, and Associates, *Preparing counselors and therapists: Creating constructivist and developmental programs* (pp. 62-76). Alexandria, VA: Association for Counselor Education and Supervision.

Mead, G. H. (1938). *The philosophy of the act*. Chicago, IL: University of Chicago Press.

Perry, W. (1970). *Forms of intellectual and ethical development in the college years*. New York: Holt, Rinehart, and Winston.

Persig, R. (1975). *Zen and the art of motorcycle maintenance*. New York: Dell.

Piaget, J. (1971). *Psychology and epistemology*. Harmondsworth, England: Penguin.

Rest, J. R. (1986). *Moral development: Advances in research and theory*. New York: Praeger.

Rogers, C. R. (1951). *Client-centered therapy*. Boston: Houghton Mifflin.

Rogers, C. R. (1969). *Freedom to learn.* Columbus, OH: Merrill.
Rogers, C. R. (1983). *Freedom to learn for the 80s.* New York: Macmillan.
Rorty, R. (1993). *Contingency, irony, and solidarity.* New York: Cambridge University
    Press.

2

Introduction to Counseling: A Preliminary Construction of the Professional Reality

Yvonne L. Callaway and Sue A. Stickel

REALITY

Counseling students and faculty sometimes want to eliminate the introductory course in counseling to make room for another requirement or an additional elective. We ourselves debated this issue as a faculty during a recent program revision. We came to the consensus that we wanted students to develop a strong professional identity and to understand the multicultural nature of counseling. An awareness of cultural pluralism enhances the overview of the profession, theories, and intervention techniques provided in the introductory course. The story of two instructors being given the task of infusing a multicultural focus into the introductory counseling course inspired this chapter. Professional counselors continue to evolve sets of parameters for practice, which include ethical guidelines, program standards, licensing requirements, and multicultural competencies. From these foundations, counselors-in-training begin to build their professional identity, exploring and establishing expectations and guidelines for their personal and professional growth. Three themes—knowledge of self and others as cultural beings, professional performance parameters, and the contemporary settings in which professional counselors work—define the course as we see it.

Of particular importance for our story is the difficulty I experienced, as a Black woman (Callaway), of sharing my perspectives about counselor education in the classrooms in which I am a minority. Such sharing often feels like swimming upstream. This was indeed my experience during my first two years of teaching the introductory course. I was committed to promoting the recognition of diverse perspectives and to presenting multiple paradigms for viewing and negotiating life experience. I viewed the introductory course as an appropriate and favorable time in the training program during which to establish this expectation.

Initially, however, I was startled and annoyed by the degree and volume of discontent expressed by both students and faculty in response to what they perceived as the "continuous talk" about multicultural views and voices. Later, my frustration fueled the search for more effective strategies for helping students learn about the profession of counseling and about their ways of developing cultural and professional competency. Both research (Aisenberg & Harrington, 1988) and experience told me that my efforts to "personalize instruction" around these themes would likely be nullified unless we, as teachers and students, were able to bridge the "tension of difference" created by my race and gender (hooks, 1994). In fact, sorting through this tension and learning to "surrender my need for immediate affirmation of successful teaching . . . and accept that students may not appreciate the value of a certain standpoint or process straightaway" (hooks, 1994, p. 42) has been very challenging.

Working with Sue (Stickel) to reconstruct this course, and subsequently to write this chapter, provided me with important insights about the ways to better model and encourage reflection in the introductory course. Through the use of constructivist methods, I have learned much about students, myself, and the dynamic interactions among us. For example, what I have discovered about students when requiring them to explore and examine ideas (both historical and contemporary) about themselves in relationship to diverse others in the context of professional helping has helped me appreciate and respond more compassionately to students' (and even faculty's) difficulty, and sometimes pain, in challenging monolithic meaning paradigms, in taking positions outside their personal frames of reference, and in developing "a high tolerance for internal contradiction and ambiguity" (McAuliffe, 2000, p. 20).

Although I remain "acutely aware that the system has not become accustomed to my presence or my physicality" (hooks, 1994, p. 135), I am now more comfortable with the challenge of infusing diversity into counseling pedagogy and training. After investing a great deal of energy in how I think about the introductory course, as well as about the training experience more globally, I have come to better understand hooks' (1994) assertion that:

We must accept the protracted nature of our struggle and be willing to remain both patient and vigilant. To commit ourselves to the work of transforming the academy so that it will be a place where cultural diversity informs every aspect of our learning, we must embrace struggle and sacrifice. We cannot be easily discouraged. We cannot despair when there is conflict. (p. 33)

Historically, the reigning zeitgeist has influenced the profession of counseling (Capuzzi & Gross, 1997). For example, the humanism of the mid-century emphasized a universal sameness or "color blindness"; which discounted the uniqueness and experiences of people of color. The changing demographics forecast for the new millennium provide a strong impetus for reconstructing what and how we teach professional counselors-in-training (Arrendondo, Toporek, Brown, Jones, Locke, Sanchez, & Stadler, 1996; Sue & Sue, 1990; Wehrly, 1995). A constructivist approach to the introductory course offers students an alternative framework, perhaps one consistent with the zeitgeist of our era, for exploring ideas and experiences as they begin the process of developing into helping professionals. I have become convinced that the constructivist principles undergirding the plan for this course enhance the learning opportunities for students and teachers, while promoting the empowerment and efficacy needed for all students to "swim upstream" toward multicultural and professional competency.

COURSE PURPOSE, PROCESS, CONTENT, AND LEARNING OBJECTIVES

During the introductory experience, learners develop a profile of the professional community and begin constructing a knowledge base, a personal growth plan, and a professional resource network. Students gain a comprehensive introduction to the profession and an understanding of how counseling interfaces with other helping professions. More importantly, students develop interpersonal relationships and begin self-development in the context of their emerging role as a professional counselor. During these and other experiences, the prospective counselor has the opportunity to increase his or her awareness of cultural pluralism, diversity, and the contextual validity of counseling theories and interventions.

Both inside and outside of the classroom we support learners in seeking new learning experiences commensurate with their developmental level and identified needs. The classroom discussions provide learners with opportunities to share divergent views concerning personal and professional approaches to helping. Experiencing the dissonance created in activities and discussions helps students to expand and transform their views of helping, and to identify the fit between their career goals and the training experience. Upon completion of the introductory experience, we hope that prospective counselors will:

1. Demonstrate awareness of differing views of human nature that serve as foundations for the helping professions and provide a format for examining multiple perspectives and models of development.

2. Demonstrate the ability to conceptualize interactions of culture, diversity, and social context that influence the applicability of counseling theories and interventions.

3. Be knowledgeable about professional communities, opportunities, responsibilities, roles, and services.

4. Take advantage of opportunities for enhancing self-awareness and personal growth.

5. Be aware of current issues and trends in the helping professions.

With so much to introduce, we find it challenging to avoid a travelogue approach in which students see highlights of each counseling locale but fail to "get off the bus" to experience how each new concept relates to their emerging professional identity. Thus we identified four learning objectives. Table 1 groups these objectives and the content, process, and learning activities with the relevant constructivist principles (Hayes & Oppenheim, 1997) that undergird our teaching of this course.

Many texts designed for the introductory class provide individual chapters covering the settings where counselors work and the content included in the counseling core courses (Capuzzi & Gross, 1997; Gibson & Mitchell, 1999; Gladding, 1996; Kottler & Brown, 1992, 1996; Nugent, 1994). Most texts now incorporate chapters outlining the multicultural nature of counseling and how to work with "special populations" such as elderly, gay, lesbian, bisexual, and disabled clients. We use one of the introductory books and *The Multicultural Counseling Competencies* (Arredondo et al., 1996) as the texts for the course.

The Multicultural Counseling Competencies (Arredondo et al., 1996), which included the "Dimensions of Personal Identity Model," provided a framework for understanding that everyone is a multicultural being possessing a personal, political, and historical culture. Cultural identity development models such as Cross (1971), Parham and Helms (1981), Kim (1981), Helms (1990), and Sue and Sue (1990) provide support for seeing clients' world views from an "emic" (internal) perspective. We also include models uniquely related to gender and sexual orientation. House and Miller (1997) constructed a model titled "The Coming Out Stages" that is derived from several systems in the literature. Downing and Roush's (1985), "Model of Feminist Identity" is useful in helping counselors discover an advocacy role.

Table 1. Course Content, Process, Learning Activities, and Constructivist Principles

Learning Objectives	Content	Processes	Learning Activities	Constructivist Principles
Demonstrate awareness of differing views of human nature that serve as foundations for the helping profession and provide a format for examining multiple perspectives and models of development	Counseling Theories Identity Development Models Multicultural Counseling Competencies (MCC)	Individual Reflection Dyads Small and Large groups Simulations Case Study Evaluation	Learning Checkpoint 1 Learning Checkpoint 3 Focused Discussions,	People construct their worldview from a context based perspective. Knowledge is derived through a social, inductive, and qualitative process. Development is contextual.
Demonstrate the ability to conceptualize interactions of culture, diversity, and social context that influence the applicability of counseling theories and interventions	Basic Counseling Process and Helping Relationship Etic and Emic Cultural References Self-Efficacy Theory History of Counseling Dimensions of Personal Identity from MCC	Individual Reflection Dyads Small and Large Groups Role Plays Guided Practice Analysis/Reaction to Counseling Videos	Learning Checkpoint 2 Individual Option B	Reality is multiform. Individuals serve as their own historians in confronting the past as an organizing framework of thought and feeling that must be assimilated into present structures.
Be knowledgeable about professional communities, opportunities, responsibilities, roles and services.	American Counseling Association, Divisions, and State Associations Ethical Standards Counseling Settings and Specialization	Journal Article Evaluation and Review Classroom Lecture Small and Large Groups Development of Ethical Dilemmas	Learning Checkpoint 4 Professional Interview	Meaning making is self evolution.
Experience opportunities for enhancing self-awareness and personal growth	Basic Counseling Process and Relationship Identity Development Models Self-Efficacy Theory Dimensions of Personal Identity from MCC	Individual reflection and assessment Dyads	Individual Options a) personal counseling b) cultural immersion c) professional conference d) student designed growth experience Self-Assessment and Goal Setting	Cognition is an active relating of events. Human development is a process of understanding what it means "to be me in a world like mine at a time like this."
Become aware of current issues and trends in the helping professions	Theories and Models MCC Professional History Counseling Settings and Specializations Ethical Standards	Individual Reflection and Assessment Dyads Small and Large Groups	Individual Goal Setting Team Teachback Presentations	Individuals are producers of their own development. Language constitutes reality.

Each goal cited thus far is attached to specific content; however, the content becomes catalyst to the student's initial mastery of the learning processes and constructivist principles that are foundations for professional counseling. The synthesis of multiple approaches and the application of learning occurs through providing opportunities for and guiding students through an experiential learning process that will allow them to begin to develop reflective as well as metacognitive skills. These experiences serve as guided practice for the incorporation of sophisticated models of problem solving and continued learning.

Experiential Learning

Kolb (1984) defined experiential learning as the process whereby knowledge is created through the transformation of experience. Experiential learning cycles through concrete experience, reflective observation, abstract conceptualization, and active experimentation. Experiential learning guides the generation of an action theory from one's own experiences. The learner is affected in three ways: (a) cognitive structures are altered, (b) attitudes are modified, and (c) the repertoire of behavioral skills is expanded (Johnson & Johnson, 1997). The experiential learning activities used in this course are included in Appendix at the end of the chapter.

An example of how we incorporate experiential learning into our course is "Learning Checkpoint 3," in which students write about their awareness of and comfort with cultural differences. Students reflect on (a) previously held ideas about culturally diverse groups, (b) new information and/or insights gained from the readings, (c) ideas about how the new information and/or insights may relate to the cultural differences between clients and counselors, and (d) ideas about how they would try to "construct" bridges to support meaningful counseling relationships. Students complete the assignment individually and then discuss their reflections in small groups. Students who elect further exploration continue experientially with an immersion activity, in which they immerse themselves in a culture that is outside of their current comfort level for difference. The questions accompanying this assignment provide a framework for reflective observation. Class discussion provides opportunities for abstract conceptualization. By the end of such an assignment, prospective counselors become more open to active experimentation as a means for expanding their world view and knowledge base.

Reflection

Reflection contributes to finding reconciliations among present troublesome situations and previous theoretical knowledge, classroom instruction, and personal experiences. Learning opportunities do not present themselves as givens, but are constructed from events that are puzzling, troubling, and uncertain (Schon, 1983). Internal self-talk about reconciling such uncertainties composes what Schon (1987) calls "knowing-in-action," or thinking-about-doing-while-doing-it. When such learning experiences are taken collectively, "knowing in action" becomes "theory in action." A central goal of reflection is to bring personal working theories into active awareness and intentional use. The process of reflection thus provides a basis for the articulation, analysis, and critique of a counselor's professional development and practice.

Reflection involves complex thought processes and is, thus, difficult to define. Goodman (1984) defined reflection as a "way of being" that focuses on substantive, rather than utilitarian, concerns. From his view, reflection must legitimate and integrate both intuitive and rational thinking. Reflection combines self-observation and analysis. Kemmis (1985) provides an operational definition of reflection:

Reflection is a dialectical process: it looks inward at our thoughts and thought processes, and outward at the situation in which we find ourselves...we pause to reflect because some issue arises which demands that we stop and take stock or consider before we act. We do so because the situation we are in requires consideration: how we act in it is a matter of some significance. We become aware of ourselves, in some small or large way, as agents of history. (p. 141)

Counselors engage in reflection by constantly monitoring their self-talk in order to prevent personal bias, value judgments, and prejudices from negatively impacting their clients. Further, counselors develop, through reflecting on knowledge and experiences, a personal framework that defines their work. Smyth (1992) proposes that action can be linked to a series of four questions: (a) describe—what do I do? (b) inform—what does this mean? (c) confront—how did I come to be like this? and (d) reconstruct—how might I do things differently?

The questions accompanying "Learning Checkpoint 3" guide students through such an inquiry-focused process after they have read about the counseling process, the counseling relationship, and diverse populations. (See Appendix for all learning activities in quotes in this chapter.) In class, students share their reflections in dyads and in small and large groups. These discussions encourage both values clarification and models for reacting to and analyzing counseling videos, role plays, or critical incidents. For example, small groups create role plays or case studies depicting professional issues and the application of theoretical propositions from the readings and lectures. These critical incidents are given to a separate group for a response, followed by a presentation and discussion that includes the entire class. This exchange provides an opportunity for students to make "connections between subject matter and personal issues" (McAuliffe & Lovell, 2000, p. 22). Students have, as a result of this activity, consistently reported an increased capacity "to attend to others and to feel related to them in spite of what may be great differences" (McAuliffe & Lovell, 2000, p. 20).

The "Professional Development Plan" assignment also encourages reflective thinking during the introductory course. This assignment guides students in the process of recognizing growth and identifying skills to be strengthened in subsequent training. Students "construct" goals for both personal and professional development by synthesizing what they have learned from reflective thinking, dialectical exchange, and feedback during the course. The Professional Development Plan assignment provides guided practice in constructing a comprehensive professional identity and reinforces the expectation and experience of empowerment and responsibility.

Metacognition

McAuliffe and Lovell (2000) alert us to the notion that metacognition, or the "conscious monitoring of one's thought processes" (Henderson, 1996, p. 21), is key for the counselor who would become a constructivist. Metacognition requires students to think about their cognitive activities rather than simply practicing them (Bandura, 1997). Bandura tells us that in constructing solutions people must channel attention, decipher environmental task demands, draw on relevant knowledge, appraise skills, and evaluate and revise plans and strategies. Counselor educators need to teach students to recognize and articulate this complex skill and to become aware of their role as change agents.

Counseling seems to be moving toward what Ivey (1986) termed a metatheoretical position of looking for commonalties among theories and recognizing that final truths are less final than once believed. Egan (1990), in practical terms, sees novice helpers as needing an integrative model or framework that helps them to borrow from available models and then to organize what they borrow. The skills needed to integrate counseling theories and other varying perspectives are too important to be left to chance. Thus, in the small and large group discussions, we encourage students to consciously examine and share the rationales that support their interpretations and assessments of self and others. The learning checkpoints can provide a focus and content for these discussions.

We also consciously attempt to model our own integrative and metacognitive skills. For instance, an ethical dilemma presented itself in one small group discussion. A school counselor was attempting to enroll a Hispanic girl, whose family members were migrant workers, in high school classes. The dilemma emerged from the counselor's attempts to assess the girl's number of credits and class standing. As the dilemma was being explained, I began mentally framing my comments for the discussion. My thoughts included the notion that the young woman had experienced many interruptions to her education and gaps in her academic knowledge. On the other hand, the student presenting the situation proceeded to talk about what the young woman would have learned as a migrant worker without the benefit of continuous formal schooling. She gave examples that included information about plants and how they grow, about geography from traveling, and about different languages. I realized that I was thinking of the student as deficient. I was thinking of what the hypothetical student didn't know and not what she did know. I shared my thinking with the class as an example of metacognitive processes.

The "Team Teachback" activity provides an opportunity for students to cooperatively examine some of their own metacognitive processes. Students self-select teams and topics about which they will construct a knowledge base and identify multiple perspectives. They select from the following course themes: knowledge of self and others as cultural beings, professional performance parameters, and the contemporary settings in which professional counselors work. For example, teams might discuss the historical or theoretical premises considered, their contemporary relevance, sources of information and training, and then offer an illustration (such as, role play, simulation exercise, critical incident scenario). The teams then debrief the class and share their metacognitive processes about methods of identifying the views presented.

INSTRUCTIONAL PROCESSES

Counselor educators "walk the walk" by constructing training experiences that themselves model the value of experience, active learning, and reflective practice. They also challenge learners and themselves to participate experientially by offering and receiving feedback, promoting egalitarianism, and inviting dialogue. In doing so, they serve as models and guides in "how to know as well as what to know," and in developing experiences to catalyze" personal revolutions in self and theoretical understanding and skill development (McAuliffe & Lovell, 2000, p. 20). By deconstructing traditional classroom power relationships, the professor can begin to position student voices as central to creating the learning environment. In fact, the following criteria might serve as a checklist for planning and evaluating instructional strategies and course interventions.

Seating Arrangements

Classroom seating configurations that promote student-to-student interactions support an open exchange of ideas and personal involvement in the learning process and community. A circle configuration seems to reinforce the equalization of voices and to promote sharing and more careful listening than traditional seating by rows. The power of this configuration as an instructional intervention is exponential (Johnson & Johnson, 1997) because it also serves to: (a) more effectively engage the group dynamics associated with formation, (b) reinforce a norm of involvement and participation in the learning process, (c) support risk-taking, and (d) increase the expression of multiple perspectives.

Small Groups

Dyadic and small group discussions, more than lecturing, may enhance the learning environment. Dyadic and small group processing allow the members of the learning group to get to know one another, and we hope to enhance, students' abilities "to accommodate difference and newness and to engage complexity" (McAuliffe & Lovell, 2000, p.18).

Participatory Lecture

We use lecture sparingly (but consistently) to clarify or supplement reading assignments, but we depend on the voices of the learners to collaboratively define the meanings derived from such lectures. Students help to determine the agenda, and their input provides a gauge for checking (and modifying as required) the level of didactic content.

Norms

We also share the process and power of constructing the learning environment by explicitly addressing the ground rules and the components of the "operative affective environment" (Graves, 1990; Wehrly, 1995). We endeavor to arrive at a group consensus concerning ground rules that will enhance involvement and growth. During the initial meeting students work in dyads, small groups, and the large group to discuss, modify, and/or offer support for behavior norms suggested by the instructor. Such discussions center on such things as the need for active involvement, respect, confidentiality, freedom from judgmentalness, and sharing personally rather than posing as an expert. Students assess their readiness for adopting these ground rules and clarify related behavioral expectations for themselves, other students, and the counselor educator. We stop class periodically to check on how we are doing at implementing these ground rules. Such discussions provide students with both a frame of reference specific to the introductory course (microcosm), and for future participatory norms in the professional community (macrocosm).

Student Input into the Course

An overview and clarification of course requirements can be incorporated into these discussions by including student voices in defining additional course content options. We begin with a course that is loosely divided into three sections. During the initial sessions (the first through the third or fourth meetings), counselor educators and prospective counselors begin to co-construct the learning environment. During the intermediate sessions (the fourth or fifth through the tenth or eleventh meetings), students begin to experience dissonance as they explore and investigate the course topics. The last four or five weeks are advanced sessions during which students demonstrate synthesis and personal framing of critical counseling issues to support their own professional development.

As already indicated, initial sessions are dedicated to co-constructing the learning environment, including developing ground rules and a sense of community. During the intermediate sessions, instructional strategies and interventions support increasingly active student engagement in defining the content and format of learning experiences, self-assessment, and individual plans for professional development. These sessions begin with a presentation of and/or a call for announcements related to current issues, news, and opportunities for professional counselors. Such a call provides on-going and salient inclusion of diverse context considerations and serves as guided practice for constructing professional awareness and advocacy.

We also open the class by "calling for content," which creates a space for discussions that are related to the overall goals of the introductory course, discussions related to the topical and reading outline, and changes of agenda based on student needs. Such changes of class focus model flexibility, the willingness to share the construction of weekly agenda-setting, the inclusion of student voices, and the equalization of power relationships in the learning community. For small group and dyadic discussions during the intermediate sessions, each student selects discussion topics that reflect his or her self-assessment from a menu of options. (See later section, "Guided Practice as a Tool for Evaluation and Goal Setting.")

During advanced sessions, students maximize their involvement in the learning process by constructing and conducting the class sessions, thus taking responsibility for getting what they need and want from these sessions. The "Individual Option," in which students assess themselves and choose an area in which to grow, and the "Team Teachback," in which students chose an area of interest and work as a group to prepare an "infomercial," both prepare students to articulate cognitive and affective developmental concerns. A sense of community seems to blossom from the team projects. This connection supports students in sharing views in large group discussions.

The instructor's primary tasks during advanced sessions include guiding the students through feedback and reflective questioning, while simultaneously facilitating student-to-student interaction about the "Team Teachback," the "Individual Options," and the "Professional Development Plan." Both counselor educators and potential counselors are jointly responsible for the consideration and appreciation of diversity. If the learning community is diverse, we can intentionally configure and/or promote the formation of groups that maximize the expression of alternative views and voices. If the class population is not sufficiently diverse, we must (ethically and intentionally) simulate the presence of alternative views and voices through classroom activities or outside assignments. Ideally, during the final sessions of the course, the class functions as a cultural and contextual sounding board for students to tryon, tryout, and construct professional meanings and metaphors.

One example of simulating the presence of alternative views in a homogenous classroom is having students assume the voice of a culturally different "other" during specific discussions. Another example is "The Cultural Artifact Exercise." This exercise asks students to bring an object to class that represents their culture. In small groups, they explain their object and its significance. The group is then asked to draw a picture that includes the meaning of each object shared while representing a unifying theme that emerged from the sharing of the cultural artifacts. Artifacts have included Ukrainian wedding rings from a grandparent, a Swiss Bible written in French, a hand carved giraffe, and a menorah brought from Germany. Diversity is revealed in close ties to immigrant backgrounds and cultures or, for some, a first thought of themselves as a part of a cultural background that is not merely "American."

Soliciting Feedback

The instructor solicits regular feedback on the course, the activities, and students' progress. Such feedback helps the instructor to determine student readiness for future activities. We have also found it helpful to periodically review the course purpose, goals, and ground rules. Such a review allows students to progressively define the meaning of developing professional counseling competency, based on growing experience with the class and the course knowledge base. Additionally, midterm and final reviews provide both formative and summative assessments of individual and group progress.

GUIDED PRACTICE AS A TOOL FOR EVALUATION AND GOAL SETTING

We provide students with preparation guidelines and evaluation criteria for each learning assignment. The overall goal in the evaluation of learning assignments is to encourage the development of the following three dimensions: personal awareness, content knowledge, and skill competency (Arredondo et al., 1996). We graduate the evaluation process from beginning to advanced sessions. That is, in beginning assignments, students receive points for merely completing the assignments. In later assignments, the instructor offers very specific feedback as a sort of a dialogue (in writing or in person) with students, which supports students in their self-appraisal, in identifying goals, and in formulating plans for professional development. A strong and continuous emphasis on self-evaluation challenges students to examine major issues related to professional counseling and their career development. The specific course assignments are as follows.

The Learning Checkpoints and Literature Review

The first three assignments, the "Learning Checkpoints," require students to explore their views of multiple counseling theories, of culture as an issue in counseling, and of a self-selected issue. For the "Literature Review" assignment, the student reviews current research literature concerning a self-selected counseling topic. The purpose of the literature review is for students to familiarize themselves with research questions, hypotheses, and methodology, and to synthesize, compare, and contrast current research on a topic of interest. This assignment also introduces them to the American Psychological Association's publication manual and professional counseling journals and provides a fund of knowledge to use in subsequent class activities and assignments.

The Individual Options

The "Individual Options" require students to: (a) evaluate their current level of self- or other awareness, knowledge, or skill; (b) identify and participate in a related "growth" activity, and (c) assess the resulting growth. The options encourage each student to explore or construct a learning experience according to his or her readiness and comfort level. The Individual Options have been reported as "the most helpful" of the course assignments, because they allow students to select their own areas of growth and development. Students choose from four options:

1. Participation in counseling (series of at least five individual or group sessions) to gain self-knowledge.

2. Cultural immersion (at least three outings) to gain knowledge of others who are culturally different and data about one's responses to such difference.

3. An option designed by the student, which includes a clear rationale and specific learning objectives. Designed options require instructor agreement and usually a learning contract.

4. Conference attendance, in order to gain knowledge of how theory translates to practice in a specific area of interest.

Of these options, the cultural immersion experience seems to be the most popular and the most powerful. In the reflective questions attached to this assignment, students share a great deal about their assumptions and attributions associated with difference and appear to reap huge cognitive and affective benefits. One student reported attending a Chinese Circus and being "pleasantly surprised" to discover the diversity of this cultural group, and even a few similarities with her own European cultural traditions. She noted that prior to this experience, her only knowledge of Chinese culture had been derived from Charlie Chan movies. She also reported a new willingness to interact with culturally different others, and an appreciation for a previously unknown group.

Several students have reported participating in Gay Pride activities and feeling more comfortable than expected and more accepting of themselves and the gay, lesbian, bisexual, and transsexual population. Similarly, students visiting the Museum of African American History and the Jewish Holocaust Center have consistently reported feeling more relaxed among members of these respective populations. They gained new awareness and insights concerning the socio-political realities for racial and ethnic minorities and an enhanced ability to define and give examples of the influence of collective histories on the cross-cultural counseling relationship. Student selection of activities ensures that initial growth experiences are based on individual readiness and sets the stage for further development in more advanced multicultural courses and practicum experiences.

REFLECTIONS ON TEACHING THE INTRODUCTORY COURSE

The excitement of having students embark on their journey towards becoming professional counselors and the power and challenge of being part of the learning community quickly banished any notion for us that this class was nonessential. However, helping students realize the contextual nature of their worldviews and much of what they have learned is not easy. As teachers try to respect "cultural diversity," hooks (1994) notes that they must confront the limitations of their training and knowledge and the possible loss of "authority." She identifies correctly that recognition of difference requires a willingness to see the classroom change, to allow for shifts in relations between students. Exposing certain truths and biases will often create chaos and confusion.

An example emerged during a Team Teachback presentation. Students compared the Latino community's Catholic religion with cognitive behavioral theory. During the large group debriefing, some conflicts emerged between counseling practices and this population group's cultural and religious practices. "Chaos" ensued during the discussion. Some students stated that they believed in both the theory and the religion and because this combination did not pose a problem for them, that "it would not be a problem" for this particular cultural group. The students were assuming that if they were able to resolve the problem, that culturally different others would automatically come to the same conclusion. Other students challenged the cultural competency of such a rationale and cited the professional standards related to working with culturally different clients. Then a student said, "This conversation has to stop right now." The group was startled and indeed the conversation did stop. As a group, we were able to acknowledge the challenge and dialogue about the cognitive dissonance and strong affective responses engendered by the discussion. The presenters thanked the group for generating such "tough" questions and said that they had experienced an epiphany. I (Calloway) was a little nervous during points of the discussion, but took the risk of giving up authority. After the presenters concluded, I pointed out the workings and associated chaos of reflective practices from both personal and professional perspectives. I focused discussion on the necessity (perhaps inevitability) of challenging our problem solving and intervention paradigms when planning cross cultural interventions. Students were able to acknowledge both frustration in trying to align traditional theory with diverse cultural frames of reference, and relief that in the future they would be able to anticipate and more competently address similar challenges in cross cultural work in their professional settings.

Counselor educators cannot necessarily anticipate the eventual professional reality that students will enter after graduation. We build this reality together. Beginning students often eagerly wait, with notebooks open, to receive a professor's words of wisdom. At the same time, they are usually ready to try new skills and behaviors and to explore the personal and social dimensions of their identity. Counselor educators may similarly experience a tension between structure and freedom, between what we want students to know (the structure) and how they need to go about understanding and deconstructing that knowledge (the freedom). The construction and continuing deconstruction in this course demonstrates our belief that, in parallel fashion, for professional counselors it is just as important to continuously identify and understand *what* to know as well as *how* to know it.

The model presented here has evolved from our collective experiences in teaching the introductory course, our evaluations of guided practice assignments, and our observations of student performance in subsequent classes. By the end of this introductory course, we hope that students will have consistently demonstrated their abilities to conceptualize and articulate dialectical tensions through their written assignments. Lively, student-directed class sessions include cognitive and affective challenges as students engage in complex reflective practices. During class, students have demonstrated the ability to tolerate disequilibrium and to generate questions and methods of inquiry. We see in students' writings their intentional application of dialectical thinking in negotiating interpersonal relationships.

Proactive as opposed to reactive thinking about diversity better positions counselors to work in varieties of communities. We resonate with Giroux's (1992) description of teachers as "cultural workers." He explains that the pedagogical dimension of cultural work lies in the process of creating "symbolic representations" and the practices within which they are engaged. Such a pedagogy concerns itself with the analysis of textual, aural, and visual representations of such practices and how such representations are organized and regulated within particular institutional arrangements. In that vein, as counselor educators we can assist both students and ourselves to unravel not only the ideological codes, representations, and practices that structure the dominant order, [and] to acknowledge those places and spaces we inherit and occupy which frame our lives in very specific and concrete ways which are as much a part of our psyches as they are a physical or geographical placement . . . . Cultural workers . . . relate to and address wider issues that affect both the immediacy of their location and the wider global context (Giroux, 1992, p. 79).

The classroom situation itself can serve as a laboratory for this "cultural work." Each experience in the introductory course is intended to be challenging and invigorating as we, instructors and students, construct our own learning community. The themes of who we are as cultural beings and who we might be as professional counselors and cultural workers become our building blocks. Our hope is that the Introduction to Counseling course will provide students with a tool kit that enables them to critically examine multiple approaches as they encounter them in subsequent course work and as they begin to construct the field with us.

Appendix

Learning Checkpoint 3
(learning activities presented in the order they were presented in the chapter)

Focus: Multicultural Counseling Competencies

Respond to the following items, supporting your comments with information from the readings. Limit your response to all three questions to no more than two pages.

1. Identify something that you have learned about members of one of the visible racial/ethnic (VREG), gay, lesbian, or bisexual groups discussed in Chapter 14. Discuss how your new learning refutes previous stereotypes and/or assumptions you have made about members of this group.

2. Provide a behavioral example of social and cultural influences on your own development and contrast it with those from another group: First identify the example and briefly describe the A, B, and C dimensions; and then contrast with a behavior that may be demonstrated by someone in another group.

3. Provide a behavioral example of how a counselor's attitudes, beliefs, and values could interfere with providing the best service to clients. First identify the example and then briefly describe the A,B, and C dimensions.

Professional Development Plan
Assignment Guidelines

The purpose of this assignment is to begin thinking through and planning for your professional development. There are three parts to this assignment and points will be assigned as follows:

Part 1: Assessment of personal strengths and skill areas targeted for improvement. 5 points

Part 2: Goals - identification of three professional development goals, one short term, one intermediate, and one long term; and an outline of the required steps / plan of how you will achieve these goals—6 points

Part 3: Counseling statement—the purpose of counseling, reasonable expectations concerning outcomes, client responsibility, and counselor responsibility—9 points

Professional Team Teach Back

The Team Teach Back is a collaborative effort by four to six people who will prepare and present a 45-60 minute "infomercial" to the rest of the class. The purpose of this assignment is to give classmates information about some specialized aspect or area of counseling. After we have seen all the presentations, we should be familiar with many of the settings in which counseling takes place. Knowing this will help us as we begin to decide what kind of counseling settings we would be comfortable working in. The presentation should cover as many of the following issues as are relevant to the topic your group has chosen.

• The history of this area

• Foundational theories or models

• Major, distinguishing features of this method of help-giving

• Expected benefits for clients

• Types of clients that would be served

• Counseling techniques likely to be employed

• Example of what this counseling setting looks like (a role-play, simulation, or case presentation)

• Current or expected need for this service (economic, socio-political issues, current news reports, etc.)

• Sources of professional development outside graduate training programs

• Representative places in this geographic area where this type of counseling takes place

Presentations will be evaluated on the degree to which they are informative, interesting and creative, organized, thorough, collaborative.

Cultural Artifacts

Students are instructed to bring an object (artifact) to class that represents their culture. The class process is as follows:

1. Form a group of 5-6 people

2. Share artifacts:
      How does the artifact represent your culture?
      What does the artifact mean to you?

3. What themes represent your group as a whole?

4. With everyone's input, make a visual representation of your group themes

5. Pick a spokesperson for the group

6. Present your picture

Learning Checkpoint 1
Focus: ACA Ethical Guidelines

Read and respond to both of the following ethical dilemmas, providing support for your response from the textbook and the ethical guidelines. Limit your response for each dilemma to one typed, double-spaced page.

For each dilemma:

Identify the nature of the dilemma

Defend the counselor's decision or describe what the counselor might have done instead.

A. A school counselor receives a phone call from the parents of a 10th grade student who is having academic problems. The parents tell the counselor that they are going to transfer their son to a private school the next school year and ask that the counselor not tell their son about the proposed move. The student loves the current school, is very involved in school activities, and would be very upset to know of his parents' plans. The counselor considers the parents' request very carefully and decides, in the best interests of the student, to tell him in the hopes that the student can talk his parents out of sending him to the private school.

B. A post master's counseling intern, seeking to fulfill the post master's supervised experience requirement for licensure arranges to volunteer at a local agency in return for clinical supervision from the only Licensed Professional Counselor (LPC) on staff at that agency. The agency director quickly agrees to this arrangement and informs the LPC that the intern will be helping her with her overwhelming caseload. The LPC indicates that she needs to first interview the intern to determine if the arrangement will work out. In the interview, the prospective intern discloses that, while she feels quite competent to work in the agency, she does need help in one related area of her own life. The LPC determines that she can in fact use the intern, agrees to provide appropriate supervision, on the condition that the LPC and the intern meet in weekly counseling sessions to work through the problem areas of the intern's life.

Learning Checkpoint 2
Focus: Chapters 3 & 10

Respond to the following items, and provide support for your response based on the readings. Limit your response to all four questions to three pages.

1. Which of the qualities/skills of effective counseling described in Chapter Three will be the easiest and/or hardest for you to learn to do well? Explain your response.

2. How do you, as the counselor, determine to what extent it may be effective for you to self-disclose to a client?

3. Under what circumstances do you as the counselor have the right to decide what you think is in the client's best interests?

4. Which of the nontraditional approaches of counseling described in Chapter Ten is most likely to "fit" with how you are as an individual and your ideas about counseling theory? Explain.

Learning Checkpoint 4
Focus: Technology and Counseling: Issues Present and Future

Respond to the following items, information from the internet and the hand-outs. Limit your response to all three questions to no more than two pages.

1. Access a professional association web site related to your area (www.counseling.org or www.studentaffairs.com will open up access to a variety). Select an item that will provide you with information relevant to a counseling professional in your field. Briefly summarize the item and then describe how it would be useful to a counseling professional.

2. Using the NBCC Web Counseling Ethical Standards and the ACA standards, develop an ethical dilemma that could result from a counseling application of the internet. Solve the dilemma providing specific support for your response from the ethical guidelines.

3. Using information learned from the above two questions, write your own checkpoint question and then answer it.

Individual Option A:
Counseling Series Experience

Guiding Questions

Requirements:

1. A minimum of five counseling sessions (individual or group), and

2. Signed compliance statement (below).

    Please respond to the following items after you have completed your counseling experience (Due Session 12). Be sure to identify the item you are responding to directly preceding your response. Respond to these items from the point of view of the client. Please note: You are *NOT* to critique the counselor.

1. What is the most potentially difficult aspect of counseling?

2. What is the most potentially rewarding aspect of counseling?

3. What personal benefits did you gain from your counseling experience?

4. Compose your own question relating to counseling and the client and then answer that question.

Be sure to type each question directly preceding your response.

Individual Option A:
Counseling Series

Compliance Statement:

I, _____, (print your name) have completed the minimum number of counseling sessions required for this optional assignment.

_____   _____
        (your signature)   (your counselor's signature)

date: _____

Individual Option B:
Cultural Immersion Experiences

Guiding Questions Requirements:

1. A minimum of three activities that are centered in a cultural experience a different from your own.

2. Prior review and approval of your itinerary by instructor (the review should be done by Session 6).

3. Programs or documentation of the immersion visits, attached to the assignment.

Please respond to the following items after you have completed your immersion experience (Due Session 12). Be sure to identify the item you are responding to directly preceding your response.

1. How have these experiences reinforced and/or changed your views about this particular cultural group or your own cultural experiences?

2. How have these experiences enhanced your potential to become a culturally competent professional counselor? Be specific about each experience.

3. What did these experiences teach you about yourself?

4. Compose your own question relating to counseling and cultural groups. Then answer that question.

Be sure to type each question directly preceding your response.

Individual Option C:
Full-Day Conference Experience

Guiding Questions Requirements:

1. Prior instructor review and approval of conference registration materials (the review should be done by Week five).

2. Programs or documentation of the presentation sessions, attached to the assignment.

Please respond to the following items after you have completed your conference experience (Due Session 11). Be sure to identify the item you are responding to directly preceding your response.

1. What was the major theme or focus of the conference and how does this theme/focus relate to your development as a professional counselor?

2. Identify and explain three key points that stand out for you from the presentation sessions you attended.

3. Identify one thing that you learned or felt reinforced in that you can/will implement immediately. How will you go about this?

4. Compose your own question relating to the conference theme and then answer that question.

Be sure to type each question directly preceding your response.

Literature Review Assignment
Helping Relationships: Basic Concepts and Services

The purpose of this assignment is to increase your knowledge of current issues in counseling and to give you some experience in reading and summarizing research literature. This review must include six sources.

To make sure that your review considers the most recent research, limit your search to publication years of 1994 and beyond. The review must be taken from professional journals and/or books. All references must present empirical evidence, for example, cite data sources for conclusions and/or recommendations. Experimental, historical, ethnographic, case study, survey, and quasi-experimental sources are appropriate. Your review should not exceed 10 pages (including the title and reference pages) and must adhere to APA guidelines. (See the APA manual for expanded definitions of the following.)

Your paper should include:

- A title   which summarizes the main idea

- An abstract   a brief comprehensive summary of the content

- An introduction   which presents the specific problem or topic under study

- Review of Literature   an integrated discussion of the sources you have reviewed, highlighting themes, similarities, and differences

- Discussion/Summary   a discussion of the major findings and recommendations; as well as any limitations and/or shortcomings of studies cited

- References   a page that identifies all sources cited in your review

Please attach a copy of the articles included in your review. Select your topic from the following list: adolescents; lesbian, gay, bisexual, transgendered clients; multiracial clients; older adults; visible ethnic minorities—American Indians, Arab Americans, African Americans, Asian Americans, Latino Americans.

REFERENCES

Aisenberg, N., & Harrington, M. (1988). *Women of academe: Outsider in the sacred game.* Amherst, MA: University of Massachusetts Press.

Arredondo, P., Toporek, R., Brown, S. P., Jones, J., Locke, D. C., Sanchez, J., & Stadler, H. (1996). Operationalization of the multicultural counseling competencies. *Association for Multicultural Counseling and Development.* Alexandria, VA: American Counseling Association.

Bandura, A. (1997). *Self-efficacy: The exercise of control.* New York: W.H. Freemam and Company.

Capuzzi, D., & Gross, D. R. (1997). *Introduction to the counseling profession* (2nd ed.). Boston, MA: Allyn and Bacon.

Cross W. E. (1971) The negro to black conversion experience: Towards a psychology of black liberation. *Black World, 20,* 13-27.

Downing, N. E. & Roush, K. L. (1985). From passive acceptance to active commitment: A model of feminist identity development for women. *The Counseling Psychologist, 13* 695-709.

Egan, G. (1990). *The skilled helper: A systematic approach to effective helping* (4th ed.). Pacific Grove, CA: Brooks Cole.

Gibson, R. L., & Mitchell, M. H. (1999). *Introduction to counseling and guidance.* Upper Saddle River, NJ: Merrill.

Gladding, S. T. (1996). *Counseling: A comprehensive profession.* Englewood Cliffs, NJ: Merrill.

Goodman, J. (1984). Reflection and teacher education: A case study and theoretical analysis. *Interchange, 15,* 9-26.

Giroux, H. A. (1992). *Border crossings: Cultural workers and the politics of education.* New York: Routledge.

Graves, S. B. (1990). A case of double jeopardy? Black women in higher education. *Initiatives, 53,* 3-8..

Hayes, R. L., & Oppenheim, R. (1997). Constructivism: Reality is what you make it. In R. L. Sexton and B. L. Griffin (Eds.), *Constructivist thinking in counseling practice, research, and training* (pp. 19-40). Teachers College, Columbia University.

Helms, J. E. (1990). *Black and white racial identity: Theory, research, and practice.* New York: Greenwood Press.

Henderson, J. G. (1996). *Reflective teaching: The study of your constructivist practices* (2nd ed.). Englewood Cliffs, NJ: Merrill.

hooks, b. (1994). *Teaching to transgress: Education as the practice of freedom.* New York: Routledge.

House, R. M. & Miller, J. L. (1997). Counseling gay, lesbian, and bisexual clients. In D. Capuzzi, & D. R. Gross, *Introduction to the counseling profession* (2nd ed.), (pp. 397-432.) Needham Heights, MA: Allyn & Bacon.

Ivey, A. E. (1986). *Developmental therapy.* San Francisco: Jossey Bass.

Johnson, D. W. & Johnson, F. P. (1997). *Joining together: Group theory and group skills* (6th ed.). Boston: Allyn and Bacon.

Kemmis, S. (1985). Action research and the politics of reflection. In D. Boud, R. Keogh, & D. Walker (Eds.), *Reflection: Turning experience into learning* (pp. 139-163). New York: Nichols.

Kim, J. (1981). The process of Asian American identity development: A study of Japanese-American women's perceptions of their struggle to achieve personal identities as Americans of Asian ancestry. *Dissertation Abstracts International, 42, 1551A.* (University Microfilms No. 81-18080).

Kolb, D. (1984). *Experiential learning: Experience as the source of learning and development.* Englewood Cliffs, NJ: Prentice Hall.

Kottler, J. A. & Brown, R. W. (1996). *Introduction to therapeutic counseling.* Pacific Grove, CA: Brooks Cole.

McAuliffe, G. J., & Lovell, C. (2000). Encouraging transformation: Guidelines for constructivist and developmental instruction. In G. McAuliffe, K. Eriksen, and Associates, *Preparing counselors and therapists: Creating constructivist and developmental programs* (pp. 14-41). Alexandria, VA: Association of Counselor Educators and Supervisors.

Nugent, F. A. (1994). *An introduction to the profession of counseling.* Columbus, OH: Merrill.

Parham, T. A., & Helms, J. E. (1981). The influence of Black students' racial attitudes on preferences for counselor's race. *Journal of Counseling Psychology, 28,* 250-257.

Schon, D. A. (1983). *The reflective practitioner: How professionals think in action.* USA: Basic Books.

Schon, D. A. (1987). *Educating the reflective practitioner.* San Francisco: Jossey-Bass.

Smyth, J. (1992). Teachers' work and the politics of reflection. *American Educational Research Journal, 29,* 267-300.

Sue, D. W. & Sue, D. (1990). *Counseling the culturally different: Theory and practice* (2nd.). New York: John Wiley & Sons.

Wehrly, B. (1995). *Pathways to multicultural counseling competence: A developmental journey.* Pacific Grove, CA: Brooks/Cole.

3

Constructing the Helping Interview

Karen Eriksen and Garrett McAuliffe

"This is a whole new way of being," said a student. "In other parts of my life I am a mother and a teacher and a boss, and I am supposed to be in charge and tell everyone else what to do. To just sit and listen, follow the client, and reflect back to them what I hear is very strange and new, and I find it very difficult."

Indeed, Constructing the Helping Interview—taught under the rubric of Interviewing Skills, Techniques of Individual Counseling, or Counseling Skills—is designed to introduce graduate or undergraduate students to ways of working and interacting with others that are different from what they have previously known. They discover that a helping interview is largely about two or more people helping each other tell a new story, one that works better than a previously told one. It often surprises students in this course that the helping interview is not directive or advice-oriented, ironically, despite its goal of influencing others toward behavior change and good decision-making. Beginning students' experiences with interviewing and helping have usually been restricted to parental admonition, religious prescription, and secondary school college advising. "Helping" for them, at its most concrete, might bring up visions of changing a flat tire for someone on the road, bandaging a wound, or washing the dishes. We cannot underestimate the pervasiveness of such a direct, "enabling" vision of helping for neophyte counselors.

Inviting Personal Evolution

In contrast, the course on the helping interview asks students, as interviewees, to put the power into the hands of the interviewee, to be ready to question all advisors, and, above all, to evoke the client's agenda. Such helping requires an epistemological leap for many beginning counseling students, as they have yet to embrace their own authority as meaning-makers (Kegan, 1994; Lovell & McAuliffe, 1996; Neukrug & McAuliffe, 1993), let alone dwell in the murky waters of a helping interview that is co-constructed.

What is therefore learned in such a course is more than mere skills, for this way of helping hinges on a worldview in which meanings are made in relationship, a relationship that reflects a respect for human beings' abilities to help themselves. Thus, the tasks of the helping skills course have the potential to challenge students in personally important ways, even as students rather mechanically learn one microskill at a time. Applying active listening skills can dramatically change students' lives in both epistemological capacity and in day-to-day relationships.

Moving from Other- to self-authorizing thinking. In the first case, this course can instigate an evolution in students' ways of knowing by inviting them to view human norms, values, and views of "reality" as socially created constructions. The cause has the potential to move students from being defined by others to defining themselves, a shift Belenky and her colleagues (1986) would call moving from a "received" or "subjective" way of knowing to a "procedural," even a "constructivist," way of knowing. Evidence exists that fewer than twenty percent of adults are able to consistently think reflectively and procedurally (Kegan, 1994). So we can assume that most of our students enter our programs fully capable of listening to authorities and delivering directives, but not yet fully capable of living in a socially constructed universe. Many will fluctuate from an authority-reliant tendency to an occasional "self-authorizing" capacity. Therefore, students may at least partially be "authority dependent" (Lovell & McAuliffe, 1996); that is, they will be:

- embedded in or subject to their relationships and to rules (For instance, saying to the instructor, "How long does the paper need to be?" "What do you want us to do this week?" "I didn't do what I wanted to on this paper because I didn't think that was what you would want.");

- able to meet their own needs, but more likely to sacrifice these to meet another's needs (For example, letting practice counseling sessions go on long beyond the required time and long beyond their comfort zone because the "client" is still distressed and seems to need to talk.);

- able to hold an inner dialogue, but likely to merely experience feelings rather than to be able to name them or think about them (For instance, when asked to name feelings during class or during counseling sessions, can only identify "bad" or "good" or "frustrated," which represents a limited awareness of or ability to identify their own feelings and a limited range of possible feelings; difficulty stepping back and examining these feelings in journals.);

- determined and defined by others (for example, difficulty saying "no" in work or personal situations; difficulty questioning the instructor or the program's authority.);

- needing to maintain relationships, be approved of, and not challenge conventions (see above examples);

- more likely to experience undifferentiated "fusion" in relationships (Intimacy requires knowing where you end and the other begins. Students' difficulties expressing or being aware of their own inner experiences in the presence of another's pain indicates a problem with this, and thus with meeting the "client" with their whole self.);

- intuitive in their approach to helping, following unexamined inner urges, sometimes reactively (For instance, difficulty standing back from a counseling session and explaining why they did what they did, and analyzing or evaluating their own or the client's behavior, or the counseling relationship; reactively jumping in with inappropriate responses, seeming to get "pulled in" by clients' ways of talking or behaving).

While each of these characteristics can be seen as strengths, in that they contribute to a student's ability to care for other people and their pain, they limit counselors' abilities to live within the ambiguity of counseling work, to set reasonable boundaries between themselves and the client (and the client's problem), to work independently and reflectively, and to plunge the very personal depths that they are trying to help clients develop.

Development-enhancing instruction. Instructors thus need to optimally "support and challenge" (Sanford, 1966) students who operate primarily from received or subjective ways of knowing in order to help them move to an evidence-based way of making meaning. *Support* might mean celebrating their kindness and ability to tune in carefully to clients. It also means offering the structure, direction, and "authority" needed by those who are more concrete and authority-reliant. *Challenge* means urging students to think about why they are doing what they are doing, to examine their multiple and even contradictory inner urges, to decide whether preserving conventions and relationships at all costs is helpful to them, to establish a separateness from others' definitions, and to be self-reflective. Such challenges have the potential to stretch students to a place of greater autonomy, to self-authoring, and to taking responsibility for their own behavior. They may come to a place in which they have a more constant identity across contexts and a greater ability to give evidence for their current beliefs and positions.

Benefits of development. Students have experienced immediate "personal" benefits from the course in the process of discovering and voicing their personal views: For instance, saying "no" for the first time in unhealthy relationships and work settings, expressing feelings for the first time in relationships, and expecting new levels of relating and of intimacy from significant others. Complementarily, students have discovered the legitimacy of others' views and, in the process, have moved from an authoritarian toward a dialogical epistemology, or from dualism to greater relativism (Benack, 1988; Neukrug & McAuliffe, 1993). Not only are these changes revolutionary for the student, but they may catch those who are in the students' lives unaware, requiring changes that those significant others had not anticipated and may not be happy about. Thus, the shock waves that can emanate from a course such as this may resound further than either the students or their significant others would have expected.

In a much more concrete sense, the helping interview course also can and should improve students' interpersonal relationships. Learning helping skills means learning basic communication skills. These are fundamental to effective family and organizational life. Such skills are immediately applicable to both professional and personal relationships in a range of settings, from the classic one-to-one counseling interview, to religious, family, medical, teaching, and administrative settings (Ivey, 1994).

Doing as we say. We would hope that instructors who understand the anxiety that can be produced in such developmentally challenging circumstances would engage students in a manner that is parallel, or "isomorphic," to the counselor-client relationship. For instance, just as the counselor-client relationship is usually grounded in the core conditions of empathy, respect, and unconditional positive regard (Carkhuff & Berenson,1977) and, in most traditions, in an egalitarian—as opposed to an authoritarian—relationship, so too the instructor might seek relationships with students based on respect, genuineness, and positive regard. Just as helpers can never change clients but can expect them to construct new meanings and try on new behaviors, the instructor, in an effort to foster progression through developmental stages, similarly encourages and challenges students to envision and try on new ways of being. Just as counselors do not expect clients to change in significant ways merely by being told "the right answer," instructors understand that merely lecturing on material seldom promotes the desired student development. Just as many counselors believe that clients' lives will be enhanced and problems will be reduced if they advance developmentally, many counselor educators believe that epistemological changes in students should improve their work (Lovell & McAuliffe, 1996). And, finally, just as counselors use the assets that clients bring into counseling sessions in creating solutions with clients, instructors value the expertise students bring into the classroom as a result of life experiences. Thus instructors refuse to serve as the sole knowledge-bearers.

THE LEARNING SEQUENCE: A BIAS TOWARD ACTIVITY

In the Helping Interview course, we have taken the "necessity of activity" for retention seriously. The sequence of activities in the course might proceed as follows (The following may be included as a list in the syllabus to help students structure their learning experience and to "share the learning method."): Read, reflect, hear, discuss, observe, critique, apply, reflect, critique. That means that, initially, students read about the topic or "skill," using a book that breaks counseling into subskills. Then, prior to class, students try the chapter's practice exercises. These written activities help the students to interact with the chapter's material. During the class period that follows such reading, instructors and students first discuss the key points of the reading briefly. Then students watch an instructor or another model demonstrate the skills, live or on videotape, and they critically evaluate the demonstration. Experimenting with the new skills follows, in practice counseling sessions with classmates and observers. Students then evaluate their own and their peers' performance. Next, students conduct an interview between class sessions with either peers or undergraduate volunteers, focusing on the designated skill or skills. Finally, following Schon (1983) and others' emphasis on reflection, students write about the feelings and thoughts that emerge during these events.

"Independent" Learning: Reading, Writing, and Quizzing

We use a book that breaks the actions of the helping interview into manageable, learnable subskills. Students progress from performing concrete and discrete tasks to combining these into more complex behaviors.

Texts like this also include writing and performance exercises which ask students to actively and independently engage the material, practicing the skills on their own between classes. We recommend that instructors further encourage active yet structured engagement with the reading by asking students to complete study questions (for instance, "What are the goals of attending behavior?" "What are the best uses for questioning?") for each reading assignment. To further the incentive to engage the reading, I (Eriksen) give "pop" quizzes which include only items from these study questions; students who are more externally-oriented (and those whose lives are very busy) may need the encouragement to study that such quizzes provide (Widick, Knefelkamp, & Parker, 1975).

With these reading and quizzing strategies, the instructor says, "This content is a beginning. It is what I consider to be important. I need you to know it in order for us to have a meaningful discussion during the next class." Such structured reading exemplifies one aspect of instructional "support" and "challenge" (Sanford, 1966). For instance, students who cannot consistently utilize a relatively autonomous way of knowing, who are more concrete or convention-dependent (Loevinger, 1976), are supported by the structure and external motivation that study questions and, perhaps quizzes, provide (Widick, Knefelkamp, & Parker, 1975). On the "challenge" front, students must generate responses to the study questions and the practice exercises. These activities ask students to "talk back" to the instructor (through written submissions), to actively engage with the material, and to think independently about how to apply it.

The between-class requirement that students practice interviewing skills sends them "out on their own." Such an assignment allows them to inductively develop their own thoughts about how helping skills work in action. This active engagement stimulates student questions about how and when to apply certain skills and the reasons for choosing them. It might also create doubt about the usefulness of specific skills. Instigating such "reflection-on-action" (Schon & Argyris, 1995) can demonstrate the value of the "pausing" and "speaking in measured tones" that are characteristic of evidence-based, procedural knowing (Belenky et al,. 1986).

Without such challenge, students operating from more external, concrete ways of knowing may merely read the material passively, as though the book is one more "authority" in a long line of "directors" in their lives. They may then passively await the next class period for the teacher-as-authority to tell them what they need to know from the chapter.

"Social" Learning: In-Class Discussions, Observations, and Experimentation. Although the counseling skills are set up to be learned by individuals, the group can be used to make new sense of what has been pondered separately. Each of the following is a "social" event. As such, it can model the

power of peers' (and one's own) insights and the constructed nature of knowledge.

"Seatwork" and Discussion: Asking for Evidence. Instructors challenge students when, during discussions, they pose questions that require students to think for themselves, to consider different perspectives, and to offer evidence for assertions. For example, in initial discussions about videotapes or live demonstrations of "paraphrasing," the instructor may challenge students to stand back from the immediate skill and think for themselves by asking at a more "macro" level, "What is the point of paraphrasing? Why do we do it?" Students might respond by saying that they really feel heard when someone listening to them uses paraphrasing, that this seems the best way to let someone know that you understand them. Through paraphrasing, a window to constructivism opens, as students see how merely restating a client's words more simply and clearly can open new meanings for the client.

A technique for teaching paraphrasing might be the following. The instructor:

a. *presents a vignette*, such this interviewee quote: "I am really upset about the grade I got in my ethics course. I worked really hard, harder than the others in my group worked, and some of them got better grades than I did. I just don't know what that teacher expects."

b. *asks students to do* "seatwork," that is, to privately write various "formulaic" responses ("You feel . . . because . . . .), such as "You are feeling really concerned about your grade and the teacher's expectations" or "You seem to feel angry that you worked so hard and it didn't pay off."

c. asks students to consider how to put these formulaic responses into *more natural feeling words* (such as, "You are saying . . . ,"and "It seems . . . ,"); and

d. asks them to *reflect* on how it would feel to them to use such responses, to *offer ideas* about other responses, and to *give evidence* for their answers.

To reiterate, the benefits of this cycle of active reading, demonstration, discussion, and activity are:

•   *Better retention* is assured when students must generate knowledge, that is, when they must produce an idea or action (McNamara, Scott, & Bess, 2000).

- *Procedural knowing* is introduced: The challenge to analyze both macro and micro dimensions of counseling skills, such as was illustrated above with paraphrasing, stimulates students to think beyond their subjective impressions and to give evidence for their evaluations. Also, posing questions often generates conflicting views, and instructors can then challenge students to fully voice their diverse opinions, offering evidence for their positions, and deciding together what to do about disagreements.

- *Better knowledge is produced in the context of a community* of learners from diverse cultures and with varied experiences. Such dialogically-generated knowledge can be more useful than the idea of any one of the participants who is working on his or her own.

- *The emergent nature of knowledge is demonstrated.* When the instructor becomes a question-poser rather than only an answer-giver, continually asking, "What do you think?" "Who agrees?" "Why or why not?" "Who feels differently?" "What if . . . (some Devil's Advocate type of question)?" students are challenged to take risks, to put themselves on the line, to offer tentative ideas rather than waiting until they discover the "right" answers. During such "unfinished discussions," out of the "space between" human beings in community, new ideas and thoughts emerge. Many are the times I (Eriksen) have entered the classroom armed with questions and a list of the particular answers I think the class should "discover," and have found that during the discussion the class has generated more and sometimes better answers than I could construct on my own. While it seems right that I, as the instructor, initially take responsibility for posing questions, and refereeing among different positions, I also need to make space for and respect the questions and answers that students generate from their own life experiences and thinking processes.

Video observation. Another layer of activity is added when students engage in critiquing demonstrations of the helping interview. The viewing of a videotape (or live demonstration) can become a participatory event. The constructivist instructor might engage students in actively watching demonstration tapes by having them look for specific counselor skills and characteristics or specific client characteristics and responses. Different members of the class would be alert for different things. For example, if "attending" is the skill of the week, some students would note eye contact, others body language, and still others vocal tone. If the course has progressed to "paraphrasing," some students might watch for attending behaviors, others questioning, some others client observations, and still others paraphrasing (using Ivey's skill progression, 1994). Students note situational choices in interviewing as they track both *when* skills were used as well as *how skillfully* they were used. The instructor may also ask students how they would feel if they had been the client, a question that recognizes both the value of student input and the fact that "real" clients would have very similar perspectives to naive students.

In addition to asking students to watch for and analyze the specific components of various subskills, the instructor can point students toward a "macro" level of understanding. For example, during viewing, instructors ask students to continually think about whether the goals of attending are being accomplished. Is the counselor demonstrating care, interest, and positive regard while performing the skills? Are these attitudes encouraging trust and promoting client verbalization? By posing questions in order to have students analyze both specific and overall goals, instructors refuse to serve as experts. Instead, by consistently asking students what they think, what they would do differently, and what they think worked best, instructors challenge students to generate answers from within, to build on what they already know, to contribute information from their own unique experiences, experiences even the instructor may not share. Such a strategy promotes an egalitarian atmosphere and challenges the students to be active in their own learning experience.

Instructors may also intentionally show what they consider to be both "bad" and "good" demonstrations of counseling skills. They can then challenge students to compare and decide which interventions seem to be more impactful, again asking for evidence for their views. Such inquiry can stimulate students to think for themselves and to evaluate what they see, which can help move them toward more "procedural" knowing (Belenky et al., 1986). Those participating as "clients" in the demonstrations are also asked to give voice to what "felt" best or worst to them. Such strategies communicate to students that their evaluations and perceptions count, that they must be active participants in deciding on the best counseling interventions.

Live demonstration. When instructors give up the "expert" role or challenge the supposed "experts," they open up the notion of the community as the creator of knowledge. Students can begin to see themselves as members of that community. For instance, in a live instructor demonstration, the supposedly expert instructor can be seen making "mistakes." She or he may acknowledge publicly how his or her efforts didn't work well and what he or she might have done differently if given another chance. The instructor can expose her own thinking process as it occurred during the session. In this way the threat level of learning counseling skills is reduced and the emerging, situation-driven use of them is demonstrated.

Role play. Instructors can also challenge students by asking them to spontaneously role play fictitious cases in small groups. The cases might be accompanied by questions that ask students to do such things as "Give three effective paraphrases a counselor might use in response to the client's concerns."

Simulation. Alternatively, students might generate planned simulations, or scripts, for demonstrating the skills. Here instructors might ask student groups to discuss, decide on, and then act out effective use of paraphrases in counseling the person in the vignette. During such activities, students must reach beyond what they have been told by the book or the instructor and generate knowledge. They also begin thinking ahead to real-world situations, preparing themselves to face professional challenges. They access many avenues and styles of learning, tapping into all three of the learning domains—namely cognition, behavior, and affect—in the process.

Viewing student role plays and simulations. Watching videotapes of student interviews brings concrete examples of both problems and counseling skills into the classroom, and is thus invaluable to skill development. However, viewing videotapes may also create obstacles to student epistemological development. That is, traditionally, the expert instructor supervising videotapes watches and evaluates the learner's performance of counseling and then offers "expert" advice about what to do next with the client. The learner is expected to be in a receptive mode in order to be considered "open to supervision." Such traditional supervision poses obstacles to student development because it supports a received way of knowing (Belenky et al., 1986) and fails to challenge students to generate their own ideas.

The more active, constructivist instructor uses videotape observation differently, actively engaging students themselves in creating possibilities, and stimulating the community of students to work together in creating possibilities. In addition to posing specific and general questions to stimulate discussion about videotapes, as was described above in response to watching demonstrations, the instructor challenges students to give effective feedback to one another. Reflecting on and specifically analyzing peers' counseling in preparation for offering feedback helps students know how to improve and think independently about their own counseling. Helpful feedback might be defined as "tentatively and specifically giving voice to one's own experience of another's behavior, usually using an 'I' statement"

(Bruck, pp. 114-115 this volume). Global negative or positive evaluations are discouraged in favor of specific observations. For instance, if a student says, "I think the counselor was very caring," the instructor asks, "What did you see specifically that led you to conclude that? And how did you feel when the counselor did what she did?" The manner of questioning is always such that it indicates, "Your view is important. Whatever your view is, we will listen. And also, if you are going to state a view, you need to give reasons for it." Again, in this manner, co-construction of knowledge is demonstrated and an environment conducive to students' expression of their own voices is created.

During the feedback process, the instructor gives the student counselor whose videotape was viewed the responsibility for soliciting feedback and doing some self-critique. The initial questions from the instructor to the student counselor are: "How did you feel during this segment of the video?" "What were you trying to accomplish?" "What did you feel successful at?" "What would you have changed if you had it to do over again?" "What help would you like from the class?" This line of questioning communicates that students have choices about what kind and how much feedback they receive.

In addition to facilitating the feedback process while viewing student videotapes, the instructor asks the students to tune into their own experiences of the counseling session. The instructor asks student counselors whose tapes were viewed how they felt during the session and asks them to trust their own internal indicators about what worked or did not work. The instructor asks a similar question of the other class members. This line of questioning communicates the importance of students' internal processes, their own voice, and their subjective experience.

During such discussions and demonstrations, the teacher poses questions to the class, challenges rigid positions, urges students to challenge each other and the teacher, and takes positions opposing those stated by students in order to get them to think about other possibilities. Again, because constructing knowledge together and constructing the best possible products are the goals of any course, the instructor poses questions that encourage expressions of multiple perspectives. In doing so, he or she communicates that without each student finding his or her voice, the answers generated might be "less than" the optimal, which only a diverse group can create.

In-Class and Out-of-Class Practice

In some helping fields, little or no practice of counseling skills occurs before the first practicum. Thankfully, that has not been the case in counseling for the past generation. However, the helping interview course is frequently taught with minimal opportunity for practice of skills. Kolb's (1984) model can remind us of the need for regular and sequential "experimentation" in learning. Such application contributes to retention (Dale, 1969), as it requires the performance, not just the recognition, of a behavior. Bandura's (1997) work has demonstrated the primacy of performance over vicarious learning.

Thus, after students have read about the skills and experimented with them independently, after they have discussed the reading and following observed and analyzed demonstrations, it behooves instructors to have students try out the skills during and after the class period. Most students find such practice to be anxiety-producing. They are asked to dwell in the "netherworld" of not quite-knowing enough yet being asked to perform. They thus discover that practice, rather than "making perfect," generates many questions and concerns. However, in the safety of the classroom, they can be immediately coached, their questions can be answered during "teachable moments," they can get relatively non-threatening feedback (because no grade is involved) from a variety of peers, and they can prepare for the longer between-class practice sessions.

As with other course assignments, instructors can build both epistemological support and challenge into classroom practice. Supporting students' need for authority, instructors provide a very clear structure for practice. For instance, they may divide the class into triads and issue the following instructions: "For five minutes, one person is the counselor, another the client, and another the observer. Then, for two minutes the counselor self-evaluates using the previous discussion of the subskills components to guide the self-evaluation. For two minutes, the client talks about how he or she felt while participating in the counseling, also using the previous discussion as a guide. And for two minutes, the observer offers feedback, using previous training in giving feedback to structure the process." (Note that in the previous discussion of feedback, we had students be specific and tentative, using "I" statements.)

Classroom practice, when conducted in this manner, challenges many students to self-author. The seed we planted at the beginning of the course now flowers. Students try on this "new" (for many of them) way of helping—by listening, caring, and reflecting, rather than by teaching or giving advice. It is now made manifest the degree to which clients are able to make their own meanings.

Further, the observation/feedback portion of the role play exercise communicates clearly that the views of each member are to be valued. I (Eriksen) have often had students indicate that they only wanted feedback from me because they somehow believed that my knowledge would be more helpful or accurate. While I believe that I have much to offer and do share my impressions with students, I also share with them my semester after semester experience: that when I read and listen to the peer feedback, I find it to be congruent with my own impressions of students' performance. They are usually surprised by this revelation. In response to their surprise, I ask them to consider that in the "real" world people just like they are the clients. And shouldn't counselors-in-training be vividly interested in their clients' opinions about helpfulness, since the clients are the ones who will choose whether or not to return for more counseling on the basis of whether they evaluate the work to be helpful and the counselor to be caring?

Students continue the benefits of classroom practice by practicing counseling between class sessions with a peer or an undergraduate volunteer. During the early part of the course, their "counseling session" is short and highly structured, designed to help them practice one microskill at a time. As the semester progresses, sessions increase in time and complexity; students add subskills, building toward a coherent session, a session with a beginning and an ending, a session that has the potential to make a difference in a client's life. These sessions allow for practicing counseling in a fairly safe environment, free from direct evaluation or observation. The aspiring counselors try on new behaviors, make mistakes, recover from their missteps, and explore the boundaries of what counseling means.

Such tryouts, while fluid and relatively spontaneous, are not amorphous, however. Instructors provide developmentally appropriate structure for these between-class practice sessions. For instance, instructors tell students that the sessions are to be a specific length of time, they are to include certain subskills, and they are to be audio- or videotaped. I (Eriksen) also provide students with Skills Feedback Sheets (see Appendix Five) to structure the feedback they offer to each other.

Self-Assessment and Reflection

Theorists (Kegan, 1982) indicate that the ability to reflect on one's life is a developmental achievement. Self-reflection requires the capacity to take oneself as "object," something that many students are not consistently able to do at the time they begin graduate school (Kegan, 1994; Neukrug & McAuliffe, 1993). Kegan calls this ability "institutional" (1982) or "modernist" knowing (1994). Belenky et al. (1986) call it procedural knowing. Many of the course activities discussed thus far have incorporated self-critique and reflection. However, here we discuss it more explicitly.

Following classroom and between-class practice sessions, we ask students to carefully consider, through self-assessment papers, what they have done, how well they have done it, and what they would do differently next time. Students must thus stand back and reflect. They write journal entries about how they felt and what they thought while practicing counseling. They also reflect on what personal, family, and/or cultural history might have contributed to the feelings they had while doing counseling. For example, because of personal history and defenses, some students have a difficult time with confrontation, others with simple listening.

For most students such reflection is a significant challenge; thus, instructors need to offer comparable levels of support. I (Eriksen) have found that offering specific guidelines and "exemplars" contributes to that support. Exemplars illustrate what I think reflection or self-assessment (or some other assignment) might look like. These serve to "hold" students who have never reflected before while they try on a new way of knowing. Appendices One and Two offer examples of the specific directions I give to students about self-assessment and reflection. Appendix Three through Six offer other guidelines and exemplars related to assignments that will be discussed later.

Since self-reflection can't be "wrong," we do not recommend giving grades for journal entries or self-assessment papers. However, instructors might, when students hand in these assignments periodically throughout the semester, offer ongoing feedback and pose questions about what students have written. This feedback creates a kind of dialogue, which gives the instructor a chance to support and challenge the student toward new developmental levels. For instance, in response to a student who reports events or facts, I (Eriksen) write such supportive statements as "You seem to have assessed what happened quite descriptively," along with challenging questions such as, "How did you feel when this happened?" "What did you think when she said that?" "What meaning do you make of this behavior?" If students offer absolutist statements or opinions without evidence, the instructor might support them by responding, "You seem very clear about what you think in this situation," while challenging them with, "What other possible ways of evaluating the situation might there be?" If the instructor is able to offer the appropriate balance of support and challenge, students ought to feel safe enough to reach more deeply into themselves in future reflections.

EVALUATION

Formative Evaluation

I (Eriksen) conceive of evaluation in this course as an ongoing dialogue, a co-constructed process, in which the entire class community participates.

Most of the evaluation is based on observable behavior and the ability to make sense of two factors: one's own and the client's behavior. Students join with their peers and the professor in first determining what form of evaluation might be most helpful, and then, in an ongoing way, in offering feedback through which they challenge each other to reach the height of their ability. Peers watch for signals about whether feedback is being perceived as helpful, own their own reactions, and try to be very specific about what worked and how they determined that it worked. The instructor makes every effort to offer both support and challenge in the feedback given.

Evaluation or feedback takes several forms. Students first self-evaluate, in order to evoke their own voices about their performance. After initial role-plays, those playing the counselor are the first ones asked about how they did, what they liked about what they did, and what they would change. After reviewing tapes of practice sessions, they reflect on the same questions. Throughout the semester they evaluate their own progress in journals and reflective papers.

Peer evaluation is also central. Following their self-evaluation of in-class role plays, students solicit input from their peers. After between-class practice sessions, counselors solicit input from their "clients." The instructor then asks students to include what they hear from peers in their written self-assessments. Students often report that they learn to value the feedback they receive from peers. Emphasizing the importance of self- and peer evaluation communicates the importance of students developing their own voice and trusting their intuition.

Instructor evaluation is, of course, also part of the ongoing dialogue. Our input as veteran and reflective helper-educators is critical. We also serve a "gatekeeping" role for the protection of future clients. When evaluating, the constructivist instructor deliberately seeks to provide an optimal balance of support and challenge. Affirmations are central for support. In reviewing class role plays and tapes of student sessions, the instructor points out and evokes strengths and competencies in each student. She or he also needs to assertively and clearly critique what seems not to be working, make suggestions about alternate interventions, and offer comment on what he or she perceives to be most or least helpful.

This sort of ongoing dialogue is usually called "formative" evaluation, and it offers students the opportunity to respond to and challenge the instructor throughout the semester. Such formative evaluation, despite the instructor's efforts to conceive of it as participation in a dialogue, can be quite threatening or challenging for some students. And yet it is difficult to conceive of helping students improve without offering them feedback on what works or what doesn't work. So, with students who do find themselves overchallenged, instructors may need to increase support (for instance, provide greater structure and direction or praise a student's "interpersonal" [Kegan, 1994] capacity). Once students feel safely supported, instructors may experience greater success in offering suggestions for improvement.

Summative Evaluation

At the middle and end of the semester, instructors typically offer "summative" evaluations. McGaghie (1993) indicates that evaluation methods ought to match both preestablished objectives and the teaching methods used to achieve those objectives. For this course, objectives primarily include the ability to perform and to think about counseling skills. Similarly then, evaluation ought to measure whether students have achieved some level of mastery in skills performance, have developed an ability to analyze or evaluate their own and others' performances, and have learned to think about what clients most need from the counselor. Thus, I (Eriksen) use a process of evaluation that merely continues what students have been doing all semester. They turn in mid-semester and end-of-the-semester taped demonstrations of an exemplary counseling session, accompanied by a transcript that explains what skills they were using and why, and also accompanied by a self-evaluation of their performance (see Appendices Five and Six for instructions and exemplars).

Prior to completing the mid-semester and final tapes, I (Eriksen) make a grading sheet available to students. The sheet lists the specific skills required in the tapes (whatever skills have been covered in class to date) and how grades will be determined (Appendices Seven and Eight). The instructor offers feedback in response to mid-semester tapes, feedback that includes the instructor's perceptions of what worked well, other possible interventions—to extend the counselor's range of possibilities, and interventions that might be better received by the client. The instructor indicates specific improvements that the student might make in order to improve his or her grade on the final tape. Such feedback offers students a sense that they have some control in the evaluation process, countering their feelings that evaluation is "done to them." Further, students are rarely surprised at their end-of-semester grades. Finally, students may redo their final tapes in order to demonstrate greater skills, if they are unhappy with their grades or their performances. Students have repeatedly evaluated this sort of specific feedback as one of the most helpful elements of this course.

Support and challenge are evident in such evaluation procedures. Providing a grading sheet that expresses specific expectations offers structure for those who need such specific guidance. Providing written, specific feedback on the transcripts (i.e., examples of the words a counselor might actually say) also supports students. On the other hand, students are challenged to speak for themselves, offering evidence, during a dialogue with us about their work and during self-evaluations.

CONCLUSION

We believe that promoting development is fundamental to educating effective counselors. While many readers may find little new in this chapter's presentation of the skills course, others may not have considered how to ground the skills course in constructivist or developmental principles or how to use the coursework to promote development. As you have reviewed our ideas—certainly not the only ideas—about how this course might be structured, we hope that you have noticed that we have attempted to make the learning experiences as active, experiential, and inductive as possible. We hope that you have seen our attempt to offer opportunities and challenges for students to develop their own voices and to access their own inner stores of knowledge. We hope that it is clear that we have valued each person's experiences and have asked them to bring such experiences to the classroom discussions. We believe that only when each person's voice is heard are we likely to come up with the best ideas, and that these ideas are continually emerging. Finally, we believe that learning communities are the best environments for creating knowledge. The Helping Interview course can be such a gathering.

Appendix

Guidelines for Self-Assessment

Ongoing personal awareness about one's ability to perform skills and about personal issues that may impact the helping process is necessary to effective helping. Therefore, you are asked each week to:

1. Review your videotaped session before class.

2. Use the evaluation forms at the end of the book's chapters to assess your performance of the week's skills.

3. Then reflect on how you felt about the session and about your performance of the skills. Journal about the feelings you experienced during different points of the session. Indicate what meaning you ascribe to those feelings—in other words, why were you feeling that way at that point in time. Explore historical experiences that might have contributed to your feelings. Examine what impact these historical experiences and feelings might have on future helping. Reflect on what you want to do about what you have discovered.

4. Prepare yourself to have your video reviewed in class or by a peer (different peers each week, please) each week. When you have received feedback on your tape, put their feedback and your reflections together into a self assessment paper related to that particular skill. Do this each week, and keep for reference in writing the final self-assessment paper.

5. At the midterm, review your weekly self-assessments and personal reflections. Hand in the peer and self assessments and the writing you have done reflecting on your feelings, skills, and personal issues (include the reflections for the tape being handed in).

6. For the final self-assessment paper, put the weekly assessments together into a well-written, comprehensive paper that gives a clear sense of the progress you have made on each of the subskills, your feelings about the helping process, and your developing awareness of personal issues and history that will impact on your abilities as a helper.

Guidelines for Reflection

The purpose of reflection is to think about or introspect about the material you are learning and the experiences you are having in class and outside of class. Reflection means many things to many people; however, in our rushed lifestyle we do not often stop to reflect, and thus we live an unexamined life. For the purposes of this assignment, you will keep a journal, and will communicate with your classmates by contributing some of your reflections as input to the class listserve. Plan to spend a minimum of an hour a week in reflection. Reflection, for the purposes of this assignment, may be composed of four parts:

1. Statement of the situation: This includes a sentence or two of "what happened." For instance, "When I was practicing reflective listening today with my best friend, I found it hard to keep listening and not make suggestions about what she should do to solve her problem." It may be tempting to include a lot more than a sentence or two. In fact, it may be tempting to journal only about events. Make every attempt to contain yourself.

2. Your thoughts about the situation: This includes your interpretation of what was going on when you noticed the above situation. Beyond the actual "facts" of the situation is your interpretation or the meaning you make about it. Your interpretation impacts both your feelings about it and your decisions about how to respond. An example of thoughts about the above situation might be: "I had thought previously that I was a good listener. And now I realize that while I care a lot about my friends, I am usually putting a lot of input *into* our conversations, rather than allowing space for them to talk fully about themselves."

3. Your feelings about these thoughts: Feelings are feelings, not thoughts. That is, feelings are angry, sad, hurt, happy, exuberant, discouraged, etc. If you find yourself saying, "I feel *that* . . . ." or "I feel *as though* . . . ." or "I feel *like* . . . .", you are expressing a thought or opinion, *not a feeling*. An example of a feeling reaction to the thought expressed above in #2 might be: "I am *disappointed* when I look back on all the conversations I have had with friends, when I think I might not have been as caring as I wanted to be. I feel *hopeful* that now I can care more effectively. I also am *excited* about trying these skills out on friends and on 'real' clients. I feel *encouraged* that something relatively simple might help people a lot."

4. Your related issues or reasons: This includes your ideas about how your experiences, and your thoughts and feelings about your experiences, might be related to your own "issues" or history. It is important to understand that experiences, feelings, and thoughts do not just happen, for you or for your "clients" and loved ones. They have some roots in a person's history, culture, gender, religion, or other previous experiences. Understanding yourself and why you respond in certain ways is the first step to making choices and having greater control in the future about how you respond. It is particularly important in the mental health field to understand yourself, because clients and mental health organizations will "push many buttons" if you don't (and perhaps even if you do) understand and have some conscious control over yourself. Further, if you find yourself in "trouble," it will probably be necessary to understand your responses to the troubling situation in order to get yourself out of trouble. And example of issues or history related to the situation expressed above might be: "I realize that in my family people didn't listen very much. In fact, people felt that the most loving thing to do was to provide a solution to the problem that the other person was expressing. Many times we would end up arguing over why it wasn't or was a good solution. I often felt as though no one really cared about why I was bringing up the problem in the first place. Now I know that it was because even though people cared, they were not expressing to me their understanding of what I was saying. So, in those moments, I didn't think they cared very much."

Sample Journal Entry

This week in class we were talking about reflective listening. I found it hard to keep listening and not make suggestions about what my partner should do to solve her problem. I spent some time watching people outside of class too, and found that many people don't really listen. I was also noticing that an awful lot of people don't make eye contact or maintain an open position. Sometimes they don't ask many questions before they respond either.

I also tried in my practice session and with my friends to do the reflective listening. While it was hard not to give solutions or suggestions, I found that the other person talked more if I listened. A couple of people actually expressed to me that they appreciated my listening instead of giving solutions. I had thought previously that I was a good listener. And now I realize that while I care a lot about my friends, I am usually putting a lot of input into our conversations, rather than allowing space for them to talk fully about themselves.

I am disappointed when I look back on all the conversations I had with friends before, when I think I might not have been as caring as I wanted to be. I feel hopeful that now I can care more effectively. I also am excited about trying these skills out on friends and on 'real' clients. I feel encouraged that something relatively simple might help people a lot. I realize that in my family people didn't listen very much. In fact, people felt that the most loving thing to do was to provide a solution to the problem the other person was expressing. Many times we would end up arguing over why it wasn't or was a good solution. I often felt as though no one really cared about why I was bringing up the problem in the first place. Now I know that it was because even though people cared, they were not expressing to me their understanding of what I was saying. So, in those moments, I didn't think they cared very much.

I have also been wondering about what the value of all this is. I mean, if most people don't do this attending and probing and listening, why should we? Is it normal? Is this what it means to be a counselor? Are we supposed to be different from other people. I mean, it isn't really just something you do at work, like some computer person would do computer skills. We are talking here about a way of being, a change in us personally. I can't imagine that we can just do it at work and not do it in the rest of our lives. So will people think we are weird? Will people think we are psychoanalyzing them? Are we asking questions and paying attention to things that no one really wants us to? Might we be embarrassing them to focus in on such personal things?? Somehow it seems okay to do this with clients or patients. But I don't know about doing it in my personal life.

And yet, when I think of the people who have made the most impact on my life, they seem to ask these kinds of questions and have paid attention to me and listened to me in the ways this class is teaching. I feel kind of confused about which way to go. But I am challenged to find out what seems right. I guess it is no surprise given the way my family is that I would wonder about this. And it certainly has not helped to be this new way in my family. They don't notice that I am listening. They just ask me why I am being so quiet. What's wrong with me. I guess I will have to practice on friends for now.

Example of Final Self-Evaluation Paper

As I look back over the semester, I am surprised by what I was unable to do initially and what comes quite easily now. I suppose that is the way it is with new skills. They seem so foreign initially. But I am happy with what I have accomplished. I find that attending comes quite easily now. I am able to keep eye contact and to maintain an open body position. I find myself able to communicate clearly that I am with the person and to follow in a more relaxed way what they are saying. I do question sometimes whether I should do this with everyone. I mean, if I attend this way, won't it mean that even people I won't want to listen to will be hanging on me??? I am not sure I want that. I may have to develop some non-attending skills—of course, not when I am working as a counselor—but for those times when I really don't have time or when it is someone I don't want to encourage.

Questioning is something I have never had a problem with. My mother used to tell me that I asked more questions than anyone she knew. I find that I never run out of questions because I am really interested in what people have to say. I am finding that I am better now at asking open questions. I also have learned a little better how to ask questions that will help the client explore, rather than questions that are just to satisfy my curiosity. I think I will probably have to remember to use fewer questions and to use the other skills more.

[Evaluate yourself on each of the skills, identifying strengths and areas to work on, while examining the progress you have made.]

Sample Feedback Sheet

The feedback sheets you use in class to evaluate your peers' skills and that you use outside of class to evaluate your own skills are designed to help you focus on the specifics of what you are watching, to help you keep track of what you have seen, and to help you learn to analyze the component parts of each skill. Please use the information from the texts and from classroom discussions and demonstrations as you complete these forms. A sample is included here as a guide. Feel free to add whatever else you feel is important or might be helpful.

Skills Feedback Sheet

Name of
Interviewer _____

Feedback giver _____

1. What is your gut reaction to the interviewer's style and way of being? How would (do) you feel if you were (as) the client? *I liked the way she did the skills. I would have felt accepted and cared for if she responded that way to me. I liked her warmth.*

2. Identify the specific (assigned) skills the interviewer did? Which of these did the interviewer do particularly well? *As she asked questions, she gave enough time to answer. She asked questions that were on target and clear. She asked one question at a time. She attended between questions and restated what she heard the "client" say. She didn't ask too many questions.*

3. Identify the skills done that were not specifically assigned. Did these interfere with time to do the assigned skills? Did they seem natural? Necessary? *Her eye contact was good. She maintained an open body position. She nodded her head in a way that indicated she was listening. She said "uh-huh" and other such things to indicate she was with the client and wanted to hear more. I thought all of these were done naturally and were necessary.*

4. Identify 2-3 things you would have done differently. *I might have asked more about the client's feelings about her mother, as I thought she said a lot about her thoughts, but not her feelings. I also might have asked for clarification on a few things, because I didn't understand and didn't think the client was expressing herself very clearly.*

Guidelines for the Final Tape

For your final tape, please conduct a 20-minute counseling session demonstrating Ivey's five attending subskills. Video tape the session. Type a transcript of the session. In the transcript, following each of your interventions, indicate what type of skill you were demonstrating and why you felt it was appropriate or helpful to use it at that point in the session.

Next, evaluate the session:

1. Did you feel connected with the client?

2. Did the client feel cared for and respected by you?

3. Were you able to perform the subskills smoothly and easily?

4. Did you focus on what was most important about the client's issue?

5. Did you see some movement in the client's way of being or movement toward solving the problem? Explain.

6. What might you have done differently if you had it to do over again?

Hand in:

1. Videotape

2. Transcript

3. Session evaluation

4. Self-assessment paper

Exemplar of Transcript

This is an example of what a page of your transcript might look like. Notice that all of the clients' words are included. If the client speaks in "paragraphs," you may just include the first and last sentences with "..." in between. Then the counselor's words (include all of these, please) are included, followed by naming the skill that has been used and by including some explanation of why that skill seemed appropriate at that time. If it seems as though some other skill might have been appropriate, or as though you might have said it differently or more clearly, include that also.

Client:

I really want to talk about my roommate. She has been giving me all kinds of trouble lately.

Counselor:

Uh huh (*Minimal Encouragement*)

Client:

I come in at night and she is waiting for me at the door with complaints of some kind: I have eaten some of her food, or I have left some dishes in the sink, or I was making too much noise last night on the computer, or with my stereo or talking on the phone.

Counselor:

You are upset that she has so many complaints (*Paraphrase. Could have been clearer on the feeling, as upset is a rather ambiguous feeling*).

Client:

Right! I can't believe she is so constant about the complaints, and has so many, and about so many picky things. I find myself dreading coming home at night, wondering what she is going to be upset about next. I find myself wondering if I am going to get evicted and not have a place to live, because she will complain to the landlord. I'm not sure I would even care at this point because it is so awful living with her right now.

Counselor:

You are not just upset, but you also worry about a place to live and whether you will be in trouble with the landlord (*Reflection of feelings. Takes to deeper level*).

Client:

And yet, I know she has problems. She has OCD. Do you know what that is?

Counselor:

Yes.

Client:

I think it makes it hard for her to let little things go. I think she has to think about all these small things all the time. It isn't really her fault. She is in counseling herself to try to get over this. I even think she takes medication. So I understand why this is happening. And I want to be kind and not make it worse. But I sure don't like it!!!

Counselor:

So, while it makes you angry and worried that she greets you at the door each night with complaints, and while you wonder if you shouldn't find another place to live sometimes, you are really trying to be understanding of someone who you know has some rather serious problems. (*Summarization*)

Skills Evaluation Sheet

---

1. Attending (*forward lean, appropriate eye contact, open position, other indications of interest in client; overall connectedness, emotional depth of relationship*):

Quality of Performance:	0	1	2	3	4	5
	Not Performed	Very Poor	Poor	Adequate	Good	Excellent

2. Open & Closed Questions

Quality of Performance:	0	1	2	3	4	5
	Not Performed	Very Poor	Poor	Adequate	Good	Excellent

3. Voicing of Client Observations

Quality of Performance:	0	1	2	3	4	5
	Not Performed	Very Poor	Poor	Adequate	Good	Excellent

4. Encouragers / Paraphrases

Quality of Performance:	0	1	2	3	4	5
	Not Performed	Very Poor	Poor	Adequate	Good	Excellent

5. Reflection of feelings / exploration of deeper meanings, values, beliefs

Quality of Performance:	0	1	2	3	4	5
	Not Performed	Very Poor	Poor	Adequate	Good	Excellent

6. Focusing skills used to track on appropriate issue

Quality of Performance:	0	1	2	3	4	5
	Not Performed	Very Poor	Poor	Adequate	Good	Excellent

7. Ivey's five stage session structuring

Quality of Performance:	0	1	2	3	4	5
	Not Performed	Very Poor	Poor	Adequate	Good	Excellent

8. Confrontation

Quality of Performance:	0	1	2	3	4	5
	Not Performed	Very Poor	Poor	Adequate	Good	Excellent

9. Other intervention skills

Quality of Performance:	0	1	2	3	4	5
	Not Performed	Very Poor	Poor	Adequate	Good	Excellent

10. Changing processes that are not helpful

Quality of Performance:	0	1	2	3	4	5
	Not Performed	Very Poor	Poor	Adequate	Good	Excellent

11. Interventions consistent with chosen school of counseling

Quality of Performance:	0	1	2	3	4	5
	Not Performed	Very Poor	Poor	Adequate	Good	Excellent

Comments:

Grade Structure

A. Students will receive an A if they perform the requisite subskills with ease, demonstrate ease in establishing a caring relationship, clearly and correctly identify that subskills they are using and why, identify personal issues which may impact the process of helping, demonstrate the ability to help clients move forward during the counseling session, receive supervision and feedback willingly and reflectively, and get greater than 90% of the answers correct on quizzes and/or the final.

B. Students will receive a B if they perform the requisite subskills, but are less "smooth" about it, if they establish a caring relationship with clients, if they identify which subskills they are using, even if they are not always sure why, if they identify some—but not all—personal issues which may impact the process of helping, if they are open to supervision and feedback, and if they get greater than 80% of the answers correct on quizzes and/or the final. Session should demonstrate that clients receive some assistance, even if session is not as organized or forward moving as those performed by the A student.

C. Students will receive a C if they perform all except one of the requisite subskills, if they identify all but one of the subskills they use, if they do not seem aware of personal issues that may impact the process of helping, if they are intermittently open to receiving supervision or feedback, and if they get greater than 70% on quizzes and/or final.

F. Students will receive an F if they demonstrate less than four of the requisite subskills, if they are unable to identify at least four of the subskills they use, if they do not seem aware of personal issues which may impact the process of helping, if they are not open to receiving supervision or feedback, and if they get less than 70% on quizzes and/or final.

REFERENCES

Bandura, A. (1997). *Self-efficacy: The exercise of control.* New York: W.H. Freemam and Company.

Belenky, M., Clinchy, B., Goldberger, N., & Tarule, J. (1986). *Women's ways of knowing.* New York: Basic Books.

Benack, S. (1988). Relativistic thought: A cognitive basis for empathy in counseling. *Counselor Education and Supervision, 27* (3), 216-232.

Carkhuff, R. R., & Berenson, B. G. (1977). *Beyond counseling and therapy.* New York: Holt Rinehart & Winston.

Dale, E. (1969). *Audio-visual methods in teaching.* New York: Holt, Rinehart, & Winston.

Kegan, R. (1982). *The evolving self.* Cambridge, MA: Harvard University Press.

Kegan, R. (1994). *In over our heads.* Cambridge, MA: Harvard.

Kolb, D. (1984). *Experiential learning.* Englewood Cliffs, NJ: Prentice-Hall.

Ivey, A. E. (1994). *Intentional Interviewing and Counseling,* (3rd ed.). Pacific Grove, CA: Brooks/Cole.

Loevinger, J. (1976). *Ego development.* San Francisco: Jossey-Bass.

Lovell, C., & McAuliffe, G. (1996). From non-constructivist to constructivist counseling. Paper presented at the quadrennial meeting of the Association for Counselor Education and Supervision. Portland, OR. October 1996.

McAuliffe, G., & Lovell, C. (2000). Encouraging transformation: Guidelines for constructivist and developmental instruction. In G. McAuliffe, K. Eriksen, and Associates (Eds.), *Preparing counselors and therapists: Creating constructivist and developmental programs* (pp.14-41). Alexandria, VA: Association for Counselor Education and Supervision.

McGaghie, W. C. (1993). Evaluating competence for professional practice. *Educating professionals: Responding to new expectations for competence and accountability.* San Francisco: Jossey-Bass.

McNamara, D. S., Scott, J., & Bess, T. (2000). Building blocks of knowledge: Constructivism from a cognitive perspective. In G. McAuliffe, K. Eriksen, and Associates, *Preparing counselors and therapists: Creating constructivist and developmental programs* (pp. 62-76). Alexandria, VA: Association for Counselor Education and Supervision.

Neukrug, E. S., & McAuliffe, G. J. (1993). Cognitive development and human service education. *Human Service Education, 13,* 13-26.

Perry, W. (1970). *Forms of intellectual and ethical development in the college years.* New York: Holt, Rinehart, and Winston.

Sanford, N. (1966). *Self and society.* New York: Atherton Press.

Schon, D. A. (1983). *The reflective practitioner.* New York: Basic Books.

Schon, D. A., & Argyris, C. (1995). *Organizational learning: Theory, method, and practice.* Boston: Addison-Wesley Longman, Inc.

Widick, C., Knefelkamp, L. L., & Parker, C. A. (1975). The counselor as a developmental instructor. *Counselor Education and Supervision, 14 (4),* 286-296.

4

Using Kelly's Personal Construct Theory as a Meta-Structure to Teach a Counseling Theories Course

Suni Petersen

Freedom from the hegemony of positivism came unexpectedly as I prepared a talk several years ago on models of health behavior change. I was scanning a book on advertising awards and was struck by the parallel between the advertisements and the regnant popular health theories of each decade. Further, the theories of each era reflected the broader sociocultural milieus in which they were created. This realization cast new light on the relativity of human behavior. The creators of the various theories, just like the advertisers, were products of their times. Context impacted both theory creation and even the effectiveness of its application.

Following on the heels of this realization came the awareness that research ideas and methods also reflect current contexts. I understood that the theories built upon such research would thus be influenced by the worldviews of both the researchers and the participants. No longer could I consider there to be one "right" way. Nor could one theory be proven more effective than others without significant qualifications. Constructivism provided an alternative to positivism and, corresponding as it did with my own evolution, lent language and legitimacy to my thinking.

Constructivism also provides a helpful framework for training counselors who, if demographic predictions about education and health care delivery prove to be true, will be serving a more diverse population of clients in the future. Flexibility will be required to respond to each type of diversity. Given that the personal qualities that the counselor brings to the work have been consistently identified as the predominant indicators of counseling effectiveness (Corey, 1996), such qualities need to be marked by openness and multiple perspective-taking. Personal qualities such as embracing pluralistic perspectives and possessing complex and flexible ways of organizing and structuring knowledge are necessary for counselors who serve diverse populations. Kelly (1955) refers to such mental structuring methods that individuals use as "constructs" or "schemata." Counselors need to be aware of their own constructs or schemata, the origins of these schemata, and how schemata change. In teaching the Counseling Theories course, my goal is to increase the cognitive complexity of the students. I hope to explore with the students any rigid, preconceived notions they may bring to their "knowing" about theories and discover with them both what drives their choices and what the consequences of those choices might be.

I use George Kelly's Personal Construct Theory (PCT; 1955) as a meta-theory in structuring this process (and this course). I believe that PCT is a theoretical umbrella large enough to encompass other theories. Kelly's notion of "constructive alternativism" indicates that as "facts" are collected, new and altered constructions occur without the necessity of rejecting those constructions already formulated. Constructive alternativism explains a counselor's ability to favor one theory's philosophical position while entertaining the use of strategies from compatible theories. Taking a constructivist approach to teaching does not, therefore, preclude exploring multiple counseling theories during the course. Many practitioners claim to be eclectic in their approach to theory utilization. Constructive alternativism provides a theoretically consistent way to become eclectic.

The postulates of PCT provide a basis for understanding how theories are created by theorists, adopted by students, and adapted for clients. PCT explains how students' constructs change in relation to the course material and how the co-constructions of their work with clients recursively affects their use of theory. Student, theorist, and client collaborate in an interactive triad undergoing continual transformation. PCT principles can both facilitate and illuminate this process.

In this chapter, the postulates of Kelly's Personal Construct Theory will both explain how I generate course activities and illustrate the process of changing students' constructions of counseling—that is, promoting student constructive development. The course opens with student introductions and an in-depth discussion of the pluralistic perspectives exemplified in these introductions. The course continues in an interactive and discussion-oriented mode. Presentation of each theory focuses first on the students' reactions to the theory and the origins of those reactions. Discussions of the multiple experiences and reactions of different students to a particular theory trigger new perspectives on the theory and its applications. A movie clip (assigned or viewed in class) then triggers discussion on the social milieu of the theorist (see appendix, p. 87, for recommended movies). Next, the tenets of each theory are placed in a framework developed by the class (more discussion later). Two role plays of the theory follow. The first role play is a professional demonstration, either by myself or by means of a video. The second role play involves one student portraying a client and the rest of the class members taking turns as counselors who are operating from the chosen theoretical perspective. At the beginning of these role plays, students begin or formulate or have already adopted a schema regarding that theory; yet as they participate in the actual counseling experience, their constructs are refined, reorganized, and changed into a deeper understanding of that theory. Students share and discuss the progressive iterations of their own constructs as theories are presented. This exposition leads students to adopt a reflective stance about their own constructs and their constructions of clients when making counseling judgements, and to choose a theory for themselves. Such self-reflectivity has consistently ranked high as an essential component of counselor effectiveness (Skovholt & Ronnestad, 1995).

RATIONALE FOR CHOICE OF THEORIES IN THE COURSE

A constructivist theories course must also attend to the types of theories taught. It may seem self-evident that given the diversity of our classes and the even greater diversity in the populations with whom the students (will) work that introducing new and emerging theories would be welcomed. However, another context influences the reception of new and emerging theories. That is, a growing number of people no longer feel connected with a legitimate system that rewards them as constituents. A growing number of people have found only illegitimacy in the prevailing dominant perspective when they have recognized that their voices have not been included. Therefore, they define their experience in terms of "victimization" (Doan & Parry, 1994). Although this position could be liberating, it may also create a conspiratorial atmosphere in the adoption of new emerging theories.

Students from oppressed groups have quite rightly challenged their marginalization, and they quickly and adamantly embrace new theories that resonate with their perspectives. In a discussion-oriented classroom, their victimization takes the form of "anger against" other, more historical theories and, by extrapolation, the proponents of those theories in the class. These proponents find their more traditional notions attacked as discriminatory, and then feel that *their* voices have been illegitimized. These proponents, who adhere to or benefit from the dominant culture's rewards, also bring with them the need to defend the legitimacy of their perspectives.

In other cases, personal tragedies may enhance the feeling of not being heard or understood. For instance, a young, white, middle-class male choosing to be in the counseling profession may feel victimized because of a personally oppressive experience, such as having been abused as a child. Thus, the difficulty faced in determining which theories to teach becomes how to penetrate the world views that drive students' narratives.

Teaching a course using postmodernism as a philosophy also raises questions about the importance of teaching the historical evolution of theory. Kenneth Gergen (1991) speaks of "social saturation," meaning that we are exposed to so many different points of view and such fast-changing ideas that we have lost a core sense of who we are and of the world in which we live. Although no one would question that a profusion of multiplicity currently exists, some regard the growing choices as being cast on a dangerous sea devoid of truth and consensus. Others regard the growing choices as avenues of inclusion, restoration of legitimacy, and as therefore comforting. If we conclude that theories are not facts to be taught but points of view to be discussed, the ensuing discourse would have to include theories valued by both "traditional" and "oppressed" perspectives.

I set the stage for the presentation of diverse and sometimes controversial theories by reading a passage from Doan and Parry (1994):

> In a world that lacks a legitimizing yardstick against which to measure one's own and others' lives, certain features become apparent. One is that each person's stories become self-legitimizing. A story told by a person in his/her own words of his/her own experience does not have to plead its legitimacy in any higher court of narrative appeal, because no narrative has any greater legitimacy than the person's own. Therefore, attempts by others to question the validity of such a story are themselves illegitimate. They are coercive, and to the extent that such methods are used to silence or discredit a person's stories, they represent a form of terrorism. We use such a strong word advisedly, for when one person tries to silence the legitimate voice of another, this is done invariably by throwing into question that person's only resource for discerning reality, her/his own judgement. All those who are thrown into that position of self-doubt are being thrown out of their own stories and robbed of their own voices. (p. 27)

I then move on to considering the theories. The purpose of counseling theories is to explain human behavior and change, and these theories view people, change, and the therapeutic process from the differing perspectives of context, behavior, cognition, or emotion. I group theories according to these perspectives, and during class discussions we consider the evolution of thinking from that perspective. The choice of theories, then, emerges partly from the desire to assure representation of each perspective.

The constructivist philosophy also influences the choice of theories discussed. Certain theories, such as systems, narrative, relational, and feminist theories, lend themselves more readily to the tenets of constructivism. Each of these theories emphasizes the construction and importance of power dynamics in relationships, encourages the taking of multiple perspectives, and accentuates egalitarian dialogue between counselor and client. These newer theories may be interspersed with the more traditional theoretical models, although the emphasis should stay on the theoretical models currently used by counselors in the field.

Constructivist teaching means that a student must identify and understand his/her own constructs in order to alter or build upon them. Consequently, an essential part of this course is assisting the student in this endeavor. Recent research demonstrates the prevalence of gender-bias among counselors, for instance (see Heesacker, Wester, Vogel, Wentzel, Mejia-Milan, & Goodholm, 1999). The results indicate that both male and female counselors hold biases about how emotion is expressed and felt by male and female clients. In order to assess such biases, students take the Biased Emotional Beliefs Questionnaire (Heesacker et al., 1999).

This exercise brings understandings to the student that serve as a foundation for relational theory, the first theory presented. Although more women seek therapy than men, the majority of the theories we use with them have been devised by men; this in spite of over two decades of evidence that women's development proceeds differently.

Jean Baker Miller and her colleagues at the Stone Center at Wellesley have researched and built relational theory since the 1970's. This theory builds on and extends the work of Carol Gilligan and Laura Brown. Miller recognized the role women's development plays in the growth of others and applied that to therapy. What emerged is recognizing and valuing the human need for connection as a source of growth in both men and women. The book used to introduce relational theory is *The Healing Connection* by Jean Baker Miller and Irene Stiver.

The second theory presented is multicultural theory. Students must identify and understand their own racial identity development as well as assessing that of their clients in order to adequately choose the role of the counselor that most fits them and their clients. Students must also be able to determine the "fit" of particular theories with different cultural groups. We superimpose the Cultural Values Chart (Sue & Sue, 1999, p. 109) onto different theories to help students determine the appropriateness of their use for different cultures.

I then present the traditional therapies, beginning with psychoanalytic and psychodynamic theories. Gestalt therapy and emotion-focused therapy next provide ways of exploring the emotion-oriented group of theories. Rogers's person-centered theory and excerpts from several existential writers—Sartre (1957), Frankl (1978), or Van Kaam (1966)—offer insight into the humanistic and existential theories.

We explore behaviorism next. The readings contain the theoretical foundation. Class demonstrations, however, focus on current behavioral interventions, such as systematic desensitization, the relaxation response, and "in vivo" exercises. These interventions are often adopted by professionals espousing other theoretical models.

We then focus on cognitive theories. I begin this segment with a brief explanation of its roots in RET, but we focus mostly on the work of Beck and Meichenbaum since they represent the cognitive theories currently in use. After these basic cognitive theories, students read an article by Mahoney and Lyddon (1988) that describes the evolution of the cognitive theories, including the addition of a constructivist dimension. Finally, we review George Kelly's personal construct theory because it is comprehensive; and although difficult at first, it provides a further foundation for understanding constructivism.

Constructivism provides a segue into teaching the systemic theories. While we overview the traditional theories (Structural, Strategic, Milan, and Satir), we primarily concentrate on Bowenian theory and narrative theory. Bowenian theory is presented first because the genogram is such a usable tool regardless of one's theoretical perspective. But more importantly, Bowenian theory, while offering many highly acceptable ideas to new counseling students, is also limited by its adherence to the "dominant perspective," a criticism that can be lodged against many traditional theories. Discussion of the theory thus invites challenge and leads to critical thinking. In contrast, the work of White and Epston (1989) addresses some of the very criticisms raised in the discussion of Bowenian theories; yet it creates its own controversy because of its brevity and ahistorical position. The last theory examined is feminist theory because it usually stimulates the most controversy and allows the class to build a sense of trust in expressing their heartfelt opinions.

KELLY'S BASIC POSTULATE AND COROLLARIES

Basic Postulate of PCT

Kelly's "Basic Postulate" states, "A person's processes are psychologically channelized by the ways in which he [sic] anticipates events" (Kelly, 1966, p. 9). By this, Kelly means that how a person construes events or views the world is determined ("channelized") by that person's constructs (or preexisting schemata). Theorists and students alike are subject to these constructs. Adopting a theoretical perspective thus becomes more of a reflexive and multiple perspective-taking task for counselors than merely discovering a point of view that matches their own. Students also need to recognize what beliefs and experiences support such matches and how their theory-of-choice must be adapted to fit the beliefs and experiences of each member in the counseling relationship.

To fully understand a counseling theorist's framework and be able to evaluate it for use in counseling sessions, students begin with the theorist's contexts. In this course, segments of movies which exemplify the sociocultural climate in which the theorist worked offer information about such contexts (see appendix, p. 87, for list of recommended films).

Following the movies, lass discussion focuses on themes that the milieu of the film might engender in a theorist, in other words, the lenses through which the theorist might have interpreted the events he or she observed. The class explores the ensuing logic that leads to an unfolding of some of the particular tenets of the theory. Each theory is seen in a complex light in which the theorist, the theory, and the milieu all interact.

The students then apply the particular theory to some aspect of their own present context, which further yields applications as diverse as the class composition itself. Students learn, in this process, that applying any theory to different people requires consideration of at least three elements: (1) the tenets of the theory, (2) the present context, and (3) the constructs of both the client and the counselor. Students also learn how to use the theories in a tentative, flexible manner, instead of "channelizing."

Construction Corollary

Kelly's "construction corollary" states, "A person anticipates events by construing their replications" (Kelly, 1955, p. 51). This means that people anticipate a future event by assigning meaning to it based on a past event. The recurrent themes in life are woven into meanings that connect the present with the past and the future.

During the first or second class, I use the movie *Stepmom* to introduce students to this concept (see appendix, p. 87, for scene used). Students usually offer intense and diverse reactions to this vignette, readily taking sides. I then challenge them to explore the beliefs and values that led to their reactions. At this point, I introduce the concept of preexisting schemata and the purpose served by those schemata. During the active discussion, students often shift their attributions of "blame" from one character to another; eventually they discard the blaming stance itself. Using this experience as an example of shifting perspectives, I encourage students throughout the course to consider their own "constructs" or preexisting notions in the ensuing role-plays and theoretical discussions and to recognize how people's pasts may lead them to interpret events through a selective desire to see their schemata supported.

Dichotomy Corollary

Another postulate helpful to the introduction of theory is the "dichotomy corollary," which states, "A person's construction system is composed of a finite number of dichotomous constructs" (Kelly, 1955, p. 59). Constructs are "black and white" with never a shade of gray, a notion that may appear as "absolutist." In fact, the black and white nature of constructs allows contrasts to be made between groups; it allows people to distinguish between events and/or to group them. The number of contrasts people make defines the complexity of their thinking. For example, a student of family therapy may counsel a couple with one depressed partner and determine that the non-depressed partner is too controlling. The inexperienced student interprets the issue of control in broadly-sweeping black and white terms. One partner is not in control; the other is in control. As the student's constructs of control are reexamined and redefined, the student notices that although the non-depressed spouse is taking overt control, the depressed spouse uses subtle nuances to exert pressure on the spouse to take responsibility. The student learns to make finer and finer discriminations regarding smaller bits of behavior as his or her constructs evolve to include more complexity.

During counselor training, students refine their discriminations among theories as they formulate or alter their constructs about a particular theory. The expansion and refinement of discriminations among theories should increase the student's ability to apply theory in creative ways and should increase their cognitive flexibility.

Thus, after exploring their preconceived ideas and the origins of these ideas, students focus on how they discriminate among aspects of the theory. Together, students generate a framework to assist in this discrimination process by creating a list of parameters that may distinguish one theory from another (For example, role of counselor, how change occurs, how problems begin). This structure is tentatively proposed with the understanding that it can be altered as new theories introduce concepts not previously addressed.

The list itself becomes a construct that is altered as the students discover new information and immerse themselves in new experiences. I construe the framework as analogous to the scaffolding used on a construction site that is reconfigured to reach different parts of the building. Throughout the course, both this framework and the meta-process of reconstructing it invite comparisons (and the use of dichotomies) among the theories. This reflective process encourages the students to increase the number of distinctions, refine existing distinctions, and increase their cognitive complexity.

Experience Corollary

The experience corollary states, "A person's construction system *varies* as he successively construes the replication of events." (Kelly, 1955, p. 72).

By this, Kelly means that personal constructs shift as events in a person's life are superimposed upon their previously-held constructs. Events may alter previously-made distinctions by altering the distinction itself, its relationship to other constructs, or one's reference position. To the extent that the alteration differs from people's expectations, they enlarge their constructs or create new constructs.

One example of the impact of experience on constructs occurs when the student continues to believe the validity of the construct, but also begins to identify circumstances in which it may not be true. For example, a counseling student who formerly learned to avoid confrontation may shift to accepting that there are times in which confrontation is valuable. In another instance, students may change how they perceive a particular concept. For instance, students' perceptions of the counseling relationship—the concept—may shift from advice-giving to facilitating client problem-solving. A third example of shifting constructs based on experience occurs when the relationship between constructs shifts. In this case, the constructs remain the same but two or more constructs are given higher priority. For example, a counseling student may have entered a course believing that encouraging the expression of emotions is the best counseling strategy. Upon being exposed to outcome research on a new theory (such as cognitive-behavioral treatments for depression), the student may shift to believing that with some clients expressing emotions may be replaced by containing emotions with thoughts.

Shifting constructs as a result of experience cycles through five phases: (1) anticipation, (2) investment, (3) encounter, (4) confirmation or disconfirmation of the construct, and (5) revision of the construct. These five phases suggest learning activities. For instance, I assigned a mini-qualitative study as a team project. Each team chose a problem area of interest. They then interviewed a person who experienced the problem and a family member, friend, or counselor associated with that person. Students coded the transcripts of their interviews and analyzed them using the constant-comparative method of identifying themes (Rafuls & Moon, 1996). The students wrote their findings using the framework of a particular theory and made a twenty minute presentation on their research.

To raise the students' awareness of how they were *anticipating* the project, or to illuminate their preconceived ideas, I asked them to write a reaction page prior to their first contact that explored their expectations of the interview. To increase their *investment* in the project, I made the project a major part of their grade and I asked students to write a summary statement about their plans, indicating why their chosen topic was important to them. Students then *encountered* the project during the interviews and the analysis of the interview. Coming face-to-face with a person telling his or her personal story generally proved to be a powerful experience for students.

The subsequent analysis then compelled students to reflect in a more objective manner than if they had merely reported on the interview. Students next applied one of the theories to the discussion of their project in the *confirmation/disconfirmation phase*. They usually found that their preconceived ideas about both a particular theory and the client population were challenged by the experience. As a result, students *revised their constructs*. Revision also occurred during the class presentation when the class asked what surprised the presenter about the experience and what former ideas had changed as a result of this experience.

Modulation Corollary

One of the most important corollaries for the theories course is the modulation corollary: "Variation in a person's construction system is limited by the permeability of the constructs within whose range of convenience the variants lie" (Kelly, 1955, p. 77). In other words, for change to occur in a person's construct system, a person must be sufficiently open to novel events to recognize when novelty is encountered. Without such recognition, the five-phase experience cycle cannot function. Also strongly held attitudes may be perceived to be infallible truths, and because they are not open to alteration, they are not permeable. Even if novel ideas were encountered, they would not be considered legitimate. Information outside a person's "range of convenience" will also not permeate a person's construct system because of its minimal interest to the person. Increasing the permeability of students' constructs increases cognitive complexity as the relaxed boundaries of perception allow more information to penetrate and to be included in students' "range of convenience."

The value of construct permeability is clear for counselors in ways beyond increasing cognitive complexity. When counseling a client, a clinician conditionally holds several possible hypotheses about that client's situation and personality, without seizing on any one idea as truth. Even as counseling proceeds and a direction emerges, concretizing earlier held conceptualizations could prevent awareness of formerly unconsidered strengths and of new changes in areas outside those initially targeted for treatment.

Counselor educators encourage permeability in students' constructs when they tentatively encourage students to appraise and provisionally accept theories. A tentative approach reduces the likelihood of provoking rigid adherence to a preexisting schemata, and students are then more likely to entertain different perspectives. Chanowicz and Langer (1981) found that when information was presented in absolute language rather than conditional language, students were more likely to accept the information as "fact" rather than "possibility," thus limiting the consideration of a variety of possibilities. Other research indicated that when students were introduced to both unfamiliar and familiar objects, either in a conditional or in an absolute way, only students presented with unfamiliar objects in a *conditional* way were able to find a novel use for that object (Langer & Piper, 1987). Research thus suggests that teaching theories in a conditional manner and portraying familiar theories in ways that encourage finer discriminations may lead to more creative applications.

However, beginning students often approach theory with preexisting ideas based on partial information, and such commitments freeze the potential for permeability. For instance, students may watch videos of someone conducting a session from a particular theoretical perspective and may react to the theory based on the dissonance or consonance between how they see themselves and how they see the demonstrator of that theory. How often has an instructor heard a student say, "I don't like Rational Emotive Behavior Therapy" or "I could never use gestalt therapy" only to find out that their decision was made because they did not identify with Ellis or Perls on the *Gloria* video? Students may react to a particular theory based on the method of presentation (Petty & Cacioppo, 1986), the messenger of that presentation (Chaiken, 1980; Petty & Cacioppo, 1986), or their preconceived ideas about themselves. Premature cognitive commitments are also more likely to be made if the information is presented by an authority (Chaiken, 1980).

By exploring the milieu in which theories are developed, the personal influences on the theorists, and the evolution of the theories over time, the theoretical concepts become more contextualized and less reified, allowing students to adapt the application of the theories to their own style. In this way, students are more likely to increase the repertoire of what they will consider using and to use the theories in novel ways.

The modulation corollary has relevance not only for how students construe theories, but for how they construe themselves. Students begin a counseling program with certain images of themselves as counselors. These images need to be permeable enough to evolve over time. We cannot, however, assume that students begin a counseling training program with the self-knowledge necessary for a clear understanding of how their unique personalities fit with specific counseling theories. In a study conducted in four universities, beginning counseling students' choices of theory were found to be unrelated to their core constructs of counseling and to their epistemologies. The results indicated a lack of self-knowledge, despite the fact that when asked the reason they favored a particular theory they overwhelmingly answered, "because it fit who I am as a person" (Petersen & Heesacker, 1997). Choice of theory and self-knowledge are inextricably linked, and so personal development requires a balanced shuttling between internal experience and external information. Yet, lack of time has often precluded a systematic appraisal of self during a theories course.

Nevertheless, a theories course needs to provide equal opportunity and direction to both theory and self-knowledge. Certain self-assessment instruments may offer students with a structure for self-exploration, which can in turn be used in selecting a theory which best fits the counselor and the client. The repertory grid (Kelly, 1955) and the laddering exercise (Neimeyer, 1993) measure core constructs and cognitive complexity. Royce and Mos's Psychoepistemology Profile (1980) designates ratios between metaphoric, empirical, or rational epistemologies, which are emphasized variously by different counseling theories (Neimeyer, Pritchard, Lyddon, & Sherrard, 1993; see appendices for directions on some of the specific exercises).

Another means of promoting theory-related self-exploration is based on Kantor & Neal's (1985, p. 17) statement that, "Knowledge of a therapist's personal paradigm or model of reality can predict the types of relationships he or she may have with families whose paradigms match or mismatch." In other words, because alternate theories suggest different types of relationships between the counselor and the client(s), instructors should help students explore their paradigms about such relationships. Kantor suggests that there are four domains in which a counselor's paradigms affect the counselor-client relationship: (1) counselor's preference for types of system: open, closed, or random; (2) psycho-political types: mover, follower, bystander, or opposer; (3) therapeutic domains: themes, feelings, or power dynamics; and (4) bystander stance: professional, disengaged, or engaged.

To explore these domains, I instigate a role play in class based on an actual practice situation in which a client finds him or herself in a conflict, takes sides, and uses self-defeating behaviors about which he or she is relatively unaware. One student begins as counselor and, when he or she feels stuck or wants to stop, he or she calls on another student to pick up the session. Students then write (1) what they see as the problem, (2) the role they wanted to take with the client, (3) those features they wanted to pursue in more depth, and 4) how engaged they felt they needed to be in order to be effective.

After students write about the role-play, I introduce Kantor's four domains and ask students to determine their preference in all four. They also complete a homework assignment exploring the roots of these preferences. The domains are then added to the framework originally used to compare theories, thereby initiating the idea of tying theory to the individual preferences of the students.

Commonality Corollary

Two corollaries, the commonality and the sociality corollaries, address the relationships between people and, therefore, apply to the counselor-client relationship. The commonality corollary states, "To the extent that one person employs a construction of experience which is similar to that employed by another, his processes are psychologically similar to those of the other person" (Kelly, 1966, p.20). For example, as clients describe an event and their experiences of that event, they disclose their constructs. In listening, counselors build their own constructs in response to the client's description. While the counselor's construction of the event may differ from that of the client, using empathic listening skills increases the likelihood of similarity between the counselor's and client's construction of the experience, allowing empathy and reflection to occur.

The group project and discussion after each role play enhance the opportunity for students to further reflect on their constructions of events and experiences. Ortega y Gasset (1985) indicates that so many things fail to interest us, simply because they don't find in us enough surfaces on which to live, and what we have to do is to increase the number of planes in our mind, so that a much larger number of themes can find a plane in it at the same time. The outcomes of the group project-role play-discussion process raise new questions and possibilities by increasing the number of planes in students' minds. Students free themselves from absolutist thinking in an atmosphere in which they see the familiar in unfamiliar ways. As a group, they work together to produce novel views.

Sociality Corollary

The sociality corollary states, "To the extent that one person construes the construction process of another, he may play a role in a social process involving the other person" (Kelly, 1966, p. 21). This corollary means that influence generates not only from observation of behavior but from attributing meaning to that behavior in ways that impact one's own psychological processes. For instance, Jane answers a question in great detail. If John merely notes that the answer was given in great detail, no real growth occurs for John. But if John attributes great brilliance to Jane, he may adopt her answer. If he consistently attributes great brilliance to Jane, he may model his actions after hers. To increase the likelihood of students learning from each other, I ask them to respond not only to the content of others' comments, but to explore their attributions. They thus allow themselves to be impacted by others' input, enhancing the group's mutual influence.

Fragmentation Corollary

The introduction of the fragmentation corollary, which states, "A person may successively employ a variety of construction subsystems that are inferentially incompatible with each other" (Kelly, 1966, p. 20), encourages students to remain open to alterations in their constructs. Fragmentation allows for the adoption and expansion of ideas without discrediting a previous idea. In other words, it increases the number of perspectives from which a person can draw information. Such a process is antithetical to making a premature commitment, and when encouraged, should ideally lead to increased cognitive complexity. The process of holding competing views is somewhat challenging to students, especially for those who have a higher need for closure and for those in earlier cognitive developmental stages (Perry, 1970). Yet in assisting a client, counselors must hold several competing hypotheses, gradually refining the co-constructed conceptualization of the client's world view.

I encourage students to hold seemingly inconsistent possibilities of themselves as counselors, the theories they use, and their views of the client. We trace interactional sequences backward within a role-play to illuminate inferences made and to explore those that might conflict with their original assumptions. The subsequent discussion centers on how their assumptions might change to accommodate the new inferences. This approach is another tool to encourage students to alter their constructs.

A culminating experience in the last class session highlights the differences among the theories as enacted in counseling sessions. Students team up in groups of three and choose one theory to portray in action. One student plays a prescribed client role for every session in that day's class. Each team then demonstrates their theory while counseling the same client. As they do so, students are typically struck by the great differences in the kinds of information elicited from the client and different directions the sessions take. They see in action the degree to which choice of theory directs the course of the counseling.

CONCLUSION

Kelly's Personal Construct Theory offers a guiding paradigm for teaching a counseling theories course. Theories are treated as tentative constructs, subject to the context in which they were created and to the construing of those who apply them. As such, theories are viewed as permeable and changeable. Rather than teaching theories as categorically distinct, with certain absolute advantages and disadvantages, the methods described in this chapter are designed to increase the recognition that liabilities and limitations of a theory can become benefits when circumstances change. Integrating this over-arching paradigm into a theories course also teaches students how to integrate counseling theories with personal inclinations. Fitting oneself into an environment (counseling a client using a theory) becomes not "finding the one best fit," but a process "by which we give form, meaning, and value to our world (Brown & Langer, 1990, p. 323).

Appendix

Ideas for Movie Clips that Demonstrate Context

I. To discuss issues of acceptance of different points of view and influence of our values on our perceptions and interpretations: *Stepmom*—the scene in which the daughter yells at the stepmother.

II. To contextualize the era in which different theories were created:

*   **Psychoanalysis**

    The Age of Innocence. The opening narration sets the social tone. Although the video is not set in Vienna, it does portray the social mores of the time.

    Blue Sky. Note the scenes from when Jessica Lange dances for the foreign soldiers to when Tommy Lee Jones talks to his children after leading her out of the fabric store. This portrayal is used as example throughout the class to help students understand this theory, especially defense mechanisms.

*   **Relational theory**

    Kramer vs. Kramer. The scene is early in the video from the point at which Meryl Streep tells Dustin Hoffman she is leaving until after Hoffman's discussion with his wife's friend.

*   **Systems theory**

    The holiday dinner table scene in *Avalon* is an example, or the entire movie *Steel Magnolias* or *Four Weddings and a Funeral* (to be viewed at home).

*   **Person-centered theory**

    Pleasantville. The scene begins when the husband comes home with a community leader, just as his wife is beginning to change to color, and ends after the husband's reaction in the aftermath of discovering his wife's change.

*   **Personal Construct theory**

    Paper Moon (to be viewed at home).

*   **Gestalt theory**

    60's. The movie can be viewed at home in order to give a full picture of the divisiveness and turmoil that occurred in the 1960s. A segment that can be used in class begins with the two white brothers playing pool and ends with the African-American father and son's confrontation in Los Angeles.

*   **Cross cultural counseling**

    Grand Canyon. The entire movie can be viewed at home since it provides a comprehensive perspective on the different worlds experienced by those from different races. For a clip for class, begin with Kevin Kline leaving the basketball game and end with the conversation between Danny Glover and Kevin Kline on the steps of the auto repair shop.

Constructivist Assessment: Laddering Exercise

The Laddering Exercise is a structured interview developed by Hinkle in 1965 (Bannister & Mair, 1968) and designed to elicit constructs regarding some important dimension in a hierarchical fashion. In this course, I use the Laddering Exercise to elicit the core constructs a student holds regarding being a counselor—in other words, what it means to the student to be a counselor. The exercise is based on the premise that we define a construct not by what it is but by what it is not. A demonstration in front of the class with a volunteer illustrates the exercise, and then students conduct the exercise in pairs.

Demonstration:

Begin by writing the word "counselor" on the board. Ask the student, "What does it mean to her to be a counselor?" The student may answer, for example, "It means being good for people." Write that in box 1 (see diagram). Next, ask the student what she considers the opposite of "good". She may answer, "bad." Write that in box 2. Ask the student, "Which do you prefer?" The student answers, "Good, of course." Mark the preference and begin from that word, asking, "And what does good mean to you?" The student may answer, "to be accepted." Write that phrase in box 3, following with, "What is the opposite of being accepted?" "Being rejected." Write that phrase in box 4. Again, ask, "Which do you prefer?" and mark the preference. Continue until the student either doesn't have any more answers or her answers become redundant. Typically students think the exercise is meaningless until they do it with each other and they are amazed when it strikes so close to home.

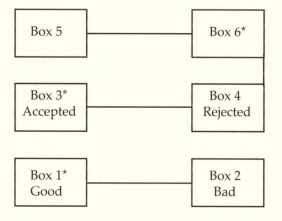

The students in the paired groups can continue the discussion of their superordinate constructs, or the students can be directed to journal their reactions. The following list of questions borrowed from Robert Neimeyer (1993) facilitate the discussion.

1. What are the superordinate values at the upper end of your ladder?

2. How are these values expressed in behaviors, traits, or roles at the lower end of the ladder?

3. What choices or alternatives are implied by your personal construct poles?

4. Did you ever hesitate in assigning a preference to one pole over the other? Why?

5. Can you imagine ways of integrating both poles in such cases?

6. What life-style might someone have who made the contrasting pole choices?

7. What would be a positive connotation for the nonpreferred pole?

8. What people in your life would criticize your pole preferences? What people would support them?

9. How would someone 10-20 years older than you live out these preferences?

These questions could be used by pairs of students or as a stimulus for journaling, but are probably too sensitive to be used in the class demonstration of laddering. This exercise reveals students' own superordinate constructs. The process is far more powerful than its simplicity suggests. If reaction papers are not a usual part of your class requirements, asking the students to submit a reaction paper after this exercise provides a mechanism to process their experience.

Constructivist Assessment: The Repertory Grid

The repertory grid was one of the first assessments developed by George Kelly (1955) to identify a person's core constructs. Ten elements are listed along the top of the page (for more information, see Kelly, 1955). These elements are used to trigger constructs. We use the repertory grid to assist students in identifying those qualities they consider most important in people. Because the role of the counselor within any theory requires particular behavior or attitudes on the part of the counselor, the personal information obtained from the repertory grid informs the students about the stance that may prove most comfortable for them.

Description:

Ten elements are provided for the students. Tell students to put the name or initials of the following people into the ten element spaces across the top of their grid. The ten elements used in this exercise are: (1) favorite person, (2) wisest person, (3) most difficult person to get along with, (4) themselves, (5) themselves when they are fully trained as counselor, (6) good friend, (7) their mother, (8) their father, (9) their sibling or cousin if the student is an only child, 10) favorite mentor/teacher. For example, I might say R.S. is my favorite person and put those initials in the first element slot.

Notice that the grid is divided into vertical columns and horizontal rows and in each row there are three circles. Invite the students to compare each group of three, designated by the three circles in that row. State, "In row one, compare the people you placed in columns _ , _ , and choose the columns according to how two are the same and one is different." You probably will have to repeat or demonstrate this before students will know what to do. For example, I could compare R.S., G.P., and X.L. and might suggest that R.S. and G.P. are both very tolerant and that X.L. is not.

Instruct the student to put the word that characterizes two of the people in Column A. Then ask the student to place the opposite of that word in Column B. For example, I would put "very tolerant" in column A and then when asked for the opposite, I might say, "insensitive to others" and place that phrase in Column B. Then ask for the student's preference. I might choose "very tolerant" and indicate this preference in some fashion. Continue until all ten constructs are completed and marked for preference. At this point my grid looks something like the following:

	favorite	wisest	most difficult	you	you as counselor	good friend	mother	father	sibling	mentor	
Tolerant*											Insensitive
Warm*											Cool
Manipulative											Honest*

The students are then instructed to evaluate each person on each preferred characteristic (*) using the following scale: -3, -2, -1, +1, +2, +3 so that there will be a score in every box on their grid. Note that there are no 0's, so that students cannot take a neutral position. This is a sample of how the grid will look when this task is completed.

	favorite	wisest	most difficult	you	you as counselor	good friend	mother	father	sibling	mentor	
Tolerant*	1	-1	1	2	2	3	-1	1	2	3	Insensitive
Warm*	2	3	-3	1	2	3	-2	-1	-1	2	Cool
Manipulative	3	3	-2	3	3	3	2	1	1	3	Honest*

Lastly, the scores for each construct of preference is added and rank ordered. Those with the highest score will represent the superordinate constructs meaning that they are stable and unlikely to change. In our example, tolerant, humorous, and honest were the preferences. By adding each row, we get the following: Tolerant, Humorous, Honest.

Next, ranking them, we find that this student's constructs are prioritized as:
  First Priority: Honest, with a score of 20
  Second Priority: Warm, with a score of 13
  Third Priority: Tolerant, with a score of 6

The student would then apply this self-knowledge to one of the theories. For instance, the student who values honest and warmth may be attracted to Rogerian therapy and less comfortable with Beck's cognitive theory. Another student whose prioritized constructs are intelligent, complex, and insightful may be more comfortable with psychoanalytic theory.

A sample grid is provided for the reader's use. Several computer programs are available to assist students in both constructing their grid and analyzing the results. Computer programs also exist that analyze the grids from a group of people. Repertory grids have been used individually and with couples and families.

Constructivist Assessment: The Psychoepistemology Profile (PEP)

The Psychoepistemology Profile (PEP) is a standardized instrument designed to measure a person's way of coming to know the world: rationalism, empiricism, or metaphorism. An epistemic style is conceptualized as a major personality integrator or higher order personality factor which determines an individual's particular world view. Each epistemic style depends upon a particular sub-hierarchy of psychological processes and involves a different criterion for truth (Royce & Mos, 1980, p. 1). Some evidence exists that clients whose counselor's epistemology matches their own are more satisfied with their sessions and report greater progress (Lyddon, 1989; 1995; Steenbarger, 1991). Some evidence also exists that counselor trainees' development is aided by choosing theories that are epistemologically similar to their own world-view (Neimeyer, Prichard, Lyddon, & Sherrard, 1993). We encourage students to use this information about themselves in choosing a theory.

The PEP is comprised of three subscales: metaphoric, rational, and empirical. Metaphorism is the approach used by people whose view of reality is metaphorically defined and tested for validity in terms of universality. Symbolism is an important cognitive process underlying this commitment. Rationalism is used by people who possess a commitment to rationality, and logical consistency would be their test of validity. Clear thinking, rational analysis, and synthesis of ideas underlie their cognitive processes. Empiricists hold a commitment to external experience; validity is established by the reliability and validity of their observations. The underlying cognitive processes are active, seeking sensory experience, and developing perceptions to interpret that experience. Most people use all three interchangeably but subscribe to one dominant epistemology in order to find truth. Therefore, each individual is given a score on all three subscales. Their dominant score represents their preferred epistemology. This self-administered test takes approximately twenty minutes to administer and has a key that can be distributed to students for self-scoring. Information is provided for the student to interpret their own epistemology profile and to apply their findings to the theories presented in the course.

REFERENCES

Bannister, D., & Fransella, F. (1971). *Inquiring man: The theory of personal constructs.* Harmondsville, England: Penquin.

Brown, J., & Langer, E. J. (1990). Mindfulness and intelligence: A comparison. *Educational Psychologist, 25* (3&4), 305-335.

Chaiken, S. (1980). "Heuristic versus systematic information processing and the use of source vs. message cues in persuasion." *Journal of Personality and Social Psychology, 39,* 752-756.

Chanowicz, B., & Langer, E. J. (1981). "Premature cognitive commitments." *Journal of Personality and Social Psychology, 41,* 1051-1063.

Corey, G. (1996). *Theory and practice of counseling and psychotherapy Fifth edition.* Pacific Grove, CA: Brooks/Cole Publishing.

Doan, A., & Parry, R. E. (1994). *Story re-visions.* New York: The Guilford Press.

Frankl, V. E. (1978). *The unheard cry for meaning.* New York: Simon & Schuster.

Gergen, K. J. (1991). *The saturated self.* New York: Basic Books.

Heesacker, M., Wester, S. R., Vogel, D. L., Wentzel, J. T., Mejia-Milan, C. M., Goodholm, C. R. (1999). Gender based emotional stereotyping. *Journal of Counseling Psychology, 46* (4), 483-495.

Kantor, D., & Neal, J. H. (1985). Integrative shifts for the theory and practice of family systems therapy. *Family Process, 24,* 13-30.

Kelly, G. (1955). *The psychology of personal constructs* (Vol. I). New York: Norton.

Kelly, G. (1966). A brief introduction to personal construct theory. In A. R. Mahrer (Ed.), *Morality and mental health,* (pp. 1-33). New York: Appleton-Century-Crofts.

Langer, E. J., & Piper, P. (1987). "The prevention of mindlessness." *Journal of Personality and Social Psychology, 53,* 280-287.

Lyddon, W. J. (1989). Personal epistemology and preference for counseling. *Journal of Counseling Psychology, 36* (4), 423-429.

Lyddon, W. J. (1995). On the relation between philosophical worldviews and theories of counseling and development: A comment. *Journal of Counseling and Development, 73,* 515- 517.

Mahoney, M. J., & Lyddon, W. J. (1988). Recent developments in cognitive theories. *The Counseling Psychologist, 16(2),* 190-234.

Miller, J. B., & Stiver, I. P. (1997). *The healing connection: How women form relationships in therapy and in life.* Boston: Beacon Press.

Neimeyer, G. J. (1993). *Constructivist assessment: A casebook.* Newbury Park: Sage Publications.

Neimeyer, G. J., Prichard, S., Lyddon, W. J., & Sherrard, P. A. (1993, May-June). The role of epistemic style in counseling preference and orientation. *Journal of Counseling and Development, 71,* 515-523.

Ortega y Gasset, J. (1985). The revolt of the masses. In A. Kerrigan (Trans.) & K. Moore (Ed.), *The philosopher's index (1940-1999)* (vol. 12, p. 357). Notre Dame,

IN: Notre Dame University Press.

Perry, W. G. (1970). *Forms of intellectual and ethical development in the college years.* New York: Holt, Rinehart, & Winston.

Petersen, S., & Heesacker, M. (1997). Student epistemology and choice of theory. Paper presented at Southeast Regional Conference of Association of Counselor Educators and Supervisors, Kentucky.

Petty, R. E., & Cacioppo, J. T. (1986). *Communication and persuasion: Central and peripheral routes to attitude change.* Englewood, NJ: Lawrence Erlbaum Press.

Rafuls, S. E. & Moon, S. D. (1996). Grounded theory methodology in family therapy research. In D. H. Sprenkle & S. M. Moon (Eds.), *Research methods in family therapy* (pp. 64-82). New York: Guilford Press.

Royce, J. R., & Mos, L. P. (1980). *Psycho-epistemological profile manual.* Edmonton, Canada: University of Alberta Press.

Sartre, J. P. (1957). *Existentialism and human emotions.* New York: The Wisdom Library.

Skovholt, T. M., & Ronnestad, M. H. (1995). *The evolving professional self.* Chichester: John Wiley & Sons.

Steenbarger, B. N. (1991). All the world is not a stage: Emerging contextualist themes in counseling and development. *Journal of Counseling and Development, 70* (2), 88-296.

Sue, D. W., & Sue, D. (1999). *Counseling the culturally different.* New York: J. Wiley and Sons.

Van Kaam, A. (1966). *The art of existential counseling.* Wilkes-Barre, PA: Dimension Books.

White, M., & Epston, D. (1989). *Literate means to therapeutic ends.* Adelaide, Australia: Dulwich Centre Publications.

Worell, J., & Remer, P. (1992). *Feminist perspectives in therapy: An empowerment model for women.* Chichester, England: John Wiley & Sons.

5

Discovering Assessment

Carolyn Oxenford

Human beings have been trying to objectively classify each other using some kind of psychological measurement for as long as there have been recorded records. Most standard assessment textbooks attribute the earliest psychological measurement to the Chinese civil service entrance exams of 2600 B.C., in which future public servants had to demonstrate their skills in such areas as poetry, archery, and calligraphy (Cohen, Swerdlik, & Phillips, 1996; Gregory, 1996). These texts then proceed to describe other early instruments designed to measure the intelligence of school children, screen military recruits, and identify personality "problems."

It is obvious that describing, selecting, and classifying individuals based on their success in answering questions and solving problems constitutes a large and profitable area for psychology and counseling. Traditionally, the assessment enterprise has been dominated by statistically-based, objectivist approaches that focus on comparing individuals to a normative sample or to an externally derived and absolute level of mastery. Because of this focus, which neglects the individual's unique world view and search for meaning and takes assessment out of the hands of the "subject," many counselors, especially the large number who were educated in the humanistic tradition, have been ambivalent or negative about formal assessment. Counseling students often perceive traditional tests and measurements courses as irrelevant to their personal and professional lives, and also as dry, technical, and boring.

Given this state of affairs, it might seem that approaching an assessment course from a constructivist framework would be a contradiction.

Constructivist theorists generally find traditional modes of assessment troublesome. Tests or procedures that attempt to objectively classify, select, or describe an individual smack of essentialism and seem to be incompatible with the constructivist world view. If we cannot know an external, objective reality, and if meaning can only be understood as the interaction between individuals and their environment, how can we presume to say that a given response or score has any objective meaning? Even more importantly, how can we, on the basis of test scores or other external criteria, make important decisions about schooling, hiring, hospitalization, or promotion? And yet, counselors who work in school, vocational, and mental health settings are asked to use "objective" test data to make exactly these kinds of decisions. And, further, must we discard all attempts to find patterns in human behavior? If, as constructivists believe, the basic assumptions of the traditional assessment enterprise are flawed, what should we teach in an assessment course and how should we teach it? This chapter attempts to address these questions.

CONSTRUCTIVISM MEETS THE ASSESSMENT COURSE

One extreme approach to teaching a constructivist-oriented assessment course would be to focus only on techniques that reflect the constructivist stance, such as participant observation and structured interviews. Certainly, educators may exist who would espouse this approach; however counselors working in the field usually cannot simply ignore traditional forms of assessment. A more useful approach, and the one advocated in this chapter, is to use constructivist principles and pedagogy to deconstruct and perhaps reconstruct the use of testing and assessment. Assessment can be a useful enterprise if it assists individuals with self-knowledge and the ability to make good decisions, and if it provides clues for the counselor.

In order to make constructivist teaching more than just a "bag of tricks," it is necessary to examine our own basic assumptions about assessment as well as about learning, teaching, and "schooling." In their book, *Mindshifts*, Caine, Caine, and Crowell (1994) suggest several questions to ask ourselves as we examine our mental models of learning. Are we blank slates to be filled or active creators of meaning? What is the role of physiology and emotion in learning? Do we have to be directly instructed in order to learn and remember? How much learning happens outside the classroom? Applying this same line of inquiry to the field of assessment yields other questions. Are test takers merely passive responders or do they actively influence the test taking situation? How do clients/students' unique cultural, biological, and social experiences influence their approach to assessment and their responses? Can we ever really assess someone meaningfully, or does the act of assessing itself alter the context and the individual?

Challenging and examining our own assumptions both about teaching and about assessment helps us create our own internal meanings about assessment and teaching, from which course decisions will flow. Like our students, we begin where we are. Perhaps we add just a few ideas as we engage in our own growth and self-reflective process. We proceed at our own pace. Our students teach us, and we teach them. They assess us, and we assess them.

What does it mean to assess someone anyway? If meaning is essentially the result of a dialogue between the "knower" and the "known," then the results of any assessment say as much about the assessor as they do about the supposed "object" of the assessment. Assessments are social constructions themselves. We must remind ourselves that they are embedded in multiple, sometimes very different, perspectives of the initial test constructors, the interpreters, and the takers. The conclusions drawn by one person based on a sample of the behavior of another are often then interpreted by others, who are themselves embedded in a given context. Therefore, even a simple assessment task quickly comes to resemble the multiple reflected images of a vanishing mirror picture.

Counseling students need to experience and understand the issues raised by the assessment enterprise if they are to be helpful to clients who must cope with the many forms of assessment that are utilized in our society. The potential and actual serious misuse of tests and test data make it particularly important for counseling students and practitioners to approach testing and assessment from a constructivist viewpoint, that is, understanding and questioning the basic assumptions which underlie traditional assessment strategies enables counselors to advocate for clients if the latter are denied access to needed or desired services based on objectivist test interpretations.

In addition to advocating for clients when tests are misused, counselors who take a constructivist perspective on testing can be more subjectivist and client-centered in helping clients use test data. Psychometrically-based tests can be integrated into a careful, full-featured assessment of the whole person. Such an assessment would include a description of the test and its assumptions and an evocation of the client's meaning-making. Then decisions can be made which reflect the unique position of the individual in a society at a particular point in time, rather than being based on a set of scores with little or no context.

Finally, students need to understand traditional assessment if they want to advocate for meaningful change in the ways tests are used. Convincing an agency, school, or other system that mass administration and rigid interpretation of "objective" test scores do not lead to client empowerment requires that students understand the assumptions and philosophy underlying traditional assessment.

In addition to examining and using existing types of assessment more mindfully, counselors can also help to create a more constructivist environment by learning about alternative forms of assessment. Assessment tasks have been developed that reflect basic constructivist assumptions, in the forms of structured interviews, repertory grids, and personal construct ladders (see Neimeyer, 1993, for examples of constructivist assessment techniques). These alternatives are more flexible and useful in counseling settings than most   traditional methods; but they also have limitations for placement and other purposes. Beginning counselors need to understand both the strengths and the limitations of these more qualitative methods of assessment.

This chapter attempts to stimulate ideas about ways to design and implement a constructivist-based course on assessment. Part I below describes the course planning process, while Part II gives specific examples of activities that can encourage students to achieve those goals. Part III focuses on evaluating students and the course to determine whether course goals have been achieved.

PART I: ESTABLISHING GOALS

What do we want future counselors to know and be able to do in the area of assessment? Four primary questions can help us determine our objectives for a course in assessment. They are:

- What do students want and need from this course?
- What does the larger community expect from graduates of this course?
- What do future clients most need and want from graduates of this course?
- What do we, as educators and "expert" practitioners, consider most important to students' future practice?

What Do Students Want and Need from This Course?

This first question is central to discussions in constructivist education. Constructivist instructors, who acknowledge that student goals, needs, and perspectives are at least as important as their own, consider how to effectively blend student and instructor goals into a cohesive whole. For the instructor teaching in a general counseling program, in which students are preparing for many different types of counseling careers, the challenge to respond to the varied personal and professional needs and interests is particularly difficult. The typical diversity among students in this course challenges us to make this learning experience relevant and comprehensive. Often, instructors opt for a mind-numbing recitation of details in trying to "cover" even a few of the specific tests and techniques required for each of the varied settings in which our students may one day practice. Far from being a burden however, such student diversity can be translated into a very positive element for the constructivist educator. For example, students' own unique experiences with assessment and the resulting attitudes they have developed can be a starting place for their critically examining and deconstructing the human assessment enterprise.

Although we can anticipate some of what our students might be interested in learning from the assessment course, we need to assess student needs and interests each time we teach it. Each unique group of students will have particular needs. This initial assessment may be as easy as asking about students' experiences with assessment, students' career goals, and students' current opinions about assessment. Or instructors may present students with some current assessment-related dilemmas drawn from relevant counseling settings. Reading and discussing such scenarios in small groups can help students generate the questions that they would like to be able to answer by the end of the course. Good sources for such testing scenarios are *Responsible Test Use* (Eyde, Robertson, Krug, Moreland, Robertson, Shewan, Harrison, Proch, Hammer, & Primoff, 1993) and the *ACA Ethics Case Book* (Herlihy, & Corey, 1996). For example, the instructor can trigger questions that students will want to answer as they progress through the course by using a synopsis of findings on racial bias in IQ testing and gender bias on the SAT, and/or having students try to explain the "Flynn effect" (the finding that IQ test scores rise with succeeding generations). These phenomena illustrate the socially constructed nature of tests and test interpretation.

What Does the Larger Community Expect from Graduates of This Course?

This question reflects the need for instructors to be aware of the many contexts within which this (or any) course must function. Where does this course fit in the larger course of study? Is this the only assessment course students take? Does the faculty mandate a designated level of expertise in the administration of particular tests? Must there also be a heavy emphasis on psychometrics and statistics? Does the course need to cover all types of tests or are there specialty courses or other opportunities for students to obtain more specialized knowledge? How much choice is there in the use of texts and other materials? Must the class meet every week at the same time? What access is there to computerized facilities, test materials, and people to assess? Is a final examination mandated? To what extent is innovative instructional practice supported (or at least tolerated) in the culture of the program? These basic program requirements, constraints, and expectations need to be considered, as well as issues affecting the entire department, school, or university.

At a broader contextual level, assessment classes must also engage current paradigms in the counseling profession. A tension exists in the field between the so-called "objectivist" and "subjectivist" paradigms. For example, a strongly constructivist instructor might argue that assessment as it has traditionally been framed is simply not possible since we can never know objective truth. How can external validity exist if one rejects the notion of objectivism? How can we understand a number that estimates an inherently objectivist concept like "intelligence" or "level of depression?" The constructivist would ask the counselor to ascertain what test items mean to the person being assessed, how they perceive the broader construct we are attempting to measure, and what role this construct plays in their lives. On the other hand, although we might feel that traditional testing concepts and techniques are irrelevant or even destructive for some of our clients, if we do not address those traditional concepts, we do our students a disservice. Constructivism is not the dominant paradigm in licensing and accreditation, as the legacy of positivism still reigns. For instance, the CACREP guidelines for assessment courses require that specific elements be included, and these elements are strikingly similar to the topics covered in traditional assessment textbooks (Council for Accreditation of Counseling and Related Educational Programs, 1994)

Another example of positivist practice is the single-minded use of the National Counselor Examination (NCE). Not only is the NCE itself rooted in an objectivist assessment practice, but it also presumes a thorough knowledge of traditional assessment concepts. Our students must understand and be able to use traditional techniques in order to enter the profession, even as we give them the tools to critically evaluate these techniques and foster change.

Students who have achieved a deeper understanding of assessment techniques and issues also have an important role to play in the community. Whether that community is the agency in which they work or the community in which they live, individuals who understand both the strengths and the limitations of various assessment methods can help to prevent misuse and misunderstanding of their results. For example, many programs for the "mentally retarded" deny services to clients if they fail to meet strict objectivist criteria (for example, IQ of 70 or below). A side effect of strict use of such criteria is that we place some clients, whom society already has labeled in a very negative way, in the position of having to "play stupid" and perhaps to define themselves as stupid in order to get the services they need. And we have done this using questionable psychometric theory, since we have not considered the standard error inherent in the measures. By helping decision-makers understand both the psychometric and the constructivist problems with this type of approach, counselors can engender a shift in social attitudes and social policy, from our present reliance on numbers toward consideration of the whole person and his or her needs and desires. Given the ubiquitous presence of test data in our society, finding opportunities to challenge similarly inappropriate uses of assessment data at work and elsewhere is not a problem. Giving students both the psychometric background and stimulating constructivist attitudes empower them for change at many levels of society.

What Do Future Clients Most Need and Want from Graduates of This Course?

If we agree that assessment is not merely something done "to" the client by the counselor and reported on to some third party, then we must encourage students to consider the needs and desires of their future assessment clients. Most assessment texts spend little or no time discussing how to give appropriate feedback to clients regarding test data, and those that do tend simply to state that feedback should be appropriate to the client's age and state of mind. Far more important is how the client and counselor will use the information provided by the test to make meaning of the client's situation. What did the client think during and after the testing, and what do they want as a result of the experience? Here it is important for students to consider their clients' developmental levels. Many clients, like the larger society, look to test results for concrete answers and may well resist open-ended feedback. On the other hand, more autonomous clients will resent their lack of participation in creating meaning if the opportunity is not there. Sensitivity and judgment are required in assessing what the client wants and striking a balance between imparting objectivist data (for example, "Your reading score is well below average") and helping clients make sense of and use the information gleaned. Further, challenging the ultimacy of data also can instigate development in the more dualistic students. Using either scenarios generated by the students or case studies provided by the instructor, the class can discuss test results and practice discussing test results with clients as a way to grow both personally and professionally.

What Do We, As Educators, Consider Most Important to Students' Future Practice?

Where do we as instructors fit in all of this? What content, concepts, and practices do we believe students need to extract from this course? What are our own preferences as educators and test users? One of the key roles of an instructor is to guide students in navigating and then choosing from a large, unfamiliar body of information. Thus, as teachers, we must first grasp the broad dimensions of the field, be able to recognize and explore the critical landmarks, and help students begin to do the same. We need to identify key issues and show students how to find and evaluate the information that they need, sifting the useful from the irrelevant. Before we can do this with students, we need to be clear about what concepts we ourselves find most critical. My personal list of topics and how to address them is as follows:

1. *Reliability and Validity:* A common concern among assessment instructors is how to balance understanding of these notions as statistical concepts with understanding of these as properties of useful assessment tools. A constructivist instructor might emphasize a conceptual approach to reliability and validity. Students who wish to explore psychometrics in more detail may be encouraged to do so, perhaps by completing an independent project to be shared with the class, or by serving as a statistics consultant for teams of students who are developing tests.

2. *Choosing and Evaluating Existing Tests:* Students need to understand different classes of assessment and be able to decide whether a test or procedure is useful for a particular individual, situation, or practice area. These classes might include objective, projective, and performance-based assessments; observational assessments; recognition or production tasks; and surveys or other assessments of attitudes and opinions. Constructivist educators will want to supplement standard texts with readings that describe qualitative assessments (for example, Goldman, 1992; Bozarth, 1991) and instruments designed to support constructivist approaches to treatment (Neimeyer, 1993), since coverage of these approaches is quite limited in standard texts.

3. *Test Construction Techniques:* While most counselors do not choose to go into the test construction business, I believe that the active experience of constructing a test helps students learn to evaluate the quality of existing tests, in a sense "deconstructing" testing by constructing a test. They learn to recognize the theoretical assumptions upon which a test is based, whether the techniques used to develop and refine the measure were appropriate, for whom the test was designed and whether it can be adapted for others, and more. Knowledge of test construction also prepares counselors to plan program evaluations and needs assessments. Understanding test construction further helps students to appreciate differences between norm- and criterion-referenced tests or between qualitative and quantitative methods, and to ultimately choose assessment techniques which suit their goals and the client's needs.

4. *Ethics in Assessment:* The ethical issues of great concern to me are those related to the abuse of standardized testing, such as fairness versus

bias in standardized test use, the effects of gender and ethnicity on test results, the rights of test takers, confidentiality of testing, and competency to give and use test results.

5. *Healthy Skepticism in Assessment:* Through administering tests, students learn a healthy skepticism about the nature of human assessment. They can learn the importance of being careful observers and accurate recorders and analyzers of information. They learn to draw conclusions from the information gathered and not to be overly impressed by numerical data. They also learn to integrate formal test data with many other types of information and assessments, and they come to understand the importance of not drawing conclusions from any single, limited source. Their final assessment reports will then be clear, accurate, and respectful of the client and his or her needs.

6. *Impact of Assessment on Society:* Through the exploration of this topic, students explore the unintended consequences of testing, such as its promotion of problematic social distinctions and discrimination. They also discuss the impact of "high stakes" testing on individuals, the problems inherent in "teaching to the test," and legal decisions which influence our use of tests and other forms of assessment.

7. *Impact of Assessment on the Individual:* Constructivist educators clearly consider the dialogue between assessor and assessee to be very important, particularly since test results can be life-altering. In constructivist test interpretation, the emphasis is on the meaning that the client makes of the results. Yet, few standard textbooks on testing and assessment ever address how to communicate with test takers, except usually to mention the need to give test takers feedback in language they can understand. Testing is portrayed as something "done to" and explained to test takers. Clients usually have little opportunity to engage in any kind of dialogue with those administering or using the assessment. Clearly a constructivist approach to the assessment course would need to supplement traditional readings with a focus on the meanings inherent in the counselor-client dialogue.

This list may be similar to that developed by other instructors. What is demanded by a constructivist approach is that the instructor confront his or her emerging values about testing, and that the course be personal, flexible and responsive to students. The next step is to choose or create materials, activities, and methods—such as those described below—which will help students achieve the objectives of the course.

PART II: TASKS, ACTIVITIES, AND METHODS

The following conditions underlie the constructivist approach to teaching the testing course. They are derived from Caine and Caine's (1994) work in cognitive psychology and neuroscience. These conditions are:

- A low-threat environment, in which risks can be taken, creativity can be unleashed, and students feel comfortable enough to allow the confusion, disorganization, and disequilibrium necessary for reorganization at a higher developmental level.

- Orchestrated immersion, in which the intense involvement of students in a personally important, real life environment in which learning can be embedded into their existing mental schema.

- Active learning, which includes the experience of personally processing course information; evaluating and choosing that which is compelling and relevant to the specific student; and the opportunity for significant self-reflection and self-evaluation.

These three conditions can guide us as we operationalize our objectives and flesh out the structure of an assessment course.

Providing a Low-Threat, Inclusive Environment

Instructors need to consider what they can do to create a low-threat environment; a place where students feel comfortable expressing opinions that may be contrary to those of others, where they can disagree with the teacher, and where they can try out new ideas. As each new group of students enters the course, the foremost question in most of their minds is "What do I have to do to be successful in this course?" We, as the educators, send many messages about this, some of them quite unintended. In a traditional first class, for example, the instructor usually spends the first few minutes of the first class handing out the syllabus and going over course objectives. This process often includes emphasizing the due dates for papers and projects, the penalties for late work or lack of participation and the conditions under which students may receive an "A." Even if we then follow up this introduction with class introductions and open-ended discussion, what message have we actually sent? We have stated pretty clearly that we alone are in charge and that we determine what the course will be about. We have encouraged passivity from the start. What if we began more inclusively and democratically? Let us try beginning with introductions, which can then lead naturally into a discussion of student and instructor experiences with assessment and various opinions about assessment. Different examples and ideas come up, and students begin to identify problems or issues they would like to learn about, leading them to formulate their goals for the course. These goals can be integrated into the course syllabus if possible, or students and instructors can co-create course contracts which capture individual goals. We have then begun to create a learning community that is invested in creating meaning by and for its members. When everyone participates in goal setting, the level of excitement and commitment to the course will be much higher.

Having set the stage in the first class for an environment which values student input, constructivist educators also must address the usual sources of anxiety for students. Is the professor fair? Does she care about my learning? Communicating openness to students and their concerns and commitment to fairness is important. Being available seems to be a key element for most students (McAuliffe, 2000).

How classroom discussion is managed also influences whether an environment is perceived as low-threat. Instructors must step in to manage discussions so that they are productive rather than aimless, respectful of others while assumptions are challenged, and inclusive. McKeachie's book, *Teaching Tips* (1994), has an excellent compendium of tips for leading discussions and creating a low threat environment. Another thought-provoking book that includes tips for using discussion effectively is Education for Judgment (Christensen, Garvin, & Sweet, 1991).

While a low threat environment is necessary for learning, it ist not sufficient. How do we create the orchestrated immersion and active learning experiences that Caine & Caine suggest are crucial? In the assessment course, opportunities are abundant.

Fostering Immersion and Active Learning

The other two conditions for optimal learning can be discussed together. Constructivist instructors can employ a variety of active learning tasks to achieve the varied objectives of an assessment course. All of the tasks described below can be integrated into a single, generalized assessment course, and each is used to achieve a different focus. Active experiences with actual test materials allow students to understand practical issues related to administering, scoring, and writing test reports, and raise questions about the validity and usefulness of tests. The simulation and the community test projects described below enlarge the context of assessment and emphasize intended and unintended consequences of test use and misuse. The test construction project asks students to conceptualize and design a meaningful assessment and highlights the difficulties of doing so. It also familiarizes students with validity and reliability issues.

Using tests: Students are powerfully motivated to explore and understand the assessment process when they take a standardized psychological test. I have used the Myers-Briggs Type Inventory or one of the many Learning Style inventories for this experience because they are short, easy to score, and relatively simple to interpret. Questions about the accuracy, usefulness, and fairness of these measures take on an immediacy during this experience which fuels discussion and critical thinking. Students also gain an appreciation for the rights and feelings of test takers when they "live" that experience.

As the course progresses, students move from being test takers to becoming test administrators. They administer their first test and bring the results to a group scoring session where they share their scoring dilemmas, gain insight into how scoring decisions are made, and practice calculating scores and analyzing their data. Once the tests are scored and analyzed, students are given copies of good professional test reports, which they use as models for their own rough drafts. Students administer two additional tests and submit only their scoring protocols and final drafts. Although it is not appropriate for students to actually give feedback based on these imperfect practice attempts, certainly they form the basis for a spirited discussion of how to use assessment results with clients. This is yet another opportunity to emphasize client-based assessment. For example, what does the client make of their performance? Can it inform their decision making, or world view? This is a real departure from typical feedback sessions in which test results are presented as immutable truths.

Using actual tests in this manner powerfully engages students due to their very real interest in understanding the meaning of their volunteers' responses. Comparing the numerical scores with their holistic perceptions of the person taking the test raises the issue of "testing" versus "assessing the person in context." The opportunity to consult with peers and the instructor throughout the process and the practice of turning in rough drafts for comments reduce the threat level in the classroom significantly. During the tasks, students also encounter real ethical and professional dilemmas regarding the provision of appropriate feedback, gaining informed consent, and maintaining test security. From a practical standpoint, the number of different tests or procedures used for this activity needs to be limited. Once students have gained skill in using and evaluating a new test or procedure, they can apply these skills independently to tests or procedures of their own choosing.

Simulations: Simulations effectively immerse students into real-world situations in which they must make decisions using assessment results. An example of such a simulation is an activity that can be called "The Eligibility Committee Meets." In this simulation students decide whether a student should receive special education services. They receive actual, disguised packets containing the reports of the teachers, the school psychologist, the school social worker, the educational consultant, and the nurse. The instructor (or a knowledgeable student) is the central office representative to the committee, while students play the roles of the school principal, the reporting professionals, and the student's parents. The remaining students in the class observe the process and formulate questions for later discussion.

Prior to beginning the simulation, students review theirs reports and ask any questions they may have about the process or the report. Then, the committee convenes. The participants give their reports, followed by discussion and debate, which is sometimes quite fiery. The committee renders a final decision. Next, the observers lead a discussion about the roles of different types of assessment in the eligibility process and the impact of non-assessment factors—such as school system politics, teacher/student personality conflicts, gender or ethnic bias, or socioeconomic bias. Similar activities could be created to simulate hiring committees, college admissions committees, or other "high stakes" users of testing.

When creating simulations or adapting real cases for simulated use, it is important for the instructor to choose or create situations that are not clear-cut. As students struggle with conflicting or ambiguous results and with the political and social realities that go into these types of decisions, they learn far more than which tests they should use to determine eligibility for special education services and the definition of a learning disability. Instead, they create an individualized, internalized understanding of the uses of assessment procedures that will help them better serve their clients' best interests when they begin their own counseling careers.

Test construction projects: As previously mentioned, students also gain valuable insight into the assessment process by creating their own tests. For this task, students form groups and decide on a question that they would like to answer using assessment procedures. Student assessments have ranged from a "knowledge of political figures" test to a "male chauvinist attitude" scale.

To help students gain the initial knowledge they need to design and implement their projects, they read, discuss, and receive mini-lectures on psychometrics, reliability, validity, and test construction. In their small groups, students conceptualize their test's format and scope. They create test items and procedures and administer pilot projects, often discarding the majority of their early attempts. Students solicit feedback from their pilot test takers, analyze the data they have collected, and revise their measure at least once. If time permits, students may readminister their revised test or procedure and analyze the new data. One important "real life" consideration for students is their need to secure appropriate permissions for conducting the project; this approval may require consultation with university institutional research boards. Often board requirements are minimal, but, even if this is the case, going through the process of obtaining necessary permissions sensitizes students to the rights of subjects and the reactions of the larger community to assessment tasks.

Toward the end of the course, each group presents its experiences and reflections on the process to the entire class. Each group earns a grade based on a jointly-written and submitted report, peer evaluations of their presentation, and a required self-reflection on the process. Required elements in this self-reflection presentation include student perceptions of the group process and their role in it, their perceptions of the process of developing their measure, ideas for improving the small group process, and a description of the personal or class learning goals they have accomplished.

Tests in the community. In order to gain a sense of how tests are used in real-world settings, students can be asked to locate an example of test use in the community. Students particularly enjoy the opportunity to find uses of assessment that are related to their interests. For example, one karate enthusiast studied the process of evaluating students during karate belt tests, and a champion tennis player studied USTA tennis rating scales. The search for nontraditional uses of assessment also encourages students to engage in some "out of the box" thinking about what constitutes an assessment tool. Students find out as much about the assessment method as possible and draw conclusions about the adequacy of the test itself and the impact of the test use on test takers, test users, and any other affected parties. The results of these investigations may be presented either as a class presentation or as a poster session. The diversity and ubiquity of tests generally intrigues students. Also some of the poor tests and poor uses of tests being promulgated in the community often horrify them (and their instructors), which leads the class very naturally into discussions of fair use, bias, and liability/legal issues in testing.

Class discussion & case methods: Instructors may write discussion questions and cases to illustrate important issues or to challenge student thinking; but they should not overlook the opportunity to have students write cases or discussion questions that reflect their thinking and interests as well. Writing the questions and cases requires students to think about an issue from several perspectives and enables them to focus on their own areas of interest. This process of conceptualizing and sharing, and of getting input and feedback from fellow students and the instructor, gives students an even broader, more inclusive perspective on an issue which has real meaning for them.

But can't I ever lecture? So far I have emphasized methods for promoting "Active learning." Sometimes descriptions of constructivist classroom practices seem to suggest (or at least imply) that didactic lecture is an ultimate evil. There are times when lectures (especially short ones) may be helpful, for instance, in explaining concepts like validity and reliability, and helping students put assessment into a historical context. In addition, when students read about or experience difficulty with concepts, brief explanatory lectures can enable them to progress more quickly. Keeping lectures short and incorporating mini-discussions, short reflection papers, or similar techniques to keep students involved with the material allows students to process lecture material more thoroughly. So hold onto those notes and see how you can make them more student-friendly.

Technology in the assessment course: Technology plays a role in the assessment course on several different levels. If possible, opportunities for students to use computer-assisted testing should be provided. One particularly interesting experience is to take the same test in both the traditional paper and pencil format and a computerized version. The Myers-Briggs Type Inventory is one easy example that can be used. There may also be students who have taken the Scholastic Aptitude Test or the Graduate Record Examinations in both computerized and traditional formats as well. Given the increasingly common use of computerized testing, any assessment course needs to alert students to the advantages and disadvantages of taking a test via computer and getting a computerized feedback report. Misuse of canned, computerized reports is also a problem with which all consumers of assessment need to be acquainted. It is usually enough to provide students with a few examples of these computerized reports for them to begin to see the problems associated with completely mechanical scoring services.

Technology can also be used as a way of enriching the learning environment. Many websites use or report on assessment of some type. These sites can be used as sources of information, but they can also be an excellent way to study how tests are used in society. Evaluating the accuracy and usefulness of these sites could be an interesting variant on the "tests in the community" project described above.

As instructors begin to see the many experiences that can be designed to develop constructivist courses, time constraints may seem tighter and tighter. But the time devoted to particular topics or activities can be modified based on student reports of understanding. Offering students a range of course content and class activity options, menu-style, allows students to demonstrate their mastery of a particular course objective in a manner of their own choosing. Additionally, requiring each student to write up an individualized course contract helps the student to take responsibility for learning, and assists the instructor in keeping track of students' progress and making sure that all course goals are addressed.

PART III: EVALUATIONS IN THE ASSESSMENT COURSE

Grading in the assessment course serves as a microcosm of constructivist approaches to assessment. If we truly see students as active creators of meaning rather than as passive recipients of knowledge, how can we evaluate them on passively-received knowledge alone? Just as students are encouraged to co-construct and share their own meanings with the guidance of their instructors as they move through course experiences, they can have opportunities to co-create the evaluation process. In course evaluation we can model our approach toward the "subjects" of assessment: Just as we do not want test takers to feel that this is something done "to" them, with no chance to have input into the process, we do not want students to feel that grading is something done to them without their understanding and input.

What to Evaluate

Deciding on what to evaluate will be easier if students and instructors have attended carefully to the goal setting phase of the course. Operationalizing the goals specified at the beginning of the course can be a joint process as students and instructor come to a mutual understanding of how these goals will be met. The learning goals that are typically evaluated seem to fall into three broad categories: (1) understanding of course content, (2) application of course concepts using higher level cognitive skills, such as analysis, synthesis, and evaluation, and (3) and personal development as demonstrated in enhanced self-reflection and creation of new internal schema. Clearly, different types of goals call for different evaluation mechanisms. A discussion of methods for evaluation in the testing course follows.

Methods for Assessing Content-Related Goals

The achievement of content-related goals can be measured in a wide variety of ways. For example, if one goal is "understanding reliability, validity, and test construction," instructors might ask students to demonstrate the ability to apply these concepts during the writing or presentation of the test construction project. Students might also respond to a written case in which they analyze how these concepts affect the choice or usefulness of a particular procedure. In either case, it is important for students and instructors to agree on what constitutes evidence of successful goal achievement. When a project is assigned, students and the instructor can jointly agree on which goals can be met by this task, and how goal attainment might be demonstrated. A student-centered scoring rubric, with clearly defined categories and examples of various performance levels, may help clarify standards and expectations. For example, if the goal is to demonstrate the ability to use and interpret reliability concepts in the context of a student-designed test, a continuum of performance from "fully met" to "partially met" to "not yet met" might be defined.

Methods of Assessing Higher Level Thinking

A student's ability to think critically about real life problems is a constructivist goal that might be assessed effectively through take-home, rather than in-class, examination questions. The artificial constraints of the usual in-class, time-limited, closed-book exam often sends the message that what students have memorized is more important than how well they can apply what they know or how well they use the data that they have available. Take-home, open-ended questions that have many possible viable responses require students to demonstrate both received knowledge from text and lecture and also internalized ideas and values from class discussion, personal reflection, and careful analysis. Instructors may discuss questions which are similar to the examination questions during class so that students can explore their understanding and receive feedback before the exam. The following examination/discussion cases and questions may be helpful in assessing critical thinking in assessment:

- You are the Assistant Superintendent for Pupil Services for your public school system. The leaders of the African-American and Hispanic communities have been putting a great deal of pressure on your school system in recent weeks, charging that the system is biased against their children. Indeed, there is an over-representation of African-American and Hispanic students in special education classes and an under-representation in the gifted/talented program. Currently you use a combination of the Wechsler intelligence tests, Iowa Tests of Basic Skills, and teacher recommendations as your means of identifying students for inclusion in these programs. Reporters have been calling you for comment. How would you explain and justify your selection procedures, particularly with regard to minority assessment. Or, in the event that you disagree with the procedures being used in your system, what alternative procedures can you suggest?

- As an Employee Assistance Provider working for IBM, you are asked to evaluate an employee whose job performance is deteriorating. You administer a battery of tests and discover no cognitive difficulties. While interviewing and administering projective tests to the employee, you discover that she is using drugs. When you discuss this with her, she admits that she is using drugs, but tells you that you do NOT have her permission to disclose this information to IBM. Identify the ethical and legal issues here and describe how you would handle the situation.

Methods of Assessing Developmental Progress

Self-evaluation. Self-evaluation complements other evaluative tools and makes evaluation dialogical. If students have not encountered meaningful self-assessment in prior classes, they usually need instruction and practice to progress beyond a surface, content-based level. Students may complete a written self-assessment as part of each major class experience. They might also keep a journal. What is particularly helpful for students at more concrete developmental levels is the instructor reading journal entries and writing responses to them as the course progresses. This feedback and gentle challenge helps the student to develop a more integrated, systemic level of knowledge and broader perspectives.

Instructor evaluation. Assigning letter grades to self-reflective tasks such as journals or self-evaluations is a difficult task. In most traditional courses grading depends on skills acquired and on the ability to understand and apply concepts. But for context-oriented constructivists, the issues of readiness and developmental level complicate the grading process. What do we do with students who, due to cognitive immaturity, lack of practice, or other factors are not ready for higher level reflection? Grading on student progress over the semester may be the most helpful approach in this case, and using the data in regular self-reflective assignments such as journals can allow us to see progress that other, more content bound and static processes do not reveal.

Self-evaluation isn't only for students. We also need to evaluate ourselves as teachers and our courses as learning experiences. Waiting until the end-of-course evaluations to begin this process means a wasted opportunity to improve the course as it progresses. By soliciting feedback from students regularly throughout the course and by sharing some of our own self-reflective process with students, we model the behaviors we seek to inspire. The feedback we solicit may take the form of a quick weekly check-in to determine whether students feel they are progressing toward meeting their goals, to more formalized feedback at certain points in the semester that could cover larger questions about course relevance, needed changes, and so forth.

CONCLUSION

Although teaching a course on assessment using constructivist principles sounds exciting and challenging, at this point it also may sound time-consuming, fragmented, and unnecessarily chaotic. After years of experiencing the traditional "downloading" model of teaching, with its underlying orientation toward student passivity, shifting our mental picture of learning into an active, independent process which is only partially under our control can be a big challenge.

In many ways, the assessment course is a natural starting place for applying constructivist learning principles because of the rich possibilities for active, hands-on learning and critical thinking. When we invite students to bring in their unique experiences, and, often their strong opinions about assessment to this cause, we are afforded many opportunities to broaden their perspectives as well as our own.

REFERENCES

Bozarth, J. (1991). Person-centered assessment. *Journal of Counseling and Development, 69,* 458-461.

Caine, G., Caine, R. N., & Crowell, S. (1994). *Mindshifts: A brain-based process for restructuring schools and renewing education.* Tucson, AZ: Zephyr Press.

Caine, R.N., & Caine, G. (1994). *Making connections: Teaching and the human brain.* Menlo Park, CA: Addison-Wesley.

Christensen, C. R., Garvin, D. A., & Sweet, A. (1991). *Education for judgment: The artistry of discussion leadership.* Boston: Harvard Business School Press.

Cohen, R. J., Swerdlik, M. E., & Phillips, S. M. (1996). *Psychological testing and assessment: An introduction to tests and measurements.* Mountain View, CA: Mayfield Publishing Company.

Council for Accreditation of Counseling and Related Educational Standards. (1994). *CACREP accreditation standards and procedures manual.* Alexandria, VA: Author.

Eyde, L. D., Robertson, G. J., Krug, S. E., Moreland, K. L., Robertson, A. G., Shewan, C. M., Harrison, P. L., Proch, B. E., Hammer, A. L., & Primoff, E. S. (1993). *Responsible test use: Case studies for assessing human behavior.* Washington, DC: American Psychological Association.

Goldman, L. (1992). Qualitative assessment: An approach for counselors. *Journal of Counseling and Development, 70,* 616-621.

Gregory, R. J. (1996). *Psychological testing: History, principles and applications,* (2nd ed.). Boston, MA: Allyn & Bacon.

Herlihy, B,. & Corey, G. (1996). *ACA ethical standards case book,* (5th ed.) Washington DC: American Counseling Association.

McKeachie, W. J. (1994). *Teaching tips: Strategies, research and theory for college and university teachers.* Lexington, MA: D.C. Heath & Co.

Neimeyer, G. (Ed.). (1993). *Constructivist assessment: A casebook.* Newbury Park, CA: Sage.

6

Teaching Group Counseling:
A Constructivist Approach

Bill Bruck

In his small yet profound book titled *How People Change*, author Alex Whelis (1973) suggests that identity consists of the integration of behavior. He says, "a young man who learns to drive a car thinks differently thereby, feels differently; when he meets a pretty girl who lives fifty miles away; the encounter carries implications he could not have felt as a bus rider. We may say, then, that he not only drives a car but has become a driver. If the action is shoplifting, we say not only that he steals from stores but that he has become a shoplifter (see p. 79)."

Similarly, in a constructivist model of counselor education we are not merely teaching discrete skills, items of knowledge, or attitudes. We are communicating a mode of being in the world—an identity for ourselves and our students. We are socializing our students into the counseling profession; helping them to *become* counselors. This is nowhere more true than in the teaching of group counseling skills.

It is a basic principle of constructivism that meaning is created, and by extension, it is good if much of that meaning can be created in dialogue. For that reason, the first principle of constructivist teaching cited by McAuliffe and Lovell (2000) is to personalize your teaching.[1] Thus, to teach group counseling from a constructivist perspective, a leader needs to engage in the process in a personal and authentic way. The instructor needs to stay in constant contact with the group; model courage, honesty, and authenticity; be willing to take risks and to self-disclose when appropriate. An example of teaching group counseling from this perspective is the following "Group Counseling Methods" course.

COURSE DESIGN

Group Counseling Methods provides graduate counseling students with the knowledge and skills needed to effectively serve as junior co-leaders of a variety of treatment groups. This course achieve this by teaching the core group worker competencies specified by the Association for Specialists in Group Work (ASGW[2]); these competencies become the learning objectives for the course. The ASGW divides core competencies into two types: knowledge competencies and skill competencies. Knowledge competencies relate to "knowing about"; skill competencies relate to things a counselor should be able to do. Sample core competencies include the ability to:

• State the advantages and disadvantages of group work and the circumstances for which it is indicated or contraindicated (knowledge competency).

• Engage in appropriate self-disclosure in a group (skill competency).

• Give and receive feedback in a group (skill competency).

The class described here includes about sixteen students and meets once a week for three hours. Usually, about half of the students in the class have had no prior experience as members or leader of any type of group. Approximately two-thirds of course time is devoted to teaching skill competencies, the other third to knowledge competencies.

We teach knowledge competencies via lecturette/discussion, independent and cooperative research projects, and small task groups. Skills are first learned in structured group exercises; then practiced and reinforced in a training group and via behavior observations, intrapersonal reflection, and (occasionally) video-tape analysis.

PROGRESSIVE SKILL TRAINING METHOD

We use a progressive, four phase method to teach skills. During the first two to three weeks, the first phase, students learn about feedback and clear communication skills during structured exercises. For example, students learn to differentiate what they directly perceive ("observations") from conclusions they draw ("thoughts") and personal values ("judgments") using an "Observe/Imagine" exercise. In the large group, one student looks at a second student, and makes an observation followed by a thought regarding some psychologically significant aspect of the second student's posture, facial expression, or body movements. For instance, the first student might say, "Henry, I notice that you're sitting with your arms crossed, and I imagine that you're feeling bored with what's going on." The instructor offers corrective feedback when the first student confuses thoughts with observations (for instance, stating, "Henry, I see that you are bored . . . ." as the observation) or inserts judgments into the statements ("Henry, I see you're wearing a beautiful sweater, and . . . "). Students may be asked to participate in learning such specific skills in full-group, small-group, or dyadic learning activities. This phase ends when the majority of the students have facility with the basic group skills.

In the second phase, students participate in a training group led by the instructor. This phase usually lasts two to three weeks, and ends when norms have started developing for positive interactions within the group. In the third phase, which again takes two to three weeks, the instructor leads the training group with students co-leading; this phase ends when the groups have progressed to the working stage, norms are solidly in place, and few if any interpersonal conflicts are observed. In the fourth and final phase, students take the leader/co-leader roles while the instructor serves as a "silent co-leader." During this phase, the instructor only steps in in certain situations (such as interpersonal conflict between group members).

THE TRAINING GROUP

The training group uses a double-fishbowl arrangement. In this format, half of the class acts as observers, while the other half of the class participates as the group; then the two groups switch. The same members remain in the two groups each week in order to allow developmental group process to build.

The training group is a real group experience. Students do not play roles or engage in didactic conversation. However, a training group differs from therapy, counseling, or support groups whose goals might include personal growth, education, symptom remediation, and the like. Instead, the goal of the training group is simply to train group counselors in the group work competencies listed in the syllabus. As it states in the syllabus, "the training group is *not* a 'therapy group.' Students are *not* required to disclose 'personal problems' or personal, historical facts about themselves. Students are required to demonstrate skills that will make them effective in group settings, which do include honest self-disclosure of feelings, thoughts, judgements and expectations arising out of occurrences in the group." Students are expected to actively participate in all phases of the course, but especially in the structured exercises and training group activities.

The class members who are outside of the fishbowl observe the demonstrated behaviors of members inside the fishbowl and use a structured form to record their observations. When the group finishes for the evening, they provide feedback to the inside members about their performance of the required skills and about the overall group process.

A question that class members often ask is, "What will we be talking about?" My approach is to have students talk about whatever emerges as most important for them. In other words, I do not come to the training group prepared with topics (aside from having a topic or exercise in my "back pocket" in case of a silent group). Instead, I structure the training group session as follows: The group begins with a "feeling round"; We go around the group and each member voices what he or she is feeling at the moment. Sometimes we go around a number of times so as to begin with vague, ambiguous feelings—for instance, bad, good and move to more vulnerable feelings—for instance, angry, sad. The feeling round helps everyone get centered and become present to each other and the group.The leader starts a second round by asking if anyone wants to briefly say anything more about their feelings. The leader starts a third round by asking if anyone has any brief unfinished business or if anyone wishes to have some time in the group that evening. The remainder of the group is divided among the people who have said they would like some group time.

I tell group members that no one needs to talk about personal problems. However, if anyone wants to, they can feel free, with certain constraints. First, unlike a counseling group, the focus of the group is not helping a person "solve" their problem. They are bringing the issue to the group as a "gift"—as something that the group can work with. Second, the nature of the group is such that the group will not have time to stay with the problem as long as it would in a counseling group, as long as it might take to solve the problem - since the overall purpose is training rather than counseling. Third, the class is told up front not to bring up certain types of issues—like child abuse, sexual abuse, or really present and significant needs —which would be beyond the group's ability to handle.

On rare occasions in which no one wants any time, I have certain stock activities that I use. For instance, feedback exercises can be especially helpful. The leader might say, "It's been a really important learning experience for me to understand what some of my strengths and weaknesses are as a counselor, particularly how I initially come across to clients. For example, some people notice the fact that I always seem to take my shoes off. Some people are bothered by it, and some aren't. But it was good to get the feedback that everyone notices it, because frankly I forget that I do it. That may seem like a silly example, but I'm wondering, since we have time tonight, if there's anyone else here who might be interested in receiving feedback on how they come across to others when they are in counseling roles, as we are here . . . ." Anyone who volunteers to receive feedback is given control of asking for it and saying when they have heard enough. The group leader supports and guides group members in giving feedback in a helpful way and in helping the volunteer process what he or she has heard.

OTHER COURSE FEATURES

Self-reflection. Students provide answers to specific questions each week on their experience of the training process. I structure the questions so as to build an increasing ability to reflect on and give voice to intrapersonal processes (such as counter-transferential issues) that counselors need to be aware of.

Ongoing feedback. In addition to the verbal feedback incorporated into the training experiences, each student regularly receives feedback from members of the observing group, based on what the observers have seen and recorded on the observation forms.

THE INSTRUCTOR'S ROLE

As described above, the instructor leads the structured exercises in phase one and provides the primary training group leadership in phases two and three. All students have the opportunity to co-lead three training group sessions and, depending on their skill and comfort, may take the primary leadership role.

The instructor also participates in exercises rather than remaining aloof. For instance, the instructor discloses during the opening "feeling check," provides feedback to students on request in the "first impressions" exercise, and the like. The instructor's participation and disclosures, however, are limited by the different roles that he or she takes. The instructor is present in the group in several roles that students do not share—for instance, as evaluator and as leader. Thus, the predominant motivation for participation is not (as it is for students) growth as a person and professional. It is facilitating the growth of the students. Thus, for example, the instructor might offer to discuss a personal issue, if he or she judges that this discussion will model the type of disclosure that would be helpful for students to experience. Similarly, disclosures of negative feelings towards students would be guided not by the instructor's merely attempting to be honest; they would be moderated by what types of disclosures will be helpful to the growth of the group and to the individual involved.

THE CONSTRUCTIVIST APPROACH

In this section, I'd like to discuss several of the elements proposed by McAuliffe in his initial chapter of this volume, elements that are most salient to the teaching of group counseling.

Personalize Your Teaching

A constructivist educator asks the questions, "Is the teacher building authentic relationships with his or her students? Is he or she promoting a learning community?" Constructivist teaching is intensely personal. It requires a instructor to be comfortable with taking risks and being transparent to his or her students; but also to be sufficiently aware of his or her personal process not to exploit students, meeting his or her personal needs under the guise of transparency. Thus, a commitment to teaching this course in a constructivist manner has implications for faculty selection and evaluation that go far beyond the traditional, behavioral methods common in academia today.

The type of relationship that is built through my group counseling courses is a mentor–student relationship. Students find that there is a significantly higher level of trust and respect between them and me, since they have in fact been transparent with one another and with me, and I've been transparent with them. We've engaged each other authentically in growth experiences.

Build Community

What type of community should we, as constructivist counselor educators, try to create? I suggest that it is more than a scholarly community of minds which has as its ideal the free and open exchange of intellectual ideas. This can be an important part of community, but for counselors, it cannot be the entire foundation.

As counselors, we are committed to growth as persons and professionals. As instructors, we should likewise be committed to facilitating the personal and professional growth of our students. The community that we create can thus be one that fosters these additional ideals—adding personal and professional growth to scholarly exchange.

The group counseling course is probably most often the place in the graduate experience that directly addresses these additional goals. In the training group, students learn to give and receive feedback on their professional skills and presentation. They learn to disclose their feelings, and they are invited (but not in any way required) to share personal problems and professional doubts. In many programs, students look back on the group counseling course as the experience in which they were the most honest with themselves and others, the experience in which the deepest and most lasting friendships were formed. In fact, the group counseling course can be a prototype for teaching the basic skills and creating the norms that can imbue the entire graduate program with the commitment to a scholarly and professionally growthful community.

Vary the Structure

For content-oriented courses, it is vital to vary the structure of the teaching activities—more than most instructors realize. Instructional consultants, whose market is teaching interactive approaches to teachers, suggest that the instructional mode be varied every eight minutes. The underlying essence of this guidline is that our teaching modality must engage and hold the learner's attention, and engage learners whose learning styles vary. In content courses, varying the mode is almost necessary to achieve this goal. In the group course, it is not.

In a group counseling course, the training group engages students powerfully. In fact, students do not lose focus, in my experience, even if the training group lasts the entire three hours of class! The focus in the group on the here-and-now experience ensures that, wherever members' attention is, the group will be there as well.

Thus, in this environment, the meta-structure of the class is governed by the instructor, but the structure is co-created by the students. In other words, the learning objectives and the fact that there will be a training group taught within a here-and-now orientation are elements of the meta-structure. The actual content of each group session depends on student needs, desires, and concerns.

Students do differ in how much they like or dislike the relative lack of structure in the training group. However, the tolerance of ambiguity becomes an issue in the professional growth of the student, as this simulates the lack of structure in groups they will lead after graduation. Coaching and supporting students in developing the ability to tolerate ambiguity also promotes cognitive development.

Value and Promote Experience

If you agree with the proposition in McAuliffe's initial chapter (this volume) that experience is defined as "sensory activity that engages the learner's attention," then the group counseling class is probably the most experiential in the curriculum of the typical counseling program.

However, learning relies on more than mere experience. It also involves, McAuliffe's words: "regular reflection and abstraction on experience in order to make greater sense of concepts." For this reason, students reflect on their own experience of the course each week (as discussed in the next section). Moreover, the final examination involves an analysis of the process of both the training group students were in and the one they observed, as well as an analysis of their own growth as persons and professionals over the course of the semester.

Teaching Counselors and Therapists

Encourage Intrapersonal Process Awareness, or "Metacognition"

Metacognition (the conscious monitoring of one's thought processes) is key for the practitioner who would become a constructivist. Group counselors need to be aware of thoughts, feelings, and judgments they experience while leading groups. Then, meta-cognitively, they need to be able to recognize the source of these issues in their personal history, introjected values, or belief systems. In Gestalt terms, group counselors need to understand their areas of blockage, so that they don't live out their own neuroses on their clients.

The structure of the course, as described, provides a concrete method for teaching the type of metacognition necessary for group counselors. Throughout the course, students reflect in writing on their experience of the training group and associated exercises. They are not, however, asked to "journal." Journals are often a collection of intellectual and emotional meanderings that have little of direction or purpose. As a student myself, I didn't really understand the point of journaling, and I learned little from the experience. As I began recognizing similar tendencies in student journals, I gradually developed a set of structured reflections that I request of students and have indeed dropped the term "journal" for these efforts.

The reflections begin with simple questions that help students to focus on their experience. "Which parts of the training group held your interest most strongly? Which held your interest least? What did you find yourself thinking about, when your attention wasn't drawn to the class?"

The reflections focus more on intrapersonal process as the weeks go on. Simpler questions give way to questions such as: "Was there any time in the group that you felt irritated, annoyed, angry, defensive, or vulnerable? Describe the situation and your interpretation of the situation that gave rise to these feelings." Thus, as the semester progresses, students learn a metacognitive skill: the ability to focus their awareness on those aspects of their intrapersonal process that affect their ability to lead groups effectively.

Accent Interpersonal Process Commentary, or "Metalogue"

Interpersonal process recall training techniques are a key to teaching students the ability to engage in "metalogue." Stop-action replay of training group videos can incorporate such recall into a group counseling class. Unfortunately, in years when I employed this technique, I found that the amount of time needed to do it effectively was excessive, so reluctantly I dropped this valuable tool.

Instead, I utilize the process observation technique, in which students in the outer fishbowl summarize everything said by the student they observe. Students take time after each training group to discuss the written feedback provided by the observer and to recall what was going on with them as they said certain things in the group.

Recognize That Conflict and Dialectic are the Norm

The meaning of this guideline is very different for a group counseling course than for a content course. In the latter, conflicts are limited to intellectual disagreements on scholarly issues, and the dialectic is a process that is used to mediate this conflict. However, intellectual conflicts have emotional and interpersonal components. The dialectic helps to mediate the intellectual part of conflict; the emotional and interpersonal parts are often ignored.

One of the explicitly stated goals of the training group is to teach students how to work with interpersonal conflict between themselves and others. The method for doing so that is taught in class involves several steps. The instructor assists each of the parties in conflict to (1) make a clear statement of their position; (2) identify and express their feelings in a clear manner; (3) identify values and beliefs that underlie their feelings, and (4) clearly express these to the other person.

Thus, the group counseling course becomes a laboratory for students to learn how to handle conflict at all levels, and in so doing to build honest and open relationships with other students. Such relationships constitute the basis for a learning community.

Show Commitment in the Face of Doubt

Counseling groups are often filled with scary ambiguity. People express anger, feelings are hurt, vulnerabilities are expressed, and secrets are revealed. Moreover, group members often don't "do things right." They judge each other and say hurtful things. They "take vacations" and talk about superficial topics. They remain silent or are aggressively intellectual.

The group leader often experiences an emotional quandary. "Will things work out?" "Should I stop this now?" "Hadn't I better take control of this session?" Beginning group leaders all too often opt for control. They structure the session, give members feedback directly, or say "Enough is enough, it's time to change the subject." Their methods often reflect their own anxieties and doubts.

Experienced group leaders have a saying: "Trust in the process." Group leaders need to recognize that groups learn to police themselves: They get tired of the obnoxious, controlling member. They don't like it when one person is ganged up on. And they institute self-correcting mechanisms.

Instructors leading training groups have the same doubts that counseling group leaders do. "Will this be a positive learning experience for my students?" It often hard for the instructor to let go and trust in the process. Its echoes the experience of the parent whose child is riding his or her bicycle around the neighborhood for the first time without the parent's accompaniment.

However, the commitment that the instructor maintains to the group process in the face of personal and professional fears is also instructional. This commitment models the type of trust in group process that he or she hopes students will have in the counseling groups that they will eventually lead themselves.

OPPORTUNITIES AND CHALLENGES
IN THE CONSTRUCTIVIST APPROACH

Using a constructivist approach to teach the group counseling course poses both opportunities and challenges at professional and ethical levels. We attempt to teach certain key attitudes throughout our programs that reflect what we see as best practices within the counseling profession. For example, these attitudes include taking responsibility for our own actions. As counselors, we know that this characteristically means not blaming others for our situation, but recognizing that we have choices that have led and continue to lead us on the path that we are taking.

A constructivist approach to group counseling can be a watershed for students in facing such areas of responsibility. The group offers them a safe and structured environment for growth as a person and professional, while providing an opportunity for the instructor to both teach and key aspects of group counseling. Instructors can observe and evaluate not only content mastery and skills, but underlying attitudes and even areas of psychological blockage that may impact on the trainee's effectiveness or their appropriateness for the field.

Herein lies the challenge. The ACA code of ethics—written from a decidedly non-constructivist point of view—forbids dual roles and relationships. At its genesis, this prohibition, in its efforts to protect clients from sexual, emotional, and financial exploitation, made sense. The prohibition also makes sense when applied to counselor trainees, but it must be balanced with another positive ethical obligation to ensure that trainees have the requisite skills and attitudes to practice their profession. One way of avoiding the "dual role" prohibition is to require counselor trainees to attend a group experience led by an adjunct faculty member, who reports nothing back to the core faculty member other than that the student did, in fact, attend the group. An instructor who teaches group methods and also sits on a national professional ethics committee recently told me that he teaches the course in exactly this way and only teaches content in the classroom. I asked him if, at the end of the program, he could tell which students had skills in group work and which did not. He replied, "No, but that's the way I must teach to abide by the ethical guidelines"

A complementary ethical challenge emerges when teaching group counseling from a constructivist point of view, however. The group counseling instructor is often caught in the dilemma of two conflicting ethical guidelines: The dual role guideline may suggest that the instructor not use information obtained about the student's personal and professional development during a training group; while other guidelines may suggest that the instructor not knowingly permit a student who is not appropriate for the profession to be promoted into the profession. Recently, during this course's training group, a student disclosed that she really didn't feel anything for her clients. In fact, she somewhat enjoyed the distress that they underwent, because it made her feel better about herself. I have also encountered students who, under the stress of being in a training group in which they are required to disclose here-and-now feelings, exhibit an inability to do so, intellectualize to the point of being counter-facilitative to the group process, or exhibit a variety of other defenses. The commonality is that many of the students who are least personally prepared to lead groups can easily pass content courses and evaluations.

The ethical challenge facing counselor educators who adopt this approach to teaching emerges during the periodic student reviews, in which faculty discuss student progress from an academic as well as personal and professional point of view. Group counseling instructors have an additional "window" into students' development. We see a side of students that, in my experience, other instructors don't, because of the unique requirements of the training group experience. The information obtained can be critical to predicting success in the profession, offering additional advisements or opportunities for development, or (if needed) recommending termination from the program.

CONCLUSION

The group counseling course teaches skills. But, when it is taught from a constructivist point of view, it can also build relationships characterized by openness, authenticity, and courage among students and between students and instructors. These relationships can then constitute the ground upon which other educational activities within the counselor education program are built. This type of educational experience forms an essential link in the chain of socializing events that contribute to a student's evolution into a counselor.

NOTES

1. In that same spirit, I will use the first person when communicating personal lessons I have learned in teaching group counseling, to foster the spirit of dialogue between you, the reader, and me, as the writer.

2. Association For Specialists In Group Work: Professional Standards For The Training Of Group Workers. *The Journal for Specialists in Group Work* (Adopted April 20, 1991), Volume 17, Number 1, March 1992, pp. 12-19.

REFERENCES

Association For Specialists In Group Work. (1992). Professional standards for the training of group workers. *The Journal for Specialists in Group Work, 17* (1), 12-19.
Whelis, A. (1973). *How people change.* New York: Harper Colophon Books

7

Teaching Counseling Research from a Constructivist Perspective

Mary Lee Nelson and Pamela O. Paisley

Teaching a counseling research course from a constructivist perspective might be viewed by some as highly challenging, in that it requires adherence to seemingly conflicting philosophies. Quantitative research has typically been viewed as a search for truth or lawfulness, the antithesis of the goals of social constructionism. Yet research does not need to be regarded as such an enterprise. From a constructivist perspective, any research, whether it is quantitative or qualitative, yields interesting and useful tentative information that can be utilized to inform the ongoing construction of pragmatic knowledge in a given content area. To us, teaching research from a constructivist perspective seems like a perfect fit, particularly when the research course is one that involves the actual conceptualization of research designs or requires real-world problem solving. The constructivist research classroom can provide a nurturing and stimulating environment in which students tackle the challenging tasks of identifying a research interest area, focusing their ideas, asking researchable questions, and designing a study to answer those questions.

The research enterprise in human sciences might be seen as the ultimate expression of the constructivist endeavor. Where else is traditional, received "truth" challenged in favor of more adequate stories? Where else is the relativity of knowledge considered in particular context? However, the social sciences have constructed empirical research in modernist terms, as a search for truths about human motivation and behavior.

Research in any of its forms is certainly a challenge to any inherited, authority-based "givens" about best practice and right thinking. Thus, the teaching of the research course is itself a call to students to give up conformist, dualistic allegiances. It can be an epistemological challenge to become a more "autonomous" thinker, a professional who practices good skepticism in the face of any blind adherence to any counseling theory or practice. It is in this spirit that we teach the counseling research courses that we will describe below.

This chapter describes three approaches to teaching counseling research using constructivist principles. Prior to describing the approaches, we present some general principles for teaching such courses from a constructivist perspective. We then outline in detail the basic structures and processes of a constructivist research course as it has been taught at the University of Washington. We also describe more briefly two other constructivist teaching approaches used at the University of Georgia. Thus both doctoral and master's degree research training is represented here.

CONSTRUCTIVIST PRINCIPLES

In a constructivist classroom, the instructor is responsible for creating a community of learners who can assist and challenge each other's thinking processes. Group interaction becomes a primary mode of discourse. Hence, the constructivist instructor must have knowledge of group process and must be able to facilitate cooperative work groups within which it is safe and acceptable to challenge and be challenged. Accordingly, students take responsibility for each other's learning by assisting each other to acquire and critique information.

Group discussions in the constructivist classroom can adopt many foci but are prompted by assigned readings and by student presentations of their work. The instructor guides the discussions around specific points in the assigned reading materials or toward specific points that emerge from student presentations. Information presented by the instructor in the form of assigned readings and mini-lectures is open for student critique. All "knowledge" shared in the course is considered tentative, including findings from quantitative investigations.

Windschitl (1997) recommends that, given the ambiguity inherent in constructionist perspectives on knowledge, instructors should provide a degree of "scaffolding," or structure, within which students may struggle with meaning making. Such structure can take the form of providing models of how to think about problems. Class assignments require students to read, write, and engage in thinking exercises designed to facilitate their progress toward learning goals.

SEMINAR IN COUNSELING RESEARCH, UNIVERSITY OF WASHINGTON

Like all constructivist endeavors, this course is an ongoing work-in-progress—owned and operated by professor and students and open at any point to critique, questioning, and revision. Because the course is intended to prepare the students for individual research projects, students have the option of designing either quantitative or qualitative studies. The course , however, focuses on the basics of qualitative research design and analysis to complement what students have already learned about experimental and correlational group designs. Constructivist procedures assist each student in arriving at specific research designs. That is, the inquiry process for each student is driven in part by interactions among group members who have an investment in each other's work. In the beginning, each student engages in some "qualitative" procedures for arriving at his or her research questions.

Goals of the Course

The purpose of the Seminar in Counseling Research is to guide students through the process of preparing to write a research proposal, either for a thesis or for a dissertation. The course is intended for doctoral or master's students in counseling who have already taken at least one course in statistics and research design. Students should be preparing to conduct independent research projects and should have roughly identified a research area before they enroll. The course assists students in exploring areas of interest, acquiring theoretical sensitivity (Strauss and Corbin, 1990), developing conceptual connections, formulating research questions, and defining a methodology. Students in this course move on to next take a final two-credit course in counseling research, wherein they will prepare actual research proposals. The intent of the first course is to facilitate each student's creation of a basic outline for that proposal. If this sequence were offered to be as a single course, students could write research proposals as their final project for the course.

Course Requirements

Assigned Readings. Readings for the course have two foci. First, students read a selection of counseling process and outcome research articles from major counseling and counseling psychology journals in order to familiarize themselves with counseling research literature. Second, students read material on designing qualitative research—current books and articles that are intellectually accessible and practical. Reading assignments are designed to provide material for class discussions on how to conceptualize qualitative research and on how to collect and analyze qualitative data.

Independent Readings. Students also conduct ongoing library research in their own interest areas and introduce material from their independent readings into class discussions.

Student Projects. In addition to the readings, students complete exercises that involve researching and thinking about problems and questions. Each student brings the results of his or her exercises to class, and the class engages with the student, inquiring about his or her area of interest, challenging the student's thinking, and providing support and suggestions for the development of the student's project. Specific exercises are outlined in the sections below.

Course Structure

Counseling Research Presentations. Strauss and Corbin (1991) stress the importance of researchers developing "theoretical sensitivity" by their understanding the extant research and theory that pertain to their areas of inquiry. This process prepares the researcher to identify what has already been investigated, what needs further investigation, and what methods have been tried to obtain information. Toward this end, a course on research in counseling might begin with an overview of prominent content areas of counseling research.

Thus, this course begins with a broad survey of process and outcome research in counseling and counseling supervision. An integral complement to that survey lies in the subsequent student presentations on the counseling research articles they have read, which are woven throughout the first two months of the course. Each student presents two articles to the entire class or to a small group within the class (depending on class size). In these presentations, students emphasize the authors' citation of relevant literature, rationale for the study, methods, results, and inferences or conclusions made. The students then lead the group or class in a critique of the study, its methods and conclusions. Students are given sample questions that they may use to critique the articles. Sample questions might include:

1. What ideas or points did you particularly like or find convincing?

2. About what conclusions or points do you feel skeptical? Why? What would you need to know before you could accept or reject the ideas? What aspects of the conceptualization, design, analysis used, or implications made seem weak to you? Why?

3. What is missing in the present state of the information? How could such information be obtained?

As students discuss the class readings, they are encouraged to bring up their own areas of research interest, tying those into the discussions.

"Thought Messes." The course also begins with an acknowledgment that knowledge creation is inherently messy. No straight linear path leads to any kind of final truth. A discussion at the first class meeting focuses on what is "bugging" each student about the state of understanding in a particular professional area. Students verbally struggle with their concerns about what is known and not known in the counseling field and allow themselves to embrace the ambiguity inherent in the "messy" state of the extant knowledge. They are, of course, also encouraged to allow the literature that they have read to bother them, excite them, frustrate them, or motivate them. Students are told that it doesn't matter how unformed their ideas are early in the course. In fact, the generation of "thought messes" is their first major task. A thought mess is a visual depiction, a diagram or graph, that represents a student's current conceptual thinking in a particular subject area. The intent of this initial process is to give students permission to play and struggle with their own and each other's ideas without the expectation that they be thinking in a linear fashion. The process aspect of the course is extremely important at this point because the "playing" and the struggle are themselves the goals. Playing and struggling with information allow students to examine and question their assumptions about what is valid or "true" and give them permission to combine ideas in unusual or creative ways.

Students are asked to suspend closure on their ideas, requiring them to tolerate a certain degree of ambiguity. They are encouraged to think in a nonlinear fashion, hopefully freeing the mind to be surprised by unexpected recognitions of conceptual relationships. The resulting thought mess is not intended to be a finished product. Rather, it is viewed as a working model, open to reevaluation and restructuring based on input from the literature and from fellow researchers. To further facilitate the conceptual process, students complete a journaling exercise, which they continue throughout the course, and in which they write their thinking as they progress through the course.

Presentation of "Thought Messes." Following the assigned presentations on counseling process and outcome research, students deliver presentations on the state of their individual thought messes to the class or to a small group within the class. Presentations demonstrate key ideas and issues of interest to the students and typically include some of the significant notations students have made in their journals. The presentations usually take the form of non-linear, visual depictions of the students' conceptual spaces. Regardless of the medium of presentation, students are invited to scribble over and revise their presented material as they interact with their class or group. Students tend to find these presentations quite exciting, as they have the opportunity to "air" their individual mental processes and get feedback from each other. They appreciate both the challenge and the support they receive.

Concept Maps. After the class examines others' thought messes, each student creates a frame or a shape that illustrates known or hypothetical relationships among concepts within the student's area of interest. A concept mapping exercise from *Qualitative Research Design* (Maxwell, 1996) may be used to help students create spatial models of conceptual relationships. After a student has completed an initial version of the concept map, he or she presents it to the class or a small group, and class members comment, question, and recommend revisions or additions. As suggestions are made, they can be noted on the presentation materials; this in turn yields visual working models. After initial concept map presentations, each student makes a follow-up presentation of the revised map, and still further revision takes place.

Development of Research Questions. As students develop their conceptual maps, they begin to get ideas about how their conceptual interests hang together and about what efforts in theory and literature have been made to investigate the relationships among the conceptual areas. The general process of arriving at research questions involves funneling concepts into questions that the researcher can answer. Helping students through this process entails getting them to ask themselves what information is missing in the extant literature, what methods have not been tried to examine the phenomenon of interest, and what the students themselves can contribute from the perspective of their own individual experiences and conceptualizations. Students must ground their research questions in the literature and justify their questions according to what is missing in the literature. Together, we critique the literature they present in class and work on how they can create new branches or fill gaps.

At this point in the course, I ask students two questions: 1) What do you want to know? and 2) What do you need to know? Sometimes those two questions yield different answers. For instance, one year the first author had two Taiwanese students in her class, both of whom intended to return to Taiwan to pursue academic careers. Because constructivist perspectives and qualitative approaches to research were highly valued in their graduate school setting, the students had taken course work that exposed them to the tangible excitement and intellectual stimulation that surround these epistemologies. Both were interested in research questions that would naturally lead to qualitative investigations. However, because academia in Taiwan is not yet receptive to post-modern approaches to inquiry, these two students needed to do quantitative dissertations. We worked on this problem as a class, and I and the other students helped them to find a compromise between what they *wanted* to ask of their research and what they *needed* to ask because of cultural constraints.

Another example of the need-to-know vs. want-to-know problem would be the case in which particular questions cannot be answered because no instruments exist that measure the construct or constructs of interest to the researcher. Before the researcher can answer a particular burning question, he or she may need to develop an instrument to measure the construct. In the first author's recent class, a student developed several hypotheses about counselors who were good at working with gay, lesbian, bisexual, and transgendered clients. He wanted to use an instrument that would measure that ability but could find no such instrument. He decided to design a qualitative study to uncover what counselor characteristics and behaviors are experienced as most helpful to the gay, lesbian, bisexual, and transgendered population. He will later use the data from that study as a basis for the development of a scale. He can then move on to use the scale to measure competency with that client population and eventually address some of his burning questions. Thus, forming useful research questions helps students to examine not only the kinds of knowledge they desire, but also the practical implications of the questions they ask.

Research Methods. As illustrated in the previous section, the students' questions determine the type of methodology they select. Questions that address relationships between or among variables will often (though not always) be answerable through a quantitative method. An example of such a question might be, "Do counseling dyads matched for ethnicity differ from non-matched dyads in their ratings of the working alliance?" Another example might be, "Which is a stronger predictor of the working alliance in counseling—similar gender or similar ethnicity between counselor and client?"

On the other hand, questions that relate to understanding observed processes, such as conversations or understanding individuals' experiences or the meaning they make of their experiences are best addressed through qualitative methods. An example of a question that lends itself to qualitative methods might be, "How do successful high school students who have been through the foster care system manage to do well in school? What internal and external resources were they able to draw on to support their studies?" Another example might be, "What are the experiences of participants in long term eating disorders groups?" The class as a group assists each student to identify what types of questions they have and to clarify what type of method would best answer the questions.

Students then specify what kinds of data they will need to answer their questions. Will they need survey data or data from standardized inventories or student-designed questionnaires? Will they need interview data or observational data? What kinds of inventories or questionnaires might they select? What types of interviews or observations would they conduct? This process generates a great deal of individual student exploration. They go back to the literature to find examples of data-producing procedures and tools. They present the results of their searches to the class for comments and suggestions.

The course then moves on to the sampling process, which addresses four questions: What kinds of participants are needed to provide the best information possible? Where and how can those participants be obtained? Whom will students contact in order to engage the participants? And how many participants will be needed? Qualitative theories of sampling – such as homogeneous vs. heterogeneous sampling, maximum variation sampling, and theoretical sampling—are presented. The class discusses rationales for each type of sampling. Students interested in quantitative studies discuss the best sampling procedures for these studies, consider issues of generalizability, and weigh external and internal validity factors.

At this point in the course, I focus on strategies for entering a system, engaging principal players, and recruiting participants. The general guidelines for this process are presented in many publications that address qualitative data collection (Maxwell, 1996; Patton, 1990), however, they are useful for students who wish to gather quantitative data as well. During class, students exchange ideas for entering systems and joining with key players.

Another key question at this point is how much data will be needed? To answer this question, students wishing to conduct quantitative investigations will be guided by principles of power and effect size; and the class is invited to engage in a discussion of those principles. Students also consider qualitative approaches to sample size, such as the principle of "saturation". Saturation holds that data collection continues until all categories of data generated are saturated; in other words, until continuing to gather data no longer provides new information (Heppner, Kivlighan, & Wampold, 1992).

In the same fashion in which they presented thought messes and conceptual maps, students bring to class a visual display of their research design to discuss with their group. Each student creates this visual representation in any way he or she desires, but is encouraged to use Maxwell's (1996) question and method matrix as an example and guide. The question and method matrix is a table composed of research questions, the types of data that will address the questions, the sources of the data, and the techniques and methods of analysis.

Data Analysis. Because the goal of this course is to bring students to the point where they are ready to write a research proposal, including methods for evaluating their data, students read about and discuss options for data analysis. Students who have already taken course work in quantitative data analysis apply what they know, if appropriate, to their questions. If students are unfamiliar with options that might be optimal for their particular methods, they are provided with alternatives and related readings. All students are given reading materials on qualitative data analysis, including a bibliography of books on data analysis procedures (Denzin & Lincoln, 1994; Giorgi, 1985; Kvale, 1996; Maxwell, 1996; Miles & Huberman, 1984; Patton, 1990; Strauss & Corbin, 1990; Yin, 1994), and are encouraged to consider what type of analysis best addresses their research questions. For example, a student wishing to map a thematic theory of counselor cognitive development in the first year of training might be interested in a grounded theory approach (Strauss and Corbin, 1990). A student wishing to uncover the phenomenological experience of children as they participate in play therapy might be interested in Giorgi's (1985) phenomenological method.

Final Project. The final project for the class is the research proposal. The written proposal should include an introduction that contains a concise review of pertinent literature, the research problem or rationale for the study, and the research questions. The proposal should also contain a methods section with subsections that describe who the participants will be and how they will be recruited, what instruments or interview protocols will be used, other procedures that will be implemented, and how the data will be analyzed. Students may then use this proposal as a basis for theses, dissertations, or other research projects they are required to undertake.

DOCTORAL-LEVEL RESEARCH GROUPS

Constructivist principles lend themselves to other creative structures as well. For example, doctoral-level research groups are used within the Counseling Psychology Program at The University of Georgia. These groups are collaborative in nature, carry academic credit, and encourage students to think about research beyond the bounds of traditional classroom instruction. Each doctoral student is required to participate in one of the teams throughout their three years of course work. Students select the team that most closely connects to their area of interest. Teams have focused on such issues as diversity, school-based research, violence prevention, juvenile offenders, psychotherapy outcome research, spirituality, and the Adlerian concept of encouragement. One of the authors (Paisley) is a member of the School Research Group (SRG). This particular group will be used as the basis for describing this team approach to teaching research.

The School Research Group meets once a week and currently consists of four faculty members and four doctoral students. Students and faculty in this group are committed to real world problem-solving with a social action orientation. Research topics cluster around three areas: (1) schools as organizations, (2) issues related to improving the lives of children and adolescents, and (3) enhancing the knowledge and skills of the adults working in schools. In this third area, particular emphasis is placed on impacting the pre-service and in-service training of school counselors.

In developing school-based research projects, group members actively involve themselves with local schools and work only on research projects that are identified within the schools. We do not "cook something up" at the university and impose it on a school. The group thus uses a collaborative model of intervention and research, rather than an expert model. That is, group members work with practitioners to identify concerns and then collaborate with these same practitioners to design interventions and collect data.

The research group serves as a clearinghouse for these projects and provides support for construction of the research design. Group members also assist each other in data analysis and writing. Each group member serves as the lead on particular projects. Currently the types of studies underway include the following:

1. A study for a local high schools on what promotes retention through graduation

2. program evaluations of a consultation project at an elementary schools and a community-based intervention to contribute to academic achievement and psychosocial development for African-American adolescents males

3. qualitative studies of a local school counselors' collaborative group and of a minority recruitment program used in the school counseling master's program

The research group is particularly helpful in formulating research purposes, questions, and choice of methodology. One of the assumptions within the group is that method will not be driven by a particular orientation to qualitative or quantitative approaches, but instead by which methodology will best answer carefully constructed research questions. The lead researcher often presents an initially vague or tentative statement of the problem and rationale as well as an abbreviated review of the literature. The group then questions, examines, and identifies weaknesses and problems, and in general helps refine the direction of the study. Group members also often pitch in to help with the time-consuming work of data analysis, as well as with mid-study corrections.

AN INTEGRATED APPROACH TO TEACHING
RESEARCH METHODS AT THE MASTER'S LEVEL

In the master's program in school counseling at the University of Georgia, the introduction to research experience is handled in an integrated or multifaceted way. As in most master's programs, a stand-alone course in research in education is required. Students take this course in the Department of Elementary and Middle Grades Education; it covers introductions to quantitative and qualitative methods and program evaluation. Students also inductively learn about research methods by encountering real world problem-solving during the foundations course in school counseling, the seminar in school counseling, and their internships.

During their first semester in the master's program, students take an introductory or foundations course in school counseling. Instructors pose questions during the course about the current "state of the art" in the school counseling specialty. In order to answer these questions, students review related literature. In addition, they interview current practitioners. Students interview counselors from a range of schools and levels of experience. They also participate in a week-long "Counselor Academy," which is a series of in-service training programs for local school counselors. During this Academy the students have the opportunity to hear the frustrations and successes associated with serving as a school counselor. Subsequent to doing outside reading and interviews and participating in the Counselor Academy, students meet in small groups to review the information they have collected. Each group develops a position statement concerning what school counseling is and how it differs by level – elementary, middle grades, and high school. Themes across groups are discussed. Without ever identifying this process as research, students are helped to understand that they have actually conducted a study together.

In the subsequent "Seminar in School Counseling," students take their "research" to the next level by conducting school profiles. Students select a school in which they interview — at a minimum — the principal, counselor, two teachers, two parents, and two students. They obtain demographic information and achievement data for the school. In these interviews they try to identify the strengths of and challenges for that school community.

They present these profiles in class. By consensus, students select one of the profiled schools as the focus for their exam. This exam consists of a group project in which students together create counseling interventions to address the challenges facing the school. This process alerts students to the logic of basing school counseling program development on identified needs rather than on some more untested, "received" framework.

During their internships, students continue this process. They select internship sites in which the supervising counselor and principal are willing to be part of such an assessment of school needs. Then, together, staff and students decide on the practical contributions that the intern might make in meeting school needs during the internship experience.

CONCLUSION

Some final comments on the qualitative-quantitative balance and the overall principles that guide constructivist teaching of research methods are in order. First, regarding balancing the qualitative-quantitative research emphases: The approaches we have discussed in this chapter are intended to be general suggestions for using social constructionist principles to help graduate students to develop research knowledge and skills. In our opinion, such approaches require faculty to be open to whatever type of research question a student wishes to address. Such faculty must be receptive to and able to be a resource for both quantitative and qualitative studies. Preparation in both research paradigms is necessary for doctoral students, as they need to be prepared to teach in departments and colleges where social constructionist perspectives have not been incorporated or where qualitative research designs are not yet supported by the faculties.

A central role of the constructivist teacher is that of process facilitator. Whether in a class or research group or across a program, the instructor can guide students "over their shoulders" so that they articulate and develop a research project from initial idea to method specification. We can create the conditions for the development of self-authorizing and empowered professionals when we treat the classroom group as a working team. The products of the research course are viewed as team products. Such a collaborative and experiential approach illustrates the constructivist principle that all knowledge is socially constructed. Further, students can, through such an experience, confidently use a model of conducting inquiry that they can later replicate in their careers.

REFERENCES

Denzin, N. K., & Lincoln, Y. S. (1994). *Handbook of qualitative research.* Thousand Oaks, CA: Sage Publications.

Giorgi, A. (1985). *Phenomenology and psychological research.* Pittsburgh: Duquesne University Press.

Heppner, P. P., Kivlighan, D. M., & Wampold, B. E. (1992). *Research design in counseling.* Pacific Grove, CA: Brooks/Cole.

Kvale, S. (1996). *InterViews.* Thousand Oaks, CA: Sage.

Maxwell, J. A. (1996). *Qualitative research design: An interactive approach.* Thousand Oaks, CA: Sage.

Miles, M. B., & Huberman, A. M. (1984). *Qualitative data analysis.* Newbury Park, CA: Sage.

Patton, M. Q. (1990). *Qualitative evaluation and research methods.* Newbury Park, CA: Sage.

Strauss, A. L., & Corbin, J. (1990). *Basics of qualitative research: Grounded theory procedures and techniques.* Newbury Park, CA: Sage.

Windschitl, M. (1997). A little knowledge is a dangerous thing: Introducing preservice teachers to constructionism. Unpublished manuscript, University of Washington.

Yin, R. K. (1994). *Case study research: Design and methods.* Thousand Oaks, CA: Sage.

8

A Constructivist Approach to the Teaching of Career Counseling

Judy Emmett

In the constructivist paradigm, human beings are, by nature, "self-orga-nizing" creatures (Peavy, 1992, 1994), as opposed to stimulus-response or-ganisms, information-processors, or sets of traits. We make sense of our lives through continuous reflection upon our experiences. It is the task of the career counselor to help the client make sense of those experiences in relation to life role choices. And it is the task of the career counselor educa-tor to demonstrate the story of career counseling.

From the constructivist lens (Hansen, 1997; Peavy, 1992, 1995; Savickas, 1993), career is much more than a job or an objective chronology of one's job history. It can be described as the telling of a life story, an internal and subjective narrative (Bateson, 1990; Cochran, 1992; Peavy, 1993), rather than an objective chronology of a person's job history. This subjectivist empha-sis is iterated, for instance, by Peavy (1995, p. 2), who has described career as an "evolving biographical narrative under continuous revision." Simi-larly, Miller-Tiedeman (1987) suggests that everyone has a career —it is their life.

But career has not always been viewed this way. For three quarters of a century, career counseling was presented as a process of "true reason-ing" by which a person's traits were matched to the requirements of an occupation (Parsons, 1909). People coming to career counselors were viewed primarily as combinations of psychometric traits to be measured and matched to single best occupations; the counselor served the role of expert technician. Counselors alone had the knowledge, hence the power, to en-able clients to identify the best occupational choices (Peavy, 1993; Savickas,

1993).

Constructivists, however, emphasize the role of individual meaning-makers in creating their own reality through continuous reflection upon their unique life experiences. Thus constructivist career counseling assumes a more facilitative, collaborative, less directive focus. Instead of counselors having the power, they empower clients (Hoskins, 1995). Constructivist career counselors help clients discern patterns, hence meaning, from previous life experiences and assist them with understanding and giving voice to their life stories. Clients become able to make decisions and to extend or modify their life stories because of new understandings about what has influenced their choices and about what meaning they have ascribed to past experiences. Cochran (1992) described constructivist career counselors as "coauthors of stories in progress."

According to Peavy (1992, 1993), constructivist career counselors value multiple realities, believing that there is no "one right way" to see the world and no one best way to go about constructing or interpreting one's life story. Constructivist counselors, therefore, value dialogue that enhances both their own understanding of the client's perspective as well as enhancing the client's understanding of his or her own world. During such dialogue, the counselor listens for and reflectively questions the internal learning and meaning-making processes of the client. Counselors help clients recognize the impact and the constraints of their individual contexts and cultures upon both their experiences and their interpretation of those experiences. During dialogue, constructivist career counselors remain authentically present to their clients and create counseling environments which balance both the security and the challenge necessary for growth. Such dialogue promotes the understanding that empowers and informs future choice making.

Peavy (1994) proposed that effective constructivist career counselors possess the following competencies: (a) Mindfulness: The ability to observe oneself; understand oneself as a constructed(ing) person, with a personal "life career" story comprised of personally and socially constructed interpretations, assumptions, and biases. To the extent that counselors are mindful, they attend to clients without imposing their own meanings or direction onto a client's emerging life story. (b) Receptive inquiry: Creating a climate in which clients feel safe when being respectfully questioned about their assumptions and interpretations of past experiences. Counselors empower clients to critically examine their actions, their beliefs, and the contextual influences on their thinking, their choices, and their lives. (c) Meaning making: Possessing a repertoire of strategies and skills necessary to assist clients in discovering themes, patterns, and meanings ascribed to their life stories.

Counselor education, then, needs to offer experiences likely to encourage the development of such characteristics. In this effort, constructivist counselor education is rich in multiple perspectives, in experiential learning and in reflection upon experience, and in recognizing the significance of both intra- and interpersonal metacognition and dialogue. Constructivist counselor educators provide safe and challenging learning environments in which students may reflect upon their life stories and understand the experiences and influences that have shaped them as counselors; they learn to be "mindful," and thus become able to encourage future clients to do the same.

In addition to such personal career reflection, students also need opportunities to engage in actual career counseling and reflect upon their interpretation of those experiences in order to recognize the emerging meanings they are making as prospective career counselors. They learn through these experiences how they already use career theory(ies), career assessment(s), and career information resources. They thus experience and practice techniques that promote "receptive inquiry" and "meaning making" (Peavy, 1994).

This chapter describes how the traditional elements of a career counseling course—such as the teaching of career theory, career assessment, career information resources, and the career counseling process—might be viewed through a constructivist lens. I offer selected learning activities and assignments that might be useful for the education of constructivist career counselors. The chapter concludes with reflections on the value of a constructivist approach for the training of career counselors. I therein propose that constructivist career counseling is, in fact, the most relevant approach to contemporary career counseling in the context of current socioeconomic and workplace realities.

INTRODUCTORY SESSION IN A CONSTRUCTIVIST CAREER COUNSELING COURSE

The introductory session, as I have structured it, sets the tone for the rest of the semester. We begin immediately with a case exploration exercise. I then share a personal and illustrative story from my experiences as a career counselor. Subsequently we review classroom guidelines, and I then introduce "Story Tech," a narrative technique which students use throughout the course.

The career counseling course begins immediately with a case exploration experience in place of an introductory lecture. This activity exposes students to multiple ways of viewing career issues and the career counseling process. It is an inductive way to help students to "create knowledge" as a group. It helps them to identify their "natural" approach to career counseling as only one of several possible approaches. In this activity, students work on one of the career counseling cases described in *Developmental Career Counseling and Assessment* (Seligman, 1994). They individually define what they believe to be the career issue(s) of the person described in the case, imagine what a desirable outcome would be for the client, and plan what they would do as counselors to facilitate that outcome. They consider how differences and similarities between themselves and the client in race, ethnicity, gender, socioeconomic background, age, sexual orientation, or physical or mental ability might affect their thinking about or working with this client. Students then meet in small groups to discuss their thinking.

As a whole class, we then discuss the approach(es) taken and the strategies chosen, and what these indicate about the meanings of career and career counseling and the roles and strategies of the career counselor. During the discussion, I highlight the multiplicity of approaches chosen and possible. I help them through empathic questioning, dialogue, production of metaphors (Peavy, 1995) to reflect on how their past experiences may have influenced them to construct their current approaches to career and to career counseling.

Next, I further introduce the course with a personal story, allowing students to see me as a co-learner along with them, a career counselor-in-process. This story illustrates the importance of career counselors knowing the meaning(s) they have ascribed to career and knowing that these meaning(s) have been constructed out of their interpretations of events that have occurred within the personal and social-cultural contexts of their lives. In this case I had constructed a definition of career which gave high priority to the values of independent choice and personal fulfillment. I attempted to assist a second generation Asian male student to choose a college major based on these same values. This student came from a family in which the eldest son was expected to choose a career that would begin the family legacy in the United States. As a result, my efforts to help him make an independent choice based on what he found most fulfilling were disrespectful and counterproductive. At that time, I did not understand that the personal meaning(s) I had ascribed to career were not universal and that my role as a career counselor was to help clients clarify the meaning of their *own* life stories. I did not serve this student well.

I tell students that I have structured their career counseling class with the hope that they will learn not to do what I did! However, I acknowledge that I can only present them with ideas and with the opportunities for experiences and for reflection upon those experiences. I cannot give them the knowledge or the skills they will use as counselors. They must, and they will, construct that knowledge and those skills themselves. The final entry on the class syllabus sums up this philosophy by saying, "It is my belief that although I can introduce and present to you in this class potentially relevant information and techniques, it is only through your interaction with the ideas and the skills presented that you will be able to construct personally and professionally relevant knowledge and skills. I look forward to working with you in this process."

Because the personal exploration I have structured into this course requires a classroom atmosphere of both challenge and support, I also offer students a list of classroom guidelines during the introductory class session. These guidelines (Brotherton, 1996), encourage students to respect persons and positions and to maintain an open mind in seriously considering perspectives different from their own. The guidelines acknowledge the courage needed to explore one's own beliefs as well as to consider those of other students, and the resistance and discomfort that they may expect to experience from time to time. Finally, the guidelines express the expectation for active participation in the work of the group and for confidentiality about what is shared during that work. I believe such guidelines help establish a climate for the honest reflection and authentic dialogue needed to create a real learning community and to educate constructivist career counselors. My modifications of Brotherton's guidelines are included in the Appendix at the end of this chapter.

The final activity of the first class session is the introductory experience with "StoryTech." The title of the experience is the term created by professor and futurist Arthur Harkins of the University of Minnesota to describe a structured visioning process. Each StoryTech instrument consists of a series of open-ended lead statements. Student responses to these leads create written visualizations (stories) featuring the student writer telling his or her own life story, enjoying a perfect day, identifying troublesome career beliefs, confronting personal feelings about the future and the overwhelming array of career information available, and functioning effectively as a career counselor with clients. This technique and its use in a career counseling class have been described in detail elsewhere (Emmett & Harkins, 1997).

Throughout this course, students complete the written visualizations. They then respond to a series of reflective questions designed to illuminate themes or patterns in their stories and to project how their personal beliefs may both help and hinder their work with some clients. Students examine their stories for insights into their personal views on life, on work, and on career. They reflect upon how their unique life experiences as persons of a particular race, gender, class, culture, sexual orientation, or age have influenced those views. In addition, they reflect on how their particular experiences and viewpoints influence how they view career counseling and how they imagine they will do career counseling. Finally, students identify areas in which to seek feedback from their classmates.

In the initial StoryTech experience, students describe themselves as children, recall how they dealt with significant life events, and characterize their approach to life as the title of a book. In reflecting on their stories, students look for central themes and for indications of contexts in which they will likely be helpful (or not) to their future clients. StoryTech One and the Reflection on Story Tech One are included in the Appendix (p. 158).

Classmates meet every two to three weeks in the same reflection group of two to four students to share their Story Techs (see other StoryTechs in the Appendix (pp. 160–67). They both give and receive feedback about how they view the role of a career counselor and how they are likely to interact with clients in a career counseling setting. At the end of the semester, students write essays in which they synthesize their life (career) stories. They reflect how their own life stories will affect how they practice as career counselors, incorporating what they have learned about themselves as counselors throughout the semester.

TEACHING CAREER THEORY

Examining several prominent career theories can powerfully illustrate the constructed nature of knowledge. When comparing career theorists' ideas and explanations about people's lives and the place of work in people's lives, students become aware that no one best or perfect explanation exists for how people make career decisions or integrate their life roles. Further, when students examine the historical and individual contexts in which the career theorists developed their theories, they find out how the varied life experiences of theorists and the theorists' varied interpretations of those experiences resulted in the construction of different career theories. Each theory potentially offers some important understandings; no theory completely explains career choice or career development for all people. Each theory is both skewed and incomplete. My hope is that students will extend this realization about the construction of career theory into their work with clients, will become aware of the career theory(ies) by which they themselves operate, and will identify the informal career theories already constructed by their clients.

One way to learn about the constructed nature of career theory is to have students engage in career interviews. Initially during these interviews, they simply listen to how people think about career. They may ask interviewees any questions they wish or engage in any topic of discussion which seems relevant to career. They bring the results of these interviews back to class and share them with classmates. We discuss and reflect upon similarities and differences in responses to similar questions.

Students examine these interviews through the lenses of different career theories (for example, typological, developmental, existential, decision-making, behavioral, social cognitive, information processing, value-based) to determine the usefulness of their theories to their work with particular clients. Students discover that they almost always favor some theoretical views more than others. They also begin to understand that clients too operate from belief systems which more closely resemble those of one theorist over another.

Finally, when students examine the interview questions they chose or the topics of discussion they chose to pursue, they begin to see how their choice of focus reveals their implicit career theories. When they intentionally change focus in successive interviews, they begin to appreciate how they are, in fact, choosing different career theories with which to work. They are in the process of constructing working theories based on their current experiences.

The final assignment for the theory section of the course is to tell the life story of their interviewee. Then, from the points of view of several theorists they "explain" the client's career development and how a counselor would use each particular theory to work with the client. Finally, they choose elements of two theories to direct their work with that client, reflecting on how their own social identity (race, gender, age, class, etc.) might influence their choice of theories and their work with that client. Thus, they synthesize and evaluate the various career theories and integrate selected elements of the theories with strategies for using them in a constructivist manner with clients.

TEACHING CAREER ASSESSMENT

Perhaps nowhere else is the distinction between an objectivist (logical positivist) and a constructivist (post-modern) approach to career counseling clearer than in the arena of career assessment. An objectivist view of assessment assumes that the counselor can evaluate or measure the client from the outside. A client becomes a "set of scores" or psychometric traits which allow a counselor to tell the client where he or she "fits" into the world of work. In contrast, a constructivist career counselor uses assessment techniques or strategies that heighten self-awareness and empowerment for clients, thus helping clients clarify who they are as whole persons, where they find meaning in life, and where they belong (Savickas, 1993). An objectivist approach to career assessment tends to focus quantitatively on how much of a trait a client possesses or how strong that trait is relative to other traits. In contrast, the constructivist career counselor helps clients make choices based on the implications of their beliefs, values, interests, and abilities. Peavy (1996) described constructivist career assessment as an intervention that is aimed at increasing clients' capacities to reconstruct their life stories. Clients use the results of their assessments to reflect upon and to explore future choices that make sense in terms of their whole lives. In essence, then, constructivist career counselors view career assessment as a collaborative counselor-client project that has the goal of clarifying clients' self-related constructs (what clients "know" about self and work) as those constructs relate to the plot of their whole life stories.

In this assessment segment of the course, students read the article "Reforming Career Appraisals to Meet the Needs of Clients in the 1990s" (Healy, 1990) in order that they might discover the contrast between "traditional" (objectivist) and "reformed" (constructivist) approaches to career assessment. In this article, Healy contrasts both the goals of these two approaches to career assessment and the role of the counselor in traditional and reformed career assessment. Healy's discussion of how the role of the counselor changes in reformed appraisal depending on the needs of the client can be especially helpful to students. Further, he describes how in traditional assessment, the counselor *explains* to a client the results of the assessment. By contrast, in reformed appraisal, counselor and client *collaborate on* (that is, construct together) the meaning of the assessment for that particular client. Similarly, traditional counselors *report scores* (that is, the traits measured by the assessment instrument), while constructivist counselors *help clients explore the contexts of their lives* which might explain these particular trends. They explore with clients how changes in life circumstances might result in different scores. In traditional assessment, counselors help clients *translate the scores to make immediate occupational choices*. In reformed appraisal, counselors both assist in that match-making and engage in the empowering process of *helping clients to learn how to assess their own abilities, values, and interests and how to use such self-assessment in a process of lifelong decision-making.*

In addition to using traditional testing as a springboard for interpretation, constructivist career counselors often utilize assessment techniques which themselves are constructivist by nature. Peavy (1996) has suggested using such self-assessment activities as journaling, autobiography, and a technique called "conceptual mapping." In a conceptual mapping exercise, clients indicate "self" in a circle in the center of a page. They proceed to fill in this page with the persons, events, and experiences that are significant in relation to their current career concerns. Finally, they draw "maps", indicating the relationships between and among these elements and the self. These "maps" become graphic representations of the meaning, hence the power, of these elements in the career decision-making process.

Other constructivist career assessment tools have been described by Forster (1992). They include portfolios and a tool he named Goals Review and Organizing Workbook (GROW). In GROW, clients identify several meaningful past activities or events. They then cluster these events into "like" groups. Clients proceed to write goals based on these "personal constructs," to prioritize these goals, and finally to rate the activities in which they are currently engaged according to how well they match the goals derived from their most meaningful personal constructs.

Another constructivist assessment technique is Neimeyer's (1992) version of Kelly's (1955) Role Construct Repertory Test ("reptest"), which Neimeyer calls "career laddering." In this activity clients are given a structured interview in which they reveal the relative importance of work-related constructs. Neimeyer gave the example of a client who identified three occupations of interest — teacher, paramedic, and musician. She then located a way in which two of these were like each other but were different from the third. She identified teacher and musician as similar (in that they were, to her, "more creative") and different from paramedic (which she described as "more technical"). She then discovered that she preferred a creative rather than a technical occupation. And the interview continued. Other clients selecting the same three occupations might choose teacher and paramedic as similar because they are service occupations, or musicians and paramedics because they have mathematical skills, or teaching as requiring less constant risk-taking than do the occupations of musician or paramedic. As clients reflect on which of the identified dimensions they prefer, they reveal personal constructs that are significant for their career decisions. Neimeyer (1993) has offered more specific details and examples of these constructivist techniques in the referenced articles, and described additional constructivist assessments and techniques in *Constructivist Assessment: A Casebook*.

Whether the particular assessment technique is a test, a narrative, or another experience, the purpose of all constructivist assessment techniques can be characterized in these three ways: to elicit (1) clients' personal constructs related to career, (2) the relationship of these constructs to each other, and (3) the relative importance of these constructs to a given client. Thus, counselors assist clients in recognizing way(s) in which they have organized their career schemas and the effects that such an organization has had upon their thoughts, feelings and dilemmas concerning career.

A constructivist counselor can also use the more conventional assessments in a constructivist manner. For example, counselors may review the results of the *Self-Directed Search* (Holland, 1994) collaboratively with clients. The counselor can evoke the story behind these results by interviewing the client about the experiences and influences on the client's life that may explain this current summary of interests and inclinations. Together, counselor and client speculate on the future, asking what might happen if the client were to make alternate choices which would provide different experiences and influences. Counselors help clients make meaning of current scores and use them to make the proximate decisions that will influence the next chapter of their life stories.

I lead the entire class in the constructivist approach to working with the *Self-Directed Search* described in the preceding paragraph. Initially, we

contrast what a counselor would say to a client if the counselor were following the traditional model of assessment versus the reformed appraisal
model (Healy, 1990). The entire class reviews sample *Self-Directed Search*
results and identifies possible areas for exploration with that client. As they
suggest questions and topics for exploration, I periodically stop the discussion, asking them to reflect on how the suggested question or topic reveals some of their own assumptions about both career assessment and
the role of a career counselor using assessments. Two simultaneous learning processes occur in this fashion. For one, students practice the
constructivist use of assessments. At the same time, they also "listen" to
themselves and to each other, thereby becoming sensitive to how their decisions about what to discuss with clients reveal their own beliefs about
the role of the career counselor relative to assessment

My students personally take both standardized and non-standardized
career assessments. They complete the Self-Directed Search, the Strong Interest Inventory (Strong & Hansen, 1994), and one of the StoryTechs in which
they write their description of "My Perfect Day". They then practice working with the results of the Self-Directed Search and the StoryTech in a
constructivist manner. Students follow the writing, reflection, and group
feedback procedures described earlier for the StoryTech. Then, in pairs,
using the Self-Directed Search results of their StoryTech partner, along with
that partner's "Perfect Day" StoryTech, they outline topics for collaborative exploration with their partners. They explore themes and discover the
meaning these themes have for that person.

For each student pair working with assessments in this fashion, another student observes and offers feedback about the success of the student counselor in conducting a reformed (constructivist) career appraisal.
When time permits, several student pairs role play their collaborative assessments for the class, asking for feedback from all class members. The
focus of the feedback is on the pair's metacognitions and the metalogue
occurring between role play partners.

Another way to both introduce a constructivist assessment technique
and promote the constructivist education of counselors is to use Neimeyer's
(1992) laddering technique in conjunction with the results of a *Strong Interest Inventory*. As described earlier, in a vocational laddering activity, a person selects any three career-related items and identifies two of the three as
being like each other but different from the third. They then identify a quality
shared by the first two, but not by the third. They then identify which quality is preferred and examine this preference. The exercise continues in a
similar fashion as students identify   some key career constructs and a hierarchy of personal values that reveal how they construct personal meanings and make career choices.

For this activity, students use the "ladder" with the ten occupations identified as "most like them" by the Strong Interest Inventory. Although many counseling students select the same occupational titles as each other, what soon becomes evident are the diverse ways in which individual students group these occupations and the multiplicity of perspectives they use to think about them. Laddering, then, provides another opportunity for counselors-in-training to appreciate differences between people in both perspectives and in the contexts which impact their constructions of meaning. Engaging in this exercise reminds students that unless they are mindful, and unless they are careful to adopt an ongoing attitude of receptive and respectful inquiry toward clients, career assessment results may take on the meaning(s) imposed on them by the counselor.

As a final requirement for the assessment section of the course, students audio- or videotape themselves discussing the results of an assessment with a "client". They critique their own tapes as to how well they have enacted the principles of reformed appraisal. They also listen for indications of the assumptions they make regarding the nature of career assessments or the role of a career counselor working with assessments. Finally, they critique a peer's taped interview using the same criteria. Students are graded on their abilities to recognize and to conduct a constructivist assessment ("reformed appraisal"), as well as on their ability to recognize how their assumptions affect their collaborative assessments with clients.

TEACHING THE USE OF CAREER INFORMATION

Constructivists do not believe that neutral or objective information can be known. The essence of constructivism is, after all, the position that people create knowledge by reflecting on and making meaning of their experiences. According to Spokane (1992), the content of career information, then, does not determine its power. He stated, "We can no longer reasonably insist that presenting simple information to a client will result in beneficial effects" (p.230). Rather, it is the processing of the information by the counselor and the client that is most critical and which becomes the focus of constructivist career counseling. Constructivist career counselors concentrate on helping clients make career information personally usable, while not neglecting ongoing attention to their own career constructs or the personal filters that affect their use of information with clients.

According to Hoskins (1995), counselors disempower clients when they simply dispense information out of context or when they do not help clients learn to access information for themselves. Thus, for constructivist career counselors, the question is not "*What* information can I give the client?", but rather, "*How* can I help the client to use this information?" This distinction is critical in an era characterized by immense quantities of easily accessible career information. The lure of offering career information through electronic or computerized sources should be particularly modified by the awareness that merely giving clients access to career information is not enough. Clients may attribute authority to the information they receive, especially from computerized systems, that goes beyond the power that this resource can confer. In this case, clients often need a counselor's assistance to deconstruct their attribution, to clarify why they need career information, to name what purpose they expect it will fulfill for them, and to learn how to make their own sense of the information accessed .

In her article, "From Career Information to Career Knowledge: Self, Search, and Synthesis," Deborah Bloch (1989) distinguished career "information" from career "knowledge." She defined career information as the facts or data that people need to know in order to make decisions for their lives. This information may be data about jobs (for example, salary or preparation needed) or about themselves (for example, personal abilities or values as they pertain to occupational choices). Data of these types are more or less constantly being presented to people as they go through life. However, people selectively attend to and selectively attribute value to career data, as they do to all other types of information. In order to process this data into personally relevant career *knowledge,* clients must be able to connect the data to cognitive frameworks, or "schemata," that are already in place (that is, they must assimilate these new bits of information into life stories that are already under construction). In other instances, clients may choose to revise cognitive schemata and rewrite their life stories in order to accommodate significant new information.

Three elements can be posed as central to a client's constructing a viable career story. In order to convert objective career information into personalized career knowledge, clients must be self-reflective and self-aware, that is, they need to become aware of the meanings of their life stories. Secondly, they need to receive sufficient bits of relevant career-related data in usable formats. Finally, clients need to actively integrate isolated bits of career-related data into their life stories. Counselors help clients with the three tasks of clarifying their sense of self, obtaining adequate and relevant career information, and synthesizing this objective information into personal career knowledge.

Several instructional strategies help counseling·students learn the process of converting career information into career knowledge. After students become familiar with multiple career information resources, as well as with the principles described in the Bloch (1989) article, we do a information request or "grab bag" exercise. Students draw out of an envelope requests for career information frequently heard by career counselors. Typical client requests may include: "What's the best school for engineering, and can I still apply to that school for next semester?" "Am I smart enough to go to the university?" "Which jobs are most secure?" "I see lots of job openings for engineering operations analyst. How long does the training for that job take?" "I know I need to go to a good school if I want to get a good job, right? So, what's the best school in the state?" Counseling students take turns reading the requests they have drawn, and they talk about how they might respond to those requests. Students not only identify the information source(s) they might use, but they access what they were thinking about the request as they made those decisions. Some students focus only on identifying an accurate source for the requested information and authoritatively answer the client with responses such as: "The deadline for application to schools can be found in the red file" or "You will need a 26 or better on the ACT to apply to that school" or "You can find the occupational outlook for that field in the book on the shelf." Other students focus more on the client's experience, seeking to understand the context in which the request for information was made. As each student responds, I ask the other students to note assumptions about the role of the career counselor that the focus of the student's response may suggest.

A variation on this exercise involves having counseling students role play career counselors who have varying core values. The instructor asks, "If a career counselor has a core value of 'helping,' how might that affect his or her use of information with a client?" and "If a counselor has a core value of 'knowledge,' or of 'respect,' how might these values affect the decisions the counselor might make both about which information sources to use and how to use those sources with a client?" This exercise helps students reflect on the constructed nature of their own career knowledge and the effects that their constructions may have on clients.

In another exercise, groups of students receive a career counseling case and put together a proposal for both the types of information they would use with the client and how they would go about helping the client convert the information into usable career knowledge. As the different groups report on their proposals, we attend to the meaning of the differences in both the information sources recommended and the counseling approaches taken.

As the final assignment for this section of the course, students identify examples of both career information and career knowledge for the "client" whose life story they told in their first essay (i.e., the assignment referred to in the Career Theory section). They then prepare a list of career information resources which they would use with that client, justifying their choice based on the individual life story and the unique needs of the client. Finally, students outline how they would use the information in such a way as to help clients convert the information into usable career knowledge.

CONCLUSION

Teaching constructivist career counseling can be isomorphic with the work of career counseling itself. Career counseling has been characterized as essentially a process of instigating client discovery (Spokane, 1992). Such counselors assist clients to examine the beliefs and the constructs they have used to create meaning in their lives. Counselors additionally help clients to hypothesize alternative constructs, to test out those constructs, and to develop action plans for implementing the constructs that promise to be useful in extending or rewriting their life stories. The constructivist teaching of career counseling follows the same process. Counseling students examine the beliefs and the constructs they have about themselves as career counselors. They experience the diversity of constructs about career counseling held by their peers. They have the opportunity during the class to hypothesize alternative constructs and to test the effects those alternate constructs have upon their conduct of career counseling sessions. As they learn to examine their own career-related constructs, they learn the process of helping clients do likewise.

Throughout the course, students have the opportunity to observe career counseling being demonstrated by the instructor and by peers. They visualize themselves doing career counseling using the StoryTech method. They role play career counseling sessions, and they tape themselves conducting actual career counseling interviews and reformed appraisal (constructivist assessment) sessions. In each of these activities, they have opportunities for self-reflection and opportunities to both give and receive instructor and peer feedback. I encourage them to become mindful and to develop the skills for receptive inquiry, which will in turn help them understand how people create meaning and purpose for themselves; that is, how people develop coherent life stories. Students learn constructivist career counseling skills, then, through constructivist learning experiences. They experience multiple perspectives with the resulting conflict and dialectic among perspectives. They learn through experience and reflection on those experiences. They focus on the metacognitions and metalogue within and among themselves. In the face of their changing constructs of themselves as career counselors, they commit to pictures of themselves as career counselors which are stable enough to be represented in their current career portfolios, yet flexible enough to allow for continued development throughout their professional careers as constructivist (career) counselors.

SOME FINAL REFLECTIONS

Many advantages accrue for constructivist educators when teaching career counseling, but they also face some difficult challenges. A major advantage lies in the constructivist paradigm being relevant to career coun-seling students, as all counseling students have "careers" themselves. The choices our students have made, both in work and in life, and the factors they have considered as they made and remake those choices are readily available "fodder" to be masticated as they learn the principles of constructivist career counseling. A further advantage lies in the ease of ac-cess that students have to clients: most people are happy to talk to career counseling students about their lives and their work and how they come to make the choices they do. There is, therefore, ample opportunity for mul-tiple experiences and perspectives to be brought into the career class. The class then provides the opportunity and the structure for reflection upon those experiences and perspectives. Through experience students learn to see themselves and others as unique individuals who are influenced by their cultural backgrounds and the contexts in which they construct their life stories.

Constructivist career counseling has a further advantage in its synchronicity with the demands of our era. Constructivism also encour-ages counselors to become competent with clientele who hold differing world views, a necessity in meeting today's mental health needs. Career clients hold world views which profoundly affect their lives and their ca-reer decisions; and, these world views may be very different from those of their counselors. To avoid inappropriately imposing their own world views on their clients counselors need to be educated to recognize their own world views, as well as the implications these have for how they do career counseling. A constructivist education that values multiple perspectives and that teaches the skills of mindfulness and receptive inquiry makes that more likely.

A final advantage lies in the applicability of a constructivist approach for social change. As recently as 1993, Peavy (1993) had proposed that the constructivist approach to counseling, and especially to career counseling, was the most appropriate response in a post-industrial society character-ized by rapid, unpredictable change. In other words, in a society in which all (objective) "truths" about life and career were being called into ques-tion, constructivism is a viable paradigm. He suggested that people would, by necessity, continually define and redefine who they were, where they fit, and what meaning they ascribed to their lives. Constructivism, with its emphasis on creating personal meaning may be the approach most helpful to our clients in a time of societal uncertainty.

As relevant as constructivist career counseling may be, however, po-tentially daunting challenges exist in teaching from a constructivist per-spective. Very young students, especially those who come into counseling programs directly from a typical undergraduate experience, have not al-ways had enough experiences or made enough life choices to be able to recognize patterns in their lives or their choices. It is also difficult for them to recognize all the contextual influences on those choices.

In addition to the challenges posed by chronological age, a constructivist approach to career can be confusing, and even upsetting, to students in a dualistic (Perry, 1970) stage of intellectual development. A more structured approach to some of the activities and assignments and to the principles of constructivist career counseling in general may be needed for those thinkers. Instructors may model self-reflective constructivist attitudes, letting students "get a peek at" their own internal dialogues. Empathic instructors will remember to be as specific as possible with instructions and as generous as possible with examples when assigning activities that may challenge the comfort level of dualistic thinkers. The instructor must exhibit genuine understanding and acceptance of students at all developmental levels, affirming them for who they are and supporting their struggles with new and challenging ideas and behaviors. In particular, many students find it difficult to translate constructivist perspectives on career to the programmatic or to a system level. Students preparing to be school counselors, for example, find it difficult to imagine ways to plan career development programs for heterogeneous groups of students, programs which are sensitive to the constructed nature of individual students' careers.

Constructivist career counseling education is best implemented in the context of counselor education programs in which constructivist principles are implemented across all curricula of the program. Perhaps the time will come when more and more counselor educators will see their role as that of organizing for learning rather than one of only directly transmitting direct information and preferred practice.

Appendix

Career Classroom Guidelines

1. Maintain *CONFIDENTIALITY*. Confidentiality is one of the most important ethical principles governing the establishment of trusting relationships. People are more likely to share information if there is a trust and a commitment to keep the information between/among those with whom it is shared. In a class, this guideline encourages the formation of a trusting, working bond between students and the instructor.

2. *ACTIVELY PARTICIPATE* in the activities, discussions, exercises. Some students are more accustomed to the "banking" method of education, where the teacher "deposits" information, and the student is a somewhat passive recipient. Learning in this course requires your active engagement with the material and with each other.

3. Exercise *RESPECT AND POSITIVE REGARD* for your co-learners in this class. Stretch your tolerance and consideration of viewpoints and experiences other than your own, and be willing to share your own viewpoints and experiences, especially if they seem to contradict or extend those of the majority in the class.

4. Maintain an *OPEN MIND* and be willing to consider views, beliefs, lifestyles, and values that are different than your own. New ideas and shifts in life views can only begin when our minds are open.

5. Acknowledge your *RESISTANCE or DISCOMFORT* to some concepts and be willing to explore (for yourself in a safe space) its meaning for you and for your career as a counselor.

6. Exercise the *COURAGE* needed to explore new ideas, as well as your own thinking, feelings, and reactions. Be *HONEST*. It takes honesty and courage to risk examining oneself and consider change. This is what you will be asking of your own future clients and students!

Story Tech #1-Life Story

It is 10 years into the future, the year 200_. Today is a very special time to gather for your family / circle of special friends. It is time when you always gather with this group of people.

- What is the event that brings you all together?
- Who would be there?

Often at these gatherings, you spend time reflecting on the past and looking ahead to a positive future. It seems to be a time for telling each other the stories of your lives—where you have been, where you are going, what has been the meaning of your lives.

At the last couple of these gatherings, you have realized that you are held in great respect by these people. Many of them seek you out for the wisdom you continue to gain in your productive and satisfying career as a counselor. Today, one of the younger members of the group sits down next to you, and with great respect and real eagerness to understand, asks you to tell a story—the story of your life. Who is this younger person?

_____

(S)he wants to know what your life has been about, and so you begin:

- "I was the little boy / girl who . . . .
- "I always loved to . . . .
- "As I grew up, more than anything else, I always wanted to . . . .
- "And I always admired people who . . . .
- "My life was not always easy, though. Some of the difficulties I faced were . . . .
- "I dealt with these difficulties by . . . .
- "I experienced times when I was very happy, and times when I was very sad. Sometimes I was excited and enthusiastic, at other times I became discouraged or frightened. As I look back now, I see my life as an attempt to . . . .
- "At the present, I am most satisfied with . . . .
- "and I'm struggling most with . . . .
- "Right now, I guess I see my life as an attempt to . . . .

- "Thank you so much for asking! Actually, I've often thought about creating something that would tell the story of my life. Most likely, I would make a . . . .
- "Currently, I am at peace with my past, energized by the present, and I can hardly wait to write the next chapter of my life! If I had to give my life story a title, I would call it :
  " _____ "
- "and very next chapter would be called : " _____ "

Reflection on Story Tech #1-Life Story

General Directions: As you reflect on your own Story Tech #1-Life Story, focus on discovering insight into the following areas. Consider what feedback from peers might help.

1. What are my views on work, on career, on life?
2. How have my unique life experiences, as a person of a particular age, gender, class, culture, religious background, sexual orientation, etc., affected these views?
3. What role do my experiences and my point of view play in how I view "career" and "career counseling"?
4. How will my experiences and my point of view affect how I do career counseling and career development?

Reflection Questions for Story Tech #1

- WHEN I THINK ABOUT MY LIFE STORY, I SEE ME DESCRIBING MYSELF AS A PERSON WHO . . . .
- A CENTRAL THEME OF THE STORY SEEMS TO BE . . . .
- WHAT I SEE IN MY OWN STORY THAT MAY HELP ME FUNCTION AS A COUNSELOR WHO HELPS OTHERS TELL THEIR OWN STORIES IS . . . .
- WHAT I NOTICE IN MY STORY THAT MIGHT MAKE IT DIFFICULT FOR ME TO HELP OTHERS TELL THEIR OWN STORIES IS . . . .
- AFTER REFLECTING ON MY OWN STORY TECH #1, I WOULD LIKE TO THINK MORE ABOUT or EXPLORE or GET FEEDBACK FROM MY PEERS OR OTHERS ON . . . .

Story Tech #3-Myself as a Career Counselor

It is 10 years from now-the year 200__. I am a competent, highly respected counselor working at my "dream job".

- Where am I working?
- Who are my students/clients; what are they like?
- What is my office/work space like?
- A "typical day" in this job will find me. . . .
- As I go through this typical day, I feel. . . .

Coming back from lunch today, I find 2 messages. One is from a former student/client. When I return the call, I find that this person wants to tell me about the latest events in his/her career/life. (S)he is so happy, and thanks me profusely for helping her/him in the past.

- What is (s)he so grateful to me for?

The second message is from a current student/client who wants to meet with you this afternoon to discuss a career issue.

- Who is this person?
- What do they want to discuss with you?

There is a knock on your door-this person has arrived.

- What do the two of you discuss?

All of your experience these last 10 years has taught you that you can help persons like this talk about their lives in ways they find useful in dealing with career issues.

- How do you go about talking with (counseling) this person.

As this person leaves, (s)he says: "Thanks so much! You really helped me. I sure feel better than when I first came to you. I really looking forward to our next meeting!"

- What has happened that results in this mutual satisfaction and anticipation of your next time together?

Reflection on Story Tech #3-Myself
as Career Counselor

General Directions: As you reflect on your own Story Tech #3-Myself as Career Counselor, focus on discovering insight into the following areas.

Consider what feedback from peers might help.

1. What are my views on work, on career, on life?
2. How have my unique life experiences, as a person of a particular age, gender, class, culture, religious background, sexual orientation, etc., affected these views?
3. What role do my experiences and my point of view play in how I view "career" and "career counseling"?
4. How will my experiences and my point of view affect how I do career counseling and career development?

Reflection Questions for Story Tech #3:

•   FROM MY RESPONSES TO THIS STORY, I APPEAR TO VIEW THE PURPOSE OF CAREER COUNSELING/DEVELOPMENT TO BE. . . .

•   HOW DOES THE PURPOSE OF CAREER COUNSELING AS REVEALED BY THE STORY TECH COMPARE TO MY STATED BELIEFS ABOUT THE PURPOSE OF CAREER COUNSELING?

•   FROM MY RESPONSES TO THIS STORY, I SEEM TO BELIEVE THAT SOME OF THE MOST HELPFUL/EFFECTIVE WAYS A COUNSELOR CAN GO ABOUT THE PROCESS OF CAREER COUNSELING/CAREER DEVELOPMENT ARE. . . .

•   FROM WHAT I'VE OBSERVED ABOUT MYSELF SO FAR THROUGH REFLECTING ON MY RESPONSES TO MY STORIES, I BELIEVE THAT SOME OF MY GREATEST STRENGTHS IN CAREER COUNSELING WILL BE. . . .

•   SOME OF THE AREAS IN WHICH I MAY HAVE DIFFICULTY MIGHT BE. . . .

Story Tech #4-My Perfect Day

"Have a nice day!" People say that to me all the time. Do they really mean it? Do they really know what a "nice day"-a perfect day- would be like for me? Well, let me tell you!

- What would make a perfect day for me would be to wake up, leisurely, in (location). . . .
- What makes this such a favorite spot for me is. . . .
- Living with me is. . . .
- I would be well-rested and eager to start my day. I've planned it to be filled with my favorite activities-those things that bring me the most energy and fulfillment.
- In the morning, I will. . . .
- While, in the afternoon, I have planned to. . . .
- In the evening, I am looking forward to. . . .
- What I most look forward to accomplishing today is. . . .
- Not everyone understands why I like days like this, but when I have one, I always feel so. . . .
- As I drift off to sleep, I smile with satisfaction, and say to myself: "I did have a nice day-actually, a perfect day. Thanks!"

Reflections on Story Tech #4-My Perfect Day

General Directions: As you reflect on your own Story Tech #4-My Perfect Day, focus on discovering insight into the following areas. Consider what feedback from peers might help.

1. What are my views on work, on career, on life?
2. How have my unique life experiences, as a person of a particular age, gender, class, culture, religious background, sexual orientation, etc., affected these views?
3. What role do my experiences and my point of view play in how I view "career" and "career counseling"?
4. How will my experiences and my point of view affect how I do career counseling and career development?

Reflection Questions for Story Tech #4

- WHEN I LOOK AT STORY TECH #4 AS A "CAREER ASSESSMENT" TOOL, IT SEEMS TO SUGGEST THAT MY INTERESTS ARE. . . .

- MY VALUES ARE. . . .

- MY PERSONALITY IS. . . .

- THE ROLES MOST SALIENT TO ME ARE. . . .

- WHAT THIS SUGGESTS TO ME IN TERMS OF WHO I AM RELATIVE TO THE WORK ASPECTS OF MY LIFE IS. . . .

- IN TERMS OF MY OVERALL CAREER DEVELOPMENT, THIS SUGGESTS. . . .

STORY TECH #5-USING CAREER INFORMATION

It is 10 years from now, the year 200___. You are about to begin your eighth year of employment at _____. Remember how thrilled you were to be hired here–having a chance to really make a difference in the lives of _____ (population you work with). These people are so eager for career information and so appreciative of your efforts. It seems that they can never get enough, and you are always on the alert for better ways to help them. Still, sometimes you feel yourself getting overwhelmed. This is, after all, the "information age". At times there seems to be no end to the information that comes to you daily via all your sophisticated telecommunications career information delivery systems. How to "get a handle" on it all?! As this new work year begins, you reflect on this concern.

- The information most of your counselees seem to be seeking is.....

- The biggest concern they have with regards to career information is.....

- Just lately, you have begun to really realize that your own view about what constitutes "good" career information and the role that it plays in career decision making greatly affects the services you provide. You jot down your personal response to the following: I believe "good" career information is. . . .

- My role with regard to that "good" career information is.....

- As you look at your own response, you realize that your students/ clients have been affected by your personal beliefs both about what good career information is and how you use it with them. It has affected them in the following ways:

- This is a real eye-opener! In fact, you are not "doing it all"! And yet, you are a very effective counselor dealing with career issues. You have the appreciation and respect of your counselees, both present and past. Perhaps, you can attribute your success with these people to believing in and living the motto you have framed and hung in your career information center:

- "_____"

REFLECTIONS ON STORY TECH #5-USING
CAREER INFORMATION

General Directions: As you reflect on your own Story Tech #5-Using Career Information, focus on discovering insight into the following areas. Consider what feedback from peers might help.

1. What are my views on work, on career, on life?
2. How have my unique life experiences, as a person of a particular age, gender, class, culture, religious background, sexual orientation, etc., affected these views?
3. What role do my experiences and my point of view play in how I view "career" and "career counseling"?
4. How will my experiences and my point of view affect how I do career counseling and career development?

REFLECTION QUESTIONS FOR STORY TECH #5:

- FROM MY RESPONSES TO STORY TECH #5, I SEEM TO BELIEVE THAT THE KIND OF INFORMATION THAT MY STUDENTS/CLIENTS NEED MOST IS. . . .
- I CAN BEST HELP THEM BY. . . .
- MY BELIEFS ABOUT HOW I CAN BE MOST HELPFUL TO OTHERS WITH THEIR CAREER INFORMATIONAL NEEDS ARE UNDOUBTEDLY BASED ON MY OWN EXPERIENCES. PERSONAL EXPERIENCE(S) THAT MAY EXPLAIN HOW I CAME TO HOLD THESE BELIEFS MIGHT BE. . . .
- WITH MY UNIQUE PERSPECTIVE(S) ON CAREER INFORMATION, THE TYPE(S) OF STUDENTS/CLIENTS I WOULD MOST LIKELY SERVE VERY WELL IS. . . .
- BASED ON MY UNIQUE PERSPECTIVE(S) ON CAREER INFORMATION, THERE ARE SOME PERSONS WHOSE CAREER INFORMATION NEEDS I MIGHT FIND IT DIFFICULT TO MEET. THESE WOULD BE PERSONS WHO. . . .

STORY TECH # 6-THE FUTURE

In your work as a counselor, dealing with career issues has been especially difficult these past few months. More and more of your counselees seem to be expressing the attitude: "Things are changing so fast! Why even bother engaging in a planful process of career exploration, career planning, career decision making, or career preparation?"

- This lack of predictability about the future has affected them so that they seem to feel . . . .
- You are empathetic; yet, dealing with them day after day has become stressful. Sometimes you find it difficult to maintain a positive attitude. What makes it especially difficult for you is . . . .
- You have given yourself the time to go on a "working retreat" to a spot that has always been energizing and refreshing to you. Where have you gone?
- Your goal for yourself in the next few hours is to clarify your own beliefs and feelings about the rapidity of change now and in the future. Not being able to help your counselees find definite "answers" makes you feel:
- You find yourself handling it by . . . .
- Actually, as you think about it more, your feelings are somewhat mixed. When you look at them negatively, you sometimes feel . . . .
- Your main concern for your counselees is . . . .
- And, yet, viewed from a more positive perspective, it also seems that . . . .
- The hopeful possibilities you can see for your counselees are . . . .
- Overall, mostly you feel . . . .
- because you believe . . . .
- It has been good to get away and take time to clarify your own thoughts and feelings. A path of action seems clearer to you now. As you return to your job, refreshed and recommitted to helping students/clients with career information issues, you plan to put your new insights and convictions into practice. The first thing(s) you will need to do . . . .

REFLECTIONS ON STORY TECH # 6-THE FUTURE

General Directions: As you reflect on your own Story Tech #6-The Future, focus on discovering insight into the following areas. Consider what feedback from peers might help.

1. What are my views on work, on career, on life?
2. How have my unique life experiences, as a person of a particular age, gender, class, culture, religious background, sexual orientation, etc., affected these views?
3. What role do my experiences and my point of view play in how I view "career" and "career counseling"?
4. How will my experiences and my point of view affect how I do career counseling and career development?

REFLECTION QUESTIONS FOR STORY TECH # 6

- WHEN I LOOK AT THE FUTURE AND THE RAPIDITY OF CHANGE AND THE EFFECTS THAT WILL HAVE ON CAREER COUNSELING/ DEVELOPMENT, MY OVERALL FEELING SEEMS TO BE . . . .
- ONE WAY THAT I MIGHT USE TO LOOK AT THOSE FEELING(S) IN A LITTLE MORE DEPTH WOULD BE . . . .
- WHEN I REFLECT BACK ON ALL MY PREVIOUS STORY TECHS ("LIFE STORY", "TROUBLESOME CAREER BELIEFS", "MYSELF AS CAREER COUNSELOR", "USING CAREER INFORMATION", AND "MY PERFECT DAY"), AS WELL AS THIS STORY TECH, 1-2 THINGS THAT STAND OUT ARE . . . .
- FROM REFLECTING ON MY "STORIES", I SEE MY GREATEST STRENGTH(S) AS A COUNSELOR DEALING WITH CAREER TO BE THE FOLLOWING:
- AND THE AREAS OF POTENTIAL DIFFICULTY MIGHT BE:

REFERENCES

Bateson, M. C. (1990). *Composing a life*. New York: Penguin.

Bloch, D. P. (1989). "From career information to career knowledge: Self, search, and synthesis." *Journal of Career Development, 16(2)*, pp. 119-127.

Brotherton, S. J. (1996). *Counselor education for the twenty-first century*. Westport, CT: Bergin & Garvey.

Cochran, L. (1992). "The career project." *Journal of Career Development, 18*, pp. 187-198.

Emmett, J. D., & Harkins, A. M. (1997). "Story Tech: Exploring the use of a narrative technique for training career counselors." *Counselor Education and Supervision, 37(1)*, 60-73.

Forster, J. R. (1992). "Eliciting personal constructs and articulating goals." *Journal of Career Development, 18*, pp. 175-185.

Hansen, L. S. (1997). *Integrative life planning: Critical tasks for career development and changing life patterns*. San Francisco: Jossey-Bass.

Healy, C. C. (1990). "Reforming career appraisals for the 90s." *Counseling Psychologist, 18(2)*, pp. 213-225.

Holland, J. L. (1994). *Self-directed search (SDS)*. Odessa, FL: Psychological Assessment Resources.

Hoskins, M. (1995). "Constructivist approaches for career counselors." *ERIC Digest ED401505*.

Kelly, G. (1955). *The psychology of personal constructs*. New York: Norton.

Miller-Tiedeman, A. (1987). *How to not make it . . . and succeed: The truth about your lifecareer*. Los Angeles: LIFECAREER Foundation.

Neimeyer, G. J. (1992). "Personal constructs in career counseling and development." *Journal of Career Development, 18*, pp. 163-173.

Neimeyer, G. (Ed.) (1993). *Constructivist assessment: A casebook*. Newbury Park, CA: Sage.

Parsons, F. (1909). *Choosing a vocation*. Boston: Houghton Mifflin.

Peavy, R.V. (1992). "A constructivist model of training for career counselors." *Journal of Career Development, 18*, pp. 215-228.

Peavy, R.V. (1993). "Envisioning the future: Worklife and counselling." *Canadian Journal of Counselling, 27(2)*, pp. 123-139.

Peavy, R.V. (1994). "Constructivist counselling: a prospectus." *Guidance and counseling, 9*, pp. 3-12.

Peavy, R.V. (1995). "Constructivist career counseling." *ERIC Digest ED401504*.

Peavy, R.V. (1996). "Constructivist career counseling and assessment." *Guidance and Counseling, 11*, pp. 8-14.

Perry, W., Jr. (1970). *Forms of intellectual and ethical development in the college years: A scheme*. New York: Holt, Rinehart & Winston.

Savickas, M. L. (1993). "Career counseling in the postmodern era." *Journal of Cognitive Psychotherapy, 7,* pp. 205-215.

Seligman, L. (1994). *Developmental career counseling and assessment.* (2nd ed.). Thousand Oaks, CA: Sage.

Spokane, A. R. (1992). "Personal constructs and careers: A reaction." *Journal of Career Development, 18,* pp. 229-236.

Strong, E. K. Jr., & Hansen, J. C. (1994). *Strong Interest Inventory.* Palo Alto, CA: Consulting Psychologists Press, Inc.

9

Educating Supervisors: A Constructivist Approach to the Teaching of Supervision

Susan Allstetter Neufeldt

Superior athletes know just how to perform on the playing field, but they often fail to become effective coaches. They know a lot about playing but little about teaching others. Likewise, excellent counselors and therapists require an additional set of skills to supervise others.[1] As one student supervisor was heard to say, "Supervision is challenging in a way that is different from working with clients. It is nice to work with trainees who are in the process of learning and not overcoming life problems. Yet at the same time, I find it more challenging in that it is necessary to keep in mind the issues of the client while working with the trainees."

Supervision has only recently been acknowledged as a task that is different from that of therapy (Bernard & Goodyear, 1998), although supervision of counselors and therapists has been required since the time of Freud. In the last decade, the American Psychological Association (1992) and the Association for Counselor Education and Supervision (1995) have developed formal standards for supervisors. To assist supervisors in carrying out its standards, the Association for Counselor Education and Supervision (ACES) developed a curriculum guide for supervision (Borders, Bernard, Dye, Fong, Henderson, & Nance, 1991). Subsequently, Neufeldt, Iversen, and Juntunen (1995; second edition, Neufeldt, 1999) offered a manual for supervising beginning counselors, and Neufeldt (1997) presented a constructivist approach to supervision. This chapter moves a step further to describe a constructivist approach to educating the supervisors themselves.

In the following pages I will describe goals for a year-long course sequence for beginning supervisors, an overview of that course with attention to power issues and reflectivity, and some specific assignments and sample activities. In addition, I will describe potential problems, including the problem of evaluation in a constructivist setting.

CONSTRUCTIVISM AND THE EDUCATION OF SUPERVISORS

In setting goals for a yearlong course in supervision theory and practice, I have integrated principles from social constructionism and constructive development (McAuliffe & Lovell, 2000). As a starting place, I take seriously the idea that college teachers have the opportunity to reconstruct aspects of the political hierarchy so prevalent in academic institutions, particularly in the classroom. Freire (1993) described the importance of a sense of equality among learners and teachers. He explicitly stated that teachers must be "teacher-students" and students must be "students-teachers" (p. 61). This drive for equality between teachers and students is especially applicable to the education of supervisors. Supervision training occurs either late in graduate programs or during internship, when students are on the verge of ending their formal training and becoming full-fledged professionals. Supervision training also occurs in other professional growth situations where supervisors and counselors are both already practicing professionals and equals by legal definition. In this vein, educators treat students in the course as "critical co-investigators," in Freire's (1993, p. 62) words, of the processes of supervision and psychotherapy. This stance enables instructors to achieve a central goal of a supervision course—the supervisee's constructive development toward "self-authorized" knowing. One road to such increased "authority" over one's supervision decisions is traveled through increased reflectivity.

REFLECTIVITY

Because developing reflectivity[2]—a quality consistent with social constructionism—is my primary goal in educating supervisors, I choose here to describe both its characteristics and its role in the professional growth of counselors and therapists. Skovholt and Rønnestad (1992) clarified the centrality of reflectivity in their landmark qualitative study of the professional development of counselors and therapists from paraprofessionals to skilled professionals. They described both the paths of those who continued to develop throughout their professional lives, and the alternative path of stagnation for those who "burned out" and either continued to work with limited pleasure and success or dropped out altogether from the mental health professions. Critical to continuing along the path of development was "continuous professional reflection," the ability to look at one's work with clients, evaluate it, place it in context, and change one's approach when suitable.

Reflectivity has also been described by Donald Schön (1983, 1987) as critical in approaching "messy" problems, the ambiguous dilemmas that are regularly faced by counselors, therapists, and supervisors. As Binder and Strupp (1997) pointed out, "The particular sort of procedural knowledge required for this type of activity Schön (1987) has called 'reflection in action.' It is the basis for the ability to improvise in problem situations in which standard principles and rules may not apply. We suggest that true therapeutic competence and effectiveness involve becoming proficient in the capacities for reflection-in-action and improvisation" (p. 58).

As we appy it to supervision, then, reflectivity begins with an initial experience of being surprised, stuck, or confused by what is occurring. We defined the reflective process as paying attention to therapist actions, emotions, and thoughts inside the session, and the interaction between therapist and client during the session. The reflector in taking the stance of "reflectivity," maintains an intention to inquire, openness to understanding, and vulnerability. Reflectors use theory, personal and professional experience, and the experience of the self to understand what is going on in counseling sessions. Finally, a useful reflection tends to be deep rather than superficial. As a result of effective reflection, reflective supervisors or therapists change their perceptions of a situation as well as their in-session behavior. Their long-term professional growth is enhanced by the reflection process.

Reflectivity seems to be a key to continued professional growth, as well as to the development of therapists from novice to expert status (which Skovholt, Rønnestad, and Jennings [1997] have claimed takes up to 15 years to achieve). Therefore, it is imperative that supervisors of therapists teach reflectivity. In turn, it follows that we who educate those supervisors must teach not only the skill of reflectivity but the means for teaching it to their supervisees. This effort to teach the activity of reflectivity is consistent with constructivist approaches to education. According to von Glasersfeld (1995), "There is no understanding without reflection, and reflection is an activity students have to carry out themselves. No one else can do it for them" (p. 383).

Reflectivity takes on even more importance when we acknowledge, with Dawes (1994), that much contemporary supervision practice is based on principles that have little or no support in either quantitative or qualitative research. Supervision practitioners often do not acknowledge this and do not attend to research that reports results contrary to their ideas.

On the other hand, supervision practitioners have little choice but to experiment; there is much that is still unknown. Binder (1993) spoke to that issue in supervision, stating, "Any discussion about problems with the supervisory process is speculative and must be based upon personal experience and relevant clinical literature. Nevertheless, such problems are sufficiently critical to the therapy training endeavor to warrant even speculative discussion" (p. 305).

The challenge for counselor educators is to know how to choose between applying positivist research results and encouraging untested experimentation. We are responsible when we tell our students, supervisees, or clients that we are speculating or testing a new strategy (for example: "I'd like to try a little experiment here; are you willing to participate?"). In like fashion, I now tell you, the reader, that I am experimenting with a course in reflective supervision, whose description follows.

THE TRAINING SEQUENCE:
SUPERVISION THEORY AND PRACTICUM

This particular training model offers a supervision theory course and a supervision practicum to advanced graduate students over a full academic year. In the first third of the course, students explore the theories and the available knowledge base about supervision. Following that, they engage in the supervision of students enrolled in their first counseling practicum.

During the first third of the year, students read literature on teaching and learning, counselor development, and theories of supervision. We structure the course as a seminar in which everyone has a voice. Meetings occur weekly, in 3-hour blocks, so that there is ample time to explore questions of concern to all members. To be ready for a thoughtful discussion in seminar, the students respond in writing to questions that tie what they have read to their professional and personal experiences with learning. The questions and discussion shared with their colleagues replace a term paper—traditionally read only by the professor—and professorial lectures.

During the rest of the year, in a supervision practicum, students continue to meet in weekly seminars, and discussion revolves around questions arising from their work with trainees. When videotaping is available, student supervisors show segments of their supervision sessions to the group for discussion. Between seminar meetings, they maintain reflective journals that they turn in weekly. In addition, they meet separately from time to time with the course instructor for individual supervision of supervision.

The course structure is not unique. However, it differs from traditional supervisor training in the subtle infusion of constructivist principles into every assignment and classroom activity. All assignments and activities are designed (1) to establish an egalitarian environment and (2) to facilitate the development of reflective processes in both the student supervisors and their trainees. A more extensive description of the course elements follows.

The Supervision Theory Course

Creation of a Collegial Environment: Introduction and Self-Disclosure. The instructor invites the student supervisors into a collegial environment from the very beginning by using the first seminar meeting for students and instructor to introduce themselves to one another. An outline, provided in advance of the first class meeting, includes questions such as the following: (1) How did you decide that you wanted to be in this profession? What do you see as your strength? What is your career goal, as best you can tell right now? (2) What is your theoretical orientation to counseling/psychotherapy or education and learning? (3) Describe some significant supervision experiences (both positive and negative) for you. What was involved? How did this impact who you are and where you are in your professional and personal life?

To set a tone for shared learning, the instructor participates. She or he is first to give a self-introduction based on the questions. This presentation models desirable self-disclosure of relevant personal experiences that have shaped the instructor's professional development. The instructor's introduction is also the opportunity to demonstrate a strong commitment, consistent with constructivism, to mutuality in learning, in that the instructor is also willing to do what she or he asks students to do (for example: present a biography, perform a spontaneous role-play, present a role-play on video for comment and criticism).

Counselors may provide limited self-disclosure to clients in order to deepen the therapeutic relationship (Hill, 1989). However, supervisors can productively provide even more such self-disclosure to supervisees. For example, supervisors report professional successes and failures to novice therapists in order to illustrate the "learning curve" through which developing counselors progress. A professional mentor may also offer a mix of professional and personal self-disclosure to the graduate student supervisors who are on the verge of becoming colleagues. I offer such self-disclosure in the initial supervision seminar, as an invitation. However, there is no expectation that students will disclose anything they do not wish to.

In addition to stimulating a collegial atmosphere, the discussion of past personal and professional histories provides the opportunity to make explicit the environments that have shaped everyone's ideas about teaching and learning. This awareness makes possible the further integration of personal experiences throughout the year and in subsequent professional life. Personal sharing often consists of telling about good and bad happenings in our own therapy or supervision work. It also can include sharing influential novels, popular non-fiction, films, or theater we may have encountered, and professional reading or training that we have valued, as all of these influences contribute to therapists' development (Skovholt & Rønnestad, 1992).

Reading Assignments. To lay the groundwork for open inquiry and mutuality, I suggest beginning the course in supervision theories by reading Paulo Freire (1993) and Donald Schön (1987). The political hierarchy in academic life is thereby exposed and the possibility for open discussion about power becomes explicit. We can discuss questions raised by these "unorthodox" readings, such as: Do they feel "oppressed" as students? Do they believe that important questions about counseling and psychology can be answered by positivist research? The goal of these discussions is to make the power and dominance topics for open discussion before the students begin to supervise less advanced counseling students. For instance, many graduate students think that much research is useless and is simply done to advance a professor's career. By opening that subject up for explicit discussion, we make it possible to discuss which research might be useful and which might not.

Subsequent readings incorporate a mix of theoretical and research materials. Texts can include Bernard and Goodyear's *Fundamentals of Clinical Supervision* (1998), Watkins' *Handbook of Psychotherapy Research* (1997), and Skovholt and Rønnestad's *The Evolving Professional Self* (1992). As students read the chapters and articles, they respond to questions that relate the readings to their own experiences, and they are asked to raise their own questions. In devising such questions, the instructor would wisely raise dilemmas that student supervisors will face in practicum. Such questions might include "When therapists perform what you think are inappropriate interventions with clients, how do you respond in a way that supports therapist experimentation and at the same time encourages a reflective look at what they have done?" or "When one member of a supervision group provides an unsuitable suggestion to another, how do you support the group's inventiveness without supporting the suggestion?" A student's effort to respond to these dilemmas creates the vicarious experience of being "stuck," which is the necessary take-off point for creative reflectivity. The questions set the tone of dialogue in the discussion of theory. This, in turn, lays the groundwork for further dialogue in the upcoming supervision practicum.

The Supervision Practicum

It is in the practicum, when student supervisors are face-to-face with counseling trainees, that supervisors bring experience, reflection, and conceptualization together. During the practicum, unlike during the theory class, the supervision student does not just analyze theory in terms of past experiences and research but incorporates it into current practice of the new skill of supervision. Declarative knowledge thus becomes procedural knowledge. The latter is the ability to apply principles to actions (Schon, 1987).

As they contemplate their new trainees, novice supervisors suddenly recognize what they have learned from their own supervised experience. They have grounded knowledge to use. They encounter what Donald Schön (personal communication, February 16, 1994) described as the heart of the difficulty faced by any experienced professional in teaching others: How do we as teachers explain what we have learned through experiences which they, the students, have not yet had? The counseling students and supervision students don't even mean the same thing when using the same words. As von Glasersfeld (1995) said so eloquently, "After some experience . . . we . . . come to realize that telling alone rarely does the trick. . . . In short, understanding is something all of us have to build up for ourselves."

Inquiry as a Strategy. The search for evidence. It is here, as "master supervisor" of supervisors, that the instructor creates a learning atmosphere that enables students to increase their understanding through making sense of their experiences. In particular, the instructor addresses the novice supervisors' frequent distress that many of their supervisees "do it [counsel] wrong." Many novice supervisors forget that just as multiple conceptions of reality exist, so too, many ways to counsel effectively exist. To my horror, after all my writing and thinking about reflectivity, I often find myself, in a parallel process, wanting to step in during the supervision practicum seminar and say to the supervisors, "You must do it this way!"

What is needed at this point, of course, is a conceptualization of the novice supervisors and the novice therapists as learners who are operating on the basis of some sort of reasoning. I am often struck by how we very quickly learn to ask ourselves and our clients why the clients do things the way that they do. We readily hypothesize the reasons, for instance, that underlie the apparently self-defeating actions taken by clients when these actions clearly thwart attainment of their own goals. We test our hypotheses. Is it frightening to succeed? Are they afraid of rejection? We understand that there is a logic here that we must discern in order to be of help.

Yet in teaching, we often forget the importance of inquiring into the reasoning behind the "errors" our student supervisors make. It is easy for educators to assume that just providing a few interventions will help the supervision students to get back on track as they supervise. But when master supervisors do that, they model unhelpful, and often remarkably useless, ways to teach and learn. Supervisors cannot help trainees without understanding the reasoning behind their decisions to make a "wrong" intervention. Such inquiry about the basis for responses does two things. First, it respects the intelligence of the reasoning process that the supervisor has used in framing the problem. Second, it provides an entré for effective teaching and learning.

Supervisors struggle harder to maintain an inquiring stance with some trainees than with others. Two examples of frequently misunderstood trainees, from my experience with novice supervisors, follow. In the *first example,* a male counseling trainee offended a client with apparently intrusive questions and explicit advice. The horrified novice supervisor immediately intervened to say that this was inappropriate, that one should not ask those questions in an early interview nor give such direct advice. When I asked the supervisor about the directive, non-reflecting approach he himself had taken, he reported that he had feared that the counselor-client working alliance would be irreparably disrupted if the intrusiveness continued. He feared that the client would leave therapy and construed the possibility as a clinical emergency. He referred to the research that directive interventions were appropriate in an emergency (Tracey, Ellickson, & Sherry, 1989). With that information, I could understand the supervisor's reasoning and praise his use of research in selecting an intervention. We were then able to discuss our perspectives on "clinical emergencies."

My principal task here, however, was to shift the novice supervisor's attention from the client's needs and motives to those of the trainee. Having modeled the usefulness of inquiry myself, I wondered aloud whether, in turn, the supervisor understood the trainee's reasoning. The trainee, he found, was operating on another assumption, also based on research—that clients of this particular ethnic group preferred a directive counseling approach.

This story vividly illustrates the necessity to further learning of inquiry into a trainee's reasoning. If we as instructors simply "correct errors," we miss opportunities. We fail to respect the student and recognize that he or she might be operating from some theoretical or research basis. We also miss the opportunity to talk with students about their efforts to turn empirical research into a formula. Such cookbook-like application of research findings is the downside of the positivism-influenced teaching approach of "manualized therapy." In contrast, professionals need to be able to read each situation, each client, each trainee, and each supervisor, and tailor their interventions to the needs of that particular person.

A *second example* of trainees who are frequently misunderstood by novice supervisors are those who have extensive experience in another counseling domain, such as the juvenile justice system. For instance, a female supervisor, on viewing a male trainee's blunt, confrontive style with clients, became critical very quickly, and the trainee in response became defensive. While my initial inclination might have been, as the supervisor's supervisor, to say, "Ease off on him," I instead explored this young woman's conceptualization of the student. Only then did I discover that both counseling trainee and supervisor inappropriately anticipated that this trainee, who had previously dealt with particularly difficult clients, would excel quickly at this "much simpler" work with voluntary clients. Once the student supervisor understood her own working hypothesis about her trainee, she could develop a new, more helpful one.

In querying this novice supervisor about her conceptualization, I was also able to integrate the expertise research into the discussion. Glaser and Chi (1988) showed that expertise in one domain does not automatically become expertise in another. I was able to provide this information at a "teachable moment," that is, one in which the information could be meaningfully related to experience.

The overall sequence of inquiry illustrated in this example demonstrates the reflective process. The novice supervisor first intervened in the session, and then examined the results of the intervention as she watched the videotaped session. In examining what transpired and how it might be viewed differently, the supervisor was able to adjust her conceptualization of this supervisee. To complete the reflectivity cycle, she could devise new interventions to test out in subsequent supervision sessions. Over time she will begin to recognize patterns in supervisees and will more accurately hypothesize reasons for their behavior. The recognition of patterns, rather than merely identifying isolated bits of trainee behavior, is the mark of an expert who can then intervene more efficiently (Glaser & Chi, 1988)

The inquiry approach is adaptable to the group supervision setting. It is often very powerful when peers in the supervision group work together with the master supervisor to examine and explore the situation. What an instructor might see as a domain-transfer issue, for instance, a peer might understand as a cultural phenomenon. The peer might ask, "In this trainee's cultural or ethnic background, might that be a pertinent intervention?" This could lead to a whole different line of inquiry with the trainee, one that would be framed not by the novice-expert literature but by literature on supervision by supervisors of one ethnic group, of counseling by a member of another ethnic group. In group settings, then, the instructor and students can be seen as co-investigators who bring varying life experiences, multicultural training, and scholarly research to bear on the work. Together they can effectively construct a better-defined problem than they would alone or in a dyad.

Deliberate Encouragement of Reflectivity. The exploration of student supervisors' intentions in constructivist supervision training is quite deliberate. As Willis Copeland (personal communication, May 5, 1994) stated in an interview with me, just thinking about something is not reflectivity in the sense of reflective practice. "You go out and act," he said, "and then you have to examine your action in the light of its purposes, and then you have to act again." That is reflectivity.

Instructors can choose to follow a particular line of inquiry. For example, supervisors might ask: What were you hoping for? How did you decide to make that intervention at that time? Did the results of the intervention fit your hypotheses? If not, what new thing about the trainee did you learn? Questions about what one has done and how it has worked illuminate a particular situation and permit new hypotheses. Such questions lay the groundwork for asking what supervisors intend to do in their next supervision session to test out their new hypotheses.

The examples above illustrate the reflective process as practiced in a supervision seminar. But how might the instructor assist novice supervisors when they face dilemmas between class meetings? How can students do further analysis and take action when a supervisor is not immediately available?

Reflective Journals. Students can pursue the points at which they are "stuck" in their journals, which in this course are written between seminar meetings. The instructor can design a series of open questions to which students can respond (Joan Rosenberg, personal communication, December 29, 1997) in order to elicit reflective exploration, such as, "What dilemma did you encounter in conducting supervision this week?" Student supervisors can also quite capably develop their own questions when left to do so. An example of creative reflectivity from an unguided student journal follows:

> In terms of promoting [trainee] Ellen's development as a therapist, I am increasingly aware of how her animated and optimistic responses to engaging in clinical work may actually inhibit my exploration of her perceptions and hypotheses about clients. I noticed this when I asked Ellen how she felt about this first session and her reactions to the client. As she responded so enthusiastically about how 'great' and 'energized' she felt about her session, I found myself validating her feelings but also neglecting to probe at a deeper level about topics such as possible difficulties in working with this client, her process of attending to client information, and her goals for development. I wonder if my expectations of Ellen are high, and thus my surprise when her presentation of her clinical work does not involve a 'deeper' sense of her ability to access what personal and client processes may be activated in session! Hmm . . . I will have to contemplate this a bit more.

In this example, the student supervisor described her trainee's behavior and then proceeded to explore her own response to it. Taking a classic reflective stance, she was surprised and confused by what was occurring. She then attended to her own actions, emotions, and behaviors in the session, and to her interaction with the trainee. And she changed her perception of the situation.

Journals offer the opportunity not only for student exploration but for dialogue between the instructor and student. Papers returned to students with few or no comments are like ideas tossed into a void. An example from a student's journal appears below at the left, with my comments attached at the right.

Supervisor Journal Entries	*Instructor Comments*
It was really interesting to have "real" clients there and reminded me of my own first experiences. As a supervisor I was feeling some of those same ways: extremely tuned into the client and the nuances of what was going on.	*It's the great discovery of supervision—what you now know!*
Very energizing! I'm finding that I very much enjoy the process of supervision and it was nice to be able to feel as though I had something to contribute to the process.	*Good timing is critical!*
It's hard to describe how that happened; I guess I fall back on how I remember my own supervisors interacting. Also I realize that over the past couple of years I've developed my "ear" and have a bit of a sense for when in a session it would be a good time for a certain thing to be said.	
I don't mean for that to sound boastful—I realize I've still got much, much to learn but I am realizing that I have learned some things and that is a good feeling. The tape with Carl Rogers from last quarter comes back to me, and somewhere on there he mentioned something to the effect that it was hard for him not to want to just jump into the session and conduct it. That is the challenge, I think.	*Absolutely!* *I experience it doubly with you folks—once with the client and once with the supervisee.*
Somehow promoting what you think to be the right way to do it while allowing the supervisee to get there on their own.	*I think it's even trickier than that. You don't want to "manipulate" them into place, but you do want them to explore and discover. If in addition, they see what you see, that's great; if not, you can tell them what you see. But sometimes they reveal their reasoning and that can then be built upon. This remains, for me, one of the most complex areas. I'm too accustomed to a lifetime as the "good student" who comes up with the "right" answers.*

In the responses to the journal above, I disclosed some of my own difficulties with supervision. However, I believe that the opportunity for dialogue could be carried one step further in journal-writing. Yalom (Yalom & Elkin, 1974) eloquently presented a series of journals of therapy, written by himself and a client, in *Every Day Gets a Little Closer: A Twice-Told Therapy*. While he and his client, Ginny, actually read one another's journals only every few months, an instructor could keep journals of his or her own experience of the supervision seminar and turn them over to the students each week when the students turn theirs in. This procedure offers an opportunity for sharing perceptions about the same events. Just as Yalom worried that Ginny might react negatively to his observations of her and to revelation of his own feelings and weaknesses, so an instructor might worry about a student's reaction. However, the potential benefits of learning how a well-practiced supervisor thinks are invaluable. In addition, the differences in perception of the same supervisory events provide the chance for further exploration.

THE RISKS OF CONSTRUCTIVIST SUPERVISION TRAINING

Many of the subtle strategies described above involve risk. Can a student supervisor adequately supervise a counseling trainee in practicum whose basic interpersonal skills are deficient, and, if she or he cannot, what are the instructor's responsibilities? And, given the time-consuming emphasis on reflection and experience, what if the student fails to learn "all of the important material" on supervision? What if supervisors become so involved in thinking and exploring that they cannot act effectively with trainees?

Potential Problems and Possible Resolutions

Some of the questions cited above can be answered by research in related fields of education. Evidence from educational psychology indicates that students learn best when they learn in context. For example, Bridges and Hallinger (1995) described the use of problem-based learning units in educational administration. He and his colleagues found that students initially displayed only 80% of the knowledge of their more traditionally educated colleagues who had been exposed to lectures and reading material without participation in solving real-life administrative problems. However, six months later, those who had participated in practical problem-solving could recall much more than those who had merely listened to lectures and consumed reading material. In the same way, when student supervisors integrate theory and research into their actual work with trainees, students will remember it. They may not be able to immediately cite as much theory and research, that is, as much "declarative knowledge," but their informed procedural knowledge will be greater and more useful.

Other problems, however, are best addressed by the instructor in a deliberate way. The problem of excessive student rumination and reflection is a risk for a process-oriented professor. I have at times become so enamored of a students' thoughtful reflections that I failed to notice their ineffective performance with clients or trainees. We must ask: Does the "armchair cogitation" lead to changes in supervisory action? Let us remember that attention to the last stage of reflectivity, that is, changed behavior, is necessary to complete the learning sequence.

A third problem, that of ineffective supervision and inadequate trainee performance at the end of a beginning practicum, is more serious. Novice supervisors struggle most with "difficult" counseling trainees, just as novice therapists struggle with difficult clients (Skovholt et al., 1997). And just as the supervisor of therapists is responsible for client welfare, so the supervisor of supervisors is responsible for counselor trainee learning, along with client welfare.

Two approaches might address this issue. The instructor might intensify the work with the student supervisor. In addition to group meetings, the instructor and supervisor may meet individually to review the latter's work with a trainee who most often demonstrates poor relationship skills with clients. The supervision instructor does not just encourage the supervisor to inquire into the trainee's thinking about particular clients; she or he must assist the supervisor to explore the causes of the trainee's difficulties in a broader way. To do so, the instructor asks the supervisor to provide hypotheses about the underlying reasons behind the trainee's inadequate performance. By this, I don't mean speculating about the trainee's personal history, but rather, imagining what impedes the trainee's functioning in session.

For example, with a student in our counseling practicum, a male supervisor hypothesized that the female trainee had little idea about how she affected others. Together he and I devised strategies for validating or refuting that hypothesis. The supervisor elected to ask several questions of the trainee. When watching her performance on videotape, for instance, he asked, "How did you think you came across?" To our surprise and satisfaction, the trainee accurately reported, "When I'm with the client, I don't feel as if I'm being arrogant, but when I watch myself on tape, I sound arrogant." The supervisor was then able to encourage the trainee to pay closer attention to her feelings while in session. Then she could analyze the tape for instances of arrogant presentation, relate it to her in-session feelings, and learn to recognize those times and change her behavior in future sessions.

Such interventions with the supervisor do not always lead to improvement in a trainee. If the student supervisor still cannot promote the trainee's improved performance, the instructor can meet individually with the trainee and provide direct supervision. This is not ideal because it bypasses the student supervisor. It is necessary, however, to fulfill the instructor's ultimate responsibility to provide adequate supervision for each counseling trainee and to make certain that professional therapists are competent to work with clients.

CONCLUSION

There is, of course, no universal way to help students "construct" effective strategies for supervision. Like Teyber (1997), I continue to develop ways to teach and supervise supervision by looking at the needs, goals, prior experience, and personality characteristics of the particular combination of supervisor, therapist, and client. However, I do encourage all supervision instructors to facilitate all supervisors' reflectivity. Instructors also need to evaluate the results of their teaching strategies with each individual student. When the results don't fit teaching expectations, instructors can develop new interventions based on what they have learned.

At this time, we do not know very much about the actual results of the strategies I have outlined. The overall effects of supervision itself have not been well documented, although many moment-to-moment events in supervision have been studied. We know very little about the nature and effects of reflective events in supervision, particularly since most of them are covert. And we do not yet know whether we can accomplish short-term learning and/or long-term development by encouraging reflectivity. Qualitative research on supervisor interventions and supervisee thinking might begin to answer some of these questions. Longitudinal studies of more and less reflective therapists could follow that research.

Constructivist approaches to research may launch us into a deeper understanding of supervision. However, in the meantime, we cannot be impulsive or whimsical. The training of supervisors is too critical an area to tackle randomly. We need to apply the results of clinical psychology's studies of psychotherapist development and of research on constructivist approaches to learning in education. In this way we operate from a theoretical base, with the understanding that we are experimenting, as we continually examine the results of our actions. Thus each of us becomes a researcher with each student.

NOTES

1. The words counselor and counseling are used interchangeably with the words therapist and psychotherapy.

2. Reflectivity and reflection refer to a process of thinking and not to a similarly-named verbal response to a client.

REFERENCES

American Psychological Association. (1992). Ethical principles of psychologists and code of conduct. *American Psychologist, 47,* 1597-1611.

Association for Counselor Education and Supervision. (1995). Ethical guidelines for counseling supervisors. *Counselor Education and Supervision, 34,* 270-276.

Bernard, J. M., & Goodyear, R. K. (1998). *Fundamentals of clinical supervision,* (2nd ed.). Boston: Allyn & Bacon.

Binder, J. L. (1993). Is it time to improve psychotherapy training? *Clinical Psychology Review, 13,* 301-318.

Binder, J. L., & Strupp, H. H. (1997). Supervision of psychodynamic psychotherapies. In C. E. Watkins, Jr. (Ed.). *Handbook of psychotherapy supervision,* (pp. 44-59). New York: Wiley.

Borders, D., Bernard, J. M., Dye, H. A., Fong, M. L., Henderson, P., & Nance, D. W. (1991). Curriculum guide for training counseling supervisors: Rationale, development, and implementation. *Counselor Education and Supervision, 31,* 58-80.

Bridges, E. M., & Hallinger, P. (1995). *Implementing problem based learning in leadership development.* Eugene, OR: ERIC.

Dawes, R. M. (1994). *House of cards: Psychology and psychotherapy built on myth.* New York: Free Press.

Freire, P. (1993). *Pedagogy of the oppressed* (M. B. Ramos, Trans.; Rev. ed.). New York: Continuum.

Glaser, R., & Chi, M. T. H. (1988). Overview. In M. T. H. Chi, R. Glaser, & M. J. Farr, (Eds.). *The nature of expertise,* (pp. xv-xxv). Hillsdale, NJ: Lawrence Erlbaum.

Hill, C. E. (1989). *Therapist techniques and client outcomes: Eight cases of brief psychotherapy.* Newbury Park, CA: Sage.

McAuliffe, G., & Lovell, C. (2000). Encouraging transformation: Guidelines for constructivist and developmental instruction."In G. McAuliffe, K. Eriksen, and Associates, *Preparing counselors and therapists: Creating constructivist and developmental programs,* (pp. 14-41). Alexandria, VA: Association for Counselor Education and Supervision.

Neufeldt, S. A. (1997). A social constructivist approach to counseling supervision. In T. L. Sexton & B. L. Griffin, (Eds.). *Constructivist thinking in counseling practice, research, and training,* (pp. 191-210). New York: Teachers College, Columbia University.

Neufeldt, S. A. (1999). *Supervision strategies for the first practicum,* (2nd ed.). Alexandria, VA: American Counseling Association.

Neufeldt, S. A., Iversen, J. N., & Juntunen, C. L. (1995). *Supervision strategies for the first practicum.* Alexandria, VA: American Counseling Association.

Schön, D. A. (1983). *The reflective practitioner.* New York: Basic Books.

Schön, D. A. (1987). *Educating the reflective practitioner.* San Francisco: Jossey-Bass.

Skovholt, T. M., & Rønnestad, M. H. (1992). *The evolving professional self: Stages and themes in therapist and counselor development.* Chichester, England: Wiley.

Skovholt, T. M., Rønnestad, M. H., & Jennings, L. (1997). Searching for expertise in counseling, psychotherapy, and professional psychology. *Educational Psychology Review, 9,* 361-369.

Teyber, E. (1997). *Interpersonal process in psychotherapy,* (3rd ed.). Pacific Grove, CA: Brooks/Cole.

Tracey, E. J., Ellickson, J. L., & Sherry, P. (1989). Reactance in relation to different supervisory environments and counselor development. *Journal of Counseling Psychology, 36,* 336-344.

von Glasersfeld, E. (1995). Sensory experience, abstraction, and teaching. In L. P. Steffe & J. Gale, (Eds.). Constructivism in education, (pp. 369-383). Hillsdale, NJ: Lawrence Erlbaum.

Watkins, C. E., Jr., (Ed.) (1997). *Handbook of psychotherapy supervision.* New York: Wiley.

Yalom, I., & Elkin, G. (1974). *Every day gets a little closer: A twice-told therapy.* New York: Basic Books.

10

Constructing Learning Communities in Pre-Practicum and Practicum Seminars

Kathy O'Byrne

A practicum classroom is a constructivist laboratory. Students experiment with new counseling skills. They mix theory and practice. And the process can be volatile. During practice sessions, a "chemical reaction" often emerges between clients and counselor trainees; that is, situations in which the mix of emotions, attitudes, behaviors, and cognitions create new dynamics and discoveries. Knowledge breaks through when developing creative solutions to clinical problems, problems that come from the student's own current life experience or prior knowledge, rather than through attempts to replicate the work of others.

This chapter describes my work with masters-level students who are either in a pre-practicum counseling skills class or in a first practicum.In the latter group students conduct counseling sessions in nonprofit community agencies or schools and brings videotapes of their sessions to class. In the pre-practicum students counsel peers or undergraduates, also bringing videotapes to class. In the chapter, I demonstrate how teaching philosophy, classroom strategies, and assessment tools can be used in these courses to holistically support the students' normal process of development.

THE CONSTRUCTIVIST RATIONALE: TRUSTING ONESELF IN A COMMUNITY OF LEARNERS

Constructivist theory offers a fitting framework for the optimization of learning in practicum. Students and instructors bring their prior knowledge, skills, and abilities to class and negotiate ways to shape counseling practice in the service of the client. Together we construct a conceptualization of the client and a plan to create a therapeutic relationship that offers relief for a client's struggle, a plan that fits the subjective experience of the client as it is understood by the counselor.

Together we try to address the beginning student's questions of "What do I do?" and "What do I say?" We respond to those questions with the seemingly diffident and highly contextual notion, "It all depends." It depends on who the client is and it depends on who the student is. This inevitably becomes a constructivist conversation because we do not use a "cookie cutter" approach to counseling; technique cannot provide the automatic responses that can or should be given to each client just because it's the first, third, or tenth session. Counseling itself is a constructivist laboratory because counselors act, and reflect didactically, making modifications to their therapeutic plans based on the client's response to them. The counseling interview is conducted. Students and instructors collaborate in crafting the work of helping to excavate the feelings and motivations that lie hidden behind the spoken words and body language of the client, creatively producing new levels of understanding.

The practicum course is generally seen by both students and faculty members as "different" from others in the curriculum, since it is performance-based. Here there is space to create individualized learning goals and outcomes for students, who are understandably tentative about going into that space. In this course, students learn by doing, through trial-and-error, and by developing a personal understanding of the "acceptable" standards of our profession. During this experience students often falter and know much self-doubt.

Student Myths of Incompetence

Newly emerging counselors hold four common "myths" of self-doubt: the imposter phenomenon, the quick fix fantasy, the instructor-has-a-secret belief, and the I-must-have-a-secret assumption. These myths often emerge in full force during the practicum courses. The "imposter phenomenon" may be coupled with all-or-nothing thinking. In this myth, students stop into my office to tell me they are "sure" that "everyone else" in the class is much more advanced and knows much more than they do. In the "quick fix fantasy," students worry that their clients are not "better" already and that they as counselors "should" be doing more or doing it faster in their counseling sessions. Or, students subscribe to the myth that I secretly see them as incompetent and I'm just not telling them; this myth may have roots in being shamed in other classrooms or life experiences and anticipating that again. Finally, some students espouse the myth that they will fail if anyone (client, instructor, peers) finds out that they don't have all the answers.

In order to counter these myths, I usually tell students up front that I'm certain that no one in the class knows completely what they are doing, that I worry if they DO think they have all the answers, and that I believe that counseling skills can be taught and learned. It usually helps to have students compare their first time behind the wheel of a car with their current driving style. They improved their driving with practice and experience and probably can now eat, talk on a cell phone, and/or have a conversation while driving. I ask them to "have faith" that so too will counseling become less less of an effort and more automatic, and that experience will provide them with new perspectives. Now we turn to constructing the work of counseling in practicum, a process that can also contribute to shattering these myths.

The Diverse Learning Community in the Classroom

Practicum can be organized on the constructivist understanding that each student's starting place will be different. Diversity is appreciated; conformity is not the goal. Thus instructors can give up being responsible for ensuring uniform endpoints for all students in the class at the end of a semester or quarter. What is important in this perspective is that we value each person's voice in integrating prior knowledge and that we see each person's potential for creating a frame (but not a template) for new knowledge. Others in other disciplines have described these processes. The interested reader might examine *Rousing Minds to Life* (Tharp & Gallimore, 1991); *The Feminist Classroom* (Maher & Tetreault, 1995); *Teaching to Transgress* (hooks, 1994) and *Assessment for Excellence* (Astin, 1996).

When we use this social constructionist model to operate the practicum classroom, we are more interested in examining as a unit of analysis the intersubjective space between and among members of the learning community (Wertsch, 1990). We ask the following: What is created on the first day of class? How is it created? Who did or said what to whom? What is the level of safety, structure, and respect that is constructed? What are the issues of power, hierarchy, or marginalization that are manifested in language, tone, or action? We are vigilant about whether the classroom context encourages or discourages learning, whether we maximize self-disclosure and self-reflection. We try to give up our urgency to pass on "expert" knowledge to a room full of seeming novices. We try to concentrate instead on articulating the struggles of not-knowing or dealing with incomplete knowledge.

188188 Teaching Counselors and Therapists

THEMES FOR THE CONSTRUCTIVIST PRACTICUM

Student Struggles

The notion of the classroom as a community of learners often creates some predictable struggles. For example, we know from counselor development and supervision research (O'Byrne, Clark & Malakuti, 1997; O'Byrne & Rosenberg, 1998) that students crave concrete direction and certain types of guidance in the beginning stages of practicum or internships. The need for greater guidance and structure must be honored at the same time that learners are empowered. One way to introduce students to their own potential for "knowledge creation" is to honor their already-existing knowledge.

Students are inevitably insecure, for they are apprentices who are new to this professional community. It thus helps for instructors to reference their own experiences learning the craft. My students seem to appreciate disclosures of my favorite "bloopers" or unforgettable errors, even though some occurred over twenty years ago. I offer stories from my own experiences if there seems to be a link with a student's current experiences, and I emphasize that the most "unforgettable" and difficult clients are the ones from whom we likely learn the most.

Helping Struggling Students Through Connecting with Prior Knowledge

Instructors can empower students as *knowers* by helping them to connect with their prior knowledge. For example, I ask students who struggle with intake interviews how they usually get to know someone they meet for the first time. I ask students who struggle with depressed clients to tell me what helpful things their friends do for them when they themselves are feeling down. I further encourage them to value kinds of knowing, such as using intuition or "hunches," that are based in their prior knowledge. Such sources of insight in counseling would be lost if instructors compartmentalized or dichotomized classroom and non-classroom knowledge, considering non-classroom knowledge to be less legitimate (Aronowitz & Giroux, 1993; Freire, 1994; hooks, 1994; Giroux, 1988).

In this constructed community of *learners*, we treat emerging knowledge as cyclical, in that we often have to return to certain themes more than once. Such knowledge becomes organized in most cases around the activities of planning, acting, and then reflecting on counseling practice. We conceptualize our thoughts about a client, plan an intervention, and reflect on how the experience felt. We encourage students to use their own reactions as reliable sources of data in order to begin the cycle again.

Through these and other methods of legitimizing personal knowledge and encouraging peer exchange, a community of learners eventually comes together. The instructor has to be willing to let much of the content and process emerge in this seminar. The community learning environment is one in which we will shape, create, and influence relationships, we will support one another through a group process. No one can say on the first day of class what topics will emerge in this process of discovery; in parallel fashion, it's not possible to know the exact ways in which clients will challenge us all. Now we turn to the co-construction of the course.

CREATING OBJECTIVES IN DIALOGUE

Approaching a practicum or internship class from the constructivist perspective parallels a qualitative researcher's approach to inquiry. There is not a hypothesis articulated in advance, but rather a descriptive search for meaning. We are less interested in similar or identical learning across students or sections of the course or semesters and are more concerned that each student's development is evolving from pre-professional to professional levels. Along the way, students also come to understand what is unacceptable or "unprofessional" practice and chart a course that is uniquely theirs, contained within the boundaries of ethical and legal counseling practice.

The Role of the Faculty: Setting Standards for Practice

Conversations about the minimal standards, or "general hypotheses," for student learning need to take place among faculty at the departmental level, so that there are parallel expectations for students across all sections of a practicum or internship course. We translate what we know about student learning and counselor development into learning goals in order to have reasonable expectations for students in these courses. Learning goals in the first semester of practicum need to differ from those for students in their subsequent internship, sometimes called the second semester of practicum. This distinction challenges faculty members to articulate what they think is an appropriate amount of progress to be expected in the course of a semester or quarter. We ask each other what a student will likely be able to do at the end of the course that he/she can not do at the beginning of the course.

For example, our faculty have decided that a student at the end of the first practicum should be able to manage and tolerate his/her own anxiety during sessions, demonstrate the use of active listening skills, begin to build a therapeutic relationship, and make effective use of supervision. At the end of the internship (the next semester), students have built on these basic skills so that they can articulate their conceptualizations of clients, assess clients in context, and demonstrate the consistent use of theory (or reference the theory that they are trying to use). Faculty communicate their expectations that students are to reflect upon and articulate their progress and accomplishments in the course.

These learning goals and strategies need continual attention. They evolve through conversations among faculty members who teach practicum. In order to maintain these conversations, practicum instructors meet once each semester. We share observations from our visits to agencies, discuss teaching philosophies and classroom strategies, or consult on challenging learning situations from the previous semester. We attempt to provide an equivalent experience across all sections of the class, but do not expect that sections will be identical. The triumvirate of students, faculty, and agency staff all to appreciate the links among the learning outcomes for the course, the assessment forms used by faculty and community supervisors, and the self-assessment procedures used by students.

Practicum instructors also visit each student's placement site once during the semester. We reinforce the importance of the instructor and the site supervisor working as partners on behalf of the student, and the collaborative, constructivist nature of learning that gives voice to diverse perspectives. The student, the university instructor, and the site supervisor participate in the site visit. Site supervisors describe what the student seems to have learned in the past semester. The faculty member adds another dimension to the feedback by saying what he or she has observed in the classroom and on videotapes. The student offers his or her opinion of the semester's experience. Multiple perspectives converge and an organized picture of the student's development becomes apparent. Finally, all three participants discuss what is likely to be the next skill or set of skills the student will add to his or her developing repertoire.

Co-Constructing New Objectives *In Situ*

As counselor educators, we necessarily make assumptions about what is important for students to know and about what is possible to know. However, instructors in practicum or internship courses will never be aware of all that happens with their students while those students are practicing in community agencies and placement sites. Instructors and field supervisors may have very different opinions from one another on what they consider to be the "most" important learning needs. Student-interns translate and interpret instructions from the classroom and from supervision sessions through their personal lenses.

Thus, knowledge that fits the evolving experiences of the students in the course cannot be organized in advance and dispensed according to a semester-long schedule. New challenges regularly present themselves and students react. The instructor of a pre-practicum or practicum course creates a learning environment in which the key activity is collegial examination of student practice, through continuous questioning, rather than the favoring of "correct" answers or final accomplishments. Thus the student-counselor's professional identity is co-created through shared experience. We now turn to specific dimensions of a constructivist pre-practicum and practicum.

SPECIFIC CONSTRUCTIVIST INSTRUCTIONAL PRACTICES

The Pre-Practicum Classroom

The "pre-practicum," which is often called the counseling skills or techniques class, can mimic the dynamism of the practicum by ensuring that students have a direct experience of counseling, albeit in a modified fashion. At our university, the Theatre Department and the Counseling Department collaboratively have created vivid and varied counseling roleplays for use in our pre-practicum class. This collaborative project has offered students in both programs a chance to demonstrate their learning and to experience the challenges of acting within professional roles. Faculty in the Counseling Department had been frustrated with students playing themselves with other students in pre-practicum; some faculty worried that roles touched students' own issues too closely and that vulnerable students didn't have adequate protection. Correspondingly, the faculty in the Theatre Department were frustrated with the lack of opportunities for their students to improvise roles and spontaneously create consistent personae. Thus, this project allowed counseling students to work with a "stranger" who they knew was playing a "role." The actor got to improvise a general role and respond spontaneously to the situation as it unfolded in the session.

Roles for the theatre students were written from stories in the *Los Angeles Times*. Some were stories of violence on a school campus; others were stories of families struggling with depression, health problems, economic stress, trauma, grief, or loss. Counseling students received these "real life" presenting problems (paraphrased from the newspaper account) as if they were on an intake sheet at a counseling clinic. Students were told that the person was seeking counseling to cope with her or his particular situation. Actors received coaching about how a person would likely feel or speak or behave in the wake of this event or trauma.

Counseling students and acting students alike treated this exercise as an opportunity to practice their respective professional "roles" and to construct a believable scenario. Both sets of students struggled with what to say or not to say, how much to say, and how to respond during each session, while remaining in their roles.

Classmates observing the role-plays from behind a one-way mirror were riveted to the role-play. They provided feedback on what they considered to be critical incidents or turning points in the session and explained why they selected that moment in the session as critical.

Another pre-practicum classroom exercise uses "restricted sentence stems" in order for students to experience the power of reflective listening. For example, the counselor in the role-play might only be allowed to respond to the client with sentences that begin with "You need me to understand that you are feeling [student names the feeling]." Such an exercise not only helps students learn how to name feelings, but also illustrates to them how often we underestimate the client movement that can occur through merely expressing empathic understanding. Students report being surprised that things begin to happen with the client in the role-play, saying, "But all I did was reflect!"

In another pre-practicum simulation, a faculty member coaches a student as he or she role-plays a challenging client. The two most frequently used categories of such challenge are "the hostile client" and "the withdrawn client." Pre-practicum students feel afraid that, in the first case, clients will attack them and they will be overwhelmed. In the second, they fear that the client will not talk at all! By having the chance to work on these scenarios before experiencing them with "real" practicum clients, students create useful knowledge frameworks for future practice.

The Practicum Classroom

The tension between two seemingly inconsistent sets of directions makes the practicum classroom stressful for our students. On the one hand, students are to speak the prescribed language of the counselor by using seemingly scripted active listening skills and by following ethical and legal guidelines. On the other hand, they are to bring themselves spontaneously to the session in a creative way that is true to their experience of the moment. Thus, students often experience and report the conundrum of being simultaneously asked to follow directions while engaging in original thought! Structure is needed; yet it takes various forms based on the emerging relationships with clients.

Probing students' expectations of helping. One of the first challenges in this course is to understand how the novice counselor perceives his or her role with clients. The instructor asks the question, "What do you think you are there to do?" The class typically struggles with this question both individually and as a group, bringing forth both their conceptions of counseling and of the people who seek professional help. Their typical responses include that they are there: to "fix" the client, to "analyze" the client as a problem to be solved, to "teach" the client, or to provide advice.

An alternative question posed to beginning practicum students might be "How do you think anyone would be better off by talking to you?" Students then reflect on times when they themselves felt "helped" by talking to a friend about a problem of their own. Classmates share responses, offering anecdotal evidence for how their friend looked, sounded, or seemed, and ways in which that "helped."

Videotape review. Viewing and reflecting on videotapes of sessions are central to practicum, of course. We emphasize the students' reflection on their own performance. They have control over selecting ten-minute segments to share in class. Students ponder their own fundamental reactions to the designated session in terms of the relationship they have constructed and the choices they have made. The class offers alternative strategies for working with the same client. Thus, by framing feedback in terms of "choices," we emphasize the multiplicity of options and we de-emphasize the notion of one "correct" way of responding. We also look to see if treatment plans and strategies are enacted or contradicted by the observed work. Students begin to understand the influence they exert in shaping the counseling relationship.

In viewing videotapes, we use three sensory metaphors as tools for analysis: sound, sight, and feeling. For example, the class considers how the student "sounds" in the session. If it sounds like a conversation you would overhear from the next table while out to lunch, it's probably not "counseling." We study both sequences and language to examine how relationships are created or defined by the interactions of the session. I ask students to note sequences that are at least three exchanges in length: "counselor-client-counselor," or, alternatively, "client-counselor-client." They think about what they are doing to enhance or shape the relationship by the way they sound and by the words they choose. What are they exploring as "relevant" and what are they ignoring? What do they convey with the spoken word and with their tone, inflection, and intonation?

Next, students study how they "look." Students provide several adjectives to describe how they think they seem to their client(s). Do they look stern? Friendly? Bored? Scared? Anxious? Interested? Seductive? Disapproving? Do they seem like a friend? a colleague? a neighbor? Or does the student look (and sound) like a teacher? prosecutor? preacher? or police officer?

Lastly, students describe how they were "feeling." We ask, "Could your client tell how you were feeling?" "Could we tell how you were feeling by seeing you on the videotape?" "Do you know how you were feeling and can you name it?" "What do you usually do when you feel that way and how willing are you to let this particular feeling show?" These probes usually lead to discussing how students think they are "supposed to be feeling, supposed to look, and supposed to talk, and their efforts to approximate these seeming imperatives. Often they are trying to "be like" some expert counselor whom they have seen in person, on videotape in another class, or even in a recent motion picture. Only now, in this practicum session, they are invited to and expected to construct their own version of how they will be "counselor;" they will evaluate how satisfied they are with their management of the spontaneous dynamics of the therapeutic relationship.

Peer observations. Issues of control predictably arise in the constructivist classroom, and the group process of the practicum class may privilege certain viewpoints (particularly the instructor's) over others. Students should be the central commentators in the seminar. In order for them to grow developmentally, they provide rationales to accompany their opinions. Also, for balance, we ask that self-disclosure coexist with intellectual analysis.

One method for generating self-awareness in the emerging counselor is to ask the student-observers to comment on any "surprises" in the videotape; that is, to point out unexpected things done by either the client or counselor. Students must also include an explanation of why they were surprised; that is, what they had expected. This question often triggers exploration by the group about the "preferred" or "expected" way of responding to a client. Students also share vulnerable places, those in which they fear being overchallenged by clients' issues. Often the "surprises" commentary exposes a certain level of unexamined naiveté, an assumption that everyone grew up the same way with the similar families or values or lifestyles.

Such naivete can lead to important discoveries about personal sensitivities. Practicum instructors are often practicing therapists who have been engaged in this work for decades. Because of this differing perspective, instructors may not see what their students see. For example, students in practicum often have a sensitivity for danger that is considerably different from those who are more experienced in the profession. The mere mention of suicide, sexuality, or drug use may "surprise" class members in ways that the instructor would not even notice. It becomes important to allow time for students to talk about what worries them and to experience the classroom as a safe haven in which to discuss their fears.

Classroom exercises. Through many classroom exercises we ask students to conceptualize the therapeutic relationships that might support the client's growth. For example, students view videotapes in the first practicum and count the number of topics that are discussed in the ten minute clip shown in class. If there are 30 or 40 content areas, the pace is probably too fast to deepen or build a relationship. To further demonstrate the multiple pathways to expertise, practicum instructors can try other classroom exercises. The following are some we have found some success with:

- *Drawing the situation.* Students may draw on the board or on some newsprint themselves and the client under discussion. Even the least-confident artist will portray a relationship that offers insight to the class.

- *Therapist tag.* Similarly, students may play "therapist tag", role-playing their clients with a classmate. Any of the observers can "tag" the counselor in the role-play and take his or her place if they have an idea they'd like to try. Or the student-counselor can ask for someone else to be "it," taking over the work with the client. Whatever emerges can be used on the spot to offer insight to the student about his or her client.

- *"Bumper sticker" sayings.* Another structured activity for the constructivist classroom is the use of what I call "bumper-stickers." These aphorisms consist of short, one-line reminders of generalizable knowledge. Some of the most popular "bumper stickers" are those that are easy to remember and help students with some of the most predictable and common dilemmas. For example, an anxious or insecure student often talks excessively in a beginning session, leaving no room for the client to speak. A "bumper sticker" for that student might be "Say every *other* thing" or "Say only *half* of what you think." These reminders slow the pace of the session and open up the possibility that the novice counselor can work less hard and perhaps begin to tolerate some silence.

- *Process comment stems.* Another common concern is that students will "draw a blank" and not be able to think of what to say when the client finishes their thought or simply stops talking. In those instances, we encourage students to remember that *"Your best friend is the process comment"* or *"When in doubt, make a process comment."* The group and the instructor generate examples of process comment sentence stems in class. These include the use of "I can't help but notice that . . . ." or "You seem so much different this week" or "What just happened here seems to be . . . ." When viewing videotapes in class, students and instructors alike may ask the performing student, "Who is your best friend?" which encourages students to remember that they can relieve themselves of the pressure to ask (yet) another question or the "correct" question. They can reframe their pattern of investigative reporting or journalistic interviewing into a more sensitive conversation related to the client's needs.

- *The "Colombo."* I also teach students "the Colombo," based on the past television series of the same name. By modeling tentativeness and asking clients to help the counselor understand what they are told, novice counselors take on the role of "not knowing." This happens when the practicum student asks the client questions that start with "How can it be that . . .?" or "I'm confused. I was sure you told me earlier that . . . ." Fearful students or those who avoid confrontation find this approach attractive.

- *Conceptualizing basic issues in counseling.* Finally, the practicum classroom sessions create a learning context for the particular problems posed in the course. In each meeting we return to the consideration of basic clinical questions, such as whether thinking, feeling, or behaviors are more relevant for students. Students express opinions about how people develop problems, what it takes for people to change, and what the counselor's role is in that process. Students select a conceptual "point of entry" in the first practicum that can be embellished into the beginnings of a theoretical orientation in the subsequent internship. They reflect on their own experiences of change and how they occurred. The instructor might ask "During that change, did you decide to think differently about a situation, or did you behave differently and find your feelings changed as well?"

ASSESSMENT OF LEARNING

We use a multilayered approach to assessing student learning in practicum. We ask for input from the three major stakeholders, namely students, site supervisors, and instructors. We also use multiple methods to organize the complex layers of learning that occur in this type of experiential course: gathering both qualitative and quantitative data, and using both formative and summative evaluations of student development.

Illustrative forms, evaluation checklists, guidelines for classroom presentations, and final papers are available in the appendices. These are the teaching artifacts that represent the application of the philosophies described above. They support and complement the principles of shared discovery and the creation of new knowledge. They also reiterate the importance of demonstrating ethical and legal professional conduct in providing counseling services.

CONCLUSION

Transforming practicum and internship courses requires a stance toward teaching and learning in which the person who is the learner is centralized and in which rigid, prefabricated course content is de-emphasized. Thus we turn away from a pedagogical model in which instructors determine whether a student knows something; that is, a model that implies a predetermined "correct" or absolute answer to issues that emerge in counseling sessions. Instead, instructors and students work together to articulate both (a) what the student knows, which includes prior knowledge that he or she brings to the classroom, and (b) how the student has constructed that knowledge.

In these ways, students can bring into awareness their own systems of understanding and can incorporate such prior knowing into the circle of professionally acceptable behaviors. Students articulate their current world views and integrate them into their roles as helping professionals. Students and instructors alike mutually investigate problems of the human condition that are embedded in certain contexts. Over time, students become advanced apprentices who themselves frame problems to be investigated in their work with clients.

These courses emphasize demonstrated learning and practice knowledge. We study what students do and then reveal systems of understanding and prior knowledge from which advanced counseling skills develop. The process of becoming a counselor is honored and valued over the search for perfect, complete, or universal knowledge. The constructivist practicum classroom acknowledges levels and types of knowing that come together and ignite the curiosity of instructors and students alike.

Appendix

Illustrative Forms

A. Worksheet for class to fill in while viewing videotapes:

1. What was one choice the counselor made that you would have also made? Why?
2. What was one choice the counselor made that you would not have also made? Why?
3. What was one thing that surprised you or that you did not expect? Why?

B. Mid-Semester Evaluation Checklist

Mid-semester Evaluation of First Practicum

	Strength	Growth Edge
Use of supervision _____		
Building a relationship _____		
Initial interviews/intakes _____		
Maintaining relationships _____		

Reflections and suggestions:

C. End of the Semester Evaluation Checklist

End of the Semester Evaluation for Practicum

Name of student _____   Date: _____

Practicum Instructor _____   Semester/Year _____

This form is a tool for communicating the level of a student's development as demonstrated in the practicum course. Please rate observed performance in each of the following areas. Use the rating scale to communicate the following:

#1	unacceptable performance
#2	an area of growth that needs attention
#3	appropriate performance
#4	good demonstrated performance
#5	outstanding clinical performance
NA	a skill or behavior that was not covered in this course

I. *Supervision*

Open to feedback from instructor	1	2	3	4	5	NA
Open to feedback from classmates	1	2	3	4	5	NA
Asks questions of instructor and students	1	2	3	4	5	NA
Regularly brings videotapes to class	1	2	3	4	5	NA

Additional comments:

II. *Building a relationship*

Demonstrates attending skills	1	2	3	4	5	NA
Demonstrates empathy	1	2	3	4	5	NA
Follows client's meaning; doesn't impose own agenda	1	2	3	4	5	NA
Demonstrates respect	1	2	3	4	5	NA
Perceives issues of diversity, including but not limited to gender and culture	1	2	3	4	5	NA

Additional comments:

III. *Initial interviews and intakes*

Asks questions to assess history, severity and duration of problem	1	2	3	4	5	NA
Formulates an initial impression of client and can articulate it	1	2	3	4	5	NA
Sees clients in context and demonstrates systemic thinking	1	2	3	4	5	NA

Additional comments:

IV. Maintaining a relationship

Uses multiple and varied techniques:
questions, empathic responses, silence.   1   2   3   4   5   NA
Reflects on his/her responses to client   1   2   3   4   5   NA
Sees how he/she seems to the client   1   2   3   4   5   NA
Tolerates expressions of affect or emotion
by the client   1   2   3   4   5   NA
Demonstrates sensitivity to ethical and
legal issues   1   2   3   4   5   NA
Additional comments:

V. Final case presentation

Presents an organized picture of client   1   2   3   4   5   NA
Sees strengths and weaknesses
in his/her own work   1   2   3   4   5   NA
Sees progress in learning during
the semester   1   2   3   4   5   NA
Additional comments:

VI. Overall assessment

I support this student moving on to Advanced Practicum: (check one)

YES _____   NO _____   CONDITIONAL* _____

*Indicate specific conditions or concerns: _____

_____

We have reviewed and discussed this assessment:

_____   _____
   Signature of instructor/date   Signature of student/date

D. *Guidelines for final class presentations:*

1. You have one hour of class time for your presentation.

2. Provide the class with a case history of the client(s) to be presented. You may present the your work with a single client, couple, or family.

3. Use videotapes to demonstrate your learning over the course of the semester.

4. Include examples that demonstrate the development of your own consistent style. Reflect on how your work has evolved and how your relationship with the client(s) changed over time. Focus on specific examples based on practice and experiences. What do you know (or know how to do) at the end of the semester that you did not know at the beginning?

E. *Guidelines for final papers*

1. Description of the client: age and other demographics, presenting problem and/or circumstances of the referral, how long you have been seeing the client, any previous counseling, etc.

2. Context and reflection: Why did you select this particular client? What made this an illustrative example of your own learning as a counselor?

3. Choices you made: What are some of the choices you made with this client, not only in the words you used and the things you said, but also the thoughts and feelings you had. What were you seeing, feeling, attending to? In what way were you intending to be helpful?

4. Mutual impact: What overall impact did you and this client have on one another? Be specific. Quote tapes if you can, with examples of sequences. Point to evidence of changes in your relationship with the client that was different or changed after an exchange. Illuminate patterns or sequences that show mutual impact. For example, point to "client-counselor-client" exchanges or "counselor-client-counselor" patterns.

REFERENCES

Aronowitz, S., and Giroux, H. A. (1993). *Education still under siege.* Westport, CT: Bergin & Garvey.

Astin, A. W. (1996). *Assessment for excellence: The philosophy and practice of assessment and evaluation in higher education.* Phoenix, AZ: Oryx Press.

Freire, P. (1994). *Pedagogy of hope.* New York: Continuum.

Giroux, H. A. (1988). *Schooling and the struggle for public life: Critical pedagogy in the modern age.* Minneapolis: University of Minneapolis Press.

hooks, b. (1994). *Teaching to transgress: Education as the practice of freedom.* New York: Routledge Press.

Maher, F. A., & Tetreault, M. K. (1995). *The feminist classroom.* New York: Basic Books.

O'Byrne, K., Clark, R., & Malakuti, R. (1997). Expert and novice performance: Implications for clinical training. *Educational Psychology Review, 9* (4), 321-332.

O'Byrne, K., & Rosenberg, J. (1998). The practice of supervision: A sociocultural perspective. *Counselor Education and Supervision, 38,* 23-42.

Tharp, R. G., & Gallimore, R. G. (1991). *Rousing minds to life: Teaching, learning, and schooling in social context.* Boston, MA: Cambridge University Press.

Wertsch, J. (1990). The voice of rationality in a sociocultural approach to mind. In L. Moll, (Ed.). *Vygotsky and education: Instructional implications and applications of sociohistorical psychology,* (pp.111-126). New York: Cambridge University Press.

11

Renaming and Rethinking the "Diagnosis and Treatment" Course

Victoria E. White

The counseling profession's focus on growth and development, multiculturalism, and contextual thinking tends to contradict the whole remediation notion of teaching a course in diagnosis and treatment planning, a course in which students typically learn the DSM-IV criteria and identify which treatments should be used with clients holding the different diagnoses. Yet insurance companies are unlikely to give up their requirement that counselors diagnose, and communication with other mental health professionals seems to require the use of diagnostic labels. How, then, can counselor educators incorporate their developmental, strength-based perspective of human experience into this well-established part of the mental health practitioner canon? This chapter attempts to answer that question by describing how the diagnoses and treatment planning course benefits from a postmodern perspective and a constructivist classroom.

Traditional content in diagnosis and treatment planning courses has resembled clinical psychology and psychiatry more than counseling. The words alone, "diagnosis" and "treatment," are part of the medical illness-cure tradition: Clients are "diagnosed" with a "mental disorder" and subsequently obtain "treatment" to "cure" their "illness." Diagnosis and treatment planning courses typically use two texts, an abnormal psychology textbook and the DSM (Diagnostic and Statistical Manual of Mental Disorders; APA, 1994) as sources. This course cries "objectivism" in its reliance on pinning down pathology, separate from constructing labels and the social context. Yet we can't escape the fact that students are learning about "historically contingent" and "socially-situated" moralities when they learn about "abnormal" behavior (Maracek, 1993).

The structure of this course is also typically objectivist in its focus on having students "memorize" categories that have been determined by experts. Learning categories in itself is not problematic, if the categories are understood as situated in a cultural context and if they are not reified nor universalized. We do not need to reject the idea of a diagnostic nomenclature in order to teach this course in a more inclusive, historically-sensitive fashion. Instead, we can analyze, contextualize, deconstruct, and re-construct what are commonly presented as "facts." Students who approach diagnosis from this more postmodern perspective are likely to gain a holistic understanding of their clients, and therefore to better counsel them.

In this chapter, attention will first be given to postmodern principles and to how these principles relate to the broad notions of diagnosis and treatment planning. Then, constructivist principles (McAuliffe & Lovell, 2000) will be more specifically applied to teaching the course.

In the constructivist spirit, the traditional term "treatment plan" will be replaced with the less pathologizing, and more constructivist term, "collaborative counseling plan." The word "diagnosis" will be replaced by the term "assessment" (Neimeyer, 1993), unless it specifically refers to the use of DSM diagnoses. Two reasons underlie this modification: (1) Postmodern philosophy asserts that meanings are historically situated and constructed and reconstructed through the medium of language (Gergen, 1985; Parker, Georgaca, Harper, McLaughlin, & Stowell-Smith, 1995; Rorty, 1979; Segal, 1986). (2) A constructivist approach points toward an evolving construction of the counseling plan, rather than a more structured, problem-saturated, predetermined plan, in working with clients (Hoyt, 1994).

APPLYING POSTMODERN THEORY TO ASSESSMENT
AND COLLABORATIVE COUNSELING PLAN DEVELOPMENT

So-called "postmodern thinkers" actively challenge scientific and positivist assumptions, and this has ramifications for assessment and collaborative counseling plan development. Postmodernists propose that knowledge is not a representation of facts existing in one static reality. They propose three concepts—social constructionism, contextualism, and deconstruction—that focus on the way meaning is represented, and that deny that a single meaning of reality exists. The interest in postmodern theories is part of a widespread skepticism toward the positivist tradition in science and related concretist, single-explanation theories of human behavior (Rorty, 1979; Segal, 1986). Instead, scholars propose the social constructionist notion that what people know is a "construction," or a hypothesis about reality, based on the socio-cultural and historical contexts within which they pursue knowledge (Watzlawick, 1984; Gergen, 1985). Evaluation of people's behavior should also then be considered historically situated.

Social constructionism emphasizes two primary ideas: 1) "knowledge" is constructed rather than discovered, and 2) knowledge construction is of a social nature (Bohan, 1995). This means that knowledge cannot be separated from its contexts; counselors are immersed in their own personal biases and experiences as well as their sociocultural milieu, and these impact what they know and how they come to know it (Bohan, 1995). Counselors' assessments and measures, the models used for searching, the questions asked in seeking knowledge, and the socio-political environment all affect counselors' creation of knowledge (Bohan, 1995). Further, knowledge gained is not equivalent to discovering "truth," but merely a "best guess, based on selective vision, using limited tools, shaped by the contextual forces surrounding the search" (Bohan, 1995, p. 8).

Thus, while the positivist diagnostician asks, "What are the facts?" social constructionism asks, "What are the assumptions?" While the positivist asks, "What are the answers?" social constructionists ask, "What are the questions?" Consider the following mental health illustration cited by Bohan (1995): During the turn of the century, mental health providers believed that women were incapable of engaging in serious intellectual endeavors and risked sterility if they pursued higher education. In our current socio-historical context, this seems ludicrous. At the time, the idea made "sense." In response to this historical fact, a social constructionist would ask, "What assumptions were guiding this line of inquiry and what and why were these questions being asked?"

Consider another example: Positivists label behavior as "dependent" whether it is engaged in by men or women. Such a perspective fails to consider social factors, access to resources, or societal power dynamics occurring within the culture or context. For instance, a woman who is a victim of domestic violence may exhibit muscle tension, irritability, and sleep disturbance and would meet the DSM-IV criteria for generalized anxiety disorder. A positivist or mechanistic view would assert that counseling should focus on alleviating anxiety using traditional means for doing so: medication management, individual relaxation training, and refutation of cognitions. Social constructionists would contend that the woman's individual and cultural contexts should be considered, focusing also on system change and the woman's safety. The question would at least be raised: In a context in which women are encouraged to defer to, and depend on males, should dependent behaviors be pathologized? They would ask, Where does one draw the line between "normal" dependency and "abnormal" dependency, particularly in a society that favors individualism and independence?

As another example, the positivist behavioral perspective considers anyone who avoids eye contact similarly, regardless of whether the person is, for instance, Asian American or European American. Yet clearly, the behavior means different things within these two cultures. Social constructionists propose that without considering sociocultural contexts, comparisons between social identity groups are irrelevant. Social constructionists would account for the different meanings of behavior within different cultures.

Postmodernism is one impulse behind challenges to diagnosing clients. Social constructionists have asked other questions, such as, "To what extent are diagnoses a means of social control, ensuring conformity to the interests of those in power, and denying the connection between social inequities and psychological distress?" (Marecek & Hare-Mustin, 1991, p. 525). Maracek (1993) notes that key contextual issues, such as those involving sex differences, gender roles, cultural issues, and context-related issues such as domestic violence and sexual abuse, are virtually unmentioned in the vast catalog of books that deal with diagnosis and treatment planning. Individuals aren't considered within their socio-political-cultural milieu, but are labeled and considered to have diseases within themselves, separate from their environments (Parker et al., 1995). Counseling students need to understand that many of the most debilitating diagnoses, such as schizophrenia, anorexia/bulimia, and alcoholism have well-documented differences from one culture to another and from one different historical time period to another.

In challenging traditional, mechanistic treatment ideas, social constructionists question commonly held assumptions. Because questions and assumptions are different, different realities and meanings of behavior emerge. Students benefit from considering these questions and from accounting for the context and consequences of various diagnostic labels.

Why Teach the DSM At All?

In the United States, the DSM provides the diagnostic system used for communicating among professionals and obtaining reimbursements. The DSM is used as a way of organizing client behaviors and determining what services clients need. It is one way to make meaning of clients' presenting concerns. Although from a social constructionist perspective the DSM-IV has many limitations, almost all counseling settings where community counselors work require a DSM-IV diagnosis for reimbursement of services (hospitals, community mental health, and residential settings). When used flexibly, the DSM can provide clues for the counselor to explore. Its Axes Four and Five can also tune the counselor in to situations and life contexts related to specific diagnoses. The DSM can thus be useful to and is certainly a necessity for professional practice.

My goal in teaching this course is to help students understand diagnosis from a postmodern perspective and be able to develop a collaborative assessment, but to also help them obtain the skills necessary to use the DSM and develop multi-axial diagnoses. I particularly emphasize how Axis Four psycho-social stressors affect Axis One and Two diagnoses.

In summary, the postmodern movement has challenged traditional ways of knowing and standard ways of thinking about assessment and counseling. While singleminded diagnosis and overly-structured treatment plans are antithetical to postmodern philosophies, necessity dictates that clinical counselors be trained to use the DSM and have the skills necessary to develop structured, documented plans in working with clients. The best resolution to the discrepancy between a postmodern perspective and the demands and expectations of the mental health field, is to help counselors find a balance between the abuses of traditional clinical practice and a postmodern skepticism.

APPLYING CONSTRUCTIVIST PRINCIPLES TO TEACHING CLIENT ASSESSMENT AND PLANNING

In addition to challenging traditional notions of assessment and collaborative counseling plan development, the postmodern perspective challenges counselor educators to use reflexive, inclusive, context-sensitive classroom methods. Constructivist (which will here be used interchangeably with postmodern) classroom techniques parallel students' actual work with clients. The course, as I have designed it, is largely experiential and incorporates the constructivist educational principles outlined by McAuliffe and Lovell (2000).

Varying Course Structure

Diversity in materials and methods. The constructivist perspective recognizes the importance of using "a diversity of materials and methods" (McAuliffe & Lovell, 2000, p. 26). Students differ in preferences and styles. The use of varying structures and teaching styles both matches students' styles and challenges them to use new styles of learning. Additionally, heterogeneous learning experiences may better hold students' attention and may reach and challenge students at different levels of cognitive development (Kegan, 1994; McNamara, Scott, and Bess, 2000). I mix teaching styles by combining brief lectures along with experiential activities, such as group discussions, role plays, small group activities, writing assignments, and guest speakers.

Alternative views of diagnoses and their contexts exist in other articles and books besides the DSM, and I use these to provide students with a broader understanding, thus breaking the "textbook and DSM" habit (Marecek, 1993). Using materials that express contradictory views makes students aware of the controversies surrounding the issue of diagnosis and challenges them to think for themselves. As an example, Parker et al. (1995), in *Deconstructing Psychopathology*, dispute the categorization and individualization of mental disorders and contend that diagnoses are not descriptive of "reality out there" but are constitutive. Thus they claim that the existence of diagnostic categories actually creates diagnoses.

In addition, articles that review the contextual correlates of those with various DSM diagnoses encourage students to complement the traditional individualized medical model with context. For example, instructors might choose an article about a trauma survivor that considers multiple factors before choosing a post-traumatic stress disorder diagnosis over a border-line personality disorder diagnosis or a dissociative identity disorder diagnosis. It is worth noting that the PTSD diagnosis considers developmental trauma reactions and is a less stigmatizing diagnosis. Instructors might also choose Broverman, Broverman, Clarkson, Rosenkrantz, and Vogel's (1970) classic piece, in which mental health professionals considered "normal" feminine characteristics more negatively and pathologically. Articles that discuss DSM-IV diagnoses as normal developmental reactions to stress can also provide an alternative viewpoint.

Diverse materials also open up the discussions of "treatment" planning. When considering how to develop collaborative counseling plans, instructors might use at least two types of "texts:" (1) a traditional treatment planning book that emphasizes concrete cognitive-behavioral and insight oriented interventions (Jongsman and Peterson, 1999), and (2) various articles or books that describe narrative or solution-oriented interventions and focus on client strengths (Hoyt, 1994). Again, using a variety of materials communicates to students that many approaches exist to working with clients.

Encouraging students' construction of their educational experience. I provide more structure early in the course, and as students develop cohesion and comfort with the course material, I become less structured. As the course progresses, I encourage students to actively assist in constructing the course by asking them questions such as: "Which topic or issues would you like to focus on today?" and "How would you like to go about processing this topic?" I sometimes introduce a card sort activity to encourage student involvement in constructing course goals and methods. (See Eriksen, Uellendahl, & Blacher, 2001, for specifics on this activity.) Here the students break into small groups and brainstorm a list of needs and desires for the remainder of the course. This flexible, relatively open approach challenges students to rely on their judgment and to determine what matters to them in the learning and meaning-making process. With the realization that they are active creators of knowledge, students develop the ability to reflect on others' knowledge (for example: in textbooks and in the DSM itself) and recognize it as created, not static or absolute.

Personalizing Teaching

In counseling, a premium is placed on the continual maintenance and development of the counseling relationship. While the teacher-student relationship is less intimate than the one between counselor and client where the former has an evaluative component, I still place a strong emphasis on building relationships with students. I try to remember names, know what students' personal goals are for the class, and know about their identities and professional experiences outside of class. At the beginning of the class, students answer a list of questions about their class goals, professional goals and experiences, and interests, and ways they enjoy learning :"visual," "auditory," and "experiential." Students share this information with class members. I make a point of learning these preferences so that I can pull class members' experiences and interests into the course when relevant. These attempts contribute to a sense of connectedness with students and create an environment in which students feel safe to do the work of socially creating meaning.

Additionally, building a "community" (McAuliffe & Lovell, 2000) emerges from encouraging and engaging difference and from emphasizing dialogue and interaction. To build community, I structure the class so that members sit in a circle facing each other. I encourage students to exchange ideas and concerns among themselves. As a facilitator, I display openness and genuine interest in all comments, even if they are divergent from mine. I encourage different opinions and thoughts; I consider such differences to be ripe opportunities for challenging my own and the students' ways of knowing. I encourage and reinforce this kind of risk-taking.

Also, consistent with personalizing teaching and building relationships, I disclose personal experiences from my work in various clinical settings. I share what different clients have taught me. I share the ambiguities and practical problems associated with various diagnoses and "treatments." I reveal my continuing struggle with many of the issues and concerns presented in class by students.

Further, I ask students to personalize their learning by applying class experiences to themselves (Schutz, Drogosz, White, and Distefano, 1999). Many students or their friends or family have been diagnosed or have been in counseling. Class members share what these encounters were like for them, if they feel comfortable in doing so. In one class, a student discussed her experience of being diagnosed with anorexia as a teenager and how that diagnosis and subsequent treatment, in her opinion, had further exacerbated her struggles. The class found her disclosure to be very interesting and reported many resulting shifts in their thinking.

Valuing and Promoting Experiences

Experiential learning has been described as "grounding concepts in personal life experience, illustrations, and experiments" (McAuliffe, 2000). In other words, experiential learning focuses on "saying *and* doing" (Dale, 1969) and active student meaning-making, as opposed viewing students as passive recipients. In addition to the activities already discussed, the following practices accentuate experience in this course: (1) interactive interviews and guest speakers, (2) historic illustrations, and (3) role plays.

Interviews and guest speakers. Students benefit from meeting people who are currently in some type of counseling (for example: a person diagnosed with PTSD who is participating in counseling at a rape crisis center). The instructor and the students might have access to people, such as friends and former clients, who would be able and willing speak with the class. The opportunity to hear people talk about their counseling experiences is typically fascinating to most students and provides a means of individualizing diagnoses.

However, due to the importance of confidentiality, it may be difficult to arrange this type of experience. It may be more feasible to have students invite several counselors from various mental health agencies to class. Such agencies might include an adolescent residential facility, a community mental health agency, a rape crisis center, or a private practice. I ask the counselors and guest speakers to talk about their work with clients who meet the criteria for one particular DSM diagnostic category or one pre-senting issue (for example, diagnoses and interventions with trauma sur-vivors). Speakers discuss practical and logistical issues associated with di-agnoses and treatment planning—perspectives that are not typically pre-sented in text books and so must be learned on the job.

Historic illustrations. Specific historical practices in diagnosis and treat-ment reveal much that abstractions cannot. Therefore, I invite students to discuss controversial treatments in the service of illustrating that "treat-ment" has been socially created in different contexts. Many "treatments" throughout history have been abused by persons in power and have served to victimize people (Parker, et al., 1995). For instance, in the late 19th cen-tury, Dr. S. Weir Mitchell garnered praise for his treatment of female neur-asthenia patients (those with fatigue, loss of energy and memory, and feel-ings of inadequacy), treatment that involved overfeeding the women pa-tients and depriving them of intellectual and social stimulation. At the same time, Dr. Isaac Baker Brown advocated and practiced clitoridectomy as a cure for female masturbation. He contended that the fragile women of the upper class could not survive masturbation and would succumb to idiocy and eventually death if they practiced it (Maracek, 1993). These examples provide for a rich discussion about how values, society, and history affect assumptions about how to best counsel clients.

Another lively class discussion emerges when I share the following in-formation: At one point, the DSM labeled gays and lesbians as "mentally ill." However, this designation was eventually dropped from the DSM-III. More recently, diagnoses such as paraphilic rapism, self-defeating person-ality disorder, and premenstrual syndrome were proposed for inclusion in the DSM-IV. Much debate ensued and these proposed "disorders" were not actually included in the DSM-IV (Marecek & Hare-Mustin, 1991). From this revelation emerges a discussion of what is and isn't labeled as "abnormal" behavior such as, self-defeating personality disorder and premenstrual syndrome, as well as the implications of labeling certain behaviors as "disorders" (such as, paraphilic rapism, or recurrent, intense sexual urges, fantasies, or behaviors related to rape).

Role plays. Role plays may also contribute to students' knowledge of assessment and collaborative counseling plan development. I ask students to role play presenting problems with class members and ask their partners to try to identify the DSM category that is being portrayed. In addition, they develop a collaborative counseling plan together. During plan development, they practice their listening skills and other counseling techniques, and they actively include the pseudo-clients in the process. I also ask students to tune into their own pathologizing or, conversely, normalizing of client issues, and to deconstruct their assumptions. Following role plays, students process what it was like to be the counselor and the client and discuss the challenges of applying diagnoses and working within the client's reality.

Emphasizing Multiple Perspectives

I encourage students' cognitive development through bringing in multiple perspectives on different issues. For example, I present the case of a female Puerto Rican client who initially reports experiences characteristic of depression and anxiety, and who has been subject to violence within her marriage for many years. Students at lower stages of development and "concrete, authority-reliant thinkers" (Lovell & McAuliffe, 1997) tend to contend that the client "is" dysthymic and "has" generalized anxiety, and that a goal of counseling should be for her to decrease these symptoms through counselor-generated "treatment." Students who think more constructivistically consider broader, more contextual, and less rigid possibilities. Maybe the client has PTSD secondary to the sustained violence. Perhaps the client should be encouraged to leave or radically change her relationship with her husband. A constructivist thinker would be able to consider a variety of contextual issues simultaneously. Maybe the client doesn't want to leave her husband; maybe she is safer staying with her husband; maybe the client has PTSD along with another primary diagnosis; maybe there are cultural issues contributing to the family violence.

Constructivist instructors use their counseling skills to encourage students to process how they might be changing their world views as a result of discussing such cases, and how the class is personally affecting them. Helping students to hear and respect differing experiences in the course encourages a level of tolerance and openness to other views. I attempt to model openness to various viewpoints and experiences. I try to demonstrate comfort with ambiguity and take a "not knowing" stance on various issues.

Debates. Taking multiple perspectives can also be encouraged through debates. Debates direct students, particularly students who are "multiplistic" or "subjectivistic" (in between fully non-constructivist and constructivist thinking; McAuliffe & Lovell, 2000), to carefully evaluate the usefulness of particular methods in different situations. If handled and processed thoroughly and productively, debates can reduce dualistic thinking (See Eriksen, Uellendahl, & Blacher, 2001 for specifics about conducting debates). Debate topics might include such controversies as:

- Mental disorders are located within the individual vs. mental disorders are located within society.
- Abnormal behavior can be differentiated form normal behavior vs. abnormal behavior can not be distinguished from normal behavior (See Parker et al., 1995, for a more thorough review of additional polar oppositions).
- Do diagnostic labels hinder the effective treatment of persons with mental disorders?
- Sexism and psychiatry: Do women really have higher rates of psychopathology (Slife, 2000)?
- Are we over-diagnosing certain disorders, such as attention deficit hyper-activity disorder?

Deconstructing language. Deconstruction refers to the process of taking apart meanings by examining their context (Combs & Freedman, 1994; White and Epston, 1990). Deconstructive listening contributes to both the classroom experience and the assessment process. Listening "deconstructively" requires counselors to believe that people's stories can have many possible meanings, and that the meaning the listener makes may not be what the speaker intended. Instructors and counselors develop a "not-knowing" attitude in order to encourage the discussion of possible meanings. Deconstructive listening, by definition, requires openness to multiple perspectives.

I ask students to consciously practice deconstruction in diagnostic interviews. Clients frequently come to us saying that they are "depressed," "obsessive," or "codependent." A constructivist counselor helps such clients deconstruct these labels by finding out what they mean to clients, rather than imposing the counselor's own meanings of such words.

Encouraging Intrapersonal Process Awareness

Thinking about thinking, or "metacognition," is critical to developing reflective constructivist thinkers. Videos, case studies, and instructor immediacy may encourage metacognitive thought.

Videos. In numerous videos, actor-clients who meet the DSM criteria for various diagnoses, present their "symptoms." I ask students to use Interpersonal Process Recall (Kagan, 1980) to discuss what they are thinking at various points in the tape. Metacognition is encouraged when instructors further ask students to think about their thinking, asking such questions as: "Why were you thinking that?" "Where does such thinking come from?" And, "What does such thinking tell you about yourself?"

Similarly, students can make tapes of role-played counseling sessions. They can then share their thoughts on what they were thinking and why during particular sections of the tape. To ensure that students don't forget what they were thinking or change their responses from their immediate reactions, students can stop the tape during the session and write down their thoughts. This technique helps them to be more aware of their automatic thoughts, hence encourages awareness of biases and increases reflectivity. They can then process automatic thoughts with the class. Students also benefit from hearing other students' thought processes in response to the same information and situation.

Case studies. Responding to case studies interactively also encourages awareness of multiple perspectives, experiential learning, and metacognition. Case studies can be used similarly to videos as a means of encouraging metacognition (see Eriksen, Uellendahl, & Blacher, 2001, for specifics). I use case examples from own work with clients and incorporate what my clients have taught me. Students either develop their own case studies for the class or the instructor provides a case study. I ask students to construct a diagnosis and possible collaborative counseling plan goals and to process their thoughts on the case with regard to various diagnoses and counseling strategies. I encourage students to brainstorm and to not monitor their thoughts, in an attempt to help them become more aware of what their immediate thoughts are.

After initially processing the cases, I add a contextual issue that was not initially mentioned, and a new discussion ensues. I again ask students to think about their thinking: for instance, what it means that they changed their diagnosis when different contextual information was added. This activity helps students to solidify the importance of context and challenges students to consider the course material in new ways.

WRITING ACTIVITIES

Consistent with constructivist theories of assessment, I emphasize qualitative evaluation methods, such as writing assignments, in which students learn even as they demonstrate their learning (Neimeyer, 1993). This type of writing serves a number of purposes, one of which is to personalize the learning. Writing assignments also provide an opportunity for active knowledge creation and student reflectivity between class sessions. It also acts as a catalyst for class discussions and co-creation of meaning in the social setting.

Writing assignments can be useful in helping students to understand that diagnoses are invented and not discovered (Parker, et al., 1995). When students consider the myriad of changes from version to version of the DSM and the fads and fashions that affect diagnosing, they see that diagnoses are constantly changing. For instance, Maracek (1993) points out that diagnoses such as hysteria, nymphomania, erotomania, and machoism have served to enforce culturally sanctioned ideas of female subordination to men's sexual desires, and have, over the years, changed in response to societal pressure (Maracek, 1993). Students who read such material begin to question diagnoses. Questions such as the following need to be asked: "How is the boundary drawn between disorder, on one hand, and eccentricity and/or crime on the other?" "What kinds of circumstances surround the death of some diagnoses and the birth of others?" What social contexts correlate with different diagnoses?" "Where does one draw the line between normal adaptation to stress and pathology (Parker, et al., 1995)?" I ask students to respond to such questions in a series of writing assignments.

We process students' responses as a class. Because students typically differ in their ideas about normal versus abnormal behavior, a microcosm of society is formed within the classroom. That is, students begin to see that the line between normal and abnormal behavior is not as easily drawn as many might think.

Students respond to several other questions in writing. For instance, "What is your theory on how people change and what role do you believe you play in this change process?" "List five beliefs you have about the counseling and client change process." "How can it be helpful and/or harmful to share client diagnoses with clients?" "How can you use diagnoses with clients in ways that are empowering and not reinforcing of client stories of being pathological?" And, "What are five ways you can actively involve clients in the development of a collaborative counseling plan?"

In other writing assignments, I ask students to create lists of five things in their assigned readings that were confusing, surprising, interesting, or brought up cognitive dissonance or emotions. I ask them for a list of five differences and similarities between particular diagnoses or "treatments." Students write about how they will improve their strategies for collaborative assessment and collaborative counseling planning.

Such writing assignments encourage reflective thinking and integration of the course material. Each week I call on a different student to process his or her list with the class. The students' lists provide a source of discussion and meaning making within the class and encourage further development of cohesion among students. Calling on one person each week also provides enough external structure to encourage students to reflect on the material during the week.

Another writing assignment asks students to trace the development of a diagnosis through various editions of the DSM in order to understand the contextual issues associated with diagnoses.

In another writing assignment, students research the relationship between a particular diagnosis and the socio-political-cultural milieu or the life experiences that may be related to the diagnoses. For example, anorexia nervosa, in the United States, has most commonly been diagnosed in young European-American females during the late twentieth-century. However, the demographics of this diagnosis appear to be changing and a discussion of these changes and contexts helps to expand students' ways of knowing beyond the typical perception that only certain people "get" certain "diseases" or diagnoses.

Students also participate in an in-class writing activity in which they develop a collaborative counseling plan based on a case study. They then break into small groups and process and give feedback on each other's plans.

The final paper. Throughout the class, I ask students to be considering their final paper. In this paper students consolidate their thoughts and assumptions about diagnosis, collaborative assessment, and developing collaborative counseling plans with clients. Students draw from experiences (for example, panel discussions, interviews) that they have had while in the class. Students also incorporate into their papers what they have learned in previous writing assignments. The assignment for the paper is as follows:

"Write a paper about a pseudoclient (may be a character from a movie, or book, or someone you know, etc.). In the paper, apply a DSM-IV diagnosis and outline and develop a collaborative counseling plan. The paper should be no more than twenty pages in length and should be written in APA style.

Please consider the following questions in writing your paper:

1. In what ways does your client conform to specified DSM criteria? What is your client's assessment of the presenting concerns?

2. In what ways does your client differ from the DSM criterion?

3. How might the client's cultural background/sexual orientation affect his or her diagnosis and collaborative counseling plan?

4. What historical-social-political-cultural issues do you need to consider before applying this diagnosis?

5. How does the client's gender affect his or her diagnosis and collaborative counseling plan?

6. What strengths does the client have that can be integrated into the collaborative counseling plan?

7. What specific needs does the client perceive he or she has and what specific goals would the client like to have incorporated into the collaborative counseling plan?

8. How would you integrate the client's goals with your goals as the counselor?

9. What theory or approach will help the client in reach his/her goals and objectives?

10. What is your theory of change and how would you assist your client to change?

11. How would you regularly evaluate, with the client, whether the collaborative counseling plan goals were being achieved and if the means of achieving the goals was satisfactory to the client?"

This final paper helps students pull together new meanings and gives structure to their emerging thoughts. Students share their experiences in writing the paper with the class.

CONCLUSION

Many challenges exist in teaching diagnosis and treatment planning from a postmodern perspective. It requires a comfort with ambiguity and an ability to tolerate taking a non-expert role. It requires a constant ability to reflect on the process of the class and to be attentive to student needs. Finally, it requires instructors to take a non-traditional stance, to challenge the status quo.

I believe that teaching this course using postmodern perspectives facilitates students' personal constructive-developmental growth and better enables students to develop into professional counselors. A former student stated, after reflecting on her counselor training, that she had realized that through this course she had developed a respect for her clients, their life situations, and their strengths. She discussed how, in her clinical practice, a context and strengths perspective differentiated her from many of her colleagues in other professions. She felt proud to be a counselor and to have a clear identity. In teaching this course, my intent is to provide opportunities for exactly what this student described: to encourage contextual, social constructionist, and deconstructive practices, while helping students develop their identities and grow and develop personally.

A postmodern perspective contributes to achieving a professional identity just at the time of their lives when counseling students are struggling to do so. If we teach a traditional diagnoses and treatment course, one which focuses on pathology apart from context, we contradict counseling's emphasis on normal growth and development and strength-based approaches. I propose that we be consistent with the counseling identity by instructing a course on diagnoses and treatment planning from a postmodern perspective.

REFERENCES

American Psychiatric Association. (1994). *Diagnostic and statistical manual of mental disorders* (4th ed.; DSM-IV). Washington, DC: Author.

Bohan, J. S. (1995). *Re-placing women in psychology: Readings toward a more inclusive history,* (2nd ed.). Dubuque, IA: Kendall/Hunt Publishing Company.

Broverman, I. K., Broverman, D. M., Clarkson, F. E., Rosenkrantz, P. S., & Vogel, S. R. (1970). "Sex-role stereotypes and clinical judgements of mental health." *Journal of Consulting and Clinical Psychology, 34,* 1-7.

Combs, G., & Freedman, J. (1994). Narrative intentions. In M. F. Hoyt's, editor, *Constructive therapies,* (pp. 67-91). New York: Guilford Press.

Dale, E. (1969). *Audio-visual methods in teaching.* New York: Holt, Rinehart, and Winston.

Eriksen, K., Uellendahl, G., & Blacher, J. (2001 in press). *In class group activities.* In G. J. McAuliffe and Karen Eriksen, *Strategies Teaching for Constructivist and Developmental Counselor Education.* Westport, CT: Greenwood Publishing Group.

Gergen, K. J. (1985). The social constructionist movement in psychology. *American Psychologist, 40,* 266-275.

Hoyt, M. F. (Ed.). (1994). *Constructive therapies.* New York: Guilford Press.

Jongsman, A. E., & Peterson, L. M. (1999). *The complete adult psychotherapy treatment planner.* New York: John Wiley and Sons.

Kagan, N. (1980). *Interpersonal process recall.* East Lansing, MI: author.

Kegan, R. (1994). *In over our heads: The mental demands of modern life.* Cambridge: Harvard University Press.

Lovell, C., & McAuliffe, G. (1997). Principles of constructivist training and education. In T. L. Sexton and B. L. Griffin, (Eds.), *Constructivist thinking in counseling practice, research, and training,* (pp. 211-227). New York: College Teachers Press.

Maracek, J. (1993). Disappearances, silences, and anxious rhetoric: Gender in abnormal psychology textbooks. *Journal of Theoretical and Philosophical Psychology, 13,* 115-123.

Marecek, J., & Hare-Mustin, R. T. (1991). A short history of the future: Feminism and clinical psychology. *Psychology of Women Quarterly, 15,* 521-536.

McAuliffe, G. (2000). How counselor education influences future helpers: What students say. In G. McAuliffe and K. Eriksen, (Eds.), *Preparing counselors and therapists: Creating constructivist and developmental programs,* (pp. 42-61). Alexandria, VA: Association for Counselor Education and Supervision.

McAuliffe, G., & Lovell, C. (2000). Encouraging transformation: Guidelines for constructivist and developmental instruction. In G. McAuliffe and K. Eriksen, editors, *Preparing counselors and therapists: Creating constructivist and developmental programs,* pp. 14-41. Alexandria, VA: Association for Counselor Education and Supervision.

McNamara, D. S., Scott, J., & Bess, T. (2000). Building blocks of knowledge: Cognitive foundations for constructivist counselor education. In G. McAuliffe and K.

Eriksen, (Eds.), *Preparing counselors and therapists: Creating constructivist and developmental programs*, (pp. 62-76). Alexandria, VA: Association for Counselor Education and Supervision.

Neimeyer, G. J., (Ed.). (1993). *Constructivist assessment: A casebook*. Newbury Park: Sage Publishers.

Parker, I., Georgaca, E., Harper, D., McLaughlin, T., & Stowell-Smith, M. (1995). *Deconstructing psychopathology*. London: Sage Publications.

Rorty, R. (1979). *Philosophy and the mirror of nature*. Princeton, NJ: Princeton University Press.

Schutz, P. A., Drogosz, L. M., White, V. E., & Distefano, C. (1999). Prior knowledge, attitude, and strategy use in a introduction to statistics course. *Learning and Individual Differences, 10*, 291-308.

Segal, L. (1986). *The dream of reality: Heinz von Foerster's constructivism*. New York: Norton.

Slife, B. (Ed.). (2000). Taking sides: *Clashing views on controversial psychological issues*. New York: Mc-Graw Hill Higher Education.

Watzlawick, P. (Ed.). (1984). *The invented reality: Contributions to constructivism*. New York: Norton.

White, M., & Epston, D. (1990). *Narrative means to a therapeutic ends*. New York: Norton.

12

Transformative Learning Experiences in Graduate Classes on Counseling Children and Adolescents

Ann Vernon and Toni R. Tollerud

In *To Kill A Mockingbird*, Addicus says to Scout, "If you learn a simple trick, Scout, you'll get along a lot better with all kinds of folks. You never really understand a person until you consider things from his [sic] point of view . . . until you climb into his skin and walk around in it" (Lee, 1962, p.113). As counselor educators, whose primary responsibility is to help students learn about counseling children and adolescents, we often use this quotation on the first day of class as a way of reminding future counselors that they have to step into the world of children and adolescents and see things from their perspective to have any hope of being successful with this age group. We then proceed to structure class sessions in a variety of creative ways that enable students to step "inside the skin" of children and adolescents.

This chapter identifies teaching strategies that prepare prospective counselors to work with children and adolescents. The ideas we present correspond to the principles of constructivist teaching, which in turn mirror many of the concepts proposed by Carl Rogers in 1969 in his pioneering work, *Freedom to Learn*. We wonder if we would need this discussion about transforming teaching and learning if Rogers' conditions for facilitating learning—"prizing the learner, prizing his feelings, his opinions, his person" (p. 109); stressing the importance of the learner taking responsibility for what he or she wants to achieve; valuing experiential learning; and encouraging inquiry—which all seemed revolutionary at the time, had been taken seriously: Perhaps these ideas didn't take hold because they were (and still are) such a radical departure from more traditional ways of teaching, in which the teacher was clearly in control of the learning environment and the focus was on content. Now, however, there seems to be renewed interest in learning that is student-centered, which also focuses on content; in teaching that recognizes the difference between the teacher as an expert and the teacher as a mediator who helps students discover what they need to know. As presented today, these constructivist teaching principles are more empirically grounded and developmentally-targeted than Rogers' ideas, and hopefully they will transform the way counselor educators teach.

In the following sections of this chapter we make specific suggestions for enhancing learning through McAuliffe and Lovell's (2000) five constructivist themes: (1) personalizing teaching through building a sense of community, (2) stimulating learning by varying the structure of the class, (3) emphasizing experiential learning, (4) encouraging exploration of multiple perspectives, and (5) encouraging intrapersonal process awareness and reflection.

PERSONALIZING TEACHING

One of the most fundamental ways of personalizing teaching is to create a climate of connectedness, or a sense of community in the classroom. We see this as a critical first step in establishing a classroom atmosphere conducive to learning, sharing, and reflecting. By involving students in establishing an environment where they are encouraged to share ideas, where diverse opinions are valued, and where learning can occur in a nonthreatening atmosphere, instructors may see both in-and out-of-class results. Such results include reduced absenteeism because students feel involved, and increased participation in class discussions and activities as students commit to this community of learners (Franken, Wells, & Vernon, 1983).

In courses on counseling children and adolescents, we build community while using concepts related to childhood and adolescence. We have successfully used the following class activities to promote interpersonal relationships, personal reflection, and sharing of experiences.

"Do You Remember When?"

This activity helps students to get acquainted and establish networks, as well as to begin reflecting about their own childhood and adolescence. The facilitator asks each student to imagine that the room represents a map of the United States. (The U.S. map can be extended to the world if the make-up of the class warrants this.) All students move to a spot on the map that corresponds to where they spent their early childhood, ages 4-5. Students then pair up with someone standing close to them and share a significant memory of what growing up was like in that location. Together the pair share their experiences with the total group for a few minutes.

Next, they move to a spot corresponding to where they lived (primarily) during middle childhood, ages 6-11. This time, they form a triad with the two people standing closest to them and share a significant memory from that period of development. Again, they report to the total group for a few minutes. They continue these procedures for the place where they spent their early adolescence, ages 11-14, and their mid-adolescence, ages 15-18.

Finally, the facilitator debriefs this activity by asking students to share how it felt to think about these memories, whether they were good or bad memories, and whether it was easier to think of memories for a particular period of development than for others.

"When I Was That Age . . . ."

A second activity for building community focuses on memories more specifically related to feelings and developmental issues. Divide students into four groups: early childhood, middle childhood, early adolescence, and mid-adolescence (subdivide if necessary to keep each group at approximately six students). Ask students to individually think about the following for their assigned developmental period and to privately record their responses on paper: Something they remember learning or mastering at this age; something they recall being anxious or afraid of; something they remember about their interactions with parents, teachers, or friends; and something they recall that was associated with feeling happy, excited, or proud. Next, invite them to share their responses within their small group. Debrief the activity with the total group by encouraging discussion about the specific items, what it was like to think about these issues, and which ones were the most difficult to identify. Engage students in a brief discussion about similar and different experiences expressed by those in the same developmental stage.

Other Community-Building Activities

Community building can be ongoing throughout the semester. One simple way to do this is to have a 5-minute "pair and share" session with a different partner each week. The topics can be generated by the class members and may relate to questions, concerns, observations and thoughts they have about counseling children and adolescents. Another community builder is to set up a list-serve and encourage informal dialogue among students and with the instructor by e-mail. The instructor or students can suggest specific topics and invite conversation. Emphasizing dialogue and interaction through small group work also enhances community building and personalization in the classroom.

VARYING THE STRUCTURE

The following anecdote illustrates the power of variety in the class-room. During one of my (Vernon) first years as a middle school counselor, a science teacher asked for help with some students who were inattentive, disruptive, and failing the course. It appeared that their problems resulted from their confusion and boredom. I am sure that the teacher wanted me to "fix" these problem students. However, I took a different approach. I asked for permission to observe in the classroom to get a better understanding of what was occurring. He reluctantly agreed, even though I am convinced he was suspicious about my motives. Luckily for me, he was desperate enough for help, even help that didn't come in the form he was expecting.

After I had observed his class several times, there was no doubt in my mind that if I were a young adolescent in that environment, I might be as disruptive and disaffected as these students were. Every day was the same: Students listened to a long lecture by a teacher who had very little ability to engage his students, and then they either discussed the chapter or worked on experiments. There was no variety in assignments, no small group work, and nothing to stimulate interest in the subject matter. Classroom rules, even though they weren't followed, were rigid and no personal relation-ship existed between the teacher and the individual students.

As I look back, I have to admire this teacher for allowing me to share some observations that were no doubt hard for him to hear. However, he agreed to participate with me in an experiment designed to increase par-ticipation in learning through varying the class structure. Over the year, I saw a "turned off" teacher develop energy and enthusiasm as we worked together to develop a sense of community among the students. We estab-lished teams and involved students in setting goals and designing their own methods of learning the content. The biggest transformation resulted from varying the structure of the class: No longer were students bored, because, from assignments to class activities, variety prevailed. Gradually students began to show enthusiasm, take responsibility for their own learn-ing, and work cooperatively with other students in achieving their goals. Dis-cipline problems decreased dramatically, communication among the teacher and students improved, and science was no longer a class students dreaded.

As has been discussed by McAuliffe and Lovell (2000), varying the struc-ture is an important cornerstone of the constructivist philosophy. Variety in assignments, classroom activities, and evaluation procedures may con-tribute to this goal. Students may increase their engagement when allowed to suggest assignments that would be meaningful for them, to give feed-back about class activities designed by the instructor, or to decide how they would like to learn a particular concept.

Since many college professors have never received training to teach at any level, they may not be aware that some of the same methods used by elementary and secondary teachers to stimulate interest in learning work at the college level as well. For example, in a college classroom, variety can also be key. Learners of all ages get bored if the weekly routine never varies and thus doesn't stimulate them. The following specific ideas have been used successfully to enhance learning by varying the in-class structure.

Setting the Stage for Learning

To help graduate students understand the importance of looking at children and adolescents as individuals and of developing their own style of counseling young clients, we use props such as the following: a bottle of window cleaner, paper towels, and a rag; a roll of toilet paper; and a sheet of paper and a tape recorder. First hold up the window cleaner, paper towel, and rag and ask how many of them prefer to wash windows using paper towels? Rags? Then display the toilet paper and ask how many put the toilet paper on the holder so that the paper rolls off the top? Off the bottom? Next, hold up the sheet of paper and a tape recorder, asking how many learn best by writing things down and how many by listening. Use this illustration to emphasize that everyone is an individual and that prospective counselors need to consider individual differences when counseling different children and adolescents.

Classroom instructors also need to accommodate differing learning styles and developmental stages when structuring learning experiences for graduate students. To facilitate this process, give each student an index card and ask for input on the following: "How do you learn best?" "How would you like the class to be structured?" "What kinds of learning experiences are most meaningful to you?" and "What do you think you can contribute to the class?" Have students share this information in small groups and then share key points with the instructor. Also, invite students to communicate with you periodically by phone, notes, or e-mail to share their reactions to class, what they might be struggling with, how things might be structured differently to optimize their learning, and what they are becoming aware of as a result of class activities.

Stimulus Activities

The following two learning activities help to vary the structure by providing vivid and concrete examples from which abstractions might be generated. One is the use of videotapes of popular films. For example, to introduce a lesson on the developmental characteristics of adolescents, I (Vernon) have used segments from several movies reflecting issues such as puberty (*Now and Then*), adolescent conflicts (*Pump Up the Volume*), intimate relationships (*Before and After*), and individuation and pressure from parents (*Dead Poets' Society*). This method not only helped illustrate the concepts in a very concrete way, but it also stimulated interest in the subject. Music may be used in a similar way. For instance, students might listen to the song "Father and Son" by Cat Stevens to identify developmental issues portrayed in the lyrics.

Another activity that helps stimulate interest in developmental issues is the *paper bag* activity. On the class period preceding this activity, we divide students into four groups: early childhood, middle childhood, early adolescence, and mid-adolescence. We ask each class member to bring an item they feel represents some developmental aspect of that age period. Examples of items might include, for adolescence, car keys or a college catalog to represent freedom and the future; for early adolescence, a mirror and a pack of cigarettes to represent preoccupation with appearance and experimentation; for middle childhood, a book and a scout badge to represent mastery and group participation; and for early childhood, a night light and a toy to represent fears and the importance of play.

At the next class period, we collect the items and put them into four bags, each of which correspond to the developmental periods. We redistribute the bags so that each group has a bag of items different from those they contributed. Students discuss how the items in the bag relate to the stated stage of development. They list their responses on poster paper and present them to the rest of the class.

Choosing from Alternatives

Since "one-size-fits-all" doesn't apply to how diverse graduate students learn, we offer a variety of instructional methods. We have found that some students learn best by doing, whereas others learn best by listening to a lecture or reading the material. Similarly, we offer a variety of ways for students to demonstrate what they have learned. We even allow students to design a unique approach for presenting what they have learned, as long as it meets with the approval of the instructor. The following assignment options have been developed specifically for courses in counseling children and adolescents.

- Interview two counselors who work with children and adolescents. Prior to your meeting, identify at least ten things you would like to ask them about counseling at this level. After you conduct the interviews, present your information in one of the following ways: by writing a report that summarizes the material, developing a board game which incorporates the learnings, or composing a poem or a short story that conveys the concepts.

- Select two of the following five topics: bibliotherapy, play, art, music, or writing. Find out more about the topics by reading at least three journal articles. Present your learnings by developing an activity based on the topic to present to a small group of classmates or by writing a short paper.

- Select a counseling theory and identify four interventions based on this theory which could be used effectively with children or adolescents. Present your learnings in one of the following ways: doing a short demonstration in class, illustrating the concepts through a skit or role play, or writing a paper and giving a short report on the intervention and how it is used.

- Select a topic or area of interest pertaining to counseling children and adolescents that was addressed during the course. As a small group, develop a creative way to present this information to the class. Examples might include skits, game shows, mock interviews, or talk shows. Presentations should be 15-20 minutes long.

- As a final project for the course, select a topic that is relevant to counseling children and adolescents and research it. Then imagine that the class members are participants at a conference and present your findings in a poster session, a formal presentation, or an experiential workshop.

Experiential Learning

The concept of experiential learning, or "learning by doing" was introduced by John Dewey and others (Stanford & Roark, 1974) and was advocated by the educational reformers of the late sixties and early seventies. Experiential learning "produces significant behavior change" (Stanford & Roark, 1974, p. 4), promotes retention of concepts, stimulates interest in the topic, and involves students in the learning process. Spolin (cited in Reed & Simon, 1975) contended that "we learn through experience and experiencing, and no one teaches us anything" (p. 371).

We wonder why college educators don't embrace this concept, and why so much of higher education is still dominated by traditional teaching methods. McAuliffe and Eriksen (2000) have explored some of the possible reasons for this condition. It might be because lecturing is easier; being creative, varying class structure, and designing alternative assignments can take a lot more time. Giving up the role of the "expert" may also be threatening to some college professors. In addition, giving students some of the responsibility for creating the learning environment sometimes generates anxiety in students who are used to a traditional structure where everything is "deposited" into them. However, based on our personal experience, we find teaching to be much more engaging for students and much more rewarding for us if we promote experiential learning. The following experiential learning ideas have been used in teaching graduate students about counseling children and adolescents.

Self-Esteem Fair

In this activity, students research and present to the class activities that promote self-esteem in children and adolescents. Each student selects a game, book, activity, or exercise and prepares a one to two page handout describing the specific objectives of the activity, the intended age level, the procedure, and the publication source. Or students may do the same with an activity they have created. In addition, each student decorates a space in the classroom with a poster illustrating the activity. The student brings props and activities that help demonstrate what they have described in the handout. Having balloons, music, and refreshments makes this a much more festive event!

During one class period, half of the class sets up to "present" and the other half of the class participates as attendees of the self-esteem fair. The attendees mill around the room, going from table to table to hear about the activities and to receive handouts. After attendees have visited each table (usually about an hour, depending on class size), the presenters become the attendees.

Following the fair, it is important to debrief the experience. Ask: "What did you learn?" "How can you use this information?" "Which ideas were the most helpful?" "How do you think these ideas will help children and adolescents increase their self-esteem?"

Counseling Young Clients

It is one thing to talk to students about how to counsel; it is a different story entirely for them to experience it, as Ivey (1994) and others have noted. In counseling courses, one common way to involve students in learning about counseling young clients is to have them role play a counseling session, with one student acting as a young client and another as the counselor. The rest of the class members observe. The instructor can distribute typical presenting problems for various age groups, such as friendship problems, difficulty getting along with parents, issues about school performance, or anxiety about new experiences. (Sample role play vignettes are included in the appendix.) After 15 minutes of the role play, the instructor stops the process and asks the client and the counselor to discuss what the experience was like for them. The instructor invites the observers to write both positive statements and constructive suggestions for improvement and gives these to the volunteer counselor.

A variation on this experience would be to divide the class into triads, with a client, a counselor, and observer in each group. This may decrease the anxiety that is often associated with counseling in front of an entire class.

Role playing can be an integral part of a skills course in child and adolescent counseling. However, once students have had a sufficient amount of laboratory/role playing experience in the classroom, they can further develop their skills by working with actual young clients. If there is no counseling clinic in your college, we suggest developing a partnership with local school counselors who will agree to supervise a university student as he or she practices counseling a child or an adolescent. The course instructor can write a letter to parents explaining the purpose of this activity and can include a form asking for permission for their child to be counseled by a student-in-training and for permission for the sessions to be audiotaped.

Our university students see their young clients for six sessions. After each weekly session they present their cases in class, either in small groups or in the total class, reporting on what they did, how the client responded, how they felt about the experience, and what feedback and suggestions they would like from other students and the instructor for future sessions. Three times during the semester, small groups of students play their tapes and receive feedback from the instructor or from the local counselors who have volunteered to be supervisors. By actually counseling young clients, students "learn by doing," following the philosophy of John Dewey, and they are able to improve their skills on the basis of feedback from their peers, practitioners, and the instructor.

"Learning It By Doing It" Activities

Especially in the counseling field, it is one thing to read something and know it "in our heads," but it is another thing to actually experience it. We believe that students learn best by doing, and we structure classroom learning experiences accordingly. Several examples follow:

Unfinished sentences. Instead of talking about how to use unfinished sentences in problem assessment and distributing a handout of examples, we discuss the concept, give several examples, and demonstrate it. Then we ask students to select a typical child or adolescent problem such as failing in school, relationships with parents, or feelings about friends, and write five sentences which correspond to the topic they selected. For example, if the topic selected was "Relationships with Parents," the following unfinished sentences might be developed:

> When I am with my mom, I feel . . . .
> When I am with my dad I feel . . . .
> My favorite thing to do with my parents . . . .
> If my parents and I disagree, it is about. . . .

After they have constructed their sentences, students choose a partner and take turns finishing each other's sentences, using the procedure that was demonstrated by the instructor.

Relaxation exercises. After a short discussion about the purpose and procedures involved in relaxation training, students work with a partner to develop a relaxation exercise for a high school student who is experiencing stress. After they have finished writing the script, the pair joins another partnership and take turns trying out their exercises on this small group.

Games. Share with the class several examples of commercial or self-developed board games which can be used therapeutically for a variety of different issues such as: feelings; self-esteem; behavior management; or situationally-specific issues like loss, divorce, or ADHD. Then invite students to get into small groups, select an age level and a topic, and develop a board game. After they have completed this task, have groups exchange games and play them.

Bibliotherapy. After discussing the concept of bibliotherapy and demonstrating how the process is used, give several examples of content questions (questions about the story) and personalization questions (questions that help them to apply the learnings personally). Then ask students to select their own topics and decide on a book that would appropriately address the topic. In partnerships, have students read their books and ask appropriate content and personalization questions.

After students have participated in these activities, it is important to engage them in a discussion about what they experienced, what they learned, and how they might use this procedure in their work with children and adolescents.

ENCOURAGING EXPLORATION OF MULTIPLE PERSPECTIVES

Encouraging the exploration of multiple perspectives is a key component of a constructivist teaching approach. Particularly in the counseling field, where there are few if any "absolutes," it is essential that we give voice to other perspectives and consider multiple viewpoints. However, it is sometimes easy for counselor educators to get "stuck" in thinking that there is "one right way" to counsel. For example, most counseling textbooks caution against self-disclosure and teach an "open" body posture that oftentimes doesn't look very natural. If students read these textbooks, they assume that this is "the only way" to counsel. In a recent discussion with students in a beginning counseling skills class, the topic of self-disclosure was raised. Students had read about it and had asked practitioners whom they were interviewing about their viewpoints on self-disclosure. Several students reported that their interviewees were adamantly opposed to self-disclosure, going so far as to say that when they had experienced this as a client, they were extremely uncomfortable. My (Vernon) students, who were new to the counseling field, were all nodding their heads in agreement that self-disclosure would always be a negative. Having just seen the movie *Good Will Hunting*, I encouraged students to consider an alternative perspective by watching how Robin Williams used self-disclosure and his own personal journey in his role as therapist in this movie. Certainly Williams defies some of our traditional notions about "good counseling," but what he does in the film nevertheless has a positive effect on the client. In courses on counseling children and adolescents, we invite students to consider multiple perspectives in several ways:

"What If"

Multiple perspectives can be enhanced in the classroom by building on some of the experiential learning activities previously described. For example, working in groups of six, one student can assume the role of counselor, another the client, and the rest the observers. After a 10-15-minute role play, invite the observers to give feedback to the counselor by saying, for example: "What do you suppose would have happened if you had pursued this adolescent's anger with her teacher instead of focusing on her school performance?" "What do you think would have happened if you had used role playing in the session?" These "what if" suggestions are given within a context of inquiry; they are not intended to be a judgment about what was or wasn't done. This activity has been very effective in helping students broaden their perspectives.

From This Perspective . . . .

To introduce this concept, you will need a pair of glasses, a sheet of yellow construction paper, and a sheet of gray construction paper. Cut two lenses out of each sheet of construction paper and then tape the yellow lenses to the glasses. Hold up these glasses and tell students that these glasses represent cheerfulness and hope, and that whatever problem they experience, they will see it from the perspective of cheerfulness and hope when they have on the yellow lensed glasses. Then inform them that a 15-page paper is due next week and will constitute 70 percent of their grade. Ask students to put on the yellow lensed glasses and share from the cheerfulness and hope perspective. Then tape the grey lenses to the glasses and indicate that these are the "doom and gloom" lenses; everything seems bad when they look through these lenses. Invite them to share their perspectives about the paper when they are looking at the situation through the grey lenses. Then discuss the concept of recognizing multiple perspectives and ask students to discuss about how race, gender, ethnic background, values, and social class impact work with children and adolescents. Distribute several short case scenarios to students in small groups (see Appendix). Invite group members to discuss how perspectives and counseling interventions would change relative to factors such as race, gender, ethnicity, values, or social class.

Round Robin

In another activity designed to encourage the understanding of multiple perspectives, a volunteer student assumes the role of a child or an adolescent client. Five other volunteers assume roles (on a rotating basis) as counselors. The client sits on a chair in the middle of a semi-circle, with the counselors sitting around him or her. The client begins discussing a typical child / adolescent problem with the first counselor, who works with the client for five minutes. After five minutes, the next counselor steps in, and so on, until all counselors have had an opportunity to counsel the client. The rest of the class members observe, noting the different approaches each counselor takes in working with this problem. For example, if the client was a depressed adolescent, one counselor might have the client discuss in detail events which may contribute to the depression, whereas another might ask for times when the client didn't feel depressed and what he or she could do to increase these times. After the role play, invite the counselors and the client to react, and then ask for observer feedback, emphasizing the differences in the way various counselors worked with the client.

ENCOURAGING INTRAPERSONAL AWARENESS

Patterson (1973), a pioneer in the field of humanistic education, strongly maintained that teaching focuses too much on "the teacher rather than the learner, on content rather than process" (p. 147). Educators who adopt a constructivist philosophy realize that they need to help students move from content to process in order to encourage intrapersonal process awareness. This is particularly critical in counselor education because "who a counselor is" is as important as what he or she does.

As noted in McAuliffe and Lovell (2000), monitoring one's thought processes is central to constructivist ideas. This "intrapersonal awareness" goes beyond simply reflecting about content or processing what occurred in an activity or role play scenario. It requires students to be aware of how they experienced a counseling session, a role play, or a simulation exercise. For example, a student may become aware of how intimidated she felt when counseling a belligerent adolescent and may reflect on what she was reacting to. As she thinks about herself, instead of focusing on the techniques she used or why the client was behaving in this manner, she increases her self-awareness.

We use journaling as one way to help students develop awareness of what they have experienced. Immediately after they have engaged in role plays or in actual counseling with young clients, we first ask them to write about what was going on with them as they were engaged in this activity. For example, were they bored? Stimulated? Too enmeshed in the client's problem? Did the problem tap into their own issues? We also suggest that they think about what the client might have been doing or saying that triggered that reaction, or what else might have been going on with them at the time. We allow time in class for students to share their reflections and we encourage discussion about their growing awareness of self-other issues in the counseling process. We encourage weekly journaling following both in-class and out-of class activities.

Students might also tape record what they became aware of as they were involved in a counseling session or an experiential activity as another way to increase awareness. Verbalizing into a tape recorder is especially effective for learners who are more auditory than visual and is oftentimes more spontaneous and natural than writing. We find that they tape record their reflections in an almost "stream of consciousness" manner, talking at random about what they have experienced, and asking themselves questions to help develop greater awareness. For example, they might ask themselves what pushed their buttons during the activity or session, what feelings they experienced, or what was it like to engage in this process.

CONCLUSION

As counselor educators, we try to practice what we preach: learning through doing. We believe that learning happens best if there is a sense of community in the classroom, characterized by a sense of trust and authentic interaction among students themselves and between students and the instructor. We believe that the teacher is a facilitator of learning; it is our job to co-create a stimulating environment, an environment that students want to be in because they are excited about what happens there. We believe that significant learning takes place when students feel that the content is relevant and that they have had some voice in determining what they want to learn and how they want to learn it. We believe that students learn best when they self-evaluate, reflect on their own processes, and set their own goals.

These ideas are not new. The educational reformers of the 1920's and 30's, as well as the 60's and 70's, had ideas that parallel many of the concepts presented in this book on constructivist teaching. It is our hope that this time around we can more effectively transform teaching and learning so that counselors are fully prepared to be reflective practitioners.

Appendix

Role Play Vignettes

1. Danielle is a sophomore who doesn't get along with her parents. One minute she is affectionate and the next minute she is hostile and defiant. She claims they "never" let her do anything.

2. Damien is a 5th grader who gets into fights on the playground when he doesn't get his way or when others refuse to play with him.

3. Kayla is a kindergartner who is having trouble getting to sleep at night because she is afraid there are monsters in her room.

4. Carmen is an eighth grader who is constantly upset because her friends don't include her in their activities.

Case Scenarios

1. Anna is a 16-year-old Latina who has just discovered she is pregnant. What perspectives do you need to consider in working with her on this issue?

2. Antonio's mother is coming in to discuss a resource room placement. What perspectives do you need to consider in meeting with her about this issue?

3. Sonja doesn't know what she wants to do next year after she graduates. She is a very bright student from a working class family. What perspectives do you need to consider in working with her on this issue?

4. Thad got picked up for stealing. His father, a fundamentalist minister, is coming in with Thad to talk with you. What perspectives do you need to consider when working with them?

REFERENCES

Franken, M., Wells. J., & Vernon, A. (1983). Creating community: Transforming a college classroom. Unpublished manuscript.

Ivy, A. E. (1994). *Intentional interviewing and counseling.* Pacific Grove, CA: Brooks Cole.

Lee, H. (1962). *To kill a mockingbird.* New York: Fawatt Popular Library.

McAuliffe, G. J., & Eriksen, K. P. (2000).Implementing constructivist counselor education: Pushing the zone of proximal development. In McAuliffe, G., Eriksen, K., & Associates. *Preparing counselors and therapists: Creating constructivist and developmental programs,* (pp. 196-217). Alexandria, VA: Association for Counselor Education and Supervision.

McAuliffe, G. J., & Lovell, C. W. (2000). Encouraging transformation: Guidelines for constructivist and developmental instruction. In G. McAuliffe, K. Eriksen, & Associates. *Preparing counselors and therapists: Creating constructivist and developmental programs,* (pp. 14-41). Alexandria, VA: Association for Counselor Education and Supervision.

Patterson, C. H. (1973). *Humanistic education.* Englewood Cliffs, NJ: Prentice Hall.

Reed, D. A., & Simon, S. B. (1975). *Humanistic education sourcebook.* Englewood Cliffs, NJ: Prentice Hall.

Rogers, C. R. (1969). *Freedom to learn.* Columbus, OH: Charles E. Merrill.

Stanford, G., & Roark, A. E. (1974). *Human interaction in education.* Boston, MA: Allyn & Bacon.

13

Family Counseling Training and the Constructivist Classroom

Thomas Russo

The broad swath of constructivism is currently working its way through some long-held assumptions in the mental health fields. The idea that knowledge and understanding are essentially individual cognitive events is being replaced with the social constructionist idea that knowledge and understanding inevitably take place in a social, interactional context. We no longer single-mindedly view the positivist empirical method as the path to unifying answers and to solutions to personal and social problems. We are now more aware than ever that there are multiple world views and therefore multiple solutions. The notion that knowledge and understanding must come about as a result of a strict inferential process of reasoning is being complemented by a practice and research methodology in which narrative, storytelling, and inductive reasoning. Nowhere has the importance of context, multiple perspectives, and alternative ways of knowing been more apparent than in the field of family counseling.

This chapter introduces a course in family counseling and consultation taught from a constructivist perspective. I focus on applying constructivist concepts to pedagogical practices for a single, stand alone course in family counseling and consultation. First, a brief summary points to the ways in which social constructionist thought and practice are impacting the field of family counseling and therapy. I draw some constructivism-based connections among theories and training in family therapy. Lastly, I describe several active classroom strategies that reflect the constructivist teaching guidelines discussed in McAuliffe and Lovell (2000).

SOCIAL CONSTRUCTIONISM AND MULTIPLE VOICES

The changes brought about by social constructionist perspectives are relatively new to counseling and psychology. However, we hear beginning echoes of such perspectives as early as the writings of Gordon Allport (1937). Allport distinguished between nomothetic (quantitative) and idiographic (qualitative) approaches to constructing knowledge. The nomothetic approach champions a singular viewpoint that can be supported by experimentally testing and generalizing about the nature of, in our case, the family. In family theory and practice, this process led directly to advocating a single preferred structure for the family unit (Whitehead, 1993) and interventions that promoted this abstract family configuration of biological mother, father, and offspring. Other "voices" and family structures, such as single parent families and gay and lesbian families, were considered less than optimal, or even dysfunctional, by their very deviation from the generalized and abstract model.

Stephanie Coontz (1995) challenged Whitehead's "preferred structure" as too narrowly defined. She instead emphasized the viability of various family structures for providing the support necessary for raising healthy and productive children. The danger inherent in the nomothetic approach, as she and others indicated, is that traditional, culture-bound family structures come to occupy a privileged place in society, to the exclusion of workable alternative arrangements.

Conversely, the idiographic approaches first described by Allport (1937), and more recently emphasized by social constructionists, make a much different claim. The idiographic methodology seeks out multiple, unique, and often marginalized voices and uses dialogue and conversational means to arrive at a fuller understanding of family life. This approach to counseling theory and practice raises and addresses important social, political, and ethical questions. Gergen (1985) suggests that the constructivist approach brings together, for the first time, the voices of history, culture, gender, and setting.

For the counselor educator who teaches family counseling and therapy, this constructivist inclination might mean beginning the course with an interdisciplinary discussion that includes family social history (Demos, 1986) and family demography and sociology (Stacy, 1991). Historians and sociologists have discussed at some length the evolution of family life in America, from the patriarchal society of Puritan New England, to the arrival of Africans and immigrant groups, to the rise of the modern family during the industrial nineteenth and early twentieth centuries, to the multiple ethnic and class varieties of family, and to the current changing family of our own postindustrial, technological times. The social constructionist approach suggests that we might understand families through exploring historical records, such as diaries, memoirs, letters, and short fiction, as well as other forms of first person narrative accounts. Gergen (1985) further states that such an endeavor requires collaboration and cooperation " . . . between psychologists and like-minded colleagues in sociology, anthropology, history, philosophy, and literary studies" (p. 273). Constructivist inquiry requires a "thick," detailed, and rich description of the family. It treats time, gender, ethnicity, and social class as principal organizing factors.

As constructivist educators, researchers, and counselors, we need to listen closely to the stories of family members. Quantitative methods of inquiry are not hereby replaced, but become another "type of story" (Howard, 1991). While the traditional, empirical approach adopted from the physical sciences can provide valuable insights about controlled events, understanding the lives of families within cultures and societies seems to demand a more narrative-based approach (Bruner, 1986, 1990). Belief, values, and behavior merge together in the "well-formed" story told by family members as they reflect on their past and present histories. Narrative accounts used in both family theory and practice essentially advocate a highly interactional process between the counselor and families, using everyday language as a way to reflect upon and construct a hopeful reality upon which future decisions can be based. Language and conversation become the principal means by which both family research and family counseling and therapy are conducted.

Our research and therapeutic viewpoints help society to shape its understanding of the contemporary family. Certainly the counselor who agrees with Whitehead's conception of the preferred, ideal American family will engage in family education, counseling, and consultation in a different way than would those counselors who listen attentively to alternative accounts of family life and seek to understand and support the essential dignity and integrity of alternative but viable worldviews and family forms. Constructivist educators and researchers view the family system in all its contemporary diversity, as well as from a holistic, person-in-environment perspective and context.

SOME CONSTRUCTIVIST TRENDS IN FAMILY THERAPY

Family therapy and counseling seem to be emerging out of the restraints placed upon them by the modernist perspective; that is, the perspective that posits a knowable reality that is independent of the observer, one that is objectively measurable, with clear boundaries and demarcation points. The postmodern, constructivist perspective questions the idea of knowing a reality that is separate from our language and meaning-making construction of it. The paradigmatic shift within the field of family counseling and family therapy has been gradually but persistently taking place, especially over the past two decades.

In the modernist view of family counseling and intervention, family counselors sought out general principles of practice and a gradually increasing sophistication of techniques in hopes that they might be applied across most, if not all, structures and cultures. The advent of constructivist approaches instead generated an interest in greater specificity; therefore, family counseling trainees increasingly need and want to understand the specific needs and contextual circumstances of families. Social constructionism-influenced counselors pay increasing attention to such issues such as family violence and abuse, families in urban and rural poverty, families and addiction, and families and ethnicity. Consistent with this emphasis on understanding multiple influences on families, Nichols and Schwartz (1998) state, "Taking constructivism seriously means that we can no longer judge theories by how well they match objective reality. Instead, we can only assess how well theories help us fit with our environment; that is, how useful, ethical, and ecologically sound and sensitive the theories are. An additional implication is that there isn't necessarily only one most useful theory, there may be many" (p. 319).

As previously mentioned, a number of more constructivist family counseling theories have developed over the past two decades; for instance, (1) narrative therapy (White & Epston, 1990), (2) the conversation/collaboration approaches (Andersen and Goolishian, 1988), (3) feminist family therapy (Walters, Carter, Papp, & Silverstein, 1988), and (4) solution-oriented family counseling and consultation (O'Hanlon, 1989). While they vary considerably, each of these recent innovations in family counseling theory and practice shares a respect for diversity and multiple perspectives, an emphasis on the ecological connectedness of systems, and the idea of the counselor as an advocate and facilitator of systems change.

Narrative family models take exception to the traditional family counseling models that often place the onus of the problem within the family (White & Epston, 1990). Michael White and David Epston (1990) of New Zealand, who have written extensively about narrative therapy, reject the search for general principles of diagnosis and intervention in favor of a telling of the particular and unique "storied" accounts constructed by the family. Their criticism of traditional, pathologizing approaches doesn't stop there. Consistent with their postmodernist and constructivist outlook, they suggest that traditional models of mental illness and family dysfunction are actually part of the problem itself. Therefore, instead of assessing (diagnosing) and using prescriptive techniques, narrative family therapists encourage families to state their concerns in their own language so that all may hear the rich, textured stories of their experiences. As the story unfolds, the counselor remains alert to "gaps" in the story, as every unique and complex "storied" account typically has elements of incompleteness. White and Epson suggest that the power of the family to control and to author more successful stories is contained (but frequently understated) within the original stories. In counseling, the alternative story is enlarged and expanded upon in such a fashion that new possibilities for thought and action naturally emerge from them.

The conversation/collaboration approach, first articulated by Harlene Andersen and Harry Goolishian (1988), resembles narrative therapy in many ways, particularly in its emphasis on how meaning is established through language. The counselor adopts a conversational position of respect and empathy while diminishing the traditional stance of the "expert." Conversational/collaborative family counselors enter into the conversation to co-construct the "storied" account without the use of obvious techniques or manipulative strategies. On the surface, the conversational model seems to resemble the active listening practices of Carl Rogers. However, its constructivist attention to language as meaning-making and the idea of "co-authoring" new, healing, and helping conversations distinguish it from client-centered approaches. This model subscribes to constructivist principles by rejecting grand, unifying theories ("metanarratives," in postmodern terms), by its subsequent interest in the uniqueness of each family's story, and by viewing language as reality construction.

Feminist approaches to family counseling emerged in the 1970's and 1980's primarily as a critique of male-dominated models (Walters, Carter, Papp, & Silverstein, 1988). Feminist family therapists asked family researchers and practitioners to look beyond the confines of family systems and examine larger social and political values and policies that directly impacted family life. Feminist critiques expanded ideas about social roles within families and subsequently empowered family members to experiment with and enact new roles and behaviors (Goldenberg & Goldenberg, 1996). Feminist family therapists do not maintain a neutral expert stance, carefully assessing and intervening. Instead they advocate for social justice within families. Walters and her co-authors (1988) developed a series of guidelines for feminist family therapy. They suggested that family counselors become more aware of the social constructs that help shape and even determine social roles, that they actualize the female values of caring and affirmation, and that they explore the impact of cultural and economic forces on women and families.

The solution-oriented family therapy of William O'Hanlon (1989) also clearly follows a constructivist perspective in suggesting that no single reality exists, but that multiple perspectives on problems may exist. Solution focused therapists contend that the problem exists largely, if not exclusively, within the family's language-based construction of the problem. When families alter these constructions through therapeutic dialogue and exchanges, they may reframe the problem itself. The dialogue addresses the family's meaning-making as they examine old dysfunctional assumptions and constructs. The solution-oriented therapist offers a series of language-based, conversational interventions. Some of these, as described by O'Hanlon (1989), include such strategies as "joining" the family by using the family's language meaning system, redirecting the therapeutic dialogue to examine more useful assumptions and directions, and anticipating positive future change by agreeing with the family's perspectives and offering common sense advice.

Beyond the emergence of these more constructivist theories, the constructivist mode has also renewed interest in family life education. Traditionally, a sharp separation existed between family life education and family therapy. In constructivist models of family life education, however, family members engage, through needs assessment and an active process of dialogue and reflection, in an educational dialogue about solving unique and "real life" family concerns. Such constructivist strategies are common to both family counseling and consultation, and family life education.

This is by no means an exhaustive list of the current trends in postmodern and constructivist thinking that are changing our thinking about family counseling and consultation. While these examples and others that might be offered vary considerably in their theory and practices, as well as in their points of origin, they all seem to contribute to the constructivist/postmodern family counseling paradigm shift that has occurred over the past two decades. Common constructivist themes include, (1) appreciating multiple perspectives versus a singular reality, (2) using many situationally bound theories versus searching for a "grand" narrative, (3) emphasizing the use of language and symbol systems to construct reality versus simply pointing to pre-existent forms and structures, (4) viewing the role of the family counselor as a facilitator, advocate, and partner in change rather than as a neutral observer and expert, and (5) understanding problems and concerns as they occur in particular contexts versus developing broad based interventions cutting across the specifics of context.

APPLICATIONS OF CONSTRUCTIVIST PRINCIPLES
TO FAMILY COUNSELING EDUCATION

The constructivist classroom is essentially a democratic meeting place in which all participants attempt to engage each other in the open and critical questioning of belief systems, traditional practices, and institutions. This openness to many views is particularly important in light of our society's current debate over the future of the American family. In making such a critical analysis and examining beliefs about families, we model for our students the complex and dynamic process of counseling practice. As instructors, we acknowledge alternative conceptions of family life in America and understand that value claims are temporary approaches and partial solutions to complex problems in our discipline. We understand the fragility and tentativeness of such claims. In this respect, the dialectical journey is perhaps more important than the destination or arrival at a final objective set of "truths" about family counseling and consultation. It is in this spirit that I now incorporate McAuliffe and Lovell's (2000) constructivist teaching guidelines into the family counseling classroom.

Our students arrive on the first day of class with opinions, ideas, and value-based judgments. Students' own current families and families of origin typically form the bases for deeply embedded models of family life and development. However, many students long ago learned to leave those opinions outside the classroom door in deference to passive reception of knowledge from teacher-experts. These unuttered beliefs and values are often emotionally embedded structures, and thus, students filter any information, no matter how "objectively" framed, through a lifetime of family life experience, as well as through the lenses of temperament and personality. Traditional objectivist models of teaching might view such preformed ideas and sentiments as impediments to learning in a discipline. However, counselor educators, perhaps more than many of their academic colleagues, typically engage those emotion-laden belief systems for the purpose of creating more integrated and lasting learning.

The constructivist classroom facilitates learning through shared communication and listening in intensely creative, interactive moments (Garrison, 1996). For the family counseling classroom, this often requires establishing a cooperative learning classroom environment (Johnson & Johnson, 1997). Thus, cooperative learning principles weave throughout the specific activities outlined in this chapter. Alexis Walker (1996) extensively discusses cooperative learning in family life education courses in her article "Cooperative Learning in the College Classroom." Consistent with a commitment to growth she states: "Overall, feminists strive to achieve two important goals in the classroom: creating an action-oriented environment and demonstrating care toward students . . . . Cooperative learning is an effective way to achieve these goals. It changes students" (p. 34).

Community building means understanding the complexity and diversity of American families at this time in history, which means that students need to deal with the social and political aspects of race, ethnicity, and social class and the ways they organize our family and social interactions. In family counseling, such a multicultural approach has been enthusiastically embraced for well over a decade. An example of the impact of multiculturalism's success is that family counselors have challenged the hegemony of the dominant Anglo middle-class version of the American family that places a high value on individualism and autonomy. Such hegemony viewed ethnic and social class groups that value group loyalty and subjugate autonomy to the family "good" as enmeshed in an unhealthy or dysfunctional manner.

More recently the notion of diversity has included not only race and ethnicity but social class. Social class, as an organizing factor intersecting with gender and race, has been underestimated by counselor educators and counselors; that is, family patterns can often be related directly to the family's economic class status (Hughes & Perry-Jenkins, 1996).

Understanding the American family is thus a culturally and historically mediated and constructed endeavor. Such an understanding can be co-constructed in the immediacy of meaningful classroom conversation. Thompson (1995) portrays this conversation as one that promotes and develops a strong sense of sensitivity and caring among classroom participants. She suggests a three stage process: instructors encourage student (1) attentiveness through suspending prior judgments, (2) empathy through taking the position and perspective of diverse family systems, and (3) responsiveness through engaging in informed social action.

Giroux (1992) calls these "critical" instructional dimensions "border-crossing." Border-crossing requires creating classroom and community conditions that allow us to move beyond our own "skins," to make known and understood multiple voices, particularly those that have historically been marginalized or left out of the dialogue altogether. In such a classroom, we decenter our views and cross borders to move into new spaces and ways of conceptualizing differences. Giroux (1992) calls this process "pedagogical cartography" (p. 15). The term conveys a classroom condition of both safety and challenge, one that allows students to move to other territories and conditions through their attentiveness and empathy while at the same time holding in place their own values and experiences. For example, can our students understand, at least in historical terms, the role of patriarchy and arranged marriages? Are our students able to appreciate both democratic and authoritarian child-rearing practices? These and other questions that reflect the broad spectrum of family life in America encourage us to move beyond sometimes long-held and seldomly examined, value-based positions.

SPECIFIC CONSTRUCTIVIST APPROACHES AND ACTIVITIES IN THE CLASSROOM

The activities and approaches presented here for teaching and training counseling students in family counseling concur with the guidelines described in McAuliffe and Lovell (2000) as well as with the constructivist principles described in this chapter. Eight to ten years of students in our Family Counseling and Consultation course, the only family counseling course our counselor education students generally take, have participated in these activities.

I typically start the course with a three-to-four week consideration of the history, economics, and social life of the American family from colonial times to the present. We consider religion, immigration, industrialization, and rural-to-urban shifts in demography as part of the context for the current American family. During the next several weeks, we examine family counseling theories from the perspective of history, culture, and gender. It is my hope that the previous emphasis on history and change will allow students to critically examine the relevance of various theoretical approaches to family life. During this section of the course, we use case studies, personal essays, memoirs, and selections from autobiographies and films about family life to examine changes in American family life.

During the second half of the course we aim to develop specific skills in developmental/systems interviewing and other theory-based family education and intervention strategies. The course concludes with applying context, theory, and skills to special issues and needs. Students choose the special needs and issues, typically including such issues as domestic abuse, alcoholism and family life, and step-parenting.

Constructivist Guideline One: Personalizing Your Teaching

The following three activities (Constructing New Knowledge, Writing the Family Autobiography, and Reflective Journaling) all represent attempts to personalize teaching and instruction. "Constructing New Knowledge" is more of a general set of guidelines that aim to enhance the instructor/student efforts in creating family autobiographies and in journaling. The three activities focus on gaining an awareness of personal family experience, not so much for analysis of that experience, but for perspective-taking and decentering. As the students understand how their families-of-origin shape their ideals about family life, they take perspectives about those experiences and view alternative family scenarios from a more detached viewpoint. Through respect for their own personal family experience, students begin to recognize that an expanded perspective is needed to fully comprehend the diversity and complexity of family.

Activity one: Constructing new knowledge. The constructivist classroom begins with an instructor as a facilitator and co-constructor, with other learners, of knowing and understanding. We want our students to think about, reflect upon, and perhaps most significantly, get excited and care about the kinds of open-ended and complex dilemmas that are part of our field and its everyday operations. We want our students to listen carefully to multiple voices and views, and after weighing evidence to come to thoughtful, imaginative, yet tentative decisions. Such flexible counseling decisions help orient us to future actions. Students need to hear and witness the dilemma-holding process as opposed to looking for the "finished products" of think-

ing. Most important, the instructor shows understanding that critical thinking is not an isolated set of technical skills that can be imparted separately
from the emotions engaged by complex social issues about families. That
is, a complex and dynamic interplay of past experience, environmental factors, maturation, and core values all play a crucial part in developing understanding.

The Reflective Judgment Model of King and Strohm-Kitchener (1994)
captures the essence of this reflective process and provides clear guidelines for presenting and modeling this interplay between personal experience and values, on the one hand, and external reality and conditions, on
the other. In this model, the students and instructor move along a stage-
like continuum. First, the learner appeals to authority, searching for the
"right" answer. The learner at this stage treats the instructor as a "trans-
mitter." Next, learners understand learning and understanding to be relative, that there are many opinions but no one is preferable to any other. At
this stage the instructor serves as a "manager" of knowledge who helps
process information. In the final stages of reflective judgment, students
experience many viewpoints; but evidence for particular viewpoints can
be gathered and evaluated, and a tentative decision can be made, at least
until new information is available. The instructor is now more of a co-constructor of knowledge and understanding with students, one who is equally
immersed in the dynamic process.

Family counseling and consultation presents rich and varied material
for this process of reflective judgment. Theoretical approaches are emerging, social issues are being debated at all levels of culture and society, and
family life in America continues to be a politically and socially contentious
and contested area of debate. For example, the future of family life is in
itself a complex and multi-layered issue. The question is being asked: Is
the structure of the American family eroding, thereby undermining the
welfare of children and families, and even, as some politicians and moral-
ists would contend, the very fabric of our society? Or, are we undergoing
broad economic and societal changes, and is the American family, as a dy-
namically resilient institution, undergoing a transition to multiple forms
and new structures in attempting to meet these changes in the culture? We
might appeal to the "authorities" for an answer. But what do we do when
well-informed and persuasive sources of authority, often using the same
data, disagree? We could entertain the relativist position that these contrasting perspectives are, in the final analysis, "just opinions" and that one
family model is as good as another. Another choice is to, as a class, create a
dialogue. Through such a dialogue, we will ideally all carefully listen to
opposing views and construct what is called "situated" understanding.
That is, dialogically constructed knowledge and meaning become a way
for the class to function as a temporary community (and in a larger sense

family counselors can be seen as a "community" of service providers).

Constructing new knowledge in this fashion acknowledges the validity of personal experience, critically examines and evaluates outside opinion and research, and affirms the core values of the counseling endeavor. The instructor models the tentativeness of his/her own perspectives and engages in an open inquiry that continues throughout the class and, I hope, throughout the professional careers of the students. The more specific activities described here are based on these propositions as well as on the importance of a dialogical encounter in the classroom.

Activity two: Writing the family autobiography. In writing a brief family autobiography, students develop a narrative that can be further illuminated by the application of family theory and family systems concepts. As stated above, the intent is not to critically analyze, but to enhance general understanding and perspective taking. We emphasize this aspect of the family autobiography to students from the outset to reduce anxiety about "grading" the student's family of origin.

The general procedures for the Family Autobiography follow the guidelines established by Lawson and Gaushell (1988). First, students create a genogram of at least three generations of family life. They accompany the family genogram with a time-line indicating significant passages and events in the history of the family. Producing a genogram and time-line allows students to look for and discover patterns of family life that have, in some direct or even indirect fashion, impacted them. It encourages students to see individual life choices, such as early career choice and value choices, as embedded in family constellations.

In a second step, students apply the Family Life Cycle (FLC) stages and transitions to their families. The Family Life Cycle approach suggests that families pass through a series of predictable chronological events and expectations as they develop. The FLC provides a larger, norm-based, descriptive perspective by which students can better understand their family of origin.

Third, students choose and write about theoretical concepts related to family rules and communication patterns that have surfaced from doing the genogram, time-line, and family life cycle description. Students may select such concepts as triangulation, styles of communication, and individuation, and are encouraged to select concepts that will deepen their understanding of family rules, myths, secrets, and patterns. As they examine these concepts, students begin to develop a "theory-in-action." That is, they weigh theories and theoretical constructs against direct experience and assess the extent to which such constructs expand understandings of behavior and family life events. Finally, students speculate on how family-of-origin rules, patterns, events, and values have shaped and influenced some of their most important life choices.

The Family Autobiography raises a few ethical considerations. For one, the use of an autobiographical genogram and narrative data can evoke negative discoveries and affect as well as positive ones (Slaugh-Bahr, 1990). In order to emphasize that understanding emerges from careful observation, I suggest that we not be interested in judgment but in description and understanding. In addition, I suggest that they choose to review more positive sources of influence, such as enduring values and career choices, as their examples of family systems influences. However, over the years, some painful discoveries and conclusions have emerged during the preparation of this project.

Students also sometimes raise issues of fairness in grading. I handle these concerns by explaining that grades will be given in response to the detail of the genogram and the depth of understanding theoretical constructs. Because of these ethical considerations, I make an alternative assignment available and consider it to be of equal weight. Students may construct a genogram and time-line and apply theory to a published family narrative; that is, someone else's autobiography, memoir, or extended personal essay.

Activity three: Keeping a reflective family journal. Student journals have long been part of counselor training; they encourage students to integrate personal experience with more abstract theory, research, and textbook knowledge. The purpose of the journal is for students to have an ongoing personal "conversation," or dialogue, with their readings, lectures, and discussions. In the family class, we ask students to reflect on their values, personal experiences, and family histories. At selected intervals throughout the semester, students write for ten to twelve minutes of class time about how the readings and discussions may have changed, broadened, or deepened their understanding of their family and of family life in general.

Typically, we ask students to first respond to the reading. Next, students write about any controversies or disagreements with the reading. They then consider everyday, "real life" examples that confirm or disconfirm important themes in the reading. In addition, students write questions for later class discussion. We collect the journals at least twice during the semester. The instructor reads the journals and makes comments in the margins. Such comments simulate an informal conversation with the student, such as, expressing interest, offering potential answers, asking questions, and in general modeling facilitative self-disclosure that is consistent with the student's own level of disclosure.

Because students are concerned about grading criteria for all assignments and especially about assignments that don't necessarily have clear factual parameters, we provide general guidelines for grading prior to the initiation of the journal. We let them know that grades will reflect their understanding of readings and their ability to connect essential elements of the readings to everyday behavior and personal experience.

Evoking the personal "voice" and creating expanded opportunities for students to value their own life experiences are essential to the constructivist classroom. Neither faculty nor students should leave their experiences at the classroom door and worship at the altar of dispassionate knowledge. On the other hand, we encourage students to avoid discounting complex theoretical thinking and writing as too abstract and too divorced from everyday experience. As much as we need to value personal experience, we also must honor intellectual and research-based findings that force us to reflect upon and critically examine personal experience. The family counseling classroom provides a rich and varied context for this very process of integration of the personal voice with more detached professional theory and research.

Constructivist Guideline Two: Emphasizing Multiple Perspectives

A second constructivist principle informs us that meaning is not a rigid or fixed entity. Meaning changes as our expanded perspectives are altered and modified by new information and new experiences. The notion of the "wisdom of many voices" challenges instructors and students to cross boundaries among socially constructed identities and worldviews. The critical education theorist Henry Giroux calls this process "border pedagogy" (1992). In the family course, students examine the historically constructed and socially situated dimensions of family life in America as it has evolved over the course of our history. Multiculturalism tells us that different families struggle to express their worldviews through varying family structures and norms. In this course we explore these variations.

Activity four: Searching for patterns through the family autobiography and the eco-map. Family counselors are a little like archaeologists in the sense that they dig through family history to find patterns that shape current personality and choices. Such patterns may be products of historical, ethnic, and socioeconomic trends that have taken place over three or more generations of family life. One of the most potent means for uncovering these patterns is the family genogram. The genogram is typically a "map" of three generations of family life. It names family members and major life events—normative, crisis, and/or transitional kinds. Genograms indicate births, deaths, divorces, and major moves and dislocations in a visual form.

Counselors use the genogram with individuals and families in a collaborative manner, characterized by discovery and understanding. We encourage students to use the genogram with particular sensitivity to issues of ethnic heritage, gender roles and distinctions, and family economics.

Using the genogram in the family autobiography assignment gives students a deeper understanding of how patterns of culture and ethnicity influence individual choices. Gaining a context-oriented conception of development serves as a counterpoint to many of the individualistic and self-contained theories of personal development that our students encounter.

Related to the use of the family genogram is the "Eco-map" (Nichols and Schwartz, 1998). The Eco-map places the family in a more contemporary context. It promotes understanding about the family's relationship to such individuals as friends, co-workers, and institutions (schools, workplaces, churches, neighborhoods). While the genogram reveals patterns over time, the Eco-map evokes the "social ecology" of the family in terms of its current networks of support. Both the genogram and the eco-map strongly suggest that healthy families, and therefore healthy productive individuals, emerge from reciprocal processes among environmental forces and individual choices. Social ecology, as a central theme in both activities, implies that understanding and intervention reside both in the environment and in the individual.

Activity five: Using first-person accounts. First-person accounts can be useful in a number of ways. To begin with, because families construct their own perceptions of reality by using language, I like to emphasize to students how important it is to carefully attend to the nuances of language systems. In the narrative-based approaches mentioned earlier in this chapter, language is both the means by which the problem is understood and the means by which new constructions of reality lead to behavioral change. One of the most powerful ways for students to consider the language-based construction of reality is through the use of memoirs and personal essays. Over the past several years I have used the memoir *Road Song* by Natalie Kusz (1990) as an extended "case study." In this memoir the writer considers her family history and their move to homestead in Alaska, as well as a traumatic dog attack that left her without sight in one eye. While the events are of interest in themselves, the language of storytelling very much impresses the reader with her family's deep sense of connectedness. Such accounts can transport the student from the abstract language of the traditional textbook to the search for meaning in language. By listening closely and sensitively, students begin to understand how language not only shapes reality but, in the constructivist model, constructs and reconstructs reality itself.

Constructivist Guideline Three: Valuing and Promoting Direct Experience

Engaging students in direct field service and in projects directly benefiting practice helps students integrate theory with the everyday practicalities of working with families in schools and community agencies. This interplay creates an active exploration of theories. In constructing a "theory-in-action," students simultaneously explore theory and engage in action, examination, and participation. Such practical experience evokes the kinds of ill-structured problems inherent in family work. It also brings into focus the tension between the values of the counselor and the ways in which the school or agency delivers services to families.

Activity six: Writing a parenting field manual. In this assignment, students create a self-help parenting workbook. They identify special populations in need of consultation, education, and/or information. They begin by talking with family counselors in schools and agencies and asking them to describe the most frequent concerns of parents. Students might also elicit direct input from parent focus groups. While students will often be quite accurate in their independent speculations about parents' needs, the data from the focus group adds invaluable information and the opportunity to hear parents' own voices. Further, going directly to the clients teaches students to construct family interventions on the basis of the needs and expectations of their counseling recipients.

Once students select the topics for their manuals, they design a manual format. The format and language of the "Workbook" chapters need to be directed toward the particular population for whom the manual is designed. In helping students make choices about presentation, the instructor presents and critiques examples from the best of the family life education self-help literature. Students have designed formats that included checklists, short questionnaires, fill-in-the-blank items, drawings, and various diagrams. The class decides together on a final format for the workbook so that each student will have a consistent family consultation workbook of several chapters addressing a wide diversity of parent questions and concerns.

Activity seven: Fieldwork and service learning opportunities. Traditionally, direct counseling experience was reserved for the practicum and internship experiences which followed extensive coursework. While I continue to support this process in general, I now encourage students to gain direct field experience with families during the preliminary coursework as well. Since most of our students are of the evening and weekend, part-time variety, they sometimes find the prospect of such an experience daunting. However, when they do participate, they usually do not perform traditional counseling duties and activities. Instead they participate in parenting seminars, after school programs, family service centers, homeless shelters, and other school and community agencies that serve families. Students find it valuable to engage with families through service learning and a wide range of volunteer activities.

Constructivist Guideline Four: Engaging Students in Controversy and Dialogue

The American family is, in our current political culture, a "contested" entity. Politicians and other critics on the right and left sides of the political spectrum have used changes in American family life to support widely divergent views and policy initiatives. Family counselors cannot afford the neutrality of the "detached" professional operating outside of social and political considerations. Instead, students need to immerse themselves in an open constructive dialogue that will bring family counseling into direct contact with political issues at the school, community, state, and national, and international levels (such as, international human rights for children and families).

Activity eight: Structuring in-class dialogue and debates. Class debates and discussions often start as problem-posing activities. In order to facilitate serious thought and discussion about complex family concerns, I use a five part process discussed by Ira Shor in his recent book, *When Students Have Power* (1996):

1. *Description.* What is the problem? What does it look like and feel like? Who is being affected by it and how?

2. *Diagnosis.* How did it get like this? What caused it? What are its roots? Who benefits? Who loses?

3. *Solution.* What are some answers? Propose three possible solutions to the problem.

4. *Implementation.* How would you go about implementing each of the three solutions? What do you need to get started?

5. *Evaluation.* How would you evaluate the success or failure of each solution? One year from now, what would you want to see changed? Five years from now? (Shor, 1996, p. 162).

Students consider issues and problems such as family medical leave, family and children's rights and responsibilities, community and societal approaches to family violence, divorce and single parenting, school and family relations. Students first directly express their experiences and opinions through non-graded in-class writing exercises on these issues. Next they share their individual perspectives in a discussion circle or open meeting format. The group discussion further clarifies existing problems and expands potential solutions while encouraging all class members to contribute.

Activity nine: Making critical use of new sources and the Internet. Traditional academic textbooks attempt to present a value-free description of important and controversial issues. Students often follow this pattern of "neutrality" when writing and discussing urgent issues. Therefore, they may leave personal experiences and deeply held values relatively unexamined.

However in other forums, many authors express strong points of view on family counseling issues. For example, a wide spectrum of "think tanks" and foundations that focus on family policy and family issues express their opinions on the Internet. Government census data on family structural changes is also readily available on the Internet. Such authors also publish in newspapers, political opinion magazines, and journals.

The procedures I use for incorporating such information and opinion into the classroom are very simple. I start each class with an Internet or print article or column. I also invite students to find and report on opinion pieces. We take 10-15 minutes of each weekly class for such presentations, and frequently follow them with in-class writing or general class discussion.

Activity ten: Taking a constructivist approach to family research. Students typically feel intimidated by the wide variety of family research methods available. They also find it challenging to generalize research findings to "real life" circumstances. They may find engaging in research complicated by the largely private nature of families. Therefore, when evaluating family research from a constructivist perspective, issues of privacy and the multiple influences on family counseling outcomes—such as social class, ethnicity, regional differences, and gender—need to be considered. While these considerations are not necessarily unique to family research, they do reflect the constructivist position that traditional, positivistic, linear methods of isolating single variables for the purposes of meeting the restraints of experimental design may impede a fuller understanding of the richness of family life.

In contrast, qualitative research designs are increasing our knowledge and understanding of families while at the same time bridging the gap for counseling practitioners between research and practice. In considering the counselor as a consumer of research, the constructivist perspective suggests that the validity of research in large measure depends on the practitioner's ability (and willingness) to utilize findings in a direct and meaningful way. Recent constructivist advances in research methods have made important strides in this direction. Action research, case studies, family ethnographies, surveys, focus group studies, and intensive interviewing all represent constructivist designs that reflect the complexity of family dynamics.

CONCLUSION

Constructivist thought is currently making a strong impact both on the general field of family counseling and consultation as well as on the strategies for instruction about family life. In this chapter, I have reviewed some of these trends and applications. In particular, I have noted that constructivist thought encourages a renewed interest in interdisciplinary considerations. The history and sociology of the family become important sources of exploration for future counselors. Multiple sources of influence need to be examined as well. Ethnicity, socio-economic class considerations, gender, and life trajectories all constitute important organizing factors for family life. Constructivist thought favors considering a diversity of influences and multiple outcomes over a search for the unifying scenario or grand theory.

In addition, I have attempted to offer a number of constructivist teaching activities that are consistent with these basic constructs. These activities have been designed and carried out in an introductory family counseling course for students who are preparing for generalist counseling practice in schools and community agencies. We hope that a social constructionist approach to learning family counseling will produce students who become active agents in constructing new models, models that reflect the best of traditional theory and research while at the same time creating new innovations that speak to the needs and concerns of the specific families they serve.

REFERENCES

Allen, K. R., & Farnsworth, E. B. (1993). Reflexivity in teaching about families. *Family Relations, 42*, 351-356.

Allport, G. W. (1937). *Pattern and growth in personality.* NY: Holt, Rinehart and Winston.

Andersen, H., & Goolishian, H. (1988). Human systems as linguistic systems: Preliminary and evolving ideas about the implications of clinical theory. *Family Process, 27*, 371-394.

Bruner, J. (1986). *Actual minds, possible worlds.* Cambridge, MA: Harvard University Press.

Bruner, J. (1990). *Acts of meaning.* Cambridge, MA: Harvard University Press.

Coontz, S. (1995, March). *The American family and the nostalgia trap.* (Special Kappan Report). Phi Delta Kappan, K1-K20.

Demos, J. (1986). *Past, present and personal: The family and the life course in American history.* NY: Oxford University Press.

Garrison, J. (1996). A Deweyan theory of democratic listening. *Educational Theory, 46*, 429-438.

Gergen, K. (1985). The social constructionist movement in modern psychology. *American Psychologist, 40*, 266-275.

Giroux, H. (1992). Literacy, border pedagogy and multiculturalism in the aftermath of the Los Angeles uprising. In R. Heft & O. Rovinescu, (Eds.). *Dimensions of literacy in a multicultural society.* (ERIC Publication No. 361598) Ann Arbor, MI: University of Michigan.

Goldenberg, I., & Goldenberg, H. (1996). *Family therapy: An overview,* (4th ed.). Monterey, CA: Brooks/Cole.

Howard, G. S. (1991). Culture tales. *American Psychologist, 46*, 187-197.

Hughes, R., & Perry-Jenkins, M. (1996). Social class issues in family life education. *Family Relations, 45*, 175-182.

Johnson, D. W., & Johnson, F. P. (1997). *Joining together: Group theory and group skills,* (6th ed.). Boston: Allyn & Bacon.

King, P. M., & Strohm-Kitchener, K. (1994). *Developing reflective judgment.* San Francisco: Jossey-Bass.

Kusz, N. (1990). *Road song: A memoir.* NY: Harper Perennial.

Lawson, D. M., & Gaushell, H. (1988). Family autobiography: A useful method for enhancing counselors' personal development. *Counseling Education and Supervision, 28*, 162-167.

McAuliffe, G., & Lovell, C. (2000). Encouraging transformation: Guidelines for constructivist and developmental instruction. In G. McAuliffe, K. Eriksen, and Associates, *Preparing counselors and therapists: Creating constructivist and developmental programs,* (pp. 14-41). Alexandria, VA: Association for Counselor Education and Supervision.

Nichols, M. P., & Schwartz, R. C. (1998). *Family therapy: Concepts and methods,* (4th ed). Boston: Allyn & Bacon.

O'Hanlon, W. (1989). *In search of solutions*. NY: Norton.

Shor, I. (1996). *When students have power*. Chicago: University of Chicago Press.

Slaugh-Bahr, K. (1990). Students responses to genogram and family chronology. *Family Relations, 39*, 243-249.

Stacy, J. (1991). *Brave new families: Stories of domestic upheaval from late twentieth century America*. NY: Basic Books.

Thompson, L. M. (1995). Teaching about ethnic minority families using a pedagogy of care. *Family Relations, 44*, 129-134.

Walker, A. (1996). Cooperative learning in the college classroom. *Family Relations, 45*, 327-335.

Walters, M., Carter, B., Papp, P., & Silverstein, O. (1988). *The invisible web: Gender patterns in family relationships*. NY: Guilford Press.

White, M. & Epston, D. (1990). *Narrative means to therapeutic ends*. NY: Norton.

Whitehead, B. D. (1993, April). Dan Quayle was right. *The Atlantic Monthly*, 47-84.

14

Constructivist and Developmental School Counselor Education

Shelley A. Jackson and Susan DeVaney

Last year my (DeVaney) sister took her first job as an elementary school counselor. It was a half-time position created to support the full-time counselor. That counselor provided classroom guidance, supervised special education referrals, and carried out school-wide standardized testing. Circumstances had changed the complexion of the school. Formerly an affluent, predominantly White community, redistricting had brought about the inclusion of a large number of Vietnamese and Mexican migrant families, as well as impoverished Black families residing in a public housing project. Every single faculty member at the school was White and no one there spoke either Vietnamese or Spanish. The faculty and administration were baffled; the new students did not understand teacher expectations, let alone the guidance lessons. Their parents did not understand the forms they were asked to sign, did not have telephones, and did not respond to written requests for conferences. The school was in turmoil. Could a half-time counselor, fresh from graduate school, make a difference at a school facing so many new challenges?

My sister and I had many talks that year about the theory and nature of school counseling. Using her recent experience as a prime example, we concluded that counselor education had failed many school counselors-in-training by espousing developmental counseling theory and emphasizing individual treatment strategies. Many school counselors struggle to apply developmental principles in environments where the demand for other, more reaction-oriented interventions is high. It is not uncommon for school counselors to grow so overwhelmed with requests for attention to individual problems that they are unable to implement true developmental programs. This failure can be traced back to assumptions made in graduate school training.

By applying developmental principles in a prescriptive way, group interventions lose much of their effectiveness. In the beginning of my (Jackson's) tenure as a school counselor, I struggled with the state requirement that I devote 75 percent of my time to classroom guidance lessons. At first I admittedly fudged on the monthly report figures, but as my confidence grew, I "confessed" that, when a child was in my office crying because her family had been evicted, I chose to spend my time consoling her and finding resources for her family.

We agree with Goncalves (1997) that the major task of developmental and constructivist counselor education is to "understand how the objective of clinical practice can move from the individual as entity to the narrative interspace between individuals" (p. xvi). Often counseling students become familiar with the developmental school counseling model through their course work but are not required to explore its personal, cultural, or political meaning for themselves and their schools. A developmental and constructivist approach to school counselor education moves the focus of school counseling from the individual entity to the system and transforms the role of the school counselor from that of "fixer" of individual problems (a medical model) to that of advocate (a preventive model).

In our view, before school counselors-to-be can deliver developmental school counseling services in the workplace, counselor educators must help them deconstruct the culture, history, and environment of school counseling. This chapter will discuss how we can teach school counselors from a constructivist perspective, helping counseling students to reframe their notions of what is desirable and possible in their respective schools. In this way, we can challenge counseling students to shift their primary attention from individual assessment, treatment, and outcomes to collective assessment, treatment, and outcomes. At the same time we can model the principle that in order to accommodate the developmental needs of their students, counselors must understand the system(s) in which such students exist.

Constructivist education encourages students to construct their own world views by first challenging sources of knowledge and unexamined means of understanding the world. This requires a new epistemology for most students. Developing such an epistemology, or way of knowing, is particularly important for the school counselor because many are "graduating" out of teaching positions. In 21 of the 52 states teaching experience is a requirement for obtaining a school counseling certificate (Quarto, 1999). These school teachers are likely to be initially oriented toward directiveness (versus client-centeredness), high structure (versus lower structure), and thinking (versus feeling). They are apt to be uncomfortable in the inductive and participatory learning environment of the constructivist classroom. Thus resistance to constructivist counselor education may be unusually high among teachers who are used to being "in charge," focusing on external state performance standards, and using directive teaching methods. Counselor education needs to transform these individuals from being "teachers" (in the above sense) to becoming true counselors, those who appreciate the total child (emotional and intellectual), the community of learners (students, faculty, staff, families, and administration), and the systems that children are part of (for example, social system, ethnic and local culture, and historical context).

TOWARD A CONSTRUCTIVIST AND DEVELOPMENTAL IDENTITY FOR SCHOOL COUNSELING STUDENTS: INFUSING CONTEXT, PHASE, STAGE, AND STYLE INTO THE PROGRAM

We will first provide the guiding rubric for the content and process of constructivist and developmental school counseling education. Later, we will describe the structure of a particular course in school counseling.

A central thrust of constructivist school counselor education is encouraging students to deconstruct their own personal and cultural histories and to situate themselves as social constructors. The Context-Phase-Stage-Style (CPSS) assessment model developed by McAuliffe and Eriksen (1999) lends itself to use in counselor education, much as it does for use in therapy. CPSS assessment aims at increasing client awareness and acceptance of self, promoting individuals' abilities to manage and maximize their so-called "natural" inclinations, and enhancing people's capacity to correct oppressive social conditions that contribute to their and others' distress. When applied to counselor education, the model targets school counseling student awareness along four dimensions, namely their: (1) social context, (2) life stage, (3) constructive stage, and (4) personality style.

Social Context

Through carefully chosen class activities and journal assignments, counseling students consider the impact of social contexts on their beliefs, attitudes, and behavior by reflecting on such questions as:

- How would you describe your family's social class?

- What messages did you receive from your family and your culture about work? Recreation? Love?

- How would you describe your ethnic heritage? What does it mean to you?

In class, counselors-in-training probe the influence of social contexts on their perspectives about clients. A shocking example brought home the need for such awareness one of my (DeVaney's) internship seminars. A student intern brought a tape of a counseling session to share with her peers. At the beginning of the taped session, the intern immediately commented on the visible bruises on her client's arms. The client, a 13-year-old White student, readily reported that her brother had hit her with a baseball bat. "What did you do?" asked the intern. "I went to stay with my boyfriend, Tyrone." "Tyrone!" the intern cried in disbelief. "You can't be staying with Tyrone. He's Black and you're White." She then spent the remainder of her session attempting to convince her client of the dangers of interracial mingling.

Rather than falling into the trap of lecturing my student about her unexamined biases, we spent some time using the situation to analyze how her own social context (female, Protestant, upper middle class, European-American heritage) influenced her perceptions of and responses to this situation. As others shared their perspectives, the student moved closer to understanding how her social context might blind her under certain circumstances, and, worse, might inhibit her ability to advocate for the children in her care. Boldly siezing such opportunities is essential to a socially conscious counselor education, of course. Activities also exist for anticipating such bias before students engage actual clients. Examples of social context awareness activities are found in the Appendix.

Life Phase

In the school counseling course students also address matters related to life phase. They respond to such questions as:

- What is most important to you at this time of your life?
- How satisfied are you with the current balance among work, leisure, and family?
- What do you do well? How do you demonstrate these skills to yourself and others?
- As you look back at your life, what are you most proud of? How does your answer differ from the answer you might have given 10 years ago?

Questions can also be raised to help identify students' rigid, internalized expectations.

In graduate education, life phase may be a particularly relevant concept for students to explore. Students struggle with moving out of one occupation (for example, teaching) toward another (for example, school counseling). One of our students summarized her experience of a life phase transition in her journal by stating that:

Every professional must at one time or another decide whether to change his or her career path. I guess I've hit that point in my life. Going back to school was supposed to make my life change easier. With each class there seem to be more questions. Am I really cut out to be a school counselor? Can I get past my other demons in order to help children? I find little solace in what some friends are calling "growing experiences." I have spent most of my adult life chasing my undergraduate degree. Know what? Creating new dreams to chase is not as easy as one thinks. Is life just a series of goals to be set and later attained? How do I decide which are really important?

This counseling student needed support for the "white water" that she was living in. We can help counselors-in-training to anticipate and prepare for upcoming phasic transitions by connecting assignments with developmental theories introduced in class. Students may engage in voluntary counseling duties, begin activity in professional organizations, network to obtain school counseling positions, and prepare for job interviews. In these ways, counseling students begin the process of molding a new identity as a school counselor.

McAuliffe and Eriksen (1999) also suggest the use of formal and informal tools to determine an individual's psychosocial phase. Values clarification exercises, goal setting activities, and life line charts that compare personal roles at different times during the lifespan can all enrich students' understanding of their relations with self, others, and the world (see Appendix). Especially useful with graduate counseling students may be Holland, Daiger, and Power's (1980) Vocational Identity Measure (VIM). Results from the VIM help to determine the extent to which counseling students have engaged in the sequence of age-related, psychosocial tasks expected of persons in this culture.

Constructive Stage

During the school counseling course we also have students identify and explore their constructive stage, or current epistemological orientation. During the assessment of constructive stage, counselors-in-training answer questions about how they have come to decide on their values, preferences, and assumptions, and how they make decisions based on that knowledge. We encourage progression from thinking that is narrow, restrictive, and doctrinaire to that which is adaptable, accommodating, and democratic. As counseling students increase their constructive capacities, they take greater responsibility for their own knowledge creation and decision-making. In this manner they become less authoritarian and more authoritative (self-defining) in their approach to life and to counseling (Kegan, 1994). We use case examples to evoke counselors' positions, and then have them probe the basis for their views with such questions as:

- What's at stake in this situation?
- How do you come to know that this is important?
- What alternatives are available?
- Who benefits from each particular outcome? In what way(s)?
- How does this decision affect you personally?

In addition, counselors-in-training participate in classroom activities designed to enhance progression through the various constructive stages. These activities include those in which prospective counselors compare personal perspectives on issues, values, and beliefs. The Appendix contains a variety of such activities.

In one school counseling class, for example, I (Jackson) encouraged the class to explore the meaning of school-based assessments. A counseling student brought to our attention the case of a fourth grade boy whose teacher had referred him for special education evaluation. Based on a battery of school-administered tests, the psychologist recommended placement in a special classroom for emotionally disturbed children. I challenged students in my class to move from conformist thinking to a more flexible, self-authoring way of thinking by deconstructing the meaning of testing in public schools. For example, counselors identified how testing and its resultant labeling may benefit the school system through increased funding or removal of disruptive children from classrooms. Such labeling might ignore important cultural and socioeconomic factors contributing to a child's behavior. Counseling students explored the danger of using labels as substitutes for knowledge of the whole person, as for example when people refer to a person with a visual impairment as "a visually impaired person," as if the person were no more than the impairment.

Personality Style

Besides social context, life phase, and constructive stage, the CPSS also asks counselors-in-training to become aware of styles, or inclinations and preferences across contexts. Personal style incorporates such constructs as personality traits, personality types, and temperament. Under nurturing conditions, people evolve through stages over time; their personal style, however, remains relatively constant (McAuliffe & Eriksen, 1999). In the school counseling course, counseling students explore how personal style interacts with the school environment through reflecting on such questions as:

- What work environments do you prefer?
- What qualities do you value in your friends and colleagues?
- How do you like to spend your time?
- What recurrent themes characterize your life?

Personal style activities may include using formal instruments such as the 16 Personality Factor Questionnaire (16 PF) and the Personal Career Development Profile. Anticipating their future relations with students, administrators, parents, and teachers, counselors-in-training explore how their personal styles interact with those in the school environment. Using the 16 PF, counseling students assess their openness to change, their self-reliance, perfectionism, and consciousness of rules. I (DeVaney) have found that as counselors explore and discuss their patterns of problem-solving, coping, and personal interactions, they identify which aspects of their personalities are assets or liabilities. For example, using independence, one of the instrument's global scale factors, one school counseling student discovered that her score placed her in the accommodating, agreeable, selfless range. She disclosed that, on one hand, administrators and parents appreciated her willingness to administer and process individual requests for counseling and testing. On the other hand, she recognized that this aspect of her personality might prevent her from fully implementing a developmental school counseling program.

INTEGRATING CONSTRUCTIVIST PRINCIPLES INTO THE INTRODUCTION TO SCHOOL COUNSELING COURSE

When developing a course in school counseling, the CACREP content areas and the national standards serve as a beginning point for discussion, a place in which to locate the school counseling profession. The actual content of the school counseling course that we will describe is closely aligned with both the CACREP (Council for the Accreditation of Counseling and Related Programs, 2000, Draft 3) Program Area Standards for School Counseling and the American School Counseling Association's (ASCA) National Standards for School Counseling Programs (Campbell & Dahir, 1997). We attempt to meet these program standards by using textbooks such as *Developmental Guidance and Counseling* by Myrick (1993), *Developing and Managing Your School Guidance Program* by Gysbers and Henderson (1988), and *Managing Your School Counseling Program: K-12 Developmental Strategies* by Wittmer (1993). In addition, students participate in a variety of experiential learning activities that lead them to deconstruct the school counseling process. This moves school counselor education away from traditional, individualistic practice toward a reflective, socially critical orientation..

Early in the class we study and deconstruct the ASCA National Standards for School Counseling Programs and the CACREP Program Area Standards. Counselors-in-training actively explore the impact of these standards and discuss their political implications. Through community projects and direct contact with individuals at various school sites, counseling students expand their cultural perspectives. They investigate the perceiptions of differing ethnic, social class, or religious groups in regard to school counseling in general and school counseling in particular. For example, instructors invite counselors to describe and explain the complex social phenomena that influenced the development of the standards. Counselors then form action plans in response to any limitations or faulty assumptions they discover in the standards or within the culture of public education in general. The action plans are meant to alleviate social inequalities in a wider arena than that of the individual child. For example, counseling students might design interventions to improve the school climate, develop a democratic discipline system, or form a network of community volunteers to help make a neighborhood safe. In this way the constructivist classroom frames the standards in context and becomes a catalyst for counselor growth.

Constructivist Guidelines for the School Counseling Course

The school counseling course, as we have developed it, follows the guidelines for constructivist counselor education as outlined by McAuliffe and Lovell (2000). The course has been designed to (1) personalize learning and teaching, (2) provide a variety of activities, (3) value and promote experience, (4) emphasize multiple perspectives, and (5) encourage intrapersonal process awareness. If faculty are successful in accomplishing these conditions, knowledge about counseling theory and practice will gradually develop along with professional identity (Winslade, Monk, & Drewey, 1997). The class environment, therefore, is non-traditional, system-centered, and visionary. We hope that our school counseling classes are live, interactive places for participatory learning and experience. Some of the constructivist-oriented activities are noted below, with the five guidelines used as a rubric. Most of the strategies, however, express more than one of the guidelines.

Personalizing learning. The instructor herself is a major factor in the constructivist classroom. By being actively engaged and present with our counseling students, learning as they are learning and discovering our own new ways of knowing, we cultivate an atmosphere of personalized learning. Providing such a constructivist environment requires an epistemological change for many instructors. Sexton and Griffin (1997) encourage instructors to assume positions "characterized not by stable knowing, but by ambiguous change that is multifaceted and contextually based" (p. 257). Our goal is, similarly, to stimulate prospective counselors to ask questions that expose the social, political, and educational conditions present in the schools and to reflect on their personal beliefs and assumptions.

In order to personalize learning on a concrete, experiential level, we ask students to identify a school to work in throughout the semester. I (Jackson) expect students to arrange a time each week to spend with the school counselor on site. Counselors-in-training interview a teacher, a child, and a parent about perceptions of school counseling and about the socio-political context of the school. They collect newsletters, brochures, school notices, and lunch menus from their sites. In addition, counseling students attend two community activities, such as a car wash, religious service, support group meeting, or garage sale. Upon completion of their assignments, counselors reflect on their experiences in their journals. In-class discussion centers on the following questions:

- What kind of people did you observe in the community?
- How are these people likely respond to you in the future?
- How are you different from these people?
- What do you have in common with them?
- How do you see yourself fitting into this school environment?
- What made you feel uncomfortable?
- When did you feel comfortable?
- What surprised you about the interviews?
- How does the school's culture mesh with your own?

Varying structure. Constructivist instruction also considers differences in counseling students' learning styles and cognitive development. The complex design of the constructivist counselor education classroom promotes the intellectual engagement of prospective counselors at all levels of cognitive development. Instructors provide an array of activities, such as lectures, discussion groups, individual reports, guest speakers, and field trips. In addition to traditional readings and assignments from school counseling texts, counseling students complete weekly projects in small groups or individually on current topics relevant to their situations. Counseling students interact with classroom guests and visit school sites over the course of the semester. Counselors-in-training are encouraged to suggest topics and special guests to invite to class. The final project consists of a portfolio of their development as school counselors.

Valuing experience. In the course, prospective counselors develop projects that explore and address real life situations. One counseling student, a special education teacher, was concerned about the number of minority children referred for special education. He developed a pre-referral intervention form that encouraged teachers to recast disruptive behavior as a sometimes logical reaction to environmental inconsistencies or power differentials (Rigazio-DiGilio, 1997). During class, we hope that counseling students will formulate questions about their own settings, exposing the conditions that lead to social, political, and educational inequities.

Promoting multiple perspectives. In class, instructors promote multiple perspectives through open discussion and guest speakers. In addition to principals and counselors, we have invited child abuse case workers, teenage parents, gay and lesbian college students, and homeless people to share their unique perspectives with the class. In all classes it is important to recognize and validate counselors-in-training with different perspectives. For example, in a recent semester a prison worker took the school counseling class as an elective. At first the class minimized and discounted his contributions to class discussions. After all, he wasn't "one of us." I (Jackson) also felt uncomfortable with his presence in this class and didn't understand why he wanted to take the course. I was soon humbled because he came to class every week with ideas that bridged school counseling and prison rehabilitation. He was excited and enthusiastic about how he could incorporate preventive school counseling theory into the prison system. Through him my counseling students and I both learned the importance and value of inviting multiple perspectives into our class.

Encouraging intrapersonal awareness. As a means of increasing intrapersonal awareness, counselors-in-training keep a weekly journal of "metacognitions." They record responses to each class meeting and consciously monitor their thought processes over the course of the semester. Their concluding entries synthesize their experience as they answer questions such as:

- How have you changed this semester?
- How has this course influenced those changes?
- What needs to happen next for you to continue to develop your professional identity?

CONCLUSION

In conclusion, the constructivist approach to school counselor education, as outlined in this chapter, moves school guidance away from focusing on purely individual solutions and toward collective solutions to school-related problems. Using the Context-Phase-Stage-Style Model, counseling students learn to deconstruct their personal and cultural histories and situate themselves as social constructors. Counselors-in-training study the national standards and apply them to real situations. We attempt to personalize learning and teaching, provide a variety of activities, value and promote experience, emphasize multiple perspectives, and encourage intrapersonal process awareness. Through these efforts we hope that school counseling students will relinquish some measure of control over others' lives, gain more authorship of their own beliefs and professional practices, know and reconsider their cultural assumptions, and engage in actions that are a partial solution to the problem of barriers to achievement for children.

Appendix

We here discuss a variety of activities that we use in our school counseling class to assist students in assessing themselves on each component of the Context-Phase-Stage-Style Model assessment. Some of the activities are original. For the others, readers may want to review the original source material for more detailed descriptions of the activities.

Drawing Your Culture

Learning Objective: Increased awareness of the more nonverbal and less rational elements, the symbols and figures important to one's cultural identity.

Activity Description: Divide the class into circles of three to five persons. Provide each group with a variety of art supplies and paper. Ask students to individually depict their cultures on paper. Symbols, doodles, and designs may be used but no words may appear on the paper. At the end of the predetermined time limit, ask each small group member to spend five minutes describing his/her product to the rest of the small group. Next, ask each small group to report to the larger group on their experiences of the activity.

Reference: Pedersen, P. (1994). *A handbook for developing multicultural awareness, Second edition,.* Alexandria: VA: American Counseling Association.

Being Normal and Abnormal

Learning Objective: Increased awareness of both positive and negative consequences of being different from others in one's reference group.

Activity Description: Participants identify and individually write down how they are different from other members of their reference group. Reference groups might be described by ethnicity, nationality, religion, language, age, gender, place of residence, social status, economic status, and educational level. Students then assess individually the impact on them of these differences. Finally, students are divided into dyads to share specifics. The class discusses as a whole what they learned from the activity.

Reference: Pedersen, P. (1994). *A handbook for developing multicultural awareness, Second edition.* Alexandria: VA: American Counseling Association.

Public and Private Self-Disclosure
Learning Objective: To increase awareness of comfortable and uncomfortable venues for sharing private information.

Activity Description: Students decide and individually and anonymously record which of the following topics they consider to be private (comfortable to discuss only with self or intimates) or public (comfortable to discuss with casual friends, acquaintances, or strangers). Topics might include attitudes and opinions, tastes and interests, work and studies, money, personality, and body image. The instructor collects and tabulates the written results and shares them with the class. The class discusses together the implications of the results.

Reference: Pedersen, P. (1994). *A handbook for developing multicultural awareness, Second edition..* Alexandria: VA: American Counseling Association.

Cultural Anthropology
Learning Objective: To investigate the heritage of one's neighborhood community.

Activity Description: Ask students to interview at least five people living in their current neighborhoods. During the interview, they should ask how their neighbors came to the area, their reasons for selecting the area, and what they do there now. In addition, interviewers should ask about previous generations of the family and their relationships to the area. Students then write a brief summary of their findings and may share their discoveries with the class.

Reference: Baruth, L. G. & Manning, M. L. (1999). *Multicultural counseling and psychotherapy: A lifespan perspective.* Upsaddle River, NJ: Merrill/Prentice Hall.

Family Mottoes
Learning Objective: To discover generational influences on self.
Activity Description: Ask students to think of the sayings or family mottoes that they heard in their families of origin (Waste not, want not; You don't have to eat it

all just because it's on the table; Spare the rod and spoil the child.). Discuss in class what cultural values are implied in these mottoes.

Reference: Baruth, L. G. & Manning, M. L. (1999). *Multicultural counseling and psychotherapy: A lifespan perspective.* Upsaddle River, NJ: Merrill/ Prentice Hall.

Life Path Paper

Learning Objective: To gain understanding of the progression of values, attitudes, and beliefs through one's life stages.

Activity Description: Students write a 5-8 page paper examining how and why their thoughts, values, attitudes, and beliefs related to teaching and learning have changed across their lifespan. They consider their thoughts and beliefs at various educational levels (elementary student, a middle and high schooler, a college student, graduate student) and at various times of life (childhood, adolescence, young adulthood, middle adulthood). In class divide into small groups. Assign one educational level and one life stage to each group. Allow 20 minutes for the small groups to discuss the factors relevant to the assigned educational level. Small groups then share their findings with the whole class (20 minutes). Repeat the process using times of life as the topic of discussion.

Reference: Original: DeVaney, S.

Assessing Interrole Relationships

Learning Objective: To increase awareness of current life roles and the energy devoted to each

Activity Description: Ask students to list the life roles in which they are involved, to estimate the amount of time spent on each role, to rank order the roles in order of importance, and to identify roles that conflict with or complement others. Roles can include, among others, student, worker, child, leisurite, citizen, volunteer, spiritual participant, spouse, lover, and parent. Discuss participant insights at each stage of the exercise.

Reference: Brown, D. & Brooks, L. (1991). *Career counseling techniques.* Needham Heights, MA: Allyn and Bacon.

The Circle of Life

Learning Objective: To increase awareness of the relative importance of various life roles at different life stages

Activity Description: 1. Provide the students with paper containing three large circles. In the first circle ask students to divide the circle as they would a pie using as a basis for division the amount of energy they are currently putting into the following life activities: grooming, sleep and rest, meals and food preparation, travel (including to and from work), study, paid employment, exercise, household chores (including errands), financial planning and paying bills, recreation, spiritual renewal, time with family, time with friends. Students may add additional categories if they choose.

2. Using the same categories, students divide the second circle according to their energy expenditure 10 (or 20) years ago. In the third circle, they envision the same "pie" 10 (or 20) years in the future.

3. Discuss student observations after each phase of the activity.

Reference: Original: DeVaney, S.

Life Line

Learning Objective: To increase awareness of how values conflicts arise during various times of life.

Activity Description: Provide students with a sheet of paper on which are drawn five parallel horizontal lines, scaled from 0 to 100. On the first line ask students to circle every age at which they have been or think they will be in school. On the second they should circle every age at which they think they will be working in their chosen occupation. On the third they circle every age at which they believe they will work at occupations other than their chosen career. On the fourth they circle every age at which they have been or think they will be married. On the fifth they circle every age at which they have had or think they will have children living in the home or dependent on them. By examining the vertical correspondence across lines, students can notice at which ages values conflicts (that is, conflicts among life roles

and responsibilities) are likely to arise. At ages
when one is in school, married, raising children,
and working, the amount of energy one can al-
lot to each area of life sets up values conflict and
resultant guilt and stress. Allow the class to discuss their observations.

Reference: Original: DeVaney, S.

Panel Discussion

Learning Objective: To discover stereotypes related to education and
counseling.

Activity Description: Arrange for a panel of counselors and social ac-
tivists to speak to the class on the topic: "The
Present Effects of Stereotyping in Counseling."
Have the panelists address the stereotypes that
they see operating in the schools and in the counseling profession, stereotypes about groups that
they themselves once held but have discarded,
and stereotypes that certain groups appear to
hold about counselors and the public schools.

Reference: Original: S. DeVaney

Attitude Awareness

Learning Objective: To become aware of the attitudes one holds toward diverse groups

Activity Description: Students to select an ethnic group or diverse
population (gays and lesbians, African-Ameri-
cans, welfare recipients, teenage parents). Ask
students to interview at least three members of
their chosen group about the purpose, efficacy,
and future of the public education system. Include one question concerning how they feel
about being interviewed. Share the information
gathered and student perceptions of their assigned population in a roundtable format in class.

Reference: Adapted from Vacc, N., DeVaney, S., & Witmer, J.
(1995). Experiencing and counseling multicultural
and diverse populations, Third edition.
Levittown, PA: Accelerated Development.

Grief and Loss

Learning Objective: To discover the meaning of physical wholeness
in one's life

Activity Description: Ask students to imagine that over the weekend they will experience a terrible accident that causes them to lose an important physical faculty. Having firmly established the specific disability in their minds, students respond to the following:

1. List four ways your life would change following your release from the hospital.

2. What parts of your identity would be transformed (for example, athletic activity, work, parenting)?

3. What would be the most difficult aspect of the loss for you?

4. Comment on your feelings regarding the loss of this faculty.

5. How do you imagine the significant others in your life would respond to the loss?

6. What would you and others do to compensate for the injury?

Reference: Adapted from Vacc, N., DeVaney, S., & Witmer, J. (1995). *Experiencing and counseling multicultural and diverse populations, Third edition.* Levittown, PA: Accelerated Development.

Famous People

Learning Objective: To increase awareness of one's values

Activity Description: Ask students to anonymously (use social security numbers so as to be able to return the papers) list 10 people who they admire and write a short paragraph about what they most admire about each person. Mix up the papers in a hat and have each student draw another student's paper. Then ask students to develop a values portrait of their anonymous writer by examining and writing about his/her selection of admirable qualities found in others. Return the values portraits to the original students. Discuss the experience as a class.

Reference: Adapted from Brown, D. & Brooks, L. (1991). Career counseling techniques. Needham Heights, MA: Allyn & Bacon.

Six-Hat Thinking

Learning Objective: To increase awareness of one's predominant style of decision making

Activity Description: Each student thinks of an important decision s/he must make that s/he feels comfortable sharing with the class. The instructor provides a volunteer with six colored hats, each representing a decision-making process. When wearing the white hat, the student may examine only the verifiable facts of their problem situation. When wearing the red hat, the student uses only unjustified hunches, impressions, or intuition. The black hat is used for negative, pessimistic, or self-critical thinking. The yellow hat represents thinking that focuses only on the benefits of the decision. When wearing the green hat, the student can think about new alternatives and creative ways to solve the problem. As the student thinks out loud about the decision, the instructor helps him/her figure out how and when to change hats as thoughts shift from one type of thinking to another.

Reference: Brown, D. & Brooks, L. (1991). Career counseling techniques. Needham Heights, MA: Allyn & Bacon.

Exploring Metacognitions

Learning Objective: To discover one's patterns of thinking in regard to career/life planning

Activity Description: Patterns of thinking, or metacognitions, are established early in life and tend to remain intact into adulthood. For this exercise, have each student complete the Career Thoughts Inventory. Use the accompanying workbook, Improving Your Career Thoughts to challenge indications of negative thinking and to develop an action plan for the future. Use class time to review the rationale for the instrument and to discuss student reactions and insights related to the assessment process.

Reference: Sampson, J. P., Jr., Peterson, G., Lenz, J., Reardon, R., & Sanders, D. E. (1996). The Career Thoughts Inventory. Odessa, FL: Psychological Assessment Resources, Inc. Sampson, J., Peterson, G., Lenz, J., Reardon, R., & Saunders, D. (1996). Improving your career thoughts: A workbook for the Career Thoughts Inventory. Odessa, FL: Psychological Assessment Resources, Inc.

REFERENCES

Baruth, L. G., & Manning, M. L. (1999). *Multicultural counseling and psychotherapy: A lifespan perspective.* Upsaddle River, NJ: Merrill/Prentice Hall.

Brown, D., & Brooks, L. (1991). *Career counseling techniques.* Needham Heights, MA: Allyn and Bacon.

Campbell, C., & Dahir, C. (1997). *The national standards for school counseling programs.* Alexandria, VA: American School Counselor Association.

Council for Accreditation of Counseling and Related Programs (CACREP) (2000). *2001 Standards for Counseling Programs, Draft 3.* Alexandria, VA: Author.

Goncalves, O. (1997). "Constructivism and the deconstruction of clinical practice." In T. Sexton & B. Griffin (Eds.), *Constructivist thinking in counseling practice, research, and training,* (pp. xi-xvii). New York: Teachers College Press.

Gysbers, N. C., & Henderson, P. (1988). *Developing and managing your school guidance program.* Alexandria, VA: American Association for Counseling and Development.

Holland, J. L., Daiger, D. C., & Power, P. G. (1980). *My vocational situation.* Palo Alto, CA: Consulting Psychologists Press.

Kegan, R. (1994). *In over our heads: The mental demands of modern life.* Cambridge, MA: Harvard University Press.

McAuliffe, G. & Eriksen, K. (1999). Toward a constructivist and developmental identity for the counseling profession: The context-phase-stage-style model. *Journal of Counseling and Development, 77,* 267-280.

McAuliffe, G., & Lovell, C. (2000). Encouraging transformation guidelines for constructivist and developmental instruction. In G. McAuliffe, K. Eriksen, and Associates, *Preparing counselors and therapists: Creating constructivist and developmental programs,* (pp. 14-41). Alexandria, VA: Association for Counselor Education and Supervision.

Myrick, R. D. (1993). *Developmental guidance and counseling: A practical approach,* (2nd ed.). Minneapolis, MN: Educational Media.

Pedersen, P. (1994). *A handbook for developing multicultural awareness,* (2nd ed.). Alexandria: VA: American Counseling Association.

Quarto, C. (1999). Teachers' perceptions of school counselors with and without teaching experience. *Professional School Counseling, 2,* 378-383.

Rigazio-DiGilio, S. A. (1997). From microscopes to holographs: Client development within a constructivist paradigm. In T. Sexton & B. Griffin, (Eds.), *Constructivist thinking in counseling practice, research, and training,* (pp. 74-97). New York: Teachers College Press.

Sampson, J. P., Jr., Peterson, G., Lenz, J., Reardon, R., & Sanders, D. E. (1996). *The Career Thoughts Inventory.* Odessa, FL: Psychological Assessment Resources, Inc.

Sampson, J., Peterson, G., Lenz, J., Reardon, R., & Saunders, D. (1996). *Improving your career thoughts: A workbook for the Career Thoughts Inventory.* Odessa, FL: Psychological Assessment Resources, Inc.

Sexton, T. L., & Griffin, B. L. (1997). The social and political nature of psychological science: The challenges, potentials, and future of constructivist thinking. In T. Sexton & B. Griffin , (Eds.), *Constructivist thinking in counseling practice, research, and training,* (pp. 249- 261). New York: Teachers College Press.

Sexton, T. L., & Griffin, B. L., (Eds.). (1997). *Constructivist thinking in counseling practice, research, and training.* New York: Teachers College Press.

Vacc, N., DeVaney, S., & Witmer, J. (1995). *Experiencing and counseling multicultural and diverse populations,* (3rd ed.). Levittown, PA: Accelerated Development.

Winslade, J., Monk, G., & Drewery, W. (1997). Sharping the critical edge: A social constructionist approach in counselor education. In T. Sexton & B. Griffin, (Eds.), *Constructivist thinking in counseling practice, research, and training,* (pp. 228- 245). New York: Teachers College Press.

Wittmer, J. (1993). *Managing your school-counseling program: K-12 developmental strategies.* Minneapolis, MN: Educational Media Corporation.

15

Community Agency Counseling: Teaching About Management and Administration

Rick Myer

One of the often-dreaded assignments in counselor education is teaching courses that are not directly tied to learning and developing counseling skills. After all, students enter our programs to learn how to do counseling or therapy, not to ponder seemingly mundane material related to other areas. One such course deals with administration and management of community agencies. Just how can this course be made interesting? Specifically, how can instructors overcome reliance on the lecture format as the primary method of instruction? A constructivist approach can be a guide for answering both questions. As McAuliffe and Lovell (2000) have suggested, this approach calls for counselor educators to break out of the lecture/"information deposit" mold on which higher education has been built. Counselor educators must be willing to take the risk that emerges from students (and themselves) not being comfortable with subordinating the role of "teacher-as-expert." A constructivist approach requires counselor educators to be creative in developing a course syllabus and assignments that challenge students to learn experientially rather than to be fed abstracted information.

This chapter describes how a course that addresses management and administrative issues for counseling agencies has been taught using a constructivist approach. The chapter is divided into three sections. The first section reviews the guidelines that have been established by the Council for the Accreditation of Counseling and Related Educational Programs (CACREP, 1994) for the introductory course in community agencies. The second section reviews research related to teaching and learning as they apply to constructivism. This review establishes the context for the course structure by examining three theories that support the constructivist impulse. The third section describes the experience of this author's effort at integrating a constructivist approach into a course on administrative and management issues for community counseling agencies.

CACREP GUIDELINES FOR EDUCATION IN COMMUNITY AGENCY WORK

The topics addressed in the CACREP guidelines for learning about community agencies can be grouped into two categories, professional identity and management, with each covering three basic themes. Each theme aims at helping students understand the basic building blocks of agencies; in other words, the context that surrounds work with clients.

Developing a Professional Identity

The first theme is the history and philosophy of the mental health movement. This theme creates a context for students as they learn about issues related to managing community counseling agencies. With such knowledge students see the influence of history on the practice of counseling and acquire a foundation for anticipating mental health needs in the future. A second theme addresses the identity, or roles and functions, of counselors within community counseling agencies. In focusing on this theme, students begin to understand the unique contribution counselors make in multidisciplinary teams. Also, students learn ways to claim their places on these teams as they seek professional positions following graduation. The third theme relates to the second, in that it concerns professional identity; students explore ethical and legal issues in community counseling.

Administration and Management of Community Agencies

The second group of themes addresses administration and management of community agencies. CACREP recognizes that simple mastery of counseling skills is necessary, but not sufficient, for full professional competence. Students also need skills that enable them to take leadership roles within community agencies. One theme within this group concerns program development, including needs assessment and program evaluation. This theme builds on understanding the historical dimensions of the mental health movement and offers students a systematic process with which to establish and assess programs. A second theme addresses organizational matters, including types of community agencies—public and private, networking among these agencies, and details associated with daily management. A focus on organizational matters helps students to appreciate all the work that undergirds seeing clients. The final theme involves fiscal management, including such topics such as budgeting and reimbursement. Again, this information helps students understand the organizational complexity of community agencies.

EDUCATIONAL RESEARCH FOUNDATIONS FOR A COURSE ON COMMUNITY AGENCIES

As mentioned previously, counselors-in-training generally do not immediately recognize the importance of the community agency course. Teaching the course using a lecture format generally results in students being even more convinced that they do not need this material. They memorize information for the test, then forget it within a few weeks. In short, the learning is decontextualized, separated from the realities of community agencies as work places. This type of learning is unacceptable if we really consider the community agency course necessary to students' success as professional counselors.

Situated Cognition

In her work on "situated cognition," Resnick (1987) compares formal education with actual work settings. In doing so, she identifies three typical differences: First, most school learning is individual while most activities outside school are shared with colleagues. Even though activities within the classroom may involve group discussion, performance is usually judged on an individual basis, using scores from tests and papers. In contrast, performance in work settings is often at least partially based on the successful completion of a project by a team. Second, students in courses usually perform tasks without the aid of external tools, such as reference material, computers, and expert help. In actual work settings, however, it is expected that counselors will use all tools available. Third, school learning focuses on general, widely transferable theoretical principles and skills, while, in the workplace, individuals develop very situation-specific competencies.

Using Constructivist Teaching Guidelines

The challenge for the instructor of the community agency course, therefore, is to use Resnick's (1987) principles to develop a course that more closely mirrors actual work settings. Students must be persuaded that they are learning material that is needed in actual work settings rather than simply memorizing information for the next test (Peterson & Myer, 1995). Brown, Collins, and Duguid (1989) argue that to construct this type of knowledge, students must (1) be involved in authentic problem solving, (2) access multiple sources of information as tools in solving these problems, and (3) work collaboratively with other students.

Several constructivist teaching guidelines articulated by McAuliffe and Lovell (2000) provide a base for creating this type of learning environment. First, instructors establish a sense of community. Instructors also vary the structure of the course. A diversity of materials and class formats is an important element in maintaining students' interest throughout the course. Reinforcing imaginative problem solving strategies is also critical to students' learning processes. Further, instructors reward students for their efforts to master the material by building in opportunities for improvement and reflection. Finally, students experience opportunities to correct mistakes and enhance their skills so that meaningful long-term learning takes place.

Cooperative Learning

I feel that three additional learning-related theories are helpful in guiding my teaching of this course: cooperative learning, Vygotsky's sociohistorical theory of development, and project-based learning. Each of these perspectives contribute various elements to a course designed to help students not only learn the material related to management and administration of community counseling agencies, but also to appreciate the learning process (Peterson & Myer, 1997).

Three types of student learning goals are identifiable when thinking in terms of the relative level and type of interaction among learners: cooperative, competitive, and individualistic (Deutsch, 1949). My focus in this course is on cooperative learning. Such learning is characterized by small groups of students experiencing positive interdependence; that is, perceiving that they can achieve their own goals only when others in the group also achieve their goals. Proponents of this perspective argue that collaboration, rather than competition, is often more characteristic of real-life settings, and that competition in classroom settings has detrimental motivational effects on many students (Johnson, Johnson, & Holubec, 1986). A substantial body of research evidence points to the positive benefits of cooperative learning on student achievement, inter-racial relations, acceptance of mainstreamed handicapped students, self-esteem, motivation, time on-task, cooperative behavior, and altruism (Slavin, 1995). Relatively little research on cooperative learning included post-secondary students, although Johnson and Johnson (1987) claim that cooperative learning positively impacts both achievement and attitudes. The research yields mixed results with respect to motivation, accomplishments, and the learning process. For example, some students, particularly high achieving students, believe that they contribute more to projects and have less control over the product (Peterson, 1992; 1993). On the other hand, students also believe that they develop skills that are needed for actual work settings through group projects (Peterson & Myer, 1995). They report that they profit from being exposed to others' viewpoints, from both providing and receiving help from others, and from enjoyment of the learning process (Peterson & Overbey, 1997).

Vygotsky's Sociohistorical Theory of Development

A second guiding perspective for the community agency course lies in Vygotsky's assertion that human beings are largely products of their cultural and social environments. Specifically, he argued that people develop complex mental functions by moving from social interaction to internalized knowledge (Vygotsky, 1978). In addition, he argued that instruction should take place within a learner's zone of proximal development (ZPD), or at a level of complexity or difficulty at which the learner can solve problems with guidance. One important implication of these two basic concepts is that instruction should provide for social interaction and negotiation. While Vygotsky's notion of the ZPD implies a more capable adult teacher providing instruction that is within a developing *child's* ZPD, Pourchot and Smith (1996) have argued convincingly that teaching practices rooted in Vygotskian perspectives may be even more appropriate for older adult learners. They point out that more recent researchers who have applied Vygotskian perspectives to adults have determined that the basic process of learning is similar between adults and children; that is, adults learn by internalizing socially mediated interactions within the learner's sociocultural context (Rogoff & Lave, 1984). These findings imply that instructional practices should focus on adults' experiences, social interaction within their cultural context, and authentic applications in adult settings (Pourchot & Smith, 1996).

One current educational model based in Vygotskian theory is what I referred to before as "situated cognition." The fundamental aim of this perspective is that learning and cognition ought to take place within a real-world activity and cultural context, rather than taking place in formal educational settings. Much of the research within this tradition has examined adults' cognition in practical settings, where much learning actually occurs. One instructional method that can be used to integrate cooperative learning and situated cognition is project-based learning.

Project-Based Learning

Project-based learning has been defined as a "comprehensive approach to classroom teaching and learning that is designed to engage students in investigation of authentic problems" (Blumenfeld, Soloway, Marx, Krajcik, Guzdial, & Palincsar, 1991, p. 369). Such projects require, first, naming an important question or problem whose solution requires students to use a variety of investigative methods, and second, producing some type of culminating product that answers the targeted question or problem.

Blumenfeld, et al (1991) claimed four advantages for project-based learning. First, students become more motivated to learn important concepts when studied within the context of an important question or problem. Second, projects allow classrooms to simulate realistic settings with real-life problems. Third, projects require use of knowledge from a variety of sources and disciplines, resulting in a broad perspective on the subject. Fourth, projects are adaptable to a variety of learners and learning situations. As with cooperative learning, research with post-secondary students using project-based learning is scarce, but results are promising (Peterson & Myer, 1997).

These frameworks provide instructors with a theoretical foundation for teaching a course on the management and administration of community counseling agencies. However, an important mediating variable affects the implementation of theory: Integrating these concepts and translating them into practical strategies requires creativity and good problem solving abilities on the part of the instructor. As McAuliffe and Lovell (2000) have stated, instructors must move beyond the traditional post-secondary classroom experience and also become learners themselves. They need to be willing to confront students who are in a "velvet rut;" that is, those who do not like the traditional lecture format class, but who also are not willing to entertain other formats, especially those that challenge and require more responsibility of them. In other words, although many students do not like the traditional lecture format, they are comfortable with it and are often more willing to maintain the status quo rather than changing to an unknown. Thus, since utilization of a constructivist approach can be threatening for students, care must be taken when implementing these strategies.

APPLICATION OF PROJECT-BASED COOPERATIVE LEARNING IN THE CLASSROOM

I developed a community agency course using the concepts and strategies described above, a course that meets the CACREP standards for environmental and specialty studies in community counseling. The key element for fashioning the course in this manner involves instructors moving away from being expert-givers-of-information to being experts-as-consultants. Students also must move beyond the traditional student role by taking more responsibility for their learning. The students potentiate their learning by being required to take on the roles of professionals in actual work settings.

The following section describes the four components of a course that meets these guidelines. First, I discuss the course syllabus. The syllabus sets the tone for the course, informing students of the departure from the typical didactic lecture format. In addition, the syllabus discusses course assignments and how these interact with course objectives. Second, I examine the structure for class meetings. Included in this discussion are the roles of the instructor and students, along with the organization of class meetings. Third, I discuss the evaluation process for the course. I use a grading system that promotes self-assessment and enhances rather than interferes with the learning process. Effective evaluation promotes quality in the team project and must also be perceived by students as fair.

Syllabus

At first glance, a course syllabus specifying project-based cooperative learning looks like any other syllabus. Included is the standard information generally found in a syllabus: course title, information about the instructor (i.e., office hours, phone number, email address), required texts, and course description. Yet other information (for instance, course objectives, class schedules, and assignments) is very different in a project-based cooperative learning syllabus. A key function of the syllabus is to inform students from the beginning about the differences between this course and the typical didactic lecture format course. By alerting students early to the differences in the course, they can anticipate the amount and type of effort the course requires. This notification at the outset helps to avoid problems throughout the course.

The objectives. Students first encounter the distinctiveness of the course when reading about the educational objectives. Since the overall goal is to help students become keenly aware of their professional identity as community counselors, objectives need to clarify how this will be accomplished. That is, objectives should provide ways for students to move from being "textbook professionals" to "practicing professionals."

Bloom, Englehart, Furst, Hill, & Krathwohl's (1956) taxonomy for the cognitive domain provides a useful resource for writing course objectives. In this work, Bloom and his colleagues organized educational objectives into six categories, from the simple to the complex: (1) knowledge, (2) comprehension, (3) application, (4) analysis, (5) synthesis, and (6) evaluation. Educational objectives for courses using project-based cooperative learning emphasize the more complex cognitive skills, such as synthesis and evaluation. The following chart illustrates how educational objectives in more traditional courses differ from those in project-based cooperative learning courses.

Traditional Course Objectives	Project Based Learning Objectives
Explain techniques of program evaluation in community agencies.	*Design a plan* for implementing program evaluation in community evaluation in community agencies.
Describe the components of a budget.	*Develop* a one year budget for an agency.

As can be seen from these examples, students do more than simply know common terms and facts. Instead, they apply and analyze material for practical use. In the first example, students are asked to *design and implement* strategies of program evaluation. This objective requires students to not only know various methods of evaluation, but also be able to use this information. Students, therefore, must recognize the benefits and drawbacks of different evaluation methods and need to judge the methods that are appropriate for various programs. The second educational objective asks students to *write a budget* for a community agency. Along with identifying obvious costs, students must also recognize costs that are not immediately apparent. Students not only need to understand the various components of a budget, but also need to know how to *utilize* this knowledge. Educational objectives, therefore, set the stage for learning in this type of course.

The assignments. Class assignments evolve out of and are directly related to educational objectives. Again, remembering that the overall goal of the course is to help students develop a professional identity as a community counselor, the instructor structures course assignments to promote that process. Assignments should promote students' regulation of the learning process and their taking responsibility for monitoring, adjusting, self-questioning, and questioning others (Tinzmann, Jones, Fennimore, Bakker, Fine, & Pierce, 1990). "Monitoring" means that students check their progress in completing the assignments; "adjusting" refers to altering the content and/or direction based on such monitoring. Project-based cooperative learning assignments also encourage students to share ideas and provide constructive feedback through self-questioning and questioning of others. Assignments of this nature challenge students not only to learn content, but also to develop skills in locating resources and in working as a team.

In a central course assignment, students work in teams of three or four to create a community agency. Two possible methods can be used to group students into teams. In the first method, students determine who will be on their team. Students thus take responsibility for themselves, which contributes to the overall goal for the course. However, the drawback of this method is that students generally choose their friends, rather than others who may have similar interests or complementary skills. A second method is to have the instructor select the teams. In this case, the instructor matches students according to project interests, such as client population, type of treatment to be used, and category of agency to be developed. While this latter type of team formation may require more time for students to become acquainted, team members quickly learn more about negotiating and allocating tasks and about becoming productive.

The "creating a community agency" project is divided into four components, each addressing a different aspect of working in a community agency. In the first component, teams propose a *purpose and rationale* for their community agency. They include a brief description of the agency's mission and its programs, a preliminary needs assessment, goals and objectives for the agency, and a plan for selecting a board of directors.

The second component of the assignment requires students to develop a "plan to fund" the agency. This portion of the assignment has two sections. Section one asks teams to describe two possible funding sources. Teams creating a nonprofit agency briefly describe two funding sources that have previously provided grant monies for their type of agency. Teams developing a for-profit agency describe expected client-generated monies, possible business loans, and buy-in or start-up arrangements for investors and partners. Section two requires teams to develop a budget for the agency. Teams generate a budget that includes ongoing costs for one year as well as start-up costs. These budgets include commodities (such as paper, postage, stationery) and contractual costs (including building rent, utilities, phone, maintenance, travel, professional development). Budgets also include detailed descriptions of one-time start up purchases, such as office furniture and equipment.

In the third component of the assignment, teams describe the "organizational structure and procedures" of the proposed agency. The organizational structure section addresses management, supervisory roles, and job descriptions of all professional and staff persons. The procedures section discusses client confidentiality, billing procedures, staff meetings, operating hours, office assignments, vacation and sick leave, crisis intervention guidelines, and relationships with other agencies. Teams may develop flow charts to illustrate their decisions.

The fourth component describes "program evaluation procedures." Students set the boundaries for evaluation and describe at least two types of evaluation procedures to be used. They also describe the types of data to be collected and an explanation of two methods that could be used to collect these data. Teams then describe how and to whom the information from the evaluation would be disseminated.

A major project such as this promotes students' learning on three levels. First, students learn the content required by CACREP. However, unlike simply memorizing the material, students *apply* the material to an authentic situation. This learning promotes students' development of a sense of professionalism, fosters a sense of accomplishment, and increases retention material. The second level of learning occurs as students master the ability to locate resources. Students are invited to be creative in gathering information and are encouraged to share strategies with other teams. Finally, students know that the team will receive a grade for the project rather than students being evaluated individually, and this serves to promote cohesion and increased effort within the teams.

Structure

A course using project-based cooperative learning requires a novel structure. Unlike the typical university course in which instructors are the experts, with knowledge flowing one way from them to the students, this type of course is more reciprocal, with knowledge flowing from instructors to students and from students to instructors. Each class period therefore requires a format in which reciprocal information flow can take place.

The initial class. The tone of the course should be set in the first class meeting. During this meeting students receive a rationale for the structure of the course and for activities and assignments (McCown, Driscoll, & Roop, 1996). Since most students will not have taken a course in which project-based cooperative learning is used as a primary teaching strategy, instructors should take time to explain and respond to questions regarding this method of course delivery. They might offer examples about how effective teamwork has solved problems, making references to projects in the world outside of the classroom. They might ask students to reflect on their work in their own places of employment, to recall the times they were asked to work totally alone on a project and had one chance to get it right. Generally, these situations are few and far between, and most students cannot remember any. This realization serves as a springboard for discussing the purpose and strategies of a course using project-based cooperative learning. Instructors, as you can see, need to be reasonably familiar with the rationale and research supporting this method of teaching and learning in order to be able to defend it as an approach.

Brainstorming. Another activity that promotes involvement in the learning process is brainstorming (Johnson & Johnson, 1994). According to Johnson and Johnson, brainstorming encourages divergent thinking, increases participation and problem solving, and reduces the possibility of negative subgrouping. One brainstorming activity asks students to identify community agencies in which counseling takes place. Usually a class will name 40 to 50 community agencies. Next students classify the agencies by category, such as provision of long-term or short-term counseling, the population served, provision of prevention or remediation, being for-profit or non-profit, and providing in-patient or out-patient care. At the completion of a brainstorming activity, students reflect on the process of brainstorming. Their discussion should focus on the amount of information they generated and their ability to think critically. Students feel empowered by this activity because it gives them a glimpse of what it is like to guide their own learning.

Active learning roles. The key to encouraging students to take responsibility for their learning is communication (McCown, Driscoll, & Roop, 1996). Instructors' interactions with students either facilitate or discourage students from taking an active part in the learning process. Students learn to either take risks in classroom discussions and in creatively completing assignments, or they learn that only one way is "correct." The instructor's role is, therefore, different from that in the traditional classroom in which lecture is the primary teaching method.

According to McCown, Driscoll, and Roop (1996), a central issue for teachers is that of power and control; how much power should be exercised for what amount of control? For project-based cooperative learning courses, instructors exercise less power to control the learning process, thereby requiring students to be active rather than passive recipients. One way to depict the instructor's role is to describe it as that of a consultant who serves as a facilitator, a model, and a coach for students (Tinzmann, et al., 1990). As *facilitators,* instructors encourage students to guide their own learning through self-regulation (See Pintrich, 1995, for a full discussion of self regulated learning). Instructors also *model* beneficial strategies that help students to understand both the content *and* the process of collaborative learning (Tinzmann, *et al.,* 1990). As *coaches,* instructors encourage students' efforts through helping them set and clarify goals, formulate plans to meet the goals, and monitor their progress; and by giving constructive feedback on their projects (McCown, Driscoll, & Roop, 1996).

The students' roles in courses that use project-based cooperative learning are also atypical. Unlike courses employing a typical lecture format to impart information and requiring students to simply be recipients of knowledge, they are now asked to be active in creating the learning environment (McCown, Driscoll, & Roop, 1996). In a sense, as instructors utilize project-based cooperative learning, students are forced into taking a more active role. Students become active through setting personal goals, being motivated to accomplish those goals, and becoming creative in discovering means to achieve the goals. A key element is a student's curiosity about finding answers to questions generated during course assignments. If students refuse or fail to take a more active role, they may become frustrated and dissatisfied with the course. They may then feel bored and indifferent about the topic. However, students who become excited and involved in the course recognize and appreciate the value of this teaching strategy.

Uses of class time. Class meeting times must be structured to encourage students to interact with and question not only themselves, but the instructor, in order to create a sense of expectancy (Slavin, 1995). Instructors should set aside time each class meeting for project-based cooperative learning tasks. I usually plan one half to two thirds of each class meeting for teams to work on their projects. By setting aside class meeting time, instructors communicate the importance of the project. Instructors also need to remain active during project work periods by circulating among teams, providing reinforcement and constructive feedback, and responding to specific requests for advice. Instructors should be careful, however, to maintain their role as a consultant offering advice rather than slipping into the role as an expert telling teams what should be done. Slipping into the role of the authority is tempting since instructors may have experience that would quickly solve a problem or overcome an obstacle. However, preserving the role of a constructivist educator is important in order for students to sustain their sense of responsibility in the learning process.

During the remainder of the class meeting time, a more traditional lecture format is used. However even in this portion of the class meeting, instructors should structure the time in order to facilitate student interaction. For example, the use of Socratic questioning can be used to engage students in the learning process. The success of this method is contingent on how well instructors know the material and how flexible they are in the presentation of the material. If instructors only have a passing familiarity with the material, they may have difficulty building on students' input. Also, the more comprehensive the instructor's knowledge, the more flexible she or he can be in recognizing critical elements over inconsequential details.

EVALUATION

Assessment for courses in which project-based cooperative learning is used must be viewed more broadly than in other courses (Tinzmann, *et al*, 1990). Two distinct dimensions that affect evaluation stand out. First, assignments for the course are actual tasks performed by teams rather than by individuals. Secondly, project-based cooperative learning courses focus on long-term, meaningful learning and skill building rather than on short-term rote memorization (Driscoll, 1994). I thus had to develop grading procedures that matched such a course design because reliance on standard grading procedures could undermine constructivist approaches to teaching a course.

One possible strategy for evaluating project-based cooperative learning is the use of a pass/fail grading system rather than standard letter grades for assignments. This grading system is advantageous if students are expected to demonstrate mastery of all course objectives (Linn & Gronlund, 2000. Mastery is desired because it contributes to students' sense of professionalism. Although students may take varying amounts of time to learn the material (Guskey, 1994), setting a standard facilitates meaningful learning as students associate obtaining information with real life application of material (Driscoll, 1994). Should instructors choose to employ this system, care must be taken to inform students verbally and in the syllabus about what constitutes a pass versus a fail grade. Instructors should carefully communicate expectations regarding content, structure, and format of assignments. Approximate percentages for each part of the assignment must be communicated to students. A major purpose for this painstaking effort is to reduce evaluation anxiety for students and to decrease the chance of misunderstandings later in the course. Students know and understand the meaning of standard letter grades: A, B, C, and F, even if they do not always agree with their grades. They do not always understand the meaning of pass/fail grading. Therefore, to reduce anxiety, instructors need to familiarize students with such a strategy.

Another method that is consistent with the overall learning goals for the course is to allow a student to resubmit assignments judged to be unsatisfactory. Just as with communicating the nature and expectations for grading assignments, instructors should be specific about how students are to resubmit assignments. Clear expectations about what is to be resubmitted and the time frame to resubmit assignments must be communicated. One suggestion is to have students resubmit assignments with (1) the original, (2) a one page summary of the changes that were made, and (3) the corrected assignment. This system helps instructors know that changes were made and reminds them of what suggestions they had made on the initial version of the assignment. Opportunities to resubmit often motivate students to improve their work and assure instructors that students have the level of knowledge and skill needed to be effective and professional community counselors.

When using project-based cooperative learning, students need to be informed upfront that all members of the team receive the same grade for assignments on which they work together. This is quite different than in traditional courses in which students receive grades based on individual performance.

A portion of students' grades, however, should be based on individual performance. Instructors can ask teams to anonymously rate the fellow members of their team. Questions about cooperativeness, effort, and participation in the assignment offer students the opportunity to rate their peers' contributions. Students may react negatively to assessing other students, however, instructors should help students understand that this type of assessment is part of accountability. Instructors might also have students complete some assignments individually. These individual assignments can help instructors differentiate among students when assigning final grades.

A modified contract method can be used to determine overall final grades for a course. Since assignments are evaluated on a pass/fail basis, instructors can use the number of satisfactory assignments completed to determine the final grade. This system assumes that in most graduate level courses students must be assigned a letter grade. Instructors can have minimum requirements for the grade of C and simply add assignments if students want a higher grade. This method helps to reduce anxiety by giving students control of what grade they receive. Used in concert with allowing students to resubmit unsatisfactory assignments, there should be no surprises about what grades will be received.

CONCLUSION

This method of offering a course is not without difficulties. Although the structure of the course aims at reducing anxiety, many students find their anxiety to be increased. Questions about depending on others for their grades are often raised. Concerns emerge about what happens if the team does not work well together. Instructors should anticipate these questions and be prepared to respond when asked. A response to the question about being dependent on others for a grade can include reminders of the requirement to complete individual assignments and of the importance of being careful about forming a team. Regarding group dysfunction, the instructor might respond by assuring students that, should problems occur in the group, the instructor will help to work out the difficulties. Such an intervention might involve a discussion with the team or possibly reassigning team members. Again, discussing the nature and expectations of the course during the first class meeting reduces anxiety.

Another issue that surfaces concerns group meeting times. For programs in which students are part-time and drive to campus, scheduling times to meet outside of class can be challenging. One method to overcome this difficulty involves the use of computers and the internet (Peterson & Myer, 1997). Surprisingly, using E-mail can increase group cohesion and help teams be more open and thoughtful regarding their input.

Project-based cooperative learning is a method for teaching counselor education courses that facilitates students' internalizing of a sense of professionalism by mirroring actual work settings. By promoting mastery of material, project-based cooperative learning strategies also help to assure agencies that students are equipped with the skills needed for entry level positions.

Since, the goal of counselor education is to prepare students for positions as professional counselors, and since research supports the use of teaching methods in which authentic work situations are mirrored, project-based cooperative learning is more likely to prepare professionals who know what they need to know when they enter the work force.

REFERENCES

Bloom, B. S., Englehart, M. D., Furst, E. J., Hill, W. H., & Krathwohl, D. R. (1956). *Taxonomy of educational objectives, Handbook I: Cognitive domains.* New York: McKay.

Blumenfeld, P. C., Soloway, E., Marx, R. W., Krajcik, J. S., Guzdial, M., & Palincsar, A. (1991). Motivating project-based learning: Sustaining the doing, supporting the learning. *Educational Psychologist, 26,* 369-398.

Brown, J. S., Collins, A., & Duguid, P. (1989). Situated cognition and the culture of learning. *Educational Researcher, 18,* 32-42.

Council for Accrediting Counseling and Related Educational Programs. (1994). *CACREP accreditation standards and procedures manual.* Alexandria, VA: American Counseling Association.

Deutsch, M. (1949). A theory of cooperation and competition. *Human Relations, 2,* 129-152.

Driscoll, M. P. (1994). *Psychology of learning for instruction.* Boston: Allyn and Bacon.

Guskey, T. (1994). Making the grade: What benefits students? *Educational Leadership, 52* (2), 14-21.

Johnson, D. W., & Johnson, F. P. (1994). *Joining together: Group theory and group skills,* (5th ed.). Boston: Allyn and Bacon.

Johnson, D. W., & Johnson, R. T. (1987). Research shows the benefits of adult cooperation. *Educational Leadership, 45* (3), 27-30.

Johnson, D. W., Johnson, R. T., & Holubec, E. D. (1986). *Circles of learning: Cooperation in the classroom.* Edina, MN: Interaction Book Co.

Linn, R. L., & Gronlund, N. E. (2000). *Measurement and assessment in teaching,* (8th ed.). Upper Saddle, NJ: Merrill.

McAuliffe, G., & Lovell, C. (2000). Encouraging transformation: Guidelines for constructivist and developmental instruction. In G. McAuliffe, K. Eriksen, and Associates, *Preparing counselors and therapists: Creating constructivist and developmental programs,* (pp.14-41). Alexandria, VA: Association for Counselor Education and Supervision.

McCown, R., Driscoll, M., & Roop, P. G. (1996). *Educational Psychology,* (2nd ed.). Boston: Allyn and Bacon.

Peterson, S. E. (1992). A comparison of causal attributions and their dimensions for individual and cooperative group tasks. *Journal of Research and Development in Education, 25* (2), 35-44.

Peterson, S. E. (1993). The effects of prior achievement and group outcome on attributions and affect in cooperative tasks. *Contemporary Educational Psychology, 18,* 479-485.

Peterson, S. E., & Myer, R. A. (1995). The use of collaborative project-based learning in counselor education. *Counselor Education and Supervision, 35* (2), 150-158.

Peterson, S. E., & Myer, R. A. (1997, August). The use of on-line communication for collaborative project-based learning. Presented at the 22nd International Conference for Improving University Learning and Teaching, Rio de Janeiro, Brazil.

Peterson, S. E., & Overbey, G. (1997, March). Relationships between perceived control and affect in motivation for collaborative projects. Paper presented at the meeting of the American Educational Research Association, Chicago, IL.

Pintrich, P. (Ed.;1995). Special Issue: Current issues in research on self-regulated learning: A discussion with commentaries. *Educational Psychologist, 30.*

Pourchot, T. L., & Smith, M. C. (1996, October). Integrating child and adult cognitive development and learning: A Vygotskian perspective on theory and practice. Paper presented at the annual meeting of the Midwestern Educational Research Association, Chicago, IL.

Resnick, L. B. (1987). Learning in school and out. *Educational Researcher, 16* (9), 13-20.

Rogoff, B., & Lave, J. (1984). *Everyday cognition: Its development in social context.* Cambridge, MA: Harvard University Press.

Slavin, R. E. (1995). *Cooperative learning,* (2nd ed). Boston, MA: Allyn & Bacon.

Tinzmann, M. B., Jones, B. F., Fennimore, T. F., Bakker, J., Fine, C., & Pierce, J. (1990). The collaborative classroom: Reconnecting teachers and learners. In M. B. Tinzmann, (Ed.). *Restructuring education to promote learning in America's schools,* (pp. 86-99). Elmhart, IL: North Central Regional Education Laboratory.

Vygotsky, L. S. (1978/1934). *Mind in society: The development of higher psychological processes.* Cambridge, MA: Harvard University Press.

16

Student Development Education as the Practice of Liberation: A Constructivist Approach

Jane Fried

In times of slower change than ours, knowledge was represented as a body, a static, transmissible collection of information, facts reified into the mental equivalents of objects. Today metaphors for knowledge are kinetic. Knowledge can change more quickly than the weather due to instantaneous communication among multinational, multiracial, multireligious, and multigendered communities. Facts, once experienced as stable, are now fluid and contextual. Patterns in phenomena are barely discernable. Competing ideas about credibility and knowledge exist simultaneously. Does matter consist of waves or particles? The answer is yes/both, depending on the viewpoint of the observer and the context of the observation.

Given these trends and their attendant "post-structuralist" epistemologies, one would expect parallel trends in teaching and learning at universities. Yet that process in many disciplines is still shaped by epistemologies that developed when knowledge was treated as a body. Today, teaching often consists of a person (the professor) relaying facts to groups of other persons (the students). Facts, and the theories that connect them to each other, are passed from teacher to student as if they were objects. When the students can pass the facts back to the teacher in reasonably accurate form, they are considered to have learned them. Such a confidence in the possibility of knowing solid truth through rational methods and communicating it to others is based on the epistemology often known as objectivism or logical positivism.

This epistemology is largely responsible for the scholarship and research that gave rise to the scientific, economic, and material dominance of the North Atlantic nations in the modern world. Ironically, the great strength of this epistemology is also its weakness. It elevates objectivity and universality while ignoring subjectivity and personal construction of meaning. Learning is expected to be factual, impersonal, and unrelated to the needs, beliefs, or cultures of the learners (Fried, 1995). For example, African American and European American students might study the slave trade as part of a course on U.S. History. From an objectivist perspective, both groups of students might be expected to learn the same facts. However, these facts, when converted into personally and culturally filtered understanding, can lead to very different learnings about self, family, and cultural history.

How might the tension between objectivist and constructivist ways of knowing affect the teacher's ideas about learning, and what are the implications of this tension for teaching graduate students to be college counselors and student affairs workers? This chapter is devoted to those inquiries.

THE UNRAVELING OF OBJECTIVIST KNOWING: CONNECTING THE KNOWER AND THE KNOWN

Objectivist epistemology has been unraveling since the early 1900's when Einstein, Bohr, and others began to discover the interchangeability of matter and energy (Capra, 1989). Time and space lost their status as objective realities. They were now understood to be situated on a continuum and each affected the other. Most importantly, Heisenberg (as cited in Capra, 1989) established the significance of the interaction between observer and observation in scientific research. Objectivity then became a frame of reference rather than a universal truth, and probability replaced predictability when making predictions.

Chaos theory was born from this research. With its images of constant, nonlinear, irreversible change, chaos theory provided a new set of metaphors for the teaching/learning process. Chaos theory has demonstrated that all knowledge is ultimately subjective because of the inevitable interactions between the observer and the observed, the knowledge and the knower (Capra, 1989).

This evolution of science has produced a new "constructivist" epistemology, which takes into account the ways in which knowers make meaning, using facts, values, beliefs, and cultural experience to create patterns that shape their understanding of the world. In the framework of constructivism, for instance, students from many cultural groups who study the history of the slave trade in the United States learn many of the same historical "facts" while interpreting these facts from many different perspectives. Such emotionally charged information can transform the nature of learning if emotions, as well as personal and cultural meaning, are allowed to enter the teaching/learning process.

THE EVOLUTION OF STUDENT DEVELOPMENT THEORY: TOWARD TRANSFORMATIVE LEARNING

In the discipline of "college student development"—a recently evolved set of theories about the psychosocial, cognitive, and moral development of college students—boundaries are also blurred. When graduate students in student development preparation programs learn about college student development, they are simultaneously learning about their own development as former undergraduate students and as emerging adults—typically from an objectivist perspective. In order to work effectively with undergraduates, graduate students must learn the theory, understand how to use the theory in applied situations, and understand enough about their own development to comprehend the interaction between themselves and the students they hope to teach or counsel. Learning about "college student development" thus means learning about oneself and others simultaneously and trying to understand the interaction between self and other in a college setting. Thus learning becomes a multifaceted process of apprehension, comprehension, and transformation. Apprehension means knowing via direct personal experience; comprehension means knowing through conceptual interpretation; and transformation means grasping the meaning of what one has come to know via reflection or experimentation (Kolb, 1984).

In order to provoke the transformative phase of learning, teaching techniques and concepts that use "fusion" constructs (Maslow, 1971) must be used in which the distinctions between facts, values, apprehension, and comprehension blur. Abraham Maslow, a major figure in the creation of humanistic psychology, provided the theoretical framework for much of the student development movement in the form of the fusion metaphor. He suggested that the idea of "full humanness" went beyond the notion of psychological health, and that neurosis should be considered "a failure of human growth" (1971, p. 28) rather than an indicator of pathology. Maslow's ideas provided a psychological framework to the evolving notion that people were motivated by goals and dreams as well as by needs and fears. Maslow went on to describe role of education in creating "peak experiences," or moments of insight and liberation for students (1971). Maslow built the foundation for the bridge over which the college student development movement has traveled. He proposed that teachers could enhance human growth and liberate human vision by fusing knowledge, inspiration, learning, and wisdom.

Burns B. Crookston, considered by many to be the founder of the student development movement, was a contemporary and colleague of Maslow. Crookston (1973) proposed a complete transformation of traditional pedagogy from a focus on information transfer to an emphasis on the integration of knowledge, meaning, and personal application. In his words:

What is needed is to transform education so that it neither focuses on subject matter requirements and syllabi, nor attempts to fit the student into a cultural heritage, but becomes a model of human development that teaches students the processes of discovering what is known and applying that knowledge to a deeper understanding of self, of enhancing the quality of relationships with others, and of coping effectively with the world. (1973, p.52)

Crookston coined the term "affective rationality" (p. 59) to suggest that one mark of a well educated person was understanding feelings and using them to shape rational action. He was particularly concerned about helping students "understand and control destructive impulses (while transforming the impulses) into growth producing experiences" (p. 59).

More recently, Parker Palmer (1997) has espoused a similar holistic and transformative approach to learning in community. His approach has been shaped more by the broader notion of adult education than by the student development movement, but his values and educational goals are quite similar to those of that movement.

Both Crookston and Palmer adopted a constructivist epistemology in their work, in that they emphasized the interactive roles of student and teacher in constructing meaning from both personal experience and empirical, "objective" data. Crookston was and Palmer is committed to the creation of learning communities in which people investigate issues of mutual concern with both discipline and passion in an environment of mutual respect.

In order to create constructivist learning communities, however, one more boundary must blur. The work of David Drum (1980) provides a bridge from counseling to teaching that completes this circle. Drum described a developmental continuum to use in conceptualizing the process of counseling college students. Remediation anchors one end of the continuum, and learning and growth or development anchors the other. Learning can occur in intrapersonal, interpersonal, or intellectual modes. Interventions occur with individuals, with small or large groups, or with an entire institution. The skills used in this kind of counseling/teaching combine active listening, group facilitation, and presentation of information in both cognitive and experiential modes. Thus the teacher/counselor must possess at least four capacities: (1) subject matter knowledge, (2) knowledge of cognitive development, (3) group facilitation abilities, and (4) active listening skills. Counseling broadens its focus from remediating the individual to enhancing the conditions in which development occurs.

INTENTIONAL STUDENT DEVELOPMENT
AS LIBERATORY EDUCATION

In this review it might be noted that thus far the student development and human growth thinkers have focused on the individual's development, although many of the early theorists had strong commitments to societal improvement as well. Another trend is now discernable, one in which socially statused relationships are included as part of college student development. The liberatory education work of Paolo Freire (1990) and his disciples (Giroux & McLaren, 1994; hooks, 1994) has been used to extend the concept of student development education, or "outreach counseling" as it is sometimes called, into the domain of power relationships and personal empowerment. In Freire's work, "personal growth" is transformed into the notion of "full humanness."

In liberatory education, students are empowered to transform their world and shape their own places in it. Freire proclaims the value of *praxis*, the process of teaching and learning by alternating action and reflection in order to transform the world. *Praxis* emphasizes experience, participation in actions that are designed to provoke thought, and reflection on the meaning of those experiences from multiple perspectives—intrapersonal, interpersonal, social, political, and economic. The goal of *praxis* learning is to encourage participants to "rename" the world, to make sense of their experiences, to make connections between events, and to transform the world in the direction of greater freedom and humanity for all, via dialogue. In contrast to earlier thinking in student development, the work of Freire and his students is avowedly political.

Education, from the liberatory perspective, is seen as the practice of freedom. The purpose of learning is to create connections between people and events and to create a community of liberation for all who engage in the dialogue. Rather than absorb the predigested explanation of any event or idea, students and teachers engage in dialogue to explore its meaning together. There is no dominating narrative in dialogue. People define problems that limit freedom and explore together various approaches to expanding humanity, freedom, and democracy.

Praxis is perceived as profoundly threatening in institutions that support the "banking deposit" (Freire, 1990) approach to education and use objectivist epistemology in the teaching/learning process. If *praxis* is used as Freire has intended, all students would participate in the discussion of issues that affect them, such as graduate school residency requirements; grading on the curve; increasing fees in times of flat inflation; and broader splits which generally exist between liberal and professional education, facts and meaning, objectivity and subjectivity.

THE CULTURAL LIMITATIONS OF STUDENT DEVELOPMENT THEORY

In the past, much student development theory has been silent about culture, about whose "voice" is heard through the theories. Freire's work calls attention to the issue of "student voice." In simplest terms, in college student development education, this problem exists on at least two levels. The first is the voices of students, often undergraduates, who are not themselves studying student development theory, but who are recipients of student development interventions. The second is the voice of graduate students who are preparing to become student affairs professionals. Both of those voices have historically been those of European American or White students. For example, Chickering's influential theory of identity formation (Chickering & Reisser, 1993) is a theory that was originally based on data gathered from the largely Anglo/Euro-American, heterosexual, able-bodied male segment of a student population in the United States. The theory is aimed at describing universal phases and tasks in young adulthood. In contrast, Baxter-Magolda's Epistemological Reflection Model (1992), which is also widely studied in graduate programs, takes gender into account. It, however, but fails to discuss class, race, or context in depth. Both of these theories are well developed within their own research paradigms, but ignore or dismiss socioeconomic and political context. Baxter-Magolda's discussion of her research methodology clearly conveys her understanding of the role that context, perspective, and voice play in describing student development, but her sample limits the influence of these factors in her writing.

Embedded in the work of Chickering and Reisser and Baxter-Magolda are two assumptions: (1) that the self is an independent entity, moving through life and making decisions more or less autonomously, and (2) that, in the process of gathering data, researchers can ignore the potential influence of themselves on the process of identity evolution. Recent recognition of cultural variations in the self-concept (Okun, Fried, & Okun, 1999) and awareness of the nonlinearity of change challenge the assumptions on which both of these theories are based.

Kaleidoscopic Identities and Selves

Scholarship on the social construction of sexual identity, race, and disability also has serious implications for both theory and practice of student development education. In the past 15 years or so, a number of theories of "minority" identity formation have been described (e.g., Atkinson, Morten and Sue, 1993; Cross, 1971; Cass, 1979). The majority of these are stage theories. They present identity formation as sequential and hierarchical, moving from efforts to deny difference, to a sense of alienation from the larger, dominant society, to resolution in which one's difference is prized and valued and self integrates both differences and commonalties with members of the dominant groups. Development is viewed as more or less linear. Context is background and identity is decontextualized and individual. For example, a person who is labeled gay or lesbian is not seen as a person with a complex sense of self or identity for whom sexual orientation is one important factor. He or she is seen as a homosexual person developing with regard to that single, defining aspect of self. The same is true for a person of color.

Current thinking on identity formation has become quite fluid (Helms, 1994). Race, class, and gender, as well as historical, political, and economic circumstances influence identity, so that it assumes many dimensions which can be considered "contradictory and are always situational" (Bailey and Hall, 1992, p. 21). The kaleidoscope is a metaphor for such fluidity. Kaleidoscopic identities do not lend themselves to description by stage theories. Contrast the following views of homosexual identity: (1) the multistage theory in which a person must struggle with the definition of self imposed by the dominant society—deviant, defective, unable, unacceptable for parenting, and unstable—upward through a hierarchy to self acceptance, with the notion that (2) "a lesbian as a type of being does not exist, but is rather actively constructed in a society which...is predicated on male subordination of women through prevailing ideas of femininity" (Kitzinger, 1987, as cited in Kitzinger, 1995, p.139). A middle ground between these two descriptions of lesbian identity posits the "dual nature of lesbian identity as an individual sexual identity that results in membership in an oppressed minority" (Carn & Fassinger, 1996, p. 509). What, or who, is a lesbian in a male, heterosexual dominated society? How can it be defined outside of that context? Who is a bisexual person in a society that rewards heterosexual behavior and punishes homosexual/affectional ties? Who, for example, is an African American man, the great grandson of slaves, who has in fact spent most of his adult life in Africa, bringing help to people in need as a United States aid worker? In what context is he a minority? Where is he a member of the majority? Who does he think he is? Whose opinion is privileged in this discussion? Such fluidity might be illustrated by the difficulty the US Census bureau is having in getting people to check an appropriate box describing ethnic/racial status.

Self versus identity. In this context-oriented light, "self" might be a richer, less culturally-bound construct for student development education. Historically, student development theory has focused on psychosocial or identity formation for college students in the 18 to 24 year old age cohort (Chickering and Reisser, 1993). For this age group, identity formation is an appropriate focal concept. However, as student demographics spread out over the life span and across cultures, the notion of self may replace identity as the appropriate organizing construct for this work. This change of focus should subsequently influence approaches to teaching and learning in student development education. Self means different things in different cultures and in different times of life. Self and identity are almost synonymous in Western cultures, particularly in adult life. In contrast, self in Eastern cultures often refers the relationship between the person and the attributes she or he shares with the larger community or derives from connection with the Divine or transcendent aspect of experience (Okun, Fried & Okun, 1999).

Every culture in the world has some self-referencing pronoun such as "I" or "me" that is used to refer to a specific person. Every culture also concerns itself with the ways in which people relate to each other, manage their affairs, and contribute to the work of the community. What varies across cultures and between cultures within the United States is the relative importance of different dimensions of self in any given context. Self is a multidimensional and dynamic construct, in contrast to identity, which is considered stable through the adult life span. Identity is burdened with historical notions of autonomy and individuality which are more significant in the United States than elsewhere in the world (Hoare, 1991).

Implementing the construct of "self": The metaphor of holon. Hierarchical theories of development are appropriate when identity is seen as the organizing construct of personality, a structure that is uniform over time and space, noncontextual, autonomous, and growing toward increasing complexity in a linear fashion. If self replaces identity as the organizing construct for student development education, practitioners will need a new, more dynamic perspective within which they can organize their interventions. Self as "holon" is one such perspective.

Holons are structures that maintain their wholeness and their "partness" simultaneously. Holons have four characteristics that contribute to these two tendencies: agency, communion, self-dissolution, and self-transcendence (Wilbur, 1996). Holons carry out their own functions and interact with other holons at the same level of complexity simultaneously, demonstrating both agency and communion. When a holon merges with another, such that a new and more complex system is created, that is self-transcendence. Occasionally complex holons disintegrate, creating dissolution of the complex holon into two complete, but less complex systems.

Self-as-holon provides us with a metaphor for understanding how students, or people in general, behave and think about themselves and their relationships in particular contexts. Different aspects of self become salient in specific situations. During each situation, students involve themselves with each other or refuse to involve themselves as they carry out what they perceive to be their purpose in the situation. For example, imagine an African American student who is a music major and serves on a programming board for a student union. If she represents all Black fraternities and sororities, she may, in decision-making about campus cultural events, feel obliged to support musicians who appeal to the majority of Black students. If the same student were elected to serve from the student body in general, she might support more European-American-based music or the creation of a foreign film series on campus. She is not betraying any part of her self. She is representing the part of her self that seems salient in two different situations. As she learns more, she becomes more complex and multidimensional, incorporating new aesthetic preferences into her sense of self, but this new self-organization is non-hierarchical. No part of her is innately more worthwhile or "true" than any other part without reference to context.

The notion of self as dynamic, nonlinear, and interactive permits us as student development educators to take a process-oriented approach to our work with inevitably multidimensional students. If we understand students as constantly manifesting different aspects of their selves as evoked in different contexts, we become more flexible in our method of responding to them and planning educational interventions for and with them. We can ask ourselves how we should enhance both agency and communion among students who are involved in various aspects of student development activities. What should we do, as counselors and advisors, to help them affirm their own perspectives, while simultaneously assisting students to learn to listen non-defensively to others who have different interests, priorities, and perspectives? These questions guide my teaching of graduate students in college student affairs preparation programs. We will turn to such teaching, after I introduce two more non-linear concepts in which the self in context is central. Each of the following can be additional foundations for student development work.

THEORIES OF MATTERING AND INVOLVEMENT

Several process-oriented theories of human development and identity formation are becoming increasingly valuable as guides to the practice of student development education. Schlossberg's works, *Counseling Adults in Transition* (1984) and *Improving Higher Education Environments for Adults* (1989; with Lynch & Chickering), demonstrate the importance of tracking the flow of change in the lives of adults, many of whom happen to be students. Schlossberg's focus on the transition process, rather than the stages of development in adult life, liberate our thinking from the time strictures of Erikson, who mapped the "normal" stages of development in adult life by age and task (1959). Her focus on the transition process permits careful inquiry into events which provoke transitions, challenges and supports necessary to make successful transitions, and the methods and environments which colleges can create to provide these challenges and supports to students at various stages of the process. Schlossberg's description of transitions resonates with chaos theory as a descriptive metaphor for both living and learning. It is not frozen into normative ideas about when people should marry or have children, what constitutes "normal" intimacy, when a person should have chosen a career and so forth.

Embedded in the Schlossberg (1989) theory is the notion that people construct meaning for their lives and activities as they go through transition after transition. The role of students-who-are-becoming-adult-development-counselors in this process is to create environments which support college students in such inevitable transitions and the important reflection, or sense-making, that accompanies them. Counselors help students who are in transition to "name the world" (Freire, 1990).

The organizing construct behind Schlossberg's (1989) approach is her theory of "mattering," which asserts that people thrive in institutions if they are convinced that they matter in the environment. If colleges organize their services in a manner that is supportive of the students' transitional process throughout, students are more likely to thrive, achieve, and accomplish their goals. Mattering is a process theory which supports the creation of environments in which persons can grow, develop, construct meaning in their lives and create an evolving and positive notion of their own realities. It can be seen as an existential approach to development conducted by the institution via policies, procedures, and programs, as well as via small group and individual counseling.

Astin's (1984) theory of "involvement" is often used to complement Schlossberg's ideas. Astin has created an elegant articulation of the adage, "You get out of an experience what you put into it." The theory of involvement states that students are satisfied with their experiences in college in direct proportion to the amount of energy, physical and emotional, that they put into creating those experiences. The more students are involved in their college experience, in any fashion that is meaningful to them, the more likely they are to be satisfied with it. The strength of Astin's (1993) theory is in the enormous amount of data he has compiled that support his very basic idea, as well as specific correlations he has observed between the types of experiences students involve themselves in and the specific areas of satisfaction they identify.

We have now reviewed the guiding notions for and the emerging "content" of student development education. Next I turn to the instructional processes that we might utilize in preparation of graduate students for the student affairs field, that is, they who are to implement student development education as professsionals.

NEW PEDAGOGIES FOR TEACHING STUDENT DEVELOPMENT THEORY

A transformation of pedagogy and assessment strategies is required if we are to apply the fluid notions of constructivism and chaos theory to teaching a student development theory course. Traditional objectivist epistemology lends itself easily to instructors presenting a "body of knowledge" which students are expected to learn, describe, and perhaps use in specific cases and situations. In contrast, constructivist epistemology assumes that students construct meaning differently from each other, based on their life experiences and belief systems.

Constructing learning as a process by which students engage with the material and each other in a manner which is simultaneously cognitive, affective, and behavioral is a departure from a teaching as a purely rational, intellectual endeavor that is centered on the teacher as expert knower who is sharing objective knowledge with apprentices. Teaching/learning, in the constructivist mode, instead "involves modeling, dialogue, practice, and confirmation" (Noddings, 1994, p.176). Each of these elements transforms learning from an intellectual process to an integrative process, one in which what one knows cannot be separated from how one feels about knowledge, how one uses knowledge, and how one chooses to rename the world in order to use knowledge to help people become more fully human.

Transformative approaches to teaching/learning in student development education have some common themes. They all integrate three domains of learning: cognitive, affective, and behavioral. They all involve "connected knowing" (Belenky, Clinchy, Goldberger & Tarule, 1986): deliberate creation of connections among students; between students and teacher; between students and knowledge, information, and meaning. Every class or learning situation becomes a learning community. Transformative approaches all require that teachers have a high degree of competency in the use of the aforementioned "fusion skills," which are used during dialogue to help students integrate content with personal values and meanings. Finally, they all involve simultaneous awareness of the borders which separate people and perspectives and the processes by which one transcends borders (Fried, 1995).

Guiding Notions

Three guiding notions for a constructivist course in college student development theory and practice follow.

Deconstructing and reconstructing theory. In the subjectivist vein, I recognize the variation in personal constructions that exists among graduate students in my teaching of an introductory student development course. However, I recognize that most students enter the graduate course with a belief in the objective validity of most theories that are presented in class. They reify theory, considering it to be an intellectual object to be "learned," like a set of "facts." I instead ask students to generate their own theories of student development.

Inclusion, caring, and reflexivity. Inclusion, caring, and reflexivity are three driving notions behind constructivist teaching. All participants are included as potential teachers and as meaning-makers. They are simultaneously included in a community of caring. For example, in the data gathering project described below, the teacher models compassion for the graduate students' own distress as they experience the distress of their interviewed undergraduate "clients" (who are also their teachers). And caring extends to the larger society. Students are also asked to consider multiple meanings of experiences, including issues of social disparity and power. The teacher demonstrates the reflective process by which students come to understand both themselves and those they serve individually and as members of disadvantaged groups, in a sociopolitical structure that shapes their opportunities. Lyons (1994) has called this dynamic "the web of self, craft, relationships, values, and ways of knowing" (p. 203). Experiencing a service learning course taught in this fashion transforms both students and teacher. This approach stands in radical contrast to traditional teaching and learning, which values "objectivity" and distance from subject matter and often separates theory from practice, thought from feeling.

Problem-posing education. A process that operationalizes this caring and reflexive pedagogy is Freire's (1990) "problem posing education". It is a process in which, above all, all participants agree on the important problems to be considered. The group describes a chosen problem in as many dimensions as it can, acquires information about the problem, brings the various value perspectives of all persons involved to the discussion, and chooses a course of action in addressing or remediating the problem. By such an inclusive and inductive approach they "rename" the world, in order to transform it and to increase possibilities for enhanced humanity or empowerment among those who grapple every day with the problem. In that process, participants come to see the world differently. They learn that their perspective is one of many, and that the skill of seeing the world through the perspective of another helps both parties experience their common humanity. They become aware of the processes of constructing knowledge, the inevitably of multiple perspectives on any problem, the difficulty and necessity of learning to remain open in the face of conflict, and the demand that people demonstrate the courage to make commitments in the face of doubt or incompleteness.

Specific Practices

Following are a number of specific methods for implementing a constructivist college student development course. A central, and initial, method is to transform theory into personal constructions and to invite students to transform their own epistemologies thereby.

Theory-making as personal transformation. Making students conscious of the theory building process is my first goal in the student development theory course. I expect students to deconstruct existing theory, to change their understanding of it as an object, and to reconstruct theory as process. They initially experience such an approach as counter-intuitive, for they have bought their texts and brought them to class expecting to "learn" the givens: the various theories of student development printed therein. They are ready to see theories as received truths and not to consider them as presentations of inferences based on specific methods of gathering and analyzing data.

In order to counter this "received" approach to learning student development theory, I first assign them to review the national demographics on college students. They are to answer: Who are today's students? Can generalizations be made about students or does one need to begin creating categories of analysis as part of the conversation—by students at large colleges, small colleges, community colleges, full-time or part-time status, age, and cultural background? They receive some prepared data but are also responsible to find new data. They must also compare data from different sources. Finally, the students must set up credibility standards for the categories on which they can agree.

The second task in constructing student development theory consists of having the graduate students generate data from undergraduates. Typically students in an introductory theory course work at area colleges and can arrange to interview undergraduates at several different types of institutions. Working in groups of four or five, the graduate students create a group of questions which each will ask of five or six undergraduates. As a group, they decide on what demographic categories matter in choosing interviewees, think about how to word and present their questions, and finally go out and actually invite students to participate in their research. The final task in this project is for the group of graduate students to pool their data, analyze it, and present it to the class. The graduate students then have to decide what they have learned from these initial reviews of both the literature and the data on college students.

The teacher plays the role of guide, mentor, and challenger in this process. At each step of the way, classroom discussions take place in which students present their inferences from the written data, the questions they intend to ask, and the students they intend to select for their sample. Previously unquestioned perceptions of simple truths and facts disappear as graduate students hear their colleagues data that is very similar to their own and come up with conflicting, competing, or even slightly different conclusions. Instead of finding answers, they are typically overwhelmed by dozens of unanticipated questions: What similarities matter in creating categories? What kind of knowledge or information is believable? When data are gathered by interviewing, does the personality or attitude of the interviewer affect the answers of the interviewee? Does time of day or time of the semester matter?

Although the primary question that this assignment attempts to answer is, "Who are today's students?" a significant learning for many of the graduate students is that there are numerous ways to answer that question. There is no "right" answer. The way questions are framed and information is categorized affects the credibility of the answers, and generalizations often have minimal credibility. Finally, they tend to realize that each graduate student has opinions about who today's students are and who they should be, and that their opinions can easily color their interpretation of the data. They become conscious of the ways in which they construct meaning from "facts," and that facts themselves are often created from combinations of perception and interpretation.

Turning in a paper which presents the research process and conclusions often creates an epistemological crisis for the novice theory-makers. How do they know what knowledge is credible? How can they live in a world with questions that have no definitive answers? If there are no definitive answers, how does one decide what to do, what policies to create, how to work with students, how to know what students need or want? What should they think about all those theories in the text books?

This last question summarizes the major point of the exercise. Students begin to become critical readers of texts and theories. They ask how data were gathered, how subjects were chosen, whether or not generalizations can reasonably be made, whether they consider conclusions accurate. Chickering and Reisser and Baxter-Magolda are transformed from their previous personae as mysterious sources of revealed "Truth" into highly skilled and credible colleagues. Students can then begin to see themselves as junior colleagues, part of whose professional responsibility is to generate knowledge and make meaning in their professional worlds.

After students generate their own theories of student development and realize that their answers are judged according to the processes they use to gather, analyze, and present data, they become peers in a search for understanding, not passive recipients of information selected by the professor. They learn to "name" their professional world. Their voice conveys a valuable perspective, but their perspective is not the only one to be considered credible. The initial experience in gathering and examining and analyzing data transforms the students and the remainder of the course. Passive, uncritical learning is no longer an option. Listening to other students is as important as listening to the teacher. Finding clear, logical ways to present arguments becomes far more important than looking for correct answers. Learning is a process in which one engages dialogically with others. Students learn to speak their minds, listen to their peers, and critique their preconceived ideas.

The remainder of this course then becomes a pleasure to teach for me. Theories of student development are now studied from the multiple perspectives of the students in the class. Theories are tested for context by having undergraduates from nondominant groups discuss their experiences in college and their sense of who they are. Every new theory is examined from multiple cultural, personal, social, economic, and empirical perspectives. The perspective of the theoretician is examined—we ask, "Who is/was this person and what unquestioned assumptions are built into the research paradigm? Did the researcher discuss the research paradigm used in analyzing the data? Does any assumption in this research disadvantage the subjects by virtue of assumptions about individualism, economic privilege, definition of family, and so forth? How would the students in this class use this theory in their work? What oversights might occur if this theory provided a single focus for student development?"

Applying the "Voice Project" method. I use several other transformative and powerful pedagogies that have been published elsewhere. They include the Voice Project and Multicultural Immersion. In Strange and Alston's (1998)Voice Project, graduate students assume responsibility for learning about a different "voice" during the course of an entire semester. These students choose a person who is significantly different from themselves by virtue of gender, age, sexual orientation, ethnicity, or combination of factors. They learn about the perspective through which that Voice understands and interprets the world by speaking with people who have one of more of the characteristics, observing members of the group in public situations like the student union, reading, attending cultural events, and finding information on the world wide web. The students assume the Voice's perspective in responding to campus events, speaking in class, reacting to situations in the wider world, and making comments in their personal journals.

By learning about their chosen Voice through multiple modalities and journaling, students direct, participate in, and reflect on their own learning process. Inevitably the complexity of their knowledge about and understanding of different cultures improves. Carney and Alston suggest that the Voice Project enhances the likelihood that students will learn to think in complex and contextual ways. Their thinking will become fluid. Their ability to adopt multiple perspectives and see difference with respect rather than negative evaluation will increase.

Multicultural immersion. A second transformative pedagogy is Evans' (1997) "Multicultural Immersion" process. It uses Kolb's experiential learning model to expose students to knowledge about the lives of members of other cultural groups. Multicultural immersion is the process of taking (or sending) students to places where another culture dominates, such as neighborhoods which are heavily populated by Chinese, Japanese, Indian, Pakistani, Caribbean, or Latin American immigrants or neighborhoods that are primarily African American. Students spend one or more days living in these neighborhoods, possibly working in a social service or church sponsored agency, visiting schools, attending religious services, and speaking with people who live in the area. They are responsible for trying to understand a different culture and paying attention their own cultural boundaries as they go through the process.

This process is similar to the one described by Strange and Alston (1998) in that it emphasizes "encouraging students to examine their feelings, fears, and stereotypes in real life situations" (Evans, 1997, p.196). It has been particularly successful in helping students understand the implications of Whiteness in the United States as a contextual factor that leads to privilege and dominance. Both of these methods can be integrated into student development theory courses by use of journaling and taking time to discuss whatever students are studying not only from their personal perspective but also from the perspective of the Voice or ethnic group they are attempting to understand.

A discussion of the means by which one has conceptualized "race" is also an excellent place to begin the examination of cultural borders. Race is a foundational element of identity among Americans (Helms, 1994). Student development courses that study identity formation are strengthened by an investigation of the role of race in identity development. Racial borders and Whiteness as constructs are pervasive, significant, confusing, and frequently blurred, particularly for White people. In short, most American students know what "race" label they carry and have some knowledge that race, as popularly defined, makes them different in some way from people of other races. A skilled teacher can draw students into the complexities of "race" as a quasi-biological construct, a sociopolitical construct, and a cultural construct (Helms, 1994). There are infinite numbers of "facts" about race available, data regarding the differential skills and accomplishments of members of various racial groups, and research studies about public perceptions of the role race plays in the life of this nation. There are few Americans who don't have preconceived opinions and feelings about these facts.

In a class discussion about race, all the elements for transformative learning are present—facts, feelings, cognitions and perceptions, values, beliefs, and relationships. During these discussions, I ask students to think about what race means to them as well as their experience of race. Was race discussed in their family, their church or synagogue, among their friends? I might also ask them what they have always wanted to ask a member of another race and how they would answer such a question if it were put to them. When classes have descendents of African and European people in them, the conversations are often challenging, frightening, and rewarding.

The means by which the teacher presents the topic, makes perspective and interpretation via the "race" lens visible. How he or she manages the dialogue determines the power of the outcome. Unfortunately, too many opportunities to use race as an opportunity to examine borders and transform understanding are missed because teachers lack the skills to manage the discussion in a productive manner. Student development educators, using counseling skills, can generally manage the predictable conflicts and misunderstandings. Unfortunately, these same educators often lack the depth of knowledge in these sociological topics to ensure that the discussion has intellectual integrity. The opposite is often true for faculty in the traditional disciplines, regardless of the radical nature of their perspectives. That is, these faculty have the depth of understanding but lack the discussion management skills. In any case, discussion of race has the potential to serve as an opportunity to enhance border crossings on at least two levels: crossings between students of different racial perspectives and collaboration between teachers who have worked from the student development and the academic perspectives.

Assessing student learning. Assessing student learning in this course consists of evaluating student class presentations, papers in which students analyze theories, their analysis of ethical dilemmas in student development, and role plays (see Appendix for examples). I evaluate student contributions in class discussions carefully. Can they express and support their point of view? Can they listen carefully to colleagues who disagree? Can they integrate theory and practice? Can they review a case and determine which theory or theories might shed the most light on the problems? Do they understand ways to balance wisdom derived from personal experience with empirical data that can be generalized, but contradicts their personal experience? In short, have their active listening, critical thinking, and communication skills developed so that they can articulate and apply what they have learned in the course?

CONCLUSION

This approach to teaching and learning is quite contrasting to teaching as imparting of the truth. It sustains a vision of hope in a complex and confusing world. It supports an endless process of inquiry, dialogue, transformation, and justice through empathy and effective conflict management. Although undergraduate student development education has traditionally been considered non-academic or co-curricular, it is central to the academic mission of any university that cares about character development or the creation of learning communities. In an era in which boundaries are collapsing, students who know information or who have technical skills, but who do not understand how to communicate across the differences of perspective shaped by ethnicity, sexual orientation, gender, race and disability are not educated people. They may "know"—but they often cannot "do." If they cannot understand others who are different from them as well as they must, then neither can they make themselves understood. If they cannot take perspective and emotion into account in decision-making, they will be forced into smaller and smaller groups of people who are just like them where the atmosphere is likely to be fraught with fear and mistrust of outsiders.

Ultimately transformative approaches to teaching student development education are transformative for the entire academic world and the epistemological assumptions on which it is based. Transformative learning does rename the world. It redefines credible knowledge. It takes perspective into account and thus overturns some of the basic assumptions about objectivity, universality, and impersonality that shaped the scientific approach to knowing (Fried, 1995). It melts the boundaries between teaching, learning, and counseling because knowledge becomes simultaneously personal and impersonal, subjective and objective. Teacher becomes student and student becomes teacher. Self worth transcends worth ascribed to role. A Buddhist aphorism states that, "No one is my friend; no one is my enemy; everyone is my teacher." In that way, everything becomes new.

Appendix

Cases in Ethics and Administration

1. For several years, the Black Students Association has been demanding that the university administration improve its support services for African American students. These students, who are less than 3% of the total student community, come primarily from urban settings and are first generation college students. Your university is in a rural area. The students who initiated these protests in their sophomore year are within three months of graduation. Despite years of promises, nothing significant has changed. One of these students decides to go on a hunger strike in her room in your residence hall. She sends an email to the president informing her of what she is doing. The president asks the Vice President of Student Affairs (VSPA) to investigate and handle the matter since the VPSA has been responding all along to the demands of this student group. The Vice President calls in the Director of Housing and gives him a note to give to you, inviting the student to come to his office and discuss the situation with him (VPSA). The student refuses to leave her room and says that she wants to talk to the President. If any talks are going to happen, they are going to happen in her room. The student tells you to deliver her message to the Director or the VP or the Pres. She doesn't care. She's had tough times before. She hasn't eaten in a week and shows no signs of giving in. The other students in your building are getting worried and you can't figure out what to do next, but you're worried too.

2. You are the new director of admissions at a large, urban university. During your first week on the job, you discover thousands of promotional brochures painting the university as a city campus with a suburban feel, lots of trees and grass and flowers. You can't find anything on the campus that looks anything like the scenes in the brochure. In addition, all of the students in the brochure are white or vaguely Asian looking. There are no African Americans or Latinos, yet you know that these students are in your market target groups. You ask about the schedule for the next revision of the brochure and discover that this brochure has been in use for years. It is printed by a company that is owned by one of the trustees. What is in the brochure fits the trustee's vision of what this campus should be. The trustee/owner edits the copy and prints the brochure.

Discussion assignment: Within your group, using an ethical decision making model, discuss your case addressing each of these questions in sequence. As you answer the questions, use your understanding of ethical principles, virtues, and context as they have been presented to you in earlier classes. At the end of the discussion period you will be expected to present your case analysis to the rest of the class. The emphasis is on your ethical reasoning. It is conceivable that different groups discussing the same case could come up with different solutions using equally valid ethical ideas.

Ethical Decision Making: Thinking Your Way Through Complex Problems

What do we mean by "ethics?" "Ethics involves making decisions of a moral nature about people and their interactions in society . . . when faced with ethical dilemmas or new issues (we) must be equipped with thinking tools that allow (us) to critically evaluate and interpret ethical codes . . . and evaluate (our) feelings as appropriate or inappropriate guides for ethical behavior." (Kitchener, 1986, p.306)

What are ethical codes? Ethical codes are systematic guidelines created by professional organizations to help members of those organizations and non-members in the specific profession to make decisions in complex or confusing areas where the "right" thing to do is unclear or ambiguous.

What are ethical dilemmas? Ethical dilemmas and issues arise when there is a conflict between two different ideas about what is right in the situation or when two different rights come into conflict.

Questions to ask yourself when faced with an ethical dilemma that requires a decision and possible action (Rion,1996)

1. Why is this bothering me?
2. Who else matters?
3. Is it my problem?
4. What is the ethical concern?
5. What do others think?
6. Am I being true to myself?

Ethical approaches to dilemmas require awareness of our thoughts, feelings, and behavioral response possibilities, and the ability to anticipate potential outcomes and consequences. Living and working with an ethical perspective is complicated. If fairness and integrity matter to you or to the people you supervise or report to, it's worth the effort.

References

Kitchener, K. (1986) "Teaching Applied Ethics in Counselor Education." *Journal of Counseling and Development. (64)*, pp. 306-310

Meara, N., Schmidt, L. & Day,D (1996) "Principles and Virtues: A foundation for Ethical Decisions, Policies and Character." *The Counseling Psychologist. (24),1*, pp. 4-77

Rion, M. (1996) *The Responsible Manager.* Amherst, MA: HRD Press

Utilizing Multiple Theories in Complex Contexts, or Making Sense of Confusing Realities

This activity is designed to integrate everything you have read for this week in a specific context.

Task: You are to design a *career counseling center or intake/orientation center or learning/academic progress center* and identify several programs or activities which will take place in that center. Your center will serve both traditional and non-traditional age groups. The students who use your center will be members of different ethnic and religious groups, including AngloAmerican Christians, males and females, gay/lesbian and heterosexual, able bodied and disabled.

Issues: Your center will address several issues for all students: gender, age, and identity group orientation(s); identifying and creating options for students' futures; helping students develop competence academically, professionally and interpersonally; and developing a sense of community among students (and possibly their families).

Process:
1. Name your center. Think of your center as a place that serves two major groups of students, traditional age and older (25 years and above).
2. Identify the developmental needs that you believe students from each group will have as they request services from this center. List the topics from particular theories that you used in deciding what kinds of developmental needs your students have.
3. Identify the learning goals that you believe your students would have if they came to your center.
4. List the types of programs and activities that you believe would help the students who use your center - what do they need to do, to research, to think about, to talk about individually with counselors or in student groups?

It would be most helpful to answer these questions in the form of a chart that you could put on the board

	Younger	*Older*
• Developmental needs		
• Relevant theory		
• Learning Goals		
• Types of Activities		

Knowing and Reasoning in College

You are all members of the Board of Governors for the Student Union. Your group has many responsibilities for student activities over the course of the year. It is now April and you are planning the major program series for next year. This program series has adopted two goals: 1) It must reflect the diversity of student tastes and interests on campus, and 2) it must bring members of diverse groups together at these events so that they can learn to understand and appreciate each other's ideas about entertainment and fun. You are to plan four events to take place during the next school year. They can be geared toward any size group. They must be entertaining. They must involve some type of educational outcome. Your budget is no problem. You have access to all campus facilities. You may even choose to rent a facility off campus if it serves your purposes.

Each of you is to role play the "way of knowing" which your group discussed in the first part of class. One of you will play the male pattern of thinking and the other will play the female pattern. Eight of you will participate in the role play. The rest of your group will sit behind you and coach when necessary. You now have a few minutes to discuss with your group your approach to this meeting - what issues would concern you, where you would seek advice in unclear areas, and any other processes which you think would be significant.

Charting Your Background : A Personal and Cultural Map

1. Think back to the time you began to attend school, or earlier if you can, and try to remember all the different cultural influences in your life. Think about your own ethnic heritage from one or both sets of grandparents, your race, your religion, your gender, other groups represented in your neighborhood. List the cultures which you believe had some influence on your own development and world view.
2. Think about the first time you realized that something about your own upbringing was different from someone else's. What was the issue? How did you feel when you realized the difference? Did you do anything about it? If so, what?
3. Identify the two cultures from question 1 that had the strongest influence on you as you were growing up.
4. Try to answer the following messages which each culture gave you:

	Culture 1	*Culture 2*

- Life Messages
- Family Relations
- Important Goals and Values
- Education
- Faith

Psychosocial Development: Key Factors and Cognitions

1. Try to remember a significant moment in your own life when you real-
    ized that you were "on your own," possibly for the first time.

    (a) Describe the event

    (b) What were the salient emotions for you?

    (c) What were the key issues you had to resolve or address?

2. Remember the first time you made friends with or learned to respect a
    person you would never have previously paid attention to.

    (a) Who was the person and why would you have ignored or avoided
        him or her previously?

    (b) Why did you change your mind or behavior?

    c) How did your emotional reactions change?

REFERENCES

Astin, A. (1984) Student involvement: A developmental theory for higher educa-
    tion. *Journal of College Student Personnel, 25,* 297-308.

Astin, A. (1993) *What matters in college.* San Francisco: Jossey Bass

Atkinson, D., Morten, G., & Sue, D. (1993) *Counseling American minorities* (4th ed.).
    Madison, WI: Brown & Benchmark

Bailey, D., & Hall, S. (1992) The vertigo of displacement: Shifts within Black docu-
    mentary practices. *Crucial Decade: Black British Photography in the 80's, (special
    issue),* 15-23.

Baxter-Magolda, M. (1992). *Knowing and reasoning in college.* San Francisco: Jossey
    Bass.

Belenky, M., Clinchy, B., Goldberger, N., & Tarule, J. (1986). *Women's ways of know-
    ing.* New York: Basic Books.

Capra, F. (1989). *Uncommon wisdom.* New York: Simon & Schuster

Carn, S., & Fassinger, R. (1996). Revisioning sexual minority identity formation: A
    new model of lesbian identity and its implications for counseling and research."
    The Counseling Psychologist, 24, 508-534.

Cass, V. (1979). Homosexual identity formation: A theoretical model. *Journal of Ho-
    mosexuality, 4,* 219-235.

Chickering, A., & Reisser, L. (1993). *Education and identity,* (2nd ed.). San Francisco:
    Jossey Bass.

Crookston, B. (1973). Education for human development. In C. Warnath's, (Ed.),
    New directions for college counselors, (pp. 47-65). San Francisco: Jossey Bass.

Cross, W. (1971). The Negro to Black conversion experience: Toward a psychology
    of Black liberation. *Black World, 20* (9), 13-27.

Drum, D. (1980). Understanding student development. In W. Morrill & J. Hurst,
    (Eds.), *Dimensions of intervention for student development,* (pp.14-38), New York:
    John Wiley & Sons.

Erikson, E. (1959). Identity in the life cycle. *Psychological Issues, 1,* 18-164.

Evans, N. (1997). Multicultural immersion: Using learning styles to educate about
    difference. *Journal of College Student Development, 38,* 195-196.

Fried, J. (1995). *Shifting paradigms in student affairs.* Lanham, MD: University Press
    of America/American College Personnel Association.

Freire, P. (1990). *Pedagogy of the oppressed.* New York: Continuum.

Giroux, H., & McLaren, P. , (Eds). (1994). *Between borders.* New York: Routledge.

Helms, J. (1994). The conceptualization of racial identity and other 'racial' constructs.
    In E. Trickett, R. Watts, & D. Birman's, (Eds), *Human diversity: Perspectives on
    people in context,* (pp. 283-311). San Francisco: Jossey Bass.

Hoare, C. (1991). Psychosocial identity development and cultural others. *Journal of
    Counseling and Development, 70,* 45-53.

hooks, b. (1994). *Teaching to transgress.* New York: Routledge.

Kitzinger, C. (1995). Social constructionism: Implications for lesbian and gay psychology. In A. D'Augelli & C. Patterson, (Eds.), *Lesbian, gay and bisexual identities over the lifespan*, (pp. 136-164). New York: Oxford University Press.

Kolb, D. (1984). *Experiential learning.* Englewood Cliffs, NJ: Prentice Hall.

Lyons, N. (1994). Dilemmas of knowing: Ethical and epistemological dimensions of teacher's work and development. In L. Stone, editor, *The education feminism reader*, (pp. 195-220). New York: Routledge.

Maslow, A. (1971). *The farther reaches of human nature.* New York: Viking Press.

Noddings, N. (1994/1988). An ethic of caring and its implications for instructional arrangements. In L. Stone, (Ed.), *The education feminism reader*, (pp. 171-183). New York: Routledge.

Okun, B., Fried, J., & Okun, M. (1999). *Understanding diversity.* Pacific Grove, CA: Brooks Cole.

Palmer, P. (1997). Teaching and learning in community. *About Campus, 2* (5), 4-13.

Schlossberg, N. (1984). *Counseling adults in transition.* New York: Springer.

Schlossberg, N., Lynch, A., & Chickering, A. (1989). *Improving higher education environments for adults.* San Francisco: Jossey-Bass.

Strange, C., & Alston, L. (1998). Voicing differences: Encouraging multicultural learning. *Journal of College Student Development, 39,* 87-99.

Wilbur, K. (1996). *A brief history of everything.* Boston: Shambala Press.

17

Teaching Substance Abuse Counseling: Constructivist Hyperlinks From Classroom to Clients

Jane J. Carroll and James A. Bazan

Vehicular homicide, robbery, spousal battery, rape, child abuse, and murder are acts that people in society condemn. We know that individuals under the influence of mind-altering drugs commit a disproportionate number of such crimes. We further know that consuming inordinate amounts of alcohol and other drugs leads to malnourishment, liver and brain damage, cardiovascular disease, and several forms of cancer. Alcohol also is associated with a significant number of suicides. Herein lies a paradox. Despite the onerous consequences of substance use, people in the United States who regularly abuse such substances number in the millions.

It is complicated and challenging work to counsel individuals who, according to Western society's standards, excessively use mind-altering, addictive substances to attain desired psychological states. Substance abuse counselors are expected to use special skills to assist clients toward the desired goal—sobriety (Hosie, West, & Mackey, 1990). Sobriety implies abstinence from alcohol and other drugs and adoption of healthful ways of thinking, feeling, and behaving.

To prepare students who might someday help clients change their "substance dependence" (American Psychiatric Association, 1994, p. 176), most counselor education programs offer academic courses and opportunities for supervised field experiences in substance abuse counseling. Some programs offer general introductory courses, and others provide a curriculum for students who want to specialize in this area. The purpose of this chapter is to stimulate thinking about the teaching of substance abuse counseling courses. These constructivist ideas can be used to teach both introductory and specialized courses in substance abuse counseling. It would not be feasible to incorporate every idea described here into any one course. We invite instructors to use the activities and ideas that they consider suitable, depending on the goals and objectives of the courses they teach.

GOALS FOR A COURSE IN SUBSTANCE ABUSE COUNSELING

Topics that instructors typically address in substance abuse counseling courses include: theoretical explanations for the etiology and maintenance of substance dependence, assessment and diagnosis of substance-related disorders, psychopharmacology, dual diagnoses, documentation and record-keeping, treatment planning for substance-dependent clients, clinical counseling skills as applied to substance abuse, and primary and relapse prevention. Additionally, instructors frequently consider cultural factors that impact all of the aforementioned areas.

Such a broad academic focus requires a host of goals; meeting all of them would be impossible in one course. Also, because philosophies regarding substance dependence and its treatment differ among scholars, scientists, practitioners, and certification-conferring entities (such as states and professional organizations), controversy exists about which goals are necessary and sufficient. Therein lies the content challenge for constructivist substance abuse instructors and their students.

We suggest, therefore, that instructors in constructivist-oriented substance abuse counseling courses assist students to reach the three broad learning goals, that we discuss in this chapter. These goals are: Students will be able to (a) communicate multiple perspectives related to substance dependence and treatment, (b) understand how individuals create knowledge about the nature of substance dependence, and (c) achieve understanding of their own dependencies and the sources of their own meaning making about substance dependence and treatment. We also suggest that instructors design course-specific objectives to empower students to be reflexive and flexible in their constructions.

The reflexive process of deconstructing and reconstructing meanings about substance dependence happens best as a recursive process at many different levels. Instructors canconsciously deconstruct and reconstruct their own perceptions of substance dependence in the classrooms. Students can examine their preconceptions about substance dependence the substance-dependent clients and consider alternative understandings under the tutelage of their instructors. New understandings can evolve as students interact with others, both informally and in structured educational environments. Students and instructors can then draw on these reconstructed meanings when working with clients and supervisees. In turn, because clients become part of a new system (treatment) that engages in these deconstruction and reconstruction interactions, they also learn to recreate their own understandings. Clients engaged in such a process, then, in turn, contribute to counselors,' supervisors,' and instructors' reformulations of the meanings given to substance dependence. A description of three major learning goals of this course and related teaching methods follows.

PERSPECTIVES ON SUBSTANCE DEPENDENCE

Explanations of Substance Dependence

Explanations work. That is, they perform tasks for those who subscribe to them. The reasons people give for using and abusing alcohol and other drugs reveal their common-sense worlds. For instance, in the following conversation a client explains the reasons why she and her family believed that she had been unable to abstain from using drugs, although she had been treated for substance dependence several times.

Counselor:
You shared with me that you've been to treatment multiple times. What do you think kept sending you back out?

Client:
Well, my family called it weakness. I need to bite the bullet. It was a lot of dealing with issues that had happened with my father. There's a lot of things, a lot of secrets in that home. Lots of secrets. And they're sick secrets. I can't believe they happened. It was like I had no power within myself. I feel that way now, I don't have what it takes not to use (Carroll & Bazan, 1997).

Explanations for why people use alcohol and other drugs differ widely according to the needs and experiences of those holding the perspectives. Generally, substance dependence is attributed to the usual suspects, such as genetic influences, weak will, learned behavior, disease process, emotional immaturity, depression, and/or anxiety. While modernists have no problem with the idea of causation, modernist substance abuse experts do not agree on how to best manage the problem. They do, however, understand "substance abuse" as referring to particular substances, as abuse, as a problem, and as manageable. Postmodernity undermines the authority of any single understanding.

Counseling students' explanations for substance dependence matter to counselor educators. Students usually present their explanatory systems as "categories" (Lakoff, 1987), such as "substance abuse" and "recreational use" and various "metaphorical concepts" (Lakoff & Johnson, 1980, p. 6). For example, consider the metaphorical concept that addiction is a disease. In this view, addicted individuals may pass through various stages of illness, in which they feel sick and helpless. Using the disease metaphor, clients are (a) in an abnormal state of health possibly requiring hospitalization, (b) at the mercy of an external agent, (c) not responsible for the cause of the addiction, and (d) obliged to seek help from others if they want to recover. In contrast, if students explain addiction metaphorically as "sin," they would claim that addiction is (a) abnormal behavior, (b) controlled by exercising self-restraint, (c) characterized by weakness, and (d) deterred by punishment.

Categories and metaphors create narrative links (Gubrium & Holstein, 1997) between the explanations and other important areas of the students' worlds. Students use these links to align realities of behavior with the stock of knowledge they have already constructed about the meanings of such behavior. These links are important in students' conceptions of clients and psychological difficulties. The understandings they hold in common with others help to define their membership in a group. The group is "those who understand such behavior in this way." Given the charged rhetoric surrounding substance abuse, students in constructivist-oriented classrooms often are surprised by the notion of "understandings as group-creating systems."

Explanations for Treatment

Similarly, different philosophies underlie the diverse ways substance dependence is treated or managed. Approaches to treating substance dependence include medical and psychological treatment, "boot camps," incarceration, religion, education, and simply ignoring the state of affairs. Although they do not propose to offer formal treatment, organized self-help groups have their own philosophies and guiding systems. Women for Sobriety (WFS) has its thirteen Statements of the "New Life" Program (Kirkpatrick, 1977), and Alcoholics Anonymous (AA) has its 12 Steps to Recovery (*Alcoholics Anonymous*, 1976).

In summary, because no agreement exists among professionals about the etiology of substance dependence or how to help substance-dependent individuals, no course content in substance abuse counseling can be based on universally accepted principles. Counselor educators can, however, help students develop awareness about their grounding perspectives on substance dependence and substance-dependent clients. We now move to implications of these worldview notions for teaching the course in substance dependence counseling.

THE CONSTRUCTIVIST TEACHING
OF SUBSTANCE ABUSE COUNSELING

Constructivist counselor educators and supervisors may initially need to provoke student creation of knowledge. They also may need to create academic environments in which students together examine and share concepts, viewpoints, and experiences; environments which support knowledge construction.

Creating an environment in which students are willing and eager to voice their viewpoints serves three purposes. First, when they share thoughts and feelings with peers and instructors, students learn to trust their abilities to formulate points of view and to speak and be heard. Second, students experience a way to help clients who fear talking in groups or who may be "stuck" in one way of contemplating the many problems associated with alcohol and other drug dependence. Substance-dependent clients often feel helpless and hopeless; therefore, if counselors provide safe and stimulating environments in which clients can explore their thoughts and feelings, clients may construct new meanings for their lives and move toward different ways of living. Third, if students recognize that people hold multiple perspectives on substance dependence, they may reject the notion of a single answer to problems and glimpse the nature of a constructed universe.

Course Objectives

Examining, or deconstructing, socially determined perspectives about substance dependence means challenging the viability of the old "truths" students have assumed. It means developing new constructs and new understandings in the process. Constructivist instructors may want to include such objectives in their design of substance abuse counseling courses; such objectives are consistent with the three previously-discussed major goals for the course. Examples of content-oriented objectives that meet current standards of many substance abuse counseling curricula and also encourage students to be reflexive and flexible follow. We describe course objectives in these terms. Students will:

- demonstrate understanding of cultural factors when discussing and applying models of the etiology of substance dependence.
- communicate understanding of various theoretical, philosophical, and historical perspectives from which treatment and prevention of substance dependence emerge.
- examine their own history related to perspectives on assessment, treatment planning, counseling, relapse prevention, and aftercare for substance dependence.

- discuss their perspectives on the social, economic, political, psychological, biological, and cultural factors which may contribute to the etiology and maintenance of substance dependence.
- describe their perspectives and those of others about how the biological, psychological, and sociological effects of using psychoactive drugs contribute to the etiology and maintenance of substance dependence.

Implementing Social Construction in the Classroom

Counselor educators who teach substance abuse counseling courses may collaborate with students to generate constructivist learning environments. Instructors can model and facilitate the self-reflective behaviors that encourage students to progress toward goals. By so doing, instructors aid students to become constructivist counselors themselves, counselors who can be self-reflectively in collaborative relationships with clients.

McAuliffe and Lovell (2000) recommend that instructors help to create classroom atmospheres in which students are unafraid to express doubt or skepticism. By encouraging unencumbered and straightforward communication in classrooms, instructors heighten students' experience of the social construction of knowledge in classrooms and in society in general. Students may be unaccustomed to focusing on *how* they make sense of the label "substance dependence" (American Psychiatric Association, 1994, p. 176) as a notion that represents some set of client behaviors and beliefs. Constructivist instructors, therefore, have as a primary responsibility to depict by example the sense-making process. They offer propositions or questions for discussion and model how to study others' arguments and viewpoints.

Students may struggle in such uncharted epistemological territories. Consciously social constructionist environments are often unfamiliar. They are places in which teachers and students together pose concepts and queries, not for the purpose of obtaining routine or rehearsed answers, but to inspire reflection and analysis on such emerging knowledge. In constructivist-oriented classrooms, students collectively engage in the social effort of interacting with clients and peers, while being individually introspective. Students find themselves initially mystified and confused by having to consciously perform multiple roles.

"Reflexivity" (Bourdieu & Wacquant, 1992; Gergen & Gergen, 1991) directs individuals" attention to the larger narratives in which their specific meanings are embedded. The first task is for students to understand the cultural and other contexts of their previous constructions. Then they can consciously create new understandings of substance dependence by engaging in class discussions and activities, reading articles and books written from various theoretical positions, and having authentic clinical experiences in the field and simulated clinical experiences in the laboratory. Through such explorations, they will likely see that each person's perceptions, life experiences, systems for logical reasoning, and emotional responses will determine his or her interpretations and conclusions.

Why is it important for educators to promote knowledge of this meaning-making process during the substance abuse course? Because the openness or narrowness of one's constructions influence the conceptualization of clients and the attendant work of counseling. In the end, all substance abuse counselors implement their understandings of substance dependence in their work with clients. A constructivist classroom inspires students to become self-authoring agents who are sensitive to their own and their clients' constructions of substance dependence.

We (Carroll and Bazan (1997) studied clients who sought treatment for substance dependence. We noted their struggle for new voices with which to understand their changed social circumstances. Their early templates for survival were fashioned with the use of drugs. They needed new constructions. Being aware of the dynamics of constructivist thinking helps counselors correspondingly work in a constructivist fashion with clients when clients provide accounts such as the one that follows:

Client:
> You know, I've been using for so long—I didn't know no other way to cope with anything. So many times drugs saved my life, so many times. If I had not used, then I think–I know–I wouldn't be here . . . . He hurt me a lot. He would burn me between my legs with the cigars. He was a real sick man (Carroll & Bazan, 1997).

Here the client has constructed a positive, survival-embracing story of drug use. The counselor begins with that survival story, but moves on to help the client create a new story. Following are some course activities that enhance students' awareness of their worldviews and increase their reflexivity.

The "Quiet Conversation" activity. Some students may be reluctant to disclose their thinking about sensitive or controversial topics. They may fear their peers' scorn or their instructors' disapproval. Therefore, a classroom atmosphere in which students feel welcome and are enthusiastic about communicating is needed. An activity that instructors can introduce to any size class in order to promote communication we call "Quiet Conversation."

This activity helps students to become aware of their thought processes in response to another's thoughts. Students and instructors write responses to selected quotes, poems, propositions, or lines from films or songs that have been pre-selected by students or instructors. We collect the responses and then shuffle and redistribute them. Each person silently reads another's response and writes brief reflective comments on the first writer's observations. Because the reader's thoughts are contingent on the first writer's response, students become aware of how their perspectives are constructed in response to situations they encounter. Students then discuss their reactions to this experience in first writer-second writer pairs and later as an entire group. In a variation on this exercise, readers respond to first writers' thoughts and both writers remain anonymous. Privacy allows both writers to fully develop their reactions and to express themselves freely.

Group projects. Instructors also encourage group communication and individual self-confidence in constructivist learning environments by providing opportunities for students to collaborate on class assignments. For example, instructors may ask small groups of students to research and present on selected topics related to substance dependence. Other possible activities include student-led seminars, workshops, and lectures. Students may lead question and answer sessions on such subjects as "The Need for Awareness of Gender Differences in Substance Abuse Counseling," "Self-Help Groups: Compatibility with Counseling Theories," "Assessing Substance-Abusing Adolescents," and "Preventing Relapse to Cocaine Use." Instructors may arrange poster sessions in which all students display posters with information about recent developments in substance abuse counseling practices or research. A few students might present posters at each class session or the class can present a "poster fair" in a common area for the benefit of many students. Students provide their classmates with resource materials, such as relevant reading lists and helpful Internet sites.

Providing opportunities for application. Instructors enhance communication when students receive opportunities for simulating counseling with peers. Working in laboratory settings, students perform assessments and intakes and practice individual and group substance abuse counseling skills and interventions. Peers assume client identities for the duration of the class. Sufficient time for students and instructors to discuss and exchange viewpoints following laboratory experiences needs to be allowed.

Using personal reflection. Among the perspectives that could contribute importantly to discussions in substance abuse counseling classes are those of students who have a history of alcohol and other drug abuse or dependency or who have family members with such a history. Yet, such students' psychosocial histories may include painful and/or shameful experiences which may inhibit their participation in class discussions. A song by Prine (1971b) illustrates the emotional impact on a child of a man addicted to heroin: "There's a hole in daddy's arm where all the money goes/And Jesus Christ died for nothing I suppose/Little pitchers have big ears/Don't

stop to count the years/Sweet songs never last long/On broken radios"
(Prine, 1971b).

Students do not easily discuss such disillusionment and sadness with
relative strangers in a classroom. The stigma often associated with sub-
stance-dependence is alive and well, even among students who study substance abuse counseling. Therefore, instructors need to approach such discussions with caution and sensitivity. They might, for instance, ask students to individually write out their stories so that that their experiences
can be anonymously shared with the class.

The use of groups. Group work is central to substance abuse counseling
and to developing a constructivist worldview. Certain conditions set the
tone for the social construction of knowledge in the classroom group. For
instance, instructors can encourage group cohesiveness by (a) modeling
appropriate self-disclosure, (b) positively encouraging students' willingness to participate in discussions and other activities, (c) respecting and
showing concern for students, and (d) actively listening and appropriately
responding to students. Such behavior encourages students, in turn, to develop these attitudes and skills and to take these beliefs and practices into
their work with clients.

Group counseling provides healing (Yalom, 1985) by instilling hope,
offering a sense of safety and support, generating group cohesiveness, providing a feeling of universality, allowing vicarious learning, and providing opportunities for interpersonal learning (George & Dustin, 1988). Counselor educators model effective group leadership and help students experience positive group process during class. Students also benefit from ex-
posure to diverse perspectives and descriptions of others' experiences. Students who experience the power of these circumstances in class can encourage those same conditions in therapeutic groups that they facilitate as
substance abuse counselors.

Having guests in class. Students and instructors may invite guests to
address classes about a multitude of subjects related to substance dependence. Differing perspectives and experiences come from law enforcement
officers, detoxification counselors, social workers, pastoral counselors,
school counselors, physicians, nurses, DUI school instructors, and speakers representing various self-help groups. Clinicians who provide specialized substance abuse counseling to racial and ethnic minorities, women,
adolescents, the elderly, and the dually diagnosed (physical and mental)
offer other valuable perspectives. Students and instructors can share responsibility for identifying and inviting guest speakers.

Students can then process the viewpoints offered by guest speakers
through recording private thoughts in journals, discussing speakers' top-

ics and perspectives in class, writing reaction papers, and comparing and contrasting speakers' perspectives with those of other sources, such as those found in professional and popular literature.

Deconstructing historical perspectives. Instructors can use a variety of methods and materials to help students learn how people have, over time, constructed meanings about substance dependence. For example, viewing films and reading accounts of societal attitudes and practices involving alcohol both preceding and following Prohibition helps students become aware that society's viewpoints toward alcohol use have a historical and social context.

To gain further historical perspective, students might interview people who have memories of the 1960s and 1970s and who retain opinions about the "counter culture" of that time. One common attitude toward marijuana use was expressed in John Prine's "Illegal Smile:" "Ahhh but fortunately I have the key to escape reality / And you may see me tonight with an illegal smile / It don't cost very much, but it lasts a long while" (Prine, 1971a). Drug use in the late 1960s and early 1970s was popularized, sentimentalized, and demonized by the media and popular culture. Students may find it illustrative to search for parallel examples from current culture.

Popular cinema is also a useful means for showing how society determines which acts are unlawful and dangerous. When the motion picture *Reefer Madness* was released originally as *Tell Your Children* in the mid-1930s, its melodramatic message warned teenagers about the dangers of smoking marijuana. Now people view the film as parody. It is found in video stores on the shelves labeled "comedy." *Reefer Madness* is an exaggerated, misleading dramatization of how smoking marijuana causes ordinarily sensible people to abandon their standards of morality and indeed become homicidal. Furthermore, the film's message implies that young people whose parents divorced are at particular risk for grave consequences from smoking marijuana. Since the film was first shown, people have come to disbelieve its overstated and sensational warnings. People now know from experience that what was once considered to be an accurate representation of the effects of certain drugs is hyperbolic and misleading, if not altogether inaccurate information.

It may be useful to invite a speaker to deconstruct historical perspectives on substance use. For example, the speaker might talk to classes about the role of xenophobia (the association of marijuana with a perceived alien menace) and the survival needs of the Bureau of Narcotics in the mid-1930s. As students compare and contrast the messages in *Reefer Madness* with more recent films that feature alcohol and other drug dependence as their themes, they can discern the impact societal attitudes have on how individuals conceive of substance use and abuse.

Evidence of societal influence on people's thinking about substance dependence can be brought to light in small group discussions, written papers, or panel discussions. For example, students can contrast historical differences in attitudes and in social and psychological principles and practices as they relate to substance dependence. The many theories—moral, medical, disease, humanistic, developmental, and psychoanalytic—explaining the etiology of substance dependence are rich with propositions to compare and contrast. Material to feed discussions about how these models previously were accepted or rejected and currently are used or discounted is abundant in professional journals and popular literature.

Deconstructing current perspectives. As students construct meaning about alcohol and other drug use, panel discussions supporting and rejecting relevant public policy issues can be valuable for sorting out perspectives. Questions for discussion could include the role of government in regulating addictive drugs, whether drug abuse should be treated as a health or a criminal justice matter, if needle exchanges are desirable, whether controlled drinking is a treatment option, and if alcohol advertisements should be illegal. Panelists can be asked to obtain reliable information; support and refute particular points of view; provide useful handouts such as relevant Internet sites and reading lists to other class members; and respect other panel members' viewpoints by not engaging in debate, but rather courteously presenting alternative perspectives.

Students can learn about the perspectives of people with histories of substance dependence and the multiple interpretations of the "truths" which they defend by attending open 12-Step meetings or other support or educational group meetings. Students can write reaction papers about their experiences. General guidelines for attending 12-Step meetings and an outline of a format we suggest students use to write a reaction paper to a 12-Step meeting is included in the Appendix.

By attending self-help group meetings, students become acquainted first-hand with why support groups are so named. Moreover, perceptions of self-help groups as gatherings of "losers" may be altered when they observe how attendees accomplish their goals by reframing the meanings of their alcohol and other drug use.

Examining personal constructs about substance use. At some point, students need to think about the personal meaning for them of substance dependence. Their personal history of substance use and that of family and friends influence their thinking. To see how students' perceptions change, counselor educators only have to compare students' descriptions of "alcoholics" and "addicts" in early class sessions with descriptions in later sessions. In early sessions, students will offer popular social constructions,

such as "grungy," "weak-willed," "criminal," and "irresponsible," and categorical concepts such as "men like my uncle," "people with addictive
personalities," and "kids who can't resist peer pressure." Such labels or
categories reflect conceptualizing substance dependence as (a) caused by
or leading to poor personal hygiene, (b) not present in people who are
resolute and honorable, (c) absent in people who are dependable, (d) found
only in people who are predisposed psychologically, or (e) particular to
people readily distinguished by comparison with one's uncle.

Instructors help students become aware of the limitations and implications of such constructs about substance dependence. By paying attention
to factors that may be implicated in peoples' drug use such as gender, race,
ethnicity, age, socioeconomic status, self-concept, and family and social
history students may develop more holistic, constructivist understandings.
Keeping journals in which students and instructors record their thoughts,
observations, and unanswered questions can stimulate introspection and
consideration of others' perspectives. Discussion of journal entries that students and instructors find most striking can take place throughout the semester.

Exercise in practicing behavior reduction. Another activity that helps students examine their constructs is the Behavior-Reduction Exercise. Students
first identify a substance or activity they want to eliminate or, at least, with
which they want to reduce their involvement. They should consider the
activity or use of the substance harmful, compulsive, self-destructive, or
non-beneficial. Students then write about their history of involvement with
the substance or activity, their reasons for choosing the particular substance
or activity as the focus of the Behavior Reduction Exercise, and the goals
they hope to achieve by eliminating or reducing the use of the substance or
behavior.

During the first phase, the "Baseline Period," students record the extent of their involvement with the substance or activity. They note information such as amounts consumed, amount of time engaged in the activity, number of times engaged in the activity, where the acts occurred, time
the acts occurred, and any physiological, psychological, or sociological stressors related to the activity. They note predisposing or contributing conditions and physical and/or emotional reactions to these stressors and to
using the substance or engaging in the activity.

During the next stage, the "Reduction Period," students attempt to abstain from the substance or activity. They continue to record the same
information they recorded during the Baseline Period, except they also
record reactions to and successes in reducing or eliminating the substance
or activity.

During the final stage, the "Follow-up Period," students may use the substance or engage in the activity to the extent they choose. Students record their consumption or activity patterns as outlined above.

After completing the three phases, students discuss with classmates and instructors their reactions, speculations, and thoughts about the implications of the experience. Students compare and contrast their experiences with their previously held perceptions of what substance-dependent individuals experience when attempting to withdraw form alcohol and other drug use.

The "Who are we and what are we doing here?" activity. During this interactive exercise students talk about their own and others' substance use, after the group has become fairly well acquainted and students have dared to risk self-disclosure. Each student enters one of three groups, "Abstainers," "Social Users," and "Partiers." These divisions describe the typical ways society characterizes people's substance use. Students choose a group based on the "label" with which they currently most closely identify. Once students commit to groups, they discuss with their fellow group members their reasons for choosing that group. After thoroughly discussing their choices, each group talks among themselves about their perceptions of why the people in the other two groups abstain or use as they do. They often talk about what it must be like to be a member of those groups.

Next, each group respectfully shares the content of its discussion about the other two groups with the class as a whole. Dialogue, questions, and ultimately greater understanding among class members generally result. Sometimes students also develop greater understanding of friends or family members not present. Always, students are surprised to hear how they are perceived and how others perceive themselves.

Students also may be enlightened by discussing the implications of labeling other people as "straight arrows," "dope fiends," "drunks," "nerds," "addicts," "burnouts," "potheads," and "alkies." While these categories may have negative connotations too great to be used for self-reference, class discussion reveals the powerful role in "othering" that metaphoric systems play.

CONCLUSION

In constructivist-oriented substance abuse counseling classrooms instructors provide opportunities for students to explore their and others' experiences in meaning-making. They engage in activities designed to help them deconstruct socially constructed concepts, and they learn how they create their knowledge. They learn that people respond to objects, events, actions, and circumstances on the basis of the meaning those things have for them. For example, substance dependence does not exist as a "real" entity, but is created through meanings developed during social interaction. Meanings made by different people will not be identical, but will vary according to individual cultural frames and worldviews.

Instructors using a constructivist approach to substance abuse counseling courses could adopt for their personal purposes the three goals previously suggested for students. By being knowledgeable about the power of communication and the dynamics of meaning-making, and by being self-aware, educators have opportunities to promote understanding, not only among individuals in classrooms, but among students and their clients.

Appendix

Guidelines for Attending a 12-Step Meeting

- If you are not affiliated with a 12-Step group, attend an <u>open</u> meeting.
- If it is of concern to you, note in advance if the meeting is non-smoking/smoking and wheelchair accessible.
- Unless you are going to several different meetings, try to attend a meeting other than one in a hospital, mental health center, or drug treatment facility.
- If you are already in a recovery group, attend a meeting of a group you have never attended
- Be prompt and stay until the end of the meeting.
- Identify yourself by your first name only.
- Maintain the role of an observer who is there to learn.
- You may make a monetary contribution when the basket is passed, but it is not required.
- Join in the closing circle, but unless you want to, you need not say the closing prayer.
- In the unlikely event that someone should ask, you may reply that you are there to learn about the recovery process of AA, Al Anon, or NA.
- RESPECT THE ANONYMITY OF THE PEOPLE YOU MEET. Be mindful of your reaction if you see people you know.

Information to be included in paper describing 12-Step meeting experience

A. Introduction
    1. name of group
    2. place and time of meeting
    3. brief description of observable demographics of people in attendance
    4. reading materials available to participants
    5. number of people attending
B. Description of Meeting
    1. chronological description of events
    2. impressions of mood in the room and behavior of attendees
    3. description of structure of meeting
    4. your perceptions of individuals' mental and emotional responses to what was said
C. Critique—Using your readings as the framework from which to write, discuss
    1. your current thinking about the structure and functions of 12-Step meetings
    2. your reactions to what you heard people say
    3. how the experience was like and/or different from what you expected.
    4. how the experience was like and/or different from other self-help group meetings you have attended.
D. Conclusions

REFERENCES

Alcoholics Anonymous. (1976). New York: Alcoholics Anonymous World Services, Inc.

American Psychiatric Association. (1994). *Diagnostic and statistical manual of mental disorders,* (4th ed.) Washington, DC: Author.

Bourdieu, P., & Wacquant, L. (1992). *An invitation to reflexive sociology.* Chicago: University of Chicago Press.

Carroll, J. J., & Bazan, J. A. (1997, February). In the beginning: The genesis of substance abuse counselors through explanatory narrative. Paper presented at the meeting of the North Carolina Counseling Association, Greensboro, NC.

George, R. L., & Dustin, D. (1988). *Group counseling: Theory and practice.* Englewood Cliffs, NJ: Prentice-Hall.

Gergen, K. J., & Gergen, M. M. (1991). Toward reflexive methodologies. In F. Steier, (Ed.), *Research and reflexivity* (pp. 76-95). Newbury Park, CA: Sage.

Gubrium, J. F., & Holstein, J. A. (1997). *The new language of qualitative method.* New York: Oxford University Press.

Hosie, T. W., West, J. D., & Mackey, J. E. (1990). Perceptions of counselor performance in substance abuse centers. *Journal of Mental Health Counseling, 12,* 199 - 207.

Kirkpatrick, J. (1977). *Turnabout: Help for a new life.* New York: Doubleday.

Lakoff, G. (1987). *Women, fire, and dangerous things.* Chicago: University of Chicago Press.

Lakoff, G. & Johnson, M. (1980). *Metaphors we live by.* Chicago: University of Chicago Press.

McAuliffe, G., & Lovell, C. (2000). Encouraging transformation: Guidelines for constructivist and developmental instruction. In G. McAuliffe, K. Eriksen, and Associates, *Preparing counselors and therapists: Creating constructivist and developmental programs,* (pp.14-41). Alexandria, VA: Association for Counselor Education and Supervision.

Prine, J. (1971a). *Illegal smile.* On John Prine. (compact disk). NY: Atlantic Recording.

Prine, J. (1971b). *Sam Stone.* On John Prine. (compact disk). NY: Atlantic Recording

Yalom, I. D. (1985). *Theory and practice of group psychotherapy,* (3rd ed.). New York: Basic Books.

18

Positivism-Plus: A Constructivist Approach to Teaching Psychopharmacology to Counselors

R. Elliott Ingersoll and Cecile Brennan

"All that is, is metaphor"
—*Life Against Death*,
Norman O. Brown

Forty years ago, if you offered a case study about a depressed client to students in the behavioral sciences and asked for a hypothesis about the etiology of the client's symptoms, one student would be likely to offer a psychodynamic explanation (an unloving, rejecting mother), while another would probably offer a behavioral explanation (previous reinforcement for the behaviors we are calling symptoms). If you describe the same case to counseling students today, many would offer a biochemical explanation (not enough serotonergic activity in the brain) to explain the symptoms. Their answers would reflect the drastic changes over the last 40 years in the premises underlying the way mental and emotional disorders are conceptualized. What has not changed much in four decades is students' metacognitive evaluation of these premises during their formal training. Today, as forty years ago, students frequently respond reflexively from the paradigm of the day. Exercising the metacognitive process that underlies constructivist thinking is still the exception rather than the rule. Constructivism has yet to be widely incorporated into counselor training.

Constructivism is based in the proposition that our beliefs and assumptions are products of the meanings we make in social and psychological contexts (Nelson & Neufeldt, 1998; Sexton, 1997). Put more colloquially, our intra-psychic and social circumstances greatly influence the way we tend to see the world. Psychologist Robert Anton Wilson (1992) has called the resulting worldview a "reality-tunnel" or "reality-labyrinth." When groups of people share the same reality tunnel or labyrinth, they may establish general ways of viewing the world that in turn contribute strongly to their culture. These elements that contribute to the culture may function as the equivalent of "game rules" for members of those cultures. For Wilson, a fully functioning human ought to be able to be aware of his or her reality tunnel and able to keep it flexible enough to accommodate, and to some degree empathize with, different reality tunnels, different "game rules," different cultures. The psychoanalyst and medical researcher John Lilly (1972), using a cyber-metaphor, called this process programming and metaprogramming the human biocomputer. Constructivist thinking is the exercise of metacognition to become aware of our reality tunnels or labyrinths and the elements that "program" them. Constructivist thinking should, ideally, decrease the chance that we will confuse our map of the world with the actual world and increase the chance of remaining receptive to what other reality tunnels or labyrinths may offer when making value judgments. Certainly this philosophy began historically long before the emergence of modern Western ideas. It is currently expressed in many Eastern consciousness-exploration techniques. "Constructivism" or "postmodernism" is merely the most current formulation of this approach to living in awareness.

Because constuctivist understanding relies on abstraction across paradigms, the type of metacognition needed to think in this manner requires, at minimum, the capacity for formal operational thinking. Since we screen counselor education applicants for evidence of such abilities (for example, through requiring the liberal arts foundation of a bachelor's degree), it is safe to assume that they are present in many of our students. However, such abilities cannot be reinforced and extended by counselor education practices that focus on static models of truth.

Psychopharmacology is an apt subject to teach in a constructivist manner, due to the rapidly changing paradigms in how neurological events are modeled and the fast pace with which psychotropic agents become available. Due to its grounding in the abstractions of the "hard sciences," psychopharmacology does require students to be able to engage in formal operational thinking. Further, students' formal operational abilities should allow them to both understand the basic information in the course and to begin to engage in a constructivist approach to the material.

This chapter describes such a constructivist approach, one that we call "positivism-plus," for teaching psychopharmacology to counseling students. Through this positivism-plus notion we recognizes that, as Sexton (1997) noted, constructivism can complement and incorporate positivism where the latter is desirable. Positivism is the tradition of using experimentation and reason to "discover" the true nature of things. In contrast, constructivism sees knowledge as useful not because it corresponds to some objective reality, but because it is viable for the realities that are presumed to exist (Hayes & Oppenheim, 1997). In our positivism-plus approach, the chemical and neurobiological bases of psychopharmacology constitute a pervasive, positivist construction of a reality that influences client behavior. However, this biological version of reality must be integrated into the work of counseling, that is, it must be adapted to the environmental and intrapsychic contexts that clients and counselors co-construct. As such, our approach is akin to what Mahoney (1991) called "critical constructivism," in that we assume that people co-create personal and social realities within the biological and existential limits of the phenomenal world.

This chapter reviews the relationships among the medical model, constructivism, and counselor training, describes the general components of the psychopharmacology course, then discusses more specifically the relationship between the positivist and positivist-plus elements.

THE MEDICAL MODEL, CONSTRUCTIVISM, AND COUNSELOR TRAINING

The Medical Model

"You can lead the horse's ass to wisdom but you cannot make him think."
— *Right Where You Are Sitting Now,*
Robert Anton Wilson

In the recent past, mental health practitioners' theoretical understandings of mental and emotional disorders was strongly psychodynamic (Gabbard, 1994). At present, however, the theoretical base of most major mental/emotional disorders is becoming increasingly medical (Cohen, 1993). This medical model emphasizes the biological bases of behavior and how to change behavior by pharmacological manipulation of human biology (Gabbard, 1994; Schatzberg, Cole, & DeBattista, 1997). The conceptualization of the disorders as presented in the Diagnostic and Statistical Manual of the American Psychiatric Association (DSM-IV) (1994) is also based in the medical model, as the notion of "diagnosis" of a "disorder" is inherent in both. The current recommended treatment of many DSM-IV disorders is pharmacological (Victor, 1996), and there are more pharmacological treatments available for these disorders than ever before (Littrell & Ashford, 1995).

The medical model that underlies the DSM and psychopharmacology research is positivist in nature and established itself early in the twentieth century when the proponents of allopathy (the method of treating disease with agents that produce effects different than those produced by the disease being treated; for instance, taking aspirin for a headache) succeeded in establishing it as the dominant medical paradigm over osteopathy and homeopathy (Kovel, 1980; Ober, 1997). Despite its positivist base, the medical model is just that, however, a model. Many psychopharmacology researchers and practitioners admit that we have barely scratched the surface of understanding the relationships between the mind and the brain and between psychotropic drugs and behavior (Grilly, 1998; Schatzberg & Nemeroff, 1998). Further, because of the enormous complexity of neurological events, researchers have admitted the incompleteness of their paradigm during this change from an emphasis on the psychological to a biological etiology of mental/emotional disorders.

Constructivism: Background and Introduction to Students

"Reality is complex and complexity is our friend."
—Mantra for the psychopharmacology course inspired,
Paul Pederson's reflections on culture

The student of psychopharmacology is presented with a wealth of information that must be understood and logically organized so that it is available when needed. The information necessarily has a positivistic dimension, derived as it is from the medical model that underlies the subject matter. The challenge to the instructor of a psychopharmacology course is to communicate the medical model and what it has accomplished while encouraging the examination of its underlying premises and not presenting it as an absolute or "final" picture.

We introduce students to an expanded vision of what knowledge is for, what its place is in life through a three-stage exploration of epistemology: (1) First we ask, "What does it mean to know something?" (2) Knowing is then examined in light of what has been learned from the constructivist/ postmodern shift in the paradigm of modern science. Knowledge comes to be understood first as functional rather than representational—*how to do* rather than *what something is*—and then as intrinsically limited and partial. In both the first and second steps, useful applications of knowledge are distinguished from dysfunctional and ultimately harmful applications. (3) And finally, counselors learn how to effectively juggle their nearly simultaneous use of these very different models of knowing. The three stages of this epistemological exploration are described below.

What Does it Mean "to Know?" Just what does it mean "to know something?" We illustrate the temporality and fragility of knowledge with the following example from science. When Camillo Golgi was first staining tissue samples with silver nitrate in the late 19th century, he had not perfected the technique and, left the tissue soaking too long. The result was a sample that made neurons appear to be physically connected. We now know that this is not true and that there are small spaces (called "synaptic clefts") between neurons. This current "fact" was only discovered after Santiago Ramon y Cajal refined the Golgi staining technique so that the stain reflected, rather than distorted, the relationship between neurons (Churchland, 1995). Clearly, then, what is considered "fact" may change simply because techniques become refined.

When we think of what it means to "know," we must also ask if a fact is a fact no matter the context. We move from hard science to the interpersonal context to illustrate. Counselors may understand the example of how a well-intended gesture of sympathy may exacerbate an already raw nerve. Although well intentioned and clearly in line with the injunction to embody and express empathy, a particular remark may be off-key and prove more harmful than helpful. The sympathizer may have merely been acting out "the right thing to do" rather than letting that action grow out of an awareness of self and other. Recognizing the subjectivity of knowing is crucial for counselors. For example, in a situation in which a counselor is discussing psychotropic medication with a client, he or she may fully understand the way the medication is intended to help the client but misunderstand what taking a medication means to that client. Frequently, clients harbor such negative images of taking medication that these images outweigh any potential benefit the medication is intended to have. Without understanding the psychological context of such a client, a counselor might act insensitively at best and incompetently at worst. In the cases of both the counselor and the client, the knowers act according to what they have been taught. Counselor educators who present ideas as if they were a physical, objective reality "out there" encourage learners to apply concepts dogmatically, without regard for the nuances of context and the subtleties of individual differences.

Problems with such dogmatic knowing are well known. Counselor educators' awareness that students may tend to apply what they have learned without attention to unique circumstances and contexts has led to classes in multicultural counseling and emphases on gender on the counseling process. For example, the seemingly universally valid advice about always maintaining eye contact with a client proves not to be so absolute when one is counseling many Native-American clients. Or a young person's physical agitation and mind-wandering tendencies may be the result of Attention-Deficit Hyperactivity Disorder (ADHD), but they might also be the result of abuse occurring at home.

When we hear of cases like these, the usual response is to say that the counselor lacked necessary information, or common sense, or interpersonal intuition. However, it does not seem possible to directly teach intuition or common sense, or how to respond to the uniqueness of particular situations. So, how can the process of education begin to account not only for *what* is known but also for *how* it is known in the sense of *how* the person relates to his knowledge? How can we teach students to think in context, and apply information practically and sensitively to real life situations they encounter? How can students in psychopharmacology courses become sensitive to the need to apply what they have learned tentatively, to move from dogmatic knowing to contextual knowing? Now that we have contextualized knowledge, we move to stage two in our epistemic pedagogical endeavor, that is, exposing students to constructivist and postmodern thinking.

"Knowing" in light of constructivism/postmoderism. The following segment captures our attempt to illustrate constructivist/postmodernist knowing at this point. The central reason why it is so difficult for most of us to move beyond dogmatic knowing is that it is generally believed that, to put it in popular words, "the truth is out there." This belief arises from the amazing achievements of classical science (Kuhn, 1962). Science and the scientific method have garnered for the human race a foothold in the material world unparalleled by that of any other organism. Diseases have been cured; the frontiers of space have been conquered. It is clear that science works.

Without denying these achievements, modern historians and philosophers of science have pointed out how these successes have focused attention away from the inconsistencies, limitations, and failures of science (Briggs & Peat, 1989). In the past, occurrences which did not lend themselves to analysis by traditional scientific methods were deemed anomalous and then frequently ignored (Gleick, 1987).

Ignoring such occurrences became less prevalent when scientists more recently began to turn their attention to more complex phenomena (Waldrop, 1992). Scientists discovered that the old rules simply did not apply when studying certain occurrences in the natural world. The material world, at both its most manifest and its hidden, sub-atomic levels, does not operate according to the rules as scientists had understood them: What was presumed to be solid and predictable was found to be fluid and unpredictable. What was believed to be objective and already present was found to be subjective, dependent on the interaction between observer and observed (Capra, 1975). These new insights challenged the existing paradigm of science and called into question the ultimate validity of the scientific method (Capra, 1975; Zukav, 1979).

But students have asked at this point: "Isn't the scientific method the reason human beings are living longer, healthier lives than ever before, to cite only one important example?" and "Is it right to challenge such a successful method?" The answer to both questions is an emphatic "yes!" However, despite the marvelous fruits of this method the scientific method is compromised by occurrences which do not lend themselves to analysis via linear reductionism. Confronting this apparent paradox leads to an expanded understanding of what it means *to know*. Knowledge is now understood as functional (what is viable), rather than as absolute (what corresponds to objective reality: Jones, 1982; Sexton, 1997). Equally important is the understanding that knowing something is always partial and incomplete. Knowing something is analogous to cutting a slice of pie: We do have pie, but just a piece of the pie.

More than many professionals, counselors need to be aware of this distinction. Counseling operates from the perspective of both the pie and the slice of pie. Counselors must constantly keep in mind the big picture—the individual as part of a system of relationships, and the narrow picture—the individual as a single unique being.

Juggling perspectives. Students now are introduced to the idea of holding both perspectives simultaneously. Such juggling is particularly important when dealing with the supposed factual knowledge of science. The seduction of science is such that when positive results are produced, it is almost impossible to remember that these results need to be viewed in the context of a larger perspective. Instead, the scientific outcomes are often reified as absolute; the slice of pie is taken to be the whole pie. This danger exists in using the DSM when a client's symptoms match the symptoms in a DSM category. Students may then begin viewing that client only through the narrow definition of the category in question ("my client is a schizophrenic" as opposed to "my client suffers from schizophrenia").

In the area of psychopharmacology, the need to hold both positions simultaneously is punctuated by the fact that use of medications can only be effective when attention is given to both dimensions. That is, because psychopharmacologists operate at the interface between mind and body, they have long been aware of the power of the mind (Dubovsky, 1997; Valenstein, 1998). The many studies that show positive outcomes resulting from placebos testify to this fact.

But, not unlike the physicists who termed certain unexplainable events anomalous, scientists frequently held that these apparent "cures" proved that the disorder or disease was solely mental (Breggin, 1994). Present in this outlook is the problematic distinction between mind and body. This distinction arises out of the dualistic thinking inherent in the scientific method: A mind exists and a body exists, both exist separately and so should be treated separately (Dubovsky, 1997). We are, it seems, no closer to a solution to the mind/brain problem than we were in the seventeenth century when Descartes proposed the substance dualism theory (the theory that the mind/soul and the brain were two distinct substances).

Fields of study outside of medicine are also attempting to account for problems similar to that of mind/brain interconnectedness. Most notable is the work of systems theorists. For these investigators "Every particle, every force, affects every other. There are not separate forces and things in nature, only sets of interacting events with differentiated characteristics" (Laszlo, 1993, p.65). As a methodology, systems theory operates in a non-linear fashion. Instead of attempting to reduce actions to the kind of linear cause and effect model required by traditional science, systems theorists focus on creating a non-linear model which displays interactions among variables (Laszlo, 1993). This methodology has been applied in fields ranging from physics to engineering to psychology. Its most familiar application within the field of psychology is family-systems therapy (Roy & Frankl, 1995). In the same way that systems theorists see a whole, a field or system, as the most useful point of exploration, family therapists see the system of the family as the most useful point of reference. This, of course, does not preclude focusing on another system such as the workplace or school (Roy & Frankl, 1995).

Embracing a systems or interconnected way of knowing is valuable to the subject of psychopharmacology. While not denying the power of the traditional medical model to produce specific, intended results, a systems approach places those results in the context of the whole person and his/her psychological, social, and physical environment. The use of drugs in treating mental disorders is ideally seen as *part* of the treatment plan, not as *the* treatment plan. The counselor is central to this process. In communicating to the client, the counselor must continually make the point that the client needs to actively work towards better mental health in many dimensions of his or her life, that only waiting for the drugs to take effect, hoping for a magical cure, is not a helpful stance. Throughout this process, the counselor needs to walk a thin line between the positivism of the medical model and the relativism of a systems understanding. This balancing act requires that the counselor be both completely informed about what the medical model has to offer, and still be able to put that information into the context of the client's total life and experiences. With this expanded vision of knowing now introduced, let us turn to the place of psychopharmacology in counselor education.

Psychopharmacology and Counselor Education

Much has changed since Ponterotto (1985) wrote the first counselor's guide to understanding psychotropic medication. As more states license counselors to diagnose and treat mental and emotional disorders, a general, working knowledge of psychopharmacology becomes increasingly important for counselors as they help their clients understand treatment options (Meyer, 1996). The topic is clearly relevant to agency counselors and private practitioners (Faiver, Eisengart, & Colonna, 1995). Additionally, school counselors also benefit from a general knowledge of psychotropic medications. It is estimated that 7.5 million children in the United States experience significant mental health problems (Kratochwill, 1994) and are increasingly being prescribed psychotropic medications as part of their treatment (Gadow, 1991; Pelham, 1993). Psychotropic medications accounted for 8.8 percent of the total prescription drug market in 1994 and that percentage is rising (Pincus, et al, 1998). The number of visits to primary care physicians and psychiatrists for psychotropic medications has also increased (Pincus, *et al*, 1998). Pincus and his colleagues noted that much of the increase is attributable to the new generation of antidepressants and the increased use of stimulants to treat children and adolescents with Attention-Deficit/Hyperactivity Disorder (ADHD).

Despite this increased use as well as the fact that many clients of master's level counselors may themselves be taking some form of psychotropic medication, research studies have noted that master's-level helping professionals lack training in psychopharmacology (Bentley, Farmer, & Phillips, 1991; Kratochwill, 1994; West, Hosie, & Mackey, 1988). In response to this, courses in psychopharmacology are slowly being added to counselor education curricula. The slowness with which they are being added may result from the differences between medical and counseling training paradigms. Where the positivist, scientific, medical pedagogy has been firmly established for over nine decades, counselor education has yet to fully define a similar pedagogy (Sexton, 1998). Counselor training has been identified with an educator-practitioner model (Lanning, 1990), an educational-developmental model (Ivey & Rigazio-DiGilio, 1991), and most recently a constructivist model (Nelson & Neufeldt, 1998; Sexton & Griffin, 1997).

Why this multiplicity of proposed pedagogical models in counseling? One reason is the research difficulties posed in using a strict, positivist, scientific method in research on human behavior. Ethical concerns preclude the degree of control over and manipulation of variables that exist in other disciplines. Further, when research is conducted from a positivist model, there is evidence that it is infrequently referred to by counseling practitioners (Howard, 1986). Counselors have also resisted the medical model, as the field began its professional identification with a focus on human growth and development. However, counselors have increasingly accommodated the realities of psychopathology and the fact that third-party payers still prefer to reimburse for remediation rather than prevention. In this spirit of constructing psychopharmacology as a dimension of counseling work, we now turn to the specific course components.

COMPONENTS OF THE PSYCHOPHARMACOLOGY COURSE

"Every interpretation of nature, whether scientific, non-scientific, or anti-scientific, is based on some intuitive conception of the general nature of things."
—*The Taoist Dimension*
Michael Polanyi

Beginning with the Medical Model

The American Psychological Association (APA) has published curriculum guidelines for three levels of training in psychopharmacology. The goal of the first level is to provide an introduction to basic psychopharmacological education for non-medical students of psychology and for mental health professionals (American Psychological Association, 1995). The level-one guidelines recommend several modules or components of instruction, many of which are positivist in nature. The following components used in the course we are discussing are based on the APA guidelines: (a) biological bases of psychopharmacological treatment, (b) principles of psychopharmacological treatment, (c) general introduction to clinical psychopharmacology, and (d) six modules specific to common classes of psychotropic medication. Following is a summary of the components.

Component One. The first component is intended to help students generally identify and understand important central nervous system (CNS) structures and functions, biologically active chemicals (ligands) including hormones, neurotransmitters, neurohormones, and neuromodulators (Grilly, 1998), elements of neurotransmission, and receptor families and functions. This component is generally the most difficult for students lacking science backgrounds and is descriptive. It is important because these elements are key to the therapeutic and side effects of psychotropic medications.

Component Two. The second component addresses principles of pharmacological treatment. It includes understanding pharmacokinetics (how drugs move through the body) and pharmacodynamics (drug mechanisms of action). Pharmacokinetics involves drug absorption, distribution, binding, metabolism, and excretion (Grilly, 1998) Pharmacodynamics refers to the physical and biological effects of psychotropic medications and how they work. One example of how information on pharmacokinetics and pharmacodynamics can help counselors is in their supporting clients who are waiting for the therapeutic effects of a drug to begin. This need is common with clients who are taking antidepressants, where the time between beginning the medication and experiencing relief from depression may take up to six weeks. In addition, students should learn how the body eliminates drugs, the relationships between drug dosage and behavioral response, drug classification, and sources of individual differences in drug action, such as gender, age, physical wellness, race, ethnicity, and certain physical conditions.

Component Three. The third component is the general introduction to clinical psychopharmacology. This component is designed to address the following. a) Historical uses of medications to treat mental/emotional disorders, b) legal/ethical issues in psychopharmacological treatment, c) important issues in psychiatrist-counselor collaboration, d) the impact of cultural variables on psychopharmacological treatment, e) how psychosocial factors interact with biological drug treatment, and f) understanding the empirical support for approaches combining counseling with drug treatments.

Component Four. The fourth component contains six modules that deal with the various classes of drugs listed in Table 1, their mechanisms of action, and the mental/emotional disorders they are used to treat. The disorders addressed include schizophrenia and other psychotic disorders, anxiety disorders, mood disorders, bulimia, and Attention Deficit Hyperactivity Disorder. A component on dementia is included as well, since more counselors continue to be needed to work with the elderly. Also, there are promising psychopharmacological treatments being investigated for elderly clients who suffer from cortical and subcortical dementias (McElroy, 1997; Nussbaum, 1998).

Table 1. Six classes of psychotropic medications covered in an introductory psychopharmacology course for counseling students

Drug Class	Primary Disorders Treated with Drug Class
Antidepressants	Mood Disorders, Bulimia, Obsessive-Compulsive Disorder
Antipsychotics	Psychotic Disorders, Bipolar I Disorder
Anxiolytics (anti-anxiety)	Anxiety Disorders
Cognitive Enhancers	Alzheimer's Type Dementia
Mood Stabilizers	Bipolar I Disorder
Psychostimulants	Attention Deficit/Hyperactivity Disorder

THE POSITIVIST BASES AND POSITIVISM-PLUS: TOWARD CONSTRUCTIVIST DIRECTIONS AND METHODS

"The opposite of a trivial truth is false; the opposite of a great truth is also true."
—*Essays, 1958-1962, On Atomic Physics and Human Knowledge,*
Neils Bohr

Having generally reviewed the medical model, the course components, and the constructivist position, we now ask, "How can we integrate these into the psychopharmacology course in a constructivist fashion? If we abide by the constructivist notion that useful knowledge is viable knowledge, we must conclude that the positivism-grounded bases described in these course components are important. Without knowledge of these, students would lack the knowledge base from which to understand clients' physical responses to medications. This information can help students communicate with clients about the effects of medications. Clearly, components 1, 2, and 4 are more positivist in nature. Physiological structures, pharmacodynamics, pharmacokinetics, and drugs classed by function or molecular structure are typically presented as unchanging variables. Given that the majority of students in counselor education programs lack science backgrounds, it is important to design multiple instructional methods for communicating complex information. In teaching psychopharmacology, this challenge is complicated by a paucity of available audio-visual aids, so the instructor must use her or his creativity in correcting for this lack.

Models and Other Visual Aids

Student integration of concepts can be facilitated with visual models. Although all the instructional components are enriched with models, such models are crucial to the first two components, biological bases and principles of psychopharmacological treatment. Excellent models of the human brain are available for gross anatomy of the central nervous system (Denoyer-Geppert Science Company, Chicago IL). Other models, such as models of a neuron and models of neuronal receptors, can be constructed inexpensively with common materials (such as, paper mache and cardboard). When describing the effects of various medications on neurons, instructors invariably need to draw simplified representations of neurons. Instructors should decide beforehand which drawing best serves their purposes and consistently use that drawing throughout the course. This helps students internalize the image of the physical structure and conceptualize the action of medications on that structure.

But in true constructivist manner, this model must be viewed as only a model. After initial introduction to a model of a neuron for example, students are introduced to the reality that there is no "typical" neuron. Neurons vary in shape, size, and function. Students are encouraged to draw their own neurons and color various representations of neurons in coloring books like those of Pinel (1998) or Diamond, Scheibel, and Elson (1985). In addition, students learn that learning changes the shape of neurons (Kandel, 1983). Since then, researchers like Sperry (1988) have further noted that there is considerable evidence that mental processes not only impact the physical structure of the brain but can actually change that structure.

These hypotheses support the constructivist premise that there are multiple realities which may interact. They also support use of counseling in conjunction with psychotropic medications. In many cases the medications may provide a neurological window of opportunity that the meaning-making organism (the client) can take advantage of in working with a counselor. That work involves the clients' and counselors' entering each others' reality tunnels with the goal of helping clients to modify theirs in order that they might be more viable within their life circumstances. Based on this hypothesis that the informationally relevant components of neurons change in response to learning, students are encouraged to draw their models of neurons before and after counseling to provide a vivid image of the way a constructivist understanding may affect a positivist formulation.

Narrative and Metaphor as a Conceptual Aids

It is important to instruct students that the very positivist methods used to investigate psychotropic medications are infused with human practices. For example, every drug used therapeutically has its own history of nonrational, often serendipitous discovery. To illustrate: When Ronald Kuhn was instructed to "find a use" for a compound that was a failure as an antipsychotic medication, it was the context of his somewhat compulsive personality style that drove him to instigate the successful patenting and marketing of tricyclic antidepressants. Similarly, chemist Leo Sternbach was studying twenty different compounds in search of a tranquilizer that didn't have the drawbacks of barbiturates. After failing to find anything significant in the first nineteen he moved on to other projects. Cleaning his lab a year later he stumbled onto the twentieth compound and decided to check it "just in case." This compound led to the development of the first benzodiazapine (these and other stories are in Snyder, 1996). Counseling students' attention is held much better when the instructor weaves the very human stories of discovery into the more technical aspects of the lectures. Other topics like racial and ethnic variations in responses to medication and cultural stigmatizations of taking medication vary from disorder to disorder and drug to drug. With a constructivist base, students are more prepared to consider these complexities in their work with clients.

Counseling students, who are inclined to use the human story and dialogical interaction as therapeutic tools, may find it difficult to make sense of a strict, linear presentation of scientific findings germane to psychopharmacology. Such students will understand concepts more thoroughly if they are communicated metaphorically as well as factually. For example, a factual presentation of neurotransmitter synthesis describes the production of enzymes and transporter molecules in the neuron's nucleus, their movement down the neuron's axon, and their subsequent action in constructing neurotransmitters from precursors and storing them in synaptic vesicles. The metaphorical presentation perhaps tells the story of a factory that makes cellular phones (since neurotransmitters are chemical communication devices). The metaphor may describe the enzymes as assembly line workers, since their job is the "construction" of the neurotransmitters. Since these assembly line workers (the enzymes) are "dispatched" from the cell nucleus, the nucleus is equated with an administration/personnel office. The transporter molecules that bring basic parts into the cell (the precursors used by enzymes to create neurotransmitters) are equated with trucks delivering the basic materials for creating cell phones (the neurotransmitters) to the factory (the neuron). Since other enzymes will break down neurotransmitters unless they are placed in a protective container, they are stored in synaptic vesicles until they are released from the neuron. In the metaphor, the cell phones (the neurotransmitters) are then packaged in shrink-wrapped boxes (the synaptic vesicles) until they are opened and used.

Stahl (1996) has utilized the metaphor approach in many of the numerous colorful illustrations in his textbook. Instructors may purchase slides of these illustrations through Cambridge University Press. Again, a two-minute story often communicates the equivalent of a thirty-minute lecture. The use of metaphor also reminds the student that the theory from which the metaphor is derived is only a model. There is also a meta-strategy to the use of metaphor: that is, to provide students with models of how they might themselves talk to clients about the action of medications the client may be taking. The metaphors are frequently more compatible with clients' reality tunnels than the factual descriptions that they may get from medical personnel.

Other Issues in Teaching Students about Consulting with Clients

The constructivist approach is perhaps most important when students examine their roles in consulting with clients about medications. In this course their counseling roles are defined as (a) helping clients to process issues about taking medication; (b) being an "information broker" for the client, that is, helping the client obtain and evaluate information about medications; (c) engaging clients in relationships and dialogue conducive to exploring compliance-related issues; and (d) forging good relationships with the medical personnel who are prescribing the medication to clients.

Processing Client Issues

Many clients are naturally concerned about taking a psychotropic medication. "Will it change who I am?" "Will it cause birth defects?" "Does this mean that I'm crazy?" A constructivist, metacognitive perspective assists counselors to enter clients' reality tunnels when clients ask such questions, a process which increases the likelihood that consultation will be effective. Clearly the counselor is not trained as a medical practitioner and should not practice (or malpractice as the case may be) like one.

Information Brokering

As an information broker (in a constructivist sense), the counselor must know where to gather information about medications, understand how to evaluate such information, and be aware of the premises underlying the latter methods of evaluation. Counselors may use medical and psychology journals to gather information, as well as a number of peer-reviewed newsletters which are grounded in the medical model. One popular newsletter is *Psychopharmacology Update* published by Manisses Communication Group. This newsletter provides case studies of pharmacological "anomalies" as well as reviews of statistically based, double-blind studies. In publishing the "anomalies," the newsletter models the understanding that the pharmacological realities are complex and that complexity is ultimately our "friend." Manisses also sells a psychopharmacology desktop reference for mental health practitioners (Tornatore & Sramek, 1997).

The second step in the counselor's task of psychopharmacology information brokering, that is, knowing how to evaluate such information is a bit more complex. Clearly, the student of psychopharmacology needs to know how to read a research study and comprehend statistical conclusions. Beyond this, the same student needs to be able to critique the premises of the methods used. Just because an approach has not been explored in controlled trials (whether for lack of funding or because it is not viable) doesn't mean it can't be used. Such is the case with most counseling interventions. Such is also the case with more controversial herbal approaches to treating the symptoms of mental/emotional disorders. As Yaeger and Hendrick (1998) noted, it is hard to do controlled studies of unregulated herbal treatments (like St. John's Wort) because we can never know how much of the substance in question is contained in each "dosage." Clients, however, will ask about such treatments, and their interest needs to be honored with honest answers about both the lack of data and the anecdotal support. Often, a consultation with a physician can affirm the client's suspicion that such a treatment may not hurt them, and the client may decide to try it out. If such a "treatment" is correlated with remission or decrease in symptoms and fewer side effects than a medication, does it really matter if the ultimate underlying mechanism was placebo, homeopathic, or both? The constructivist answer would be "no."

Dealing With Compliance Issues

Although this is a variation on the theme of processing client issues around medication, it deserves special mention here. Nothing quite so starkly illustrates the difference between positivist assumptions and constructivist practices than the following item (from Patterson, 1996) posed to counseling students in a psychopharmacology course. "Raise your hand if you have ever: (a) stopped taking a medication before the prescription indicated to, (b) stopped taking a medication before consulting your physician, (c) taken more of a medication than was prescribed, and (d) taken less of a prescription than prescribed." Usually over fifty percent of the students raise their hands. This introduces the topic of "noncompliance." Between the idea of the positivist prescription and the reality of the patient's perception lies the shadow of compliance. In dialogue with students about why they did not comply with a medication regimen, they will list things like severe side effects, not liking taking medication, and believing that needing medication was a sign of weakness. These compare with the common reasons for non-compliance listed by Patterson (1996); however, when students first think about their personal experiences, they are less prone to see the negative baggage that goes with the term "non-compliant." and are more likely to enter openly into dialogue with clients who are "non-compliant" with their medications.

Forging Healthy Relationships with Medical Personnel

When we think of the medical model, we often think of the medical personnel who were trained in it. Clearly the behavior of those physicians and psychiatrists who prescribe medications to our clients may range from rigid adherence to the positivist paradigm of their training to what we would consider a healthy constructivist approach to their client's understandings of taking psychotropic medication. In true constructivist fashion, counselors need to be aware of the reality tunnels used by those who hold to rather rigid notions of the relationship between health professionals at extreme ends of the power hierarchy. In most agency settings, the hierarchy reflects adherence to the positivist values of the medical model starting with psychiatrists at the top, Ph.D. psychologists next, master's level practitioners next, and bachelor's level case managers last. Understanding that many medical professionals may in fact be wed to the positivist paradigm, the counselor can forge a healthy relationship by approaching it from a "one down" position. From this position, counselors "honor" the positivist reality tunnel by framing their queries about client medications as "learning opportunities" for themselves. This is a win-win strategy. Medical professionals who do remain primarily in the positivist reality tunnel usually respond favorably to this approach, while more constructivist medical professionals will invite further input from counselors about their unique perspectives on the client.

CONCLUSION

Numerous other topics could be addressed in this chapter, such as pharmacoeconomics, a more complete treatment of alternatives to pharmacotherapy, and client-counselor power dynamics related to medication compliance. We have just begun to scratch the surface in this chapter on how constructivist and positivist elements can combine to fashion the gestalt of a psychopharmacology course for counselors. Hopefully our positivism-plus approach has outlined how to get the best out of the positivist material that forms the basis for the course, while the constructivist beginnings we have mapped here provide further "food for thought."

REFERENCES

American Psychological Association (1995). Final report of the BEA working group to develop a level 1 curriculum for psychopharmacology education and training. Washington, DC:

Bentley, K. J., Farmer, R., & Phillips, M. E. (1991). Student knowledge of and attitudes toward psychotropic drugs. *Journal of Social Work Education, 27,* 279-289.

Breggin, P. R. (1994). *Talking back to Prozac.* New York: St. Martin's Press

Briggs, J., & Peat, F. D. (1989). *Turbulent mirror.* New York: Harper and Row.

Capra, F. (1975). *The tao of physics.* Berkeley, CA: Shambhala.

Churchland-Smith, P. (1995). *Neurophilosophy: Toward a unified science of mind/brain.* Cambridge, MA: MIT Press.

Cohen, C. I. (1993). The biomedicalization of psychiatry: A critical overview. *Community Mental Health Journal, 29,* 509-521.

Diamond, M.C., Scheibel, A. B., & Elson, L. M. (1985). *The human brain coloring book.* New York: HarperPerennial.

Dubovsky, S. L. (1997). *Mind-body deceptions.* New York: W. W. Norton & Company.

Faiver, C. M., Eisengart, S., & Colonna, R. (1995). *The counselor intern's handbook.* Pacific Grove, CA: Brooks Cole Publishing Company.

Gabbard, G. O. (Ed.) (1994). *Treatment of the DSM-IV psychiatric disorders.* Washington, DC: American Psychiatric Press.

Gadow, K. D. (1991). Clinical issues in child and adolescent psychopharmacology. *Journal of Counseling and Clinical Psychology, 59,* 842-852.

Gleick, J. (1987). *Chaos.* New York: Viking.

Grilly, D. M. (1998). *Drugs and human behavior,* (3rd ed.). Boston: Allyn & Bacon.

Hayes, R. L., & Oppenheim, R. (1997). Constructivism: Reality is what you make it. In T. L. Sexton and B. L. Griffin, (Eds.), *Constructivist thinking in counseling practice, research, and training* (pp 45-56). New York: The Teachers College Press.

Howard, G. S. (1986). *Dare we develop a human science?* Notre Dame, IN: Academic Publications.

Ivey, A. E., & Rigazio-Digilio, S. A. (1991). Toward a developmental practice of mental health counseling: Strategies for training, practice, and political unity. *Journal of Mental Health Counseling, 13* (1), 21-36.

Jones, R. S. (1982). *Physics as metaphor.* New York: Signet Classics.

Kandel, E. R. (1983). From metapsychology to molecular biology: Explorations into the nature of anxiety. *American Journal of Psychiatry, 140,* 1277-1293.

Kovel, J. (1980). The American mental health industry. In D. Ingleby (Ed.), *Critical psychiatry.* New York: Pantheon.

Kratochwill, T. R. (1994). Psychopharmacology for children and adolescents: Commentary on current issues and future challenges. *School Psychology Quarterly, 9,* 53-59.

Lanning, W. (1990). An educator/practitioner model for counselor education doctoral programs. *Counselor Education and Supervision, 30,* pp. 163-168.

Laszlo, E. (1993). *The creative cosmos.* Edinburgh: Floris Books.

Lilly, J. (1972). *Programming and metaprogramming in the human biocomputer.* New York: The Julien Press.

Kuhn, T. (1962). *The structure of scientific revolutions.* Chicago: The University of Chicago Press.

Mahoney, M. J. (1991). *Human change processes: Notes on the facilitation of personal development.* New York: Basic Books.

McElroy, S. L. (Ed.) (1997). *Psychopharmacology across the life span: Section IV of the American Psychiatric Press Review of Psychiatry: Volume 16.* Washington, DC: American Psychiatric Press.

Meyer, R. G., & Deitsch, S. E. (1996). *The clinician's handbook: Integrated diagnostics, assessment, and intervention in adult and adolescent psychopathology.* Boston: Allyn and Bacon.

Nelson, M. L., & Neufeldt, S. A. (1998). The pedagogy of counseling: A critical examination.*Counselor Education and Supervision, 38,* 70-88.

Ober, K. P. (1997). The pre-Flexnerian reports: Mark Twain's criticism of medicine in the United States. *Annals of Internal Medicine, 126* (2), 1, 57-163.

Patterson, L. E. (1996). Strategies for improving medication compliance. *Essential Psychopharmacology, 1,* 70-79.

Pelham, W. E. Jr. (1993). Guest editor's comments: Recent developments in pharmacological treatment for child and adolescent mental health problems. *School Psychology Review, 22,* 158-161.

Pincus, H. A., Tanielian, T. L., Marcus, S. C., Olfson, M., Zarin, D. A., Thompson, J., & Zito, J. M. (1998). Prescribing trends in psychotropic medications. *Journal of the American Medical Association, 279,* 526-531.

Pinel, J. P. with Edwards, M. (1998). *A colorful introduction to the anatomy of the human brain: A brain and psychology coloring book.* Boston: Allyn & Bacon.

Ponterotto, J. G. (1985). A counselor's guide to psychopharmacology. *Journal of Counseling and Development, 64,* 109-115.

Roy, R. & Frankel, H. (1995). *How good is family therapy?* Toronto: University of Toronto Press.

Schatzberg, A. F., Cole, J. O., & DeBattista, C. (1997). *Manual of clinical psychopharmacology,* (3rd ed.). Washington DC: American Psychiatric Press.

Schatzberg, A. F., & Nemeroff, C. B., (Eds.) (1998). *The American Psychiatric Association textbook of psychopharmacology,* (2nd ed.). Washington, DC: American Psychiatric Association.

Sexton, T. L. (1998). Reconstructing counselor education: Issues of our pedagogical foundation. *Counselor Education and Supervision, 38,* 66-69.

Snyder, S. H. (1996). *Drugs and the brain.* New York: Scientific American Library.

Sperry, R. W. (1988). Psychology's mentalist paradigm and the religion/science tension. *American Psychologist, 43,* 607-613.

Stahl, S. M. (1996). *Essential psychopharmacology: Neuroscientific basis and practical applications.* New York: Cambridge University Press.

Tornatore, F. L., & Sramek, J. J., (Eds.), (1996). *Psychotropic medications: A desktop reference for mental health practitioners.* Providence, RI: Manisses Communications Group.

Valenstein, E. S. (1998). *Blaming the brain.* New York: The Free Press.

Victor, B. S. (1996). Transpersonal psychopharmacology and psychiatry. In B. W. Scotton, A. B. Chinen, & J. R. Battista, (Eds.), *Textbook of transpersonal psychiatry and psychology* (pp. 327-334). New York: Basic Books.

Waldrop, M. M. (1992). *Complexity.* New York: Simon & Schuster.

West, J. D., Hosie, T. W., & Mackey, J. A. (1988). The counselor's role in mental health: An evaluation. *Counselor Education and Supervision, March,* pp. 233-239.

Wilson, R. A. (1992). *Right where you are sitting now, second edition.* Berkeley, CA: Ronin Publishing.

Yaeger, D., & Hendrick, V. (1998). The faces of depression through the female life cycle. *PsychLink video presentation, Feb. 11th.* New York: Interactive Medical Networks.

Zukav, G. (1979). *The dancing Wu Li masters.* New York: William Morrow.

Index

Active Learning, in the assessment course, 102, 104–106; in the community agency course, 285; in the course on substance abuse, 330. *See also* Experience, Experiential Learning

Allport, Gordon, 236

Ambiguity, and "thought messes," 129–130

American Psychological Association (APA), curriculum guidelines for teaching psychopharmacology, 344–346

Approximation, valuing of, 6–7

Assessment, meaning of, 95; qualitative, 96, 100; ethics in, 101, use in career counseling, 144–149. *See also* Evaluation of students' performance, Tests and Testing

Authority, role of in knowing 43–44, 46; and asking for evidence 47

Cases, Case Study, as used in the assessment course, 106–107; in the career counseling course, 141–142, 151; in the diagnosis and treatment course, 214; in the family counseling course, 248.

Categorical thinking, 4

Challenge, in instruction, 44, 46

Chaos Theory, 294

Classroom activities, in the practicum course, 194–195; for personalization and building community in the counseling children and adolescents course, 220–221; in the course on substance abuse, 330–331

Collaborative assessment, 206

College student development theory, 295; cultural limitations of, 298–299

Commitment, 5

Community, in the group counseling course, 118; in the diagnosis and treatment course, 209; in the

Dissonance, inviting into the classroom, 27

Equality, between students and teachers, 170; highlighted in the Supervision course, 174
Ethics, and the Group Counseling course, 122–123
Evaluation of Students' Performance, in the helping interview course, 54–57; in the Assessment course, 108–111; of critical thinking, 109–110; self–evaluation, 110; in the Practicum course, 196; in the community agency course, 286–287, in the college student development course, 309. *See also* Grading
Experience, Experiential Learning, 8–9; defined 18; in the introductory course, 18; corollary, 78–79; in the Group Counseling course, 115–117, 119; in the Research Methods course, 135–136; in the diagnosis and treatment course, 210–211; in the counseling children and adolescents course, 225–228; in the family counseling course, 248; in the school counseling course, 263–264; in the course on substance abuse, 326

Feedback, soliciting from students, 24–25, from students on course goals and activities, 97; to students by others, 117
Field visits, in the practicum course, 190
Feminist, approaches to family counseling, 239

Freire, Paolo, 297–298; and problem–posing education, 304–305. *See also* Liberatory Education

Gender, in counseling theory, 75. *See also* Multicultural Awareness
Grading. *See* Evaluation of students' perfromances.
Group counseling competencies, 114
Groups, use of in the research methods course, 133–135; in the course on substance abuse, 326–327

Hierarchy, 174; limits of in college student development theory, 300. *See also* Equality

Identity, limitation of as a construct for college student development theory, 299–300
Inquiry, as a method in teaching supervision, 175–177
Interpersonal process, 6, 121–122.
Intrapersonal process 9–10, 20–21, 120, in the diagnosis and treatment course, 213–214; in the counseling children and adolescents course, 230–231; in the school counseling course, 264
Involvement, as a theme in college student development, 302
Isomorphism, between teaching and counseling, 44–45

Journaling, in the family counseling course, 246

Kelly, George, 72

Learning communities, 296
Lectures, Lecturing, in the assess-

About the Editors and Contributors

Cecile Brennan is currently a visiting professor in the department of Counseling, Administration, Supervision, and Adult Learning at Cleveland State University. Her research interests have focused on integrating postmodern concepts into counselor education. She has also worked as an English teacher and a counselor in private practice.

James A. Bazan is on the Behavioral and Social Sciences faculty at Central Piedmont Community College in Charlotte, North Carolina, where he received the 1999-2000 Teaching Excellence Award. Mr. Bazan has research interests in areas related to community, diversity, and families. His doctoral research focuses on religious pilgrimages as ethnic practices. He looks forward to research that requires less walking.

Bill Bruck is a psychologist and futurist who focuses on the effects of rapid technological change on information intensive industries, integrating technical expertise with his understanding of organizational systems and the people who make them work. Dr. Bruck has written ten books on the effective use of information technology, books that have been translated and sold internationally. He is Chief Knowledge Officer of Caucus Systems, Inc., where he architects virtual collaboration solutions for Global 1000 companies. He was a former professor of psychology.

Yvonne L. Callaway is an associate professor in the Department of Leadership and Counseling at Eastern Michigan University. She has worked actively in the Michigan Counseling Association and is a past president of the Michigan Association for Multicultural Counseling and Development. Her specialized teaching interests include cross-cultural counseling and group work.

Jane J. Carroll is currently at The University of North Carolina at Charlotte where she teaches the substance abuse counseling curriculum and supervises students in clinical internships. She holds state and national credentials as a specialist in substance abuse counseling. Dr. Carroll utilizes a constructivist approach to teaching and supervision. She is a past president of the International Association of Addictions and Offender Counselors, and serves on the American Counseling Association Editorial Advisory Board, and on the Editorial Boards of the Journal of Addictions and Offender Counseling and the Journal of Teaching in the Addictions.

Susan DeVaney is associate professor of Counseling and Counselor-in-Residence at the Early Childhood Development Center (ECDC) at Texas A&M University-Corpus Christi. As Counselor-in-Residence, Susan and counseling interns provide classroom guidance lessons, individual and group counseling, play therapy, and collaborative consultation with families and staff. She co-directs a five-week summer pre-employment experience for disadvantaged adolescents. She has authored publications on topics for school counselors, such as sexual abuse reporting in schools, the school counselor as court witness, the working relationship between school counselors and family resource centers, counseling single parents, and career development in ethnic minority students.

Judy Emmett is a professor at the University of Wisconsin-River Falls. She regularly teaches the career development class, a counseling class for teacher education students, and coordinates and supervises school counseling practicum and internship students. She has research interests and has published and presented in the area of career development and school counseling. She maintains memberships in the American Counseling Association, the National Career Development Association, the American School Counselor Association, and the Association of Counselor Educators and Supervisors.

Karen Eriksen teaches counseling at Radford University and is licensed as a Professional Counselor and Marriage and Family Counselor in Virginia. She spent 18 years as a mental health and community agency counselor, gaining specialties in family therapy, addictions, survivors of sexual abuse, and the intersection of spirituality and counseling. Dr. Eriksen is a Nationally Certified Counselor, an AAMFT Clinical Member, and an AAMFT Approved Supervisor. She has written the only book on the process of professional advocacy—*Making an Impact: A Handbook on Counselor Advocacy.* She has co-authored *Preparing Counselors and Therapists: Creating Constructivist and Developmental Programs.* Her research areas are in counselor advocacy and counselor preparation. Active in leadership of several state and national professional associations, including: ACA, VAMFC, VACC, AMHCA, VCA, NVCCC, and IAMFC, she is currently President-elect of VAMFC. She presents workshops on advocacy and counselor preparation at local, state, and national conferences.

Jane Fried is an associate professor at Central Connecticut State University where she directs the master's program in student development in higher education. Dr. Fried is the author of several books on areas related to student affairs, including women's issues, ethics, and "shifting paradigms" from administration to education. She has also been a director of housing and a coordinator of staff training for a large residence hall system at the University of Connecticut.

R. Elliott Ingersoll is currently the chairperson of the Counseling, Administration, Supervision, and Adult Learning Department at Cleveland State University. He has co-authored two books, and published numerous book chapters and articles on topics ranging from counseling and spirituality to psychopharmacology. His current research interests center on developing a model of teaching psychopathology using Ken Wilber's integral model.

Shelley A. Jackson is an assistant professor of Counseling in the College of Education at Texas A & M University - Corpus Christi and is a counselor educator. She has over 10 years of school counseling experience in Georgia and Florida. Currently she is serving as a certified trainer for the National Standards for School Counseling Programs and is the technology committee chairperson for the Texas School Counselor Association. Her research interests include the effectiveness of school counseling programs, multicultural issues in school counseling, and play therapy.

Garrett McAuliffe is the Graduate Program Director of the nationally-accredited counseling program at Old Dominion University. His current work focuses on cultural diversity, especially ethnicity, social class, and sexual orientation. He has trained college faculty on cultural sensitivity at a number of forums, and has a strong interest in adult cognitive development, especially as it affects moral choices and organizations, and college student change. He has published three books on the topic of constructivism and counselor education. Recognized by receiving the Tonelson Award for Outstanding Teaching in the Darden College of Education, he was also selected as one of eight Old Dominion Faculty members nominated for the Virginia Outstanding Faculty Award, known as the SCHEV Award.

Rick Myer is a licensed psychologist in the states of Illinois and Pennsylvania and a Nationally Certified Counselor. Dr. Myer currently teaches at

Duquesne University in Pittsburgh, Pennsylvania and does private practice with the Pittsburgh Pastoral Inistitute. Dr. Myer's research interests include pedagogical issues in counselor education and crisis intervention. He has written numerous articles and presents regularly at conferences on these topics. He is currently working on his second book in the area of crisis intervention.

Mary Lee Nelson is an associate professor of counselor education in Educational Psychology at the University of Washington. She teaches master's and doctoral level courses in both clinical and research areas. Dr. Nelson has been conducting research on clinical supervision process since 1987 and has authored numerous articles and book chapters on counseling supervision and research in counseling.

Susan Allstetter Neufeldt was a teacher and a practicing psychologist before she joined the faculty at the University of California at Santa Barbara in the Clinical/Counseling/School Psychology Program as lecturer and training clinic director in 1990. She has taught and supervised numerous novice supervisors as well as therapists-in-training. Author of many articles, chapters, and a book on supervision, Dr. Neufeldt has lectured all over the country as well as abroad on the topic of supervision. Her book, *Supervision Strategies for the First Practicum*, encourages supervisors to hypothesize, act, and reflect on their work with supervisees.

Kathy O'Byrne is an associate professor in the Department of Counseling at the California State University, Fullerton. Her research interests include the development of expertise, assessment of student learning, service-learning and counselor supervision. Her teaching experience includes practicum and qualitative research courses.

Carolyn Oxenford specializes in child and family treatment and has practiced in in-patient, community, and private practice settings and has consulted extensively with parents and schools. She is particularly interested in the development of ethical behavior in students (especially in the on-line environment) and in the social-emotional development of Gifted and Talented students. Currently, Dr. Oxenford is associate professor of Psychology and Chairperson of the Department of Psychology at Marymount University.

Pamela O. Paisley is a professor and School Counseling Program Coordinator in the Department of Counseling and Human Development Services at The University of Georgia. She is Past-President of the Association for Counselor Education and Supervision, Associate Editor of the *Journal of Counseling and Development*, and principal investigator on a major national grant to transform the preparation and practice of school counselors. Dr. Paisley has published and presented extensively at the local, state, regional, national, and international levels.

Suni Petersen is currently an assistant professor in the Counseling Psychology Program at Temple University in Philadelphia. In addition to constructivism influencing her teaching, Dr. Petersen uses the constructivist philosophy as a foundation in her program of research on medical decision making among cancer patients. She has written about how illness and its treatment are other social constructions.

Thomas Russo is a professor of education in the Department of Counseling and School Psychology at the University of Wisconsin - River Falls. He teaches courses in the graduate Counselor Education program as well as the School Psychology program. He has also taught briefly in England and Scotland. He has published and presented research and professional papers in a diversity of counseling related areas, including teaching and pedagogy, cross-cultural counseling, group counseling, and school counseling. He is currently working on a book about groupwork practice in schools.

Sue A. Stickel is a professor in the Department of Leadership and Counseling at Eastern Michigan University. She is the author or publications relating to school counseling and school reform. She has served as the editor of the *Michigan Journal of Counseling and Development* and is a past president of the Michigan Association of Counselor Education and Supervision.

Toni R. Tollerud is an associate professor of Counseling in the Department of Counseling, Adult and Health Education at Northern Illinois University. She coordinates the School Counseling Program and is Faculty Coordinator. She was named Director the Illinois School Counselors' Academy, and is past-president of the Illinois School Counselors Association, The Illinois Counselor Educators and Supervisors, and is president-elect of the Illinois Counseling Association. She is a Licensed Clinical Professional Counselor, National Certified Counselor, National Certified School Counselor, Approved Clinical Supervisor.

Ann Vernon is professor and coordinator of counseling at the University of Northern Iowa in Cedar Falls, IA. She is the author of numerous books, including *Passport Programs: A Journey through Emotional, Social, Cognitive and Self Development, What Growing Up Is All About, Developmental Assessment and Intervention with Children and Adolescents,* and *Counseling Children and Adolescents.* Dr. Vernon specializes in working with children and adolescents. She conducts workshops throughout the United States and Canada including stress management, parenting, counseling techniques with children and adolescents, and rational emotive behavior therapy. She is director of the Midwest Center for RET, a member of the Board of Trustees of the Albert Ellis Institute. She was awarded a professional leadership award from the Association for Counselor Education and Supervision.

Victoria E. White is an assistant professor in the Department of Counseling and Educational Development, University of North Carolina at Greensboro. She is currently the coordinator of the Community Counseling program. In addition to constructivist theories, her research interests include intervention efficacy with sexual abuse survivors and counseling supervision.